History Alive!®
The Medieval World and Beyond

Chief Executive Officer: Bert Bower

Chief Operating Officer: Amy Larson

Director of Curriculum: Liz Russell

Managing Editor: Laura Alavosus

Editorial Project Manager: Nancy Rogier

Project Editor: Marie Norris

Copyeditor: Ava Hayes

Editorial Associates: Anna Embree, Sarah Sudano

Production Manager: Lynn Sanchez

Art Director: John F. Kelly

Senior Graphic Designer: Christy Uyeno

Graphic Designer: Don Taka

Photo Edit Manager: Margee Robinson

Photo Editor: Elaine Soares

Production Project Manager: Eric Houts

Art Editor: Mary Swab

Audio Director: Katy Haun

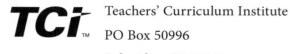 Teachers' Curriculum Institute
PO Box 50996
Palo Alto, CA 94303

Customer Service: 800-497-6138

www.teachtci.com

ISBN 978-1-58371-919-0

1 2 3 4 5 6 7 8 9 10 -EB- 14 13 12 11 10

Manufactured by Edwards Brothers, Ann Arbor, MI
United States of America, August 2010, J#20070

Program Director

Bert Bower

Program Author

Wendy Frey

Creative Development Manager

Kelly Shafsky

Contributing Writers

Lillian Duggan

Marisa A. Howard

Barbara Johnson

Christopher Johnson

Rena Korb

Joan Kane Nichols

Joy Nolan

Curriculum Developers

Joyce Bartky

April Bennett

Nicole Boylan

Terry Coburn

Sarah Cook

Julie Cremin

Erin Fry

Amy George

Anne Maloney

Steve Seely

Nathan Wellborne

Reading Specialist

Kate Kinsella, Ed.D.
Reading and TESOL Specialist
San Francisco State University

Teacher Consultants

Terry Coburn
Brookside School
Stockton, California

Randi Gibson
Stanford Middle School
Long Beach, California

Jana Kreger
Hanover Middle School
Hanover, Massachusetts

Dawn Lavond
SC Rogers Middle School
San Jose, California

Michal Lim
Borel Middle School
San Mateo, California

Alana D. Murray
Parkland Middle School
Rockville, Maryland

Stevie Wheeler
Rincon Middle School
San Diego, California

Acknowledgments

Scholars

Dr. William H. Brennan
University of the Pacific

Dr. Philippe Buc
Stanford University

Dr. Eun Mi Cho
*California State University
Sacramento*

Dr. Tom Conlan
Bowdoin College

Dr. Thomas Dandelet
University of California, Berkeley

Dr. James A. Fox
Stanford University

Gloria Frey
Ethical Culture Schools, New York

Christopher Gardner
George Mason University

Dr. Bruce Grelle
California State University Chico

Dr. Kan Liang
Seattle University

Mahan Mirza
University of Notre Dame

Dr. Merrick Posnansky
University of California, Los Angeles

Dr. John Rick
Stanford University

Dr. Melinda Takeuchi
Stanford University

Dr. Allen Wittenborn
San Diego State University

Assessment Consultant

Julie Weiss
*Curriculum and Assessment
Specialist
Elliot, Maine*

Music Consultant

Melanie Pinkert
*Music Faculty
Montgomery College, Maryland*

Cartographer

Mapping Specialists
Madison, Wisconsin

Internet Consultant

Amy George
Weston, Massachusetts

Diverse Needs Consultants

Erin Fry
Glendora, California

Colleen Guccione
Naperville, Illinois

Cathy Hix
*Swanson Middle School
Arlington, Virginia*

How to Use This Program: *History Alive! The Medieval World and Beyond*

Teaching with the TCI Approach means shifting to a student-centered, activity-based classroom. To meet this exciting challenge, this introduction to the Lesson Guide for *History Alive! The MedievalWorld and Beyond* will give you the basics you need to start teaching this program with confidence right away.

The TCI Approach

Why is the TCI Approach so effective at igniting students' passion for learning? The TCI Approach consists of a series of instructional practices that allow students of all abilities to experience key social studies concepts. It has eight features.

Theory- and Research-Based Active Instruction

Lessons and activities are based on five well-established theories.

Understanding by Design   Grant Wiggins and Jay McTighe maintain that teaching for deep understanding must begin with planning the big ideas students should learn. That's why you will see an Essential Question at the start of every chapter in *History Alive! The Medieval World and Beyond*.

Nonlinguistic Representation   Research by Robert Marzano and colleagues demonstrates that teaching with nonlinguistic activities helps improve comprehension and retention. Use of graphic organizers and movement are both key to TCI lessons.

Multiple Intelligences   Howard Gardner believes that all students are intelligent —just not in the same ways. TCI activities address Gardner's seven intelligences: verbal-linguistic, logical-mathematical, visual-spatial, body-kinesthetic, musical-rhythmic, interpersonal, and intrapersonal.

Cooperative Interaction   Elizabeth Cohen's research shows that cooperative groupwork leads to learning gains and higher student achievement. Working in small groups is a cornerstone of TCI activities.

Spiral Curriculum   Jerome Bruner championed the idea of the spiral curriculum, in which students learn progressively—understanding more difficult concepts through a process of step-by-step discovery. TCI questioning strategies spiral from simple recall to higher-order thinking skills such as analysis and evaluation.

Standards-Based Content

Dynamic lessons that integrate hands-on learning and content reading build mastery of state and national social studies standards.

Preview Assignments

Short, engaging assignments at the start of the lessons help you preview key concepts and tap students' prior knowledge and personal experience.

Multiple Intelligences Teaching Strategies

TCI activities incorporate six multiple intelligences teaching strategies:

- Visual Discovery
- Social Studies Skill Builder
- Experiential Exercise
- Writing for Understanding
- Response Group
- Problem Solving Groupwork

These six strategies are explained in detail on the following pages.

Considerate Text

Carefully structured reading materials enable students at all levels to understand what they read. Uncluttered pages present content in digestible "chunks." Engaging images reinforce content, while consistent vocabulary development improves student comprehension.

Graphically Organized Reading Notes

Easy-to-understand graphic organizers help students record key ideas and make meaning out of what they read. By using graphic organizers that display the underlying logic of and interconnections among concepts, students improve their comprehension and retention of content.

Processing Assignments

End-of-lesson assignments, involving multiple intelligences and higher-order thinking skills, challenge students to apply what they have learned in a variety of creative ways.

Assessments to Inform Instruction

Carefully designed chapter tests move students through a progression of thinking skills, from comprehension to skills application to critical thinking. Test results in these three areas show you where students are succeeding and where they need more instruction.

Multiple Intelligences Teaching Strategies

The TCI Approach uses the six teaching strategies described here to bring learning alive. All six appear in the *History Alive! The Medieval World and Beyond* Lesson Guide with detailed, step-by-step instructions. Support materials for the chapter activities appear in the Lesson Masters, visuals, and placards; on Sounds of History; and online at TeachTCI (see page xxvi).

Visual Discovery

In Visual Discovery activities, students view, touch, interpret, and bring to life compelling images as they discover key social studies concepts. Seeing and interacting with an image in combination with reading and recording notes on the content help students remember salient ideas.

Here are some tips for Visual Discovery activities:

- Arrange your classroom so that projected images will be large and clear.
- Ask carefully sequenced questions that lead to discovery.
- Challenge students to read about each image and apply what they learn.
- Have students interact with each image to demonstrate learning.

Social Studies Skill Builder

In Social Studies Skill Builders, students work in pairs or small groups on fast-paced, skill-oriented tasks such as mapping, graphing, analyzing artifacts, and forming hypotheses, to enhance their understanding of chapter content.

Here are some tips for Social Studies Skill Builders:

- Teach each skill through modeling and guided practice.
- Prepare students to work in pairs or small groups.
- Set clear expectations, allow students to practice each skill repeatedly, and give immediate feedback.
- Debrief the activity to help students make connections to key social studies concepts.

Experiential Exercise

In Experiential Exercises, participating in short, memorable experiences helps students grasp social studies concepts. Through the use of movement and introspection, students capture a moment or feeling that is central to understanding a particular concept, situation, or event.

Here are some tips for Experiential Exercises:

- Prepare students for a safe, successful experience by arranging the classroom appropriately, communicating clear behavioral and learning expectations, anticipating student reactions, and recognizing teachable moments.

- Bring authenticity to the experience by assuming an appropriate persona, hamming it up, and using simple props, costumes, music, and sound effects.
- Allow students to express their feelings immediately after the experience.
- Ask carefully sequenced questions to help students make connections between their experience and key concepts or events.

Writing for Understanding

Writing for Understanding activities give students a rich experience—such as viewing powerful images, role-playing, discussing complex issues, or acting out key events—to write about. Students develop ideas and form opinions during the experience, before beginning to write. The experience becomes a springboard for writing, challenging students to clarify ideas, organize information, and express what they have learned.

Here are some tips for Writing for Understanding activities:

- Have students record their ideas, thoughts, and feelings in prewriting activities.
- Guide students through the writing process.

Response Group

In Response Group activities, students work in small groups with thought-provoking resources to discuss critical thinking questions among themselves. A presenter then shares each group's findings with the class.

Here are some tips for Response Group activities:

- Create mixed-ability groups and a suitable classroom arrangement.
- Prepare students to answer provocative critical thinking questions.
- Allow groups time to prepare their responses.
- Facilitate a lively class discussion.

Problem Solving Groupwork

In Problem Solving Groupwork activities, students work in heterogeneous groups to create projects that require multiple abilities so that every student can contribute. Within a group, each student takes a defined role. After completing their task, groups present their projects to the class.

Here are some tips for Problem Solving Groupwork activities:

- Review ground rules for working cooperatively in groups.
- Give group members clearly defined roles and requirements.
- Give groups autonomy and time to prepare high-quality projects.
- After groups present their work, debrief each presentation for deeper meaning and accuracy.

Program Components

The components of *History Alive! The Medieval World and Beyond* work together to maximize your time and creativity. Everything you need to provide insightful and stimulating classroom experiences is included in the program. There are also plenty of opportunities to add your own resources.

Lesson Guide

"Command central" for the program includes detailed, step-by-step procedures for implementing the classroom activities, as well as the following resources:

- Planning Guides detailing materials and timing for each part of the lesson guides
- social studies and language arts objectives
- Key Content Terms and academic vocabulary
- mini lesson guides for writing assignments tied to each Reading Further case study
- listings of online resources and literature recommendations
- recommendations for differentiating instruction for English language learners, students reading and writing below grade level, special education students, and advanced learners
- Guide to Reading Notes
- answers and rubrics for assessments

Student Edition

To help students focus their learning, each chapter of the text is organized around an Essential Question. In the Student Edition, you will find

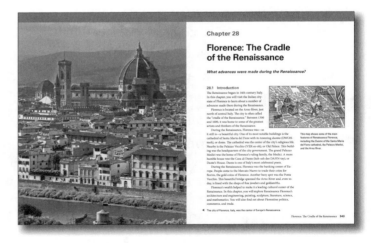

- considerate text that is uncluttered and easy to navigate.
- powerful graphic elements that support visual learning, spark student interest, and foster comprehension.
- key concepts and vocabulary terms that are highlighted in the text and defined in the Glossary.
- Setting the Stage unit introductions that provide background on how the geography of the region affected its history. Each spread includes detailed maps that students use to complete Geography Challenge lessons.
- unit timelines that appear at the end of every unit and capture the most important events of the region's history at a glance.
- High-interest Reading Further case studies that explore the chapter concepts in depth.

Interactive Student Notebook

The Interactive Student Notebook is each student's personal repository of learning, all in one place. The Interactive Student Notebook includes

- Preview activities
- graphically organized Reading Notes
- Processing activities
- Reading Further writing activities

For more information, see "Using the Interactive Student Notebook" on pages xx–xxi.

Lesson Masters

Reproducible pages support classroom activities. Follow the materials list in the Lesson Guide to know how many copies of each master to prepare before class.

- Student Handouts and Information Masters
- Station Materials and Station Directions
- chapter assessments
- sets of cards containing images for the unit timelines

Visuals and Placards

Visual support for chapter activities, including

- maps, graphs, diagrams, and tables
- photographs

Sounds of History

Audio tracks, including dramatic readings, musical recordings, and sound effects, enhance the drama and realism of many of the activities.

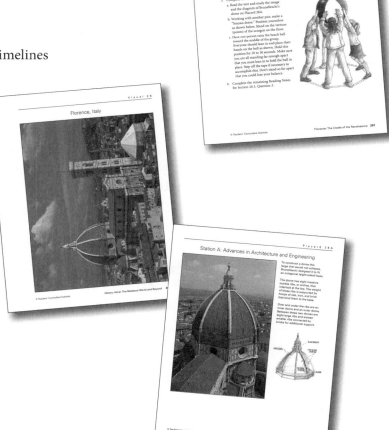

Chapter Essentials

While students look forward to the wide variety of activities they will experience in a TCI classroom, they also reap the benefits of TCI's consistent organization of learning in the chapters. Following sound pedagogical practices, each lesson begins with a Preview activity to spark interest and connect to prior learning, progresses to visually engaging Reading Notes, and concludes with a Processing activity that asks students to apply what they have learned.

Preview

The Preview activity is a short, engaging task that foreshadows upcoming content. The goal is to ignite interest, activate prior knowledge, tap a wide range of intelligences, and prepare students to tackle new concepts. Students complete most of the Preview activities in their Interactive Student Notebooks.

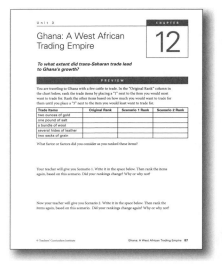

Types of Preview activities include

- connecting personal experiences with key concepts
- predicting
- analyzing artifacts, maps, photographs, paintings, drawings, political cartoons, song lyrics, and music
- responding to hypothetical scenarios
- depicting and explaining historical information
- examining the contributions of historical figures

Reading Notes

One of the most powerful ways to improve students' comprehension and retention is to have them complete graphically organized Reading Notes for each chapter. Using this format helps students see the underlying logic of and interconnections among events, facts, and concepts. When students record information in engaging, visual ways, they are better able to recall content months and even years later. Students complete the Reading Notes in their Interactive Student Notebooks.

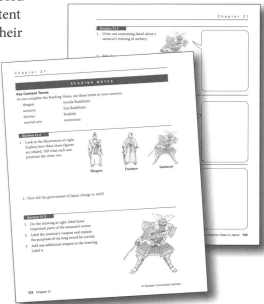

Types of graphically organized Reading Notes include

- T-charts
- labeled and annotated maps, charts, diagrams, and illustrations
- flowcharts
- spoke diagrams
- time lines
- Venn diagrams
- speech bubbles

Reading Further

For each Reading Further, students complete a two-part writing activity about what they've read. The first part prepares them to write while the second part provides them with a guiding rubric for their work. Types of writing activities include

- business letters
- diary entries
- point-of-view statements
- comparing and contrasting

Processing

Processing activities challenge students to synthesize the information in a chapter to demonstrate their understanding of it. The intent is to allow students to actively apply what they have learned so that you—and they—can assess their comprehension. Students complete the Processing activities in their Interactive Student Notebooks or on separate sheets of paper.

Products of Processing activities include

- song and poem verses
- magazine covers
- posters
- Web page designs
- storyboards
- journal entries
- interviews
- collages

- advertisements
- illustrated timelines
- T-charts
- parables
- letters
- spoke diagrams
- dialogues
- annotated maps

Using the Interactive Student Notebook

In the Interactive Student Notebook, all parts of the integrated lesson come together as students create a dynamic repository for their learning. Students should store their notebooks in a three-ring binder. Because the pages are perforated, it is easy for you to collect only selected chapters to grade a one time, rather than whole binders.

Interactive Student Notebook Guidelines for Students

One of the most important steps for helping students to create successful notebooks is establishing clear guidelines. Decide ahead of time what you expect your students to produce in their notebooks. Clearly communicate your expectations on a single sheet of paper that students can glue into the inside front cover of their notebooks. Here are example guidelines that you might adapt for your own students.

Purpose   Your Interactive Student Notebook will help you to become a creative, independent thinker and writer. You will use your notebook in class for completing all chapter Preview, Reading Notes, Reading Further, and Processing activities. It will also help you study for tests.

Materials   You will need colored pencils, a glue stick, highlighters, scissors, tape, and a zipper pouch.

Grading   To earn an A– or higher grade, you must keep a complete, neat notebook, produce quality work, and consistently take the time to extend your learning beyond classroom assignments. Notebooks will be checked for completeness periodically—usually every three to four weeks, except during the first few weeks of class, when they will be checked more regularly. You must keep an updated assignment sheet listing all class assignments, due dates, and point values. Also include columns for recording self-assessment points and teacher-assessment points.

Absence   If you are absent, check the class assignment sheet the teacher has placed in the large envelope in the front of the class. It will list all assignments that are due.

Managing Assessment of Interactive Student Notebooks

If you teach four or five classes a day, you could have 150 or more student notebooks to monitor. Because so much of students' work appears in these notebooks, you will need an efficient and accurate system for assessing them.

Informal Assessment   Monitor student notebooks aggressively in the first few weeks of the course. Look at notebooks as you walk around, making positive comments and helpful suggestions. Here are some additional ideas:

- While students work on another assignment, conduct a quick review of the previous night's homework, giving students checks or special stamps to denote completed assignments.
- Provide a model of outstanding work for an assignment or set of class notes.
- Allow students to use their notebooks on a quiz or test. This will come as a pleasant surprise and reward for students with well-organized notebooks.

Formal Assessment   At the beginning of the course, clearly explain the criteria on which notebooks will be assessed, such as quality and completeness of assignments, visual appearance, neatness, higher-order thinking, and organization. Here are some additional ideas for assessing student work:

- Create a simple rubric that identifies the criteria you feel are most important.
- Stagger notebook collection so that you correct only one class set at a time.
- Grade selectively. Don't feel compelled to grade every notebook entry.
- Create an evaluation sheet like the one below to support your expectations of student work.

Notebook Assignment	Due Date	Possible Points	Student Assessment	Teacher Assessment
Chapter 6 Preview	11/8	5	3	4
Chapter 6 Reading Notes	11/9	20	19	17
Chapter 6 Processing	11/10	10	8	10
Chapter 9 Reading Notes	11/15	20	18	19
Chapter 9 Processing	11/16	10	9	8
Totals		65	57	58
Student Comments: I'm not used to these kinds of assignments, but I'm trying my best.				
Teacher Comments: Your work is solid. Think about creating some of your excellent visuals for extra credit.				

Organizing a TCI Classroom

Most of the activities in *History Alive! The Medieval World and Beyond* require students to move into small groups of two, three, or four. With a brief training exercise, you can teach them how to do so quickly without wasting valuable time.

Moving Your Classroom Furniture

Tell students that they will be working in small groups of different sizes throughout the course. They must know how to move into each grouping quickly and efficiently with all their materials. When working in pairs, they should place their desks either side by side or face to face, with the edges touching. For groups of three or more, the front corners of the desks must touch.

With these expectations clear, allow students to practice moving into groups. Randomly assign students to groups and indicate where they should meet. Then say "Go!" and time them. If necessary, allow the class to discuss what went wrong and brainstorm ideas for getting into groups more efficiently. Have students repeat the process until they can do it in "record time."

Be prepared for students to think this exercise is silly. However, if you spend 20 minutes at the beginning of the course teaching this skill, you will save hours of instructional time. Your goal should be for students to be able to form various group configurations in less than one minute, without your needing to touch any student furniture.

Organizing Your Teacher Resources

History Alive! The Ancient World comes with all of the materials you need to excite your students about the history and legacy of the the ancient world. It will be up to you, however, to gather the materials for each chapter and organize them in a way that makes it fast and easy to conduct activities year after year. Here are some tips to save you time and make running your classroom much easier:

1. Begin preparation for each activity by gathering everything on the materials list, such as placards, visuals, and the audio tracks.

2. Make all the copies you will need of classroom masters, such as Student Handouts, Information Masters, and Station Materials. Consider creating these copies from the online resources at TeachTCI.

3. When you finish each activity, place all the printed materials in a clear, resealable plastic bag (an ideal size is 10 by 12 in. and 4 mm thick) with the Lesson Guide on top as a "label." This will keep the many individual activity pieces together and will ensure that next year's preparation takes virtually no time.

4. Prepare the equipment you will use, including projectors and computers.

Creating a Cooperative, Tolerant Classroom

The interactive, experiential, and stimulating learning at the heart of the TCI Approach can happen only when students feel comfortable sharing ideas, taking risks, working cooperatively, tolerating differences, and disagreeing honestly and respectfully with you and their classmates. Thus you need to take purposeful steps to develop a "safe" community in your classroom.

Here are some tips for creating a cooperative, tolerant classroom:

- Greet your students at the door every day to make a personal connection with them as they enter your classroom.

- Explain your expectations for classroom behavior, using specific examples. You may also involve students in shaping class rules.

- Stage an icebreaker at the beginning of the course to help students feel more comfortable with their new classmates. For example, make a list of descriptions (likes to dance, speaks another language, and the like), give each student a copy, and ask the class to get the autograph of one person who fits each profile.

- Convince students that learning to work effectively with others will benefit them throughout their lives.

- Teach students how to move efficiently into groups of various sizes.

- Use role-playing activities to teach students cooperative skills.

- Form mixed-ability groups.

- Allow newly formed groups to engage in team-building activities to promote group cohesion.

- Allow students to engage in groupwork activities without unnecessary interventions by you.

Assessing Learning

Effective assessment requires many approaches—individual and group, informal and formal—to create a well-rounded understanding of student performance. Here are some tips for evaluating student work.

Informal Assessment

Assessment of day-to-day activities benefits both you and your students. You send the message that every activity is important. And by identifying what works and what doesn't, you are able to adjust your instructional plans. Try these methods:

- Make your expectations known in advance so students will know how they will be rated.
- Note students' answers to questions, both oral and written.
- Evaluate participation in act-it-outs and class discussions.
- Look for students' level of cooperation in pairs and small groups.
- Ask students to assess their own work.
- Skim Interactive Student Notebooks as students work in class.

Groupwork Assessment

Evaluating groupwork presents a lot of questions: Should you rate the product or the process? The individual or the group? The amount of effort or the quality of the result? Here are five steps that will help you assess groupwork equitably:

1. Set clear criteria for evaluation.

2. Make both individuals and groups accountable.

3. Record notes as groups work and while they present their final products.

4. Have students complete self-assessments to evaluate their individual contributions as well as the group's performance.

5. Determine group and individual grades.

Formal Assessment

In addition to classroom observations and evaluation of student notebooks, you will need formal measurements of how much your students have learned. Research has shown that the TCI Approach improves student comprehension and retention. (For research results, visit www.teachtci.com.)

History Alive! The Medieval World and Beyond provides an assessment for each chapter. You will find reproducible test pages in the Lesson Masters and answers in the Lesson Guide. Each chapter assessment has three parts.

Mastering the Content   The first part contains multiple-choice questions that check students' understanding of the main concepts and content introduced in the chapter. These questions range from simple comprehension to application, analysis, and evaluation. They use the wording and formats most commonly found on standardized tests.

Applying Social Studies Skills   The second part has short-answer tasks designed to assess how well students have mastered a wide range of history skills. Students are asked to read, compare, and analyze selected passages as well as a great variety of graphic elements, including maps, diagrams, illustrations, graphs, and tables of data. These skill assessments are scaffolded to guide students from simple tasks, such as identifying data, to more complex critical thinking tasks.

Exploring the Essential Question   The third part returns to the Essential Question, asking students to apply what they have learned to a constructed-response task. Each writing task is accompanied by a prompt that provides information for students to draw upon and is carefully scaffolded to help students gather and organize the information they will need to complete the task. The final work product may be a written piece or a visual representation of information, similar to those called for in state assessments that include constructed-response tasks.

You will find digital versions of the assessments online at TeachTCI (see page xxvi). You can use the tests as they are, randomize the order of questions, edit questions, or add your own questions.

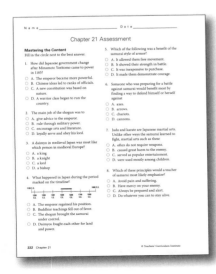

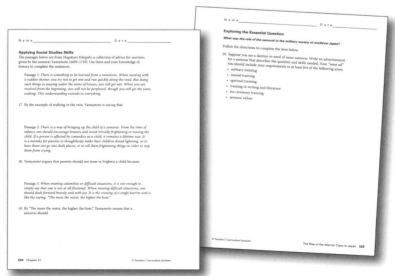

Enhancing Instruction with TeachTCI

Support for *History Alive! The Medieval World and Beyond* extends beyond the box of print and audiovisual materials to a wealth of technology components. With a subscription to TeachTCI providing access to exclusive online resources, you will have the following tools to help you plan and extend lessons and customize assessments.

Teacher Resources Materials Online

Access digital versions of components—such as the Lesson Guide, Lesson Masters, and Interactive Student Notebook—all organized by chapter. Preview, print, and project items as needed.

Classroom Presenter

Project a digital lesson guide for each classroom activity from your internet-connected computer. Hidden teaching notes pop up for your eyes only, while animated visuals show students what to do.

Student Edition

You and your students can view the Student Edition text and images online. You'll see what your students are reading as you assign them chapters and Reading Challenges.

Reading Challenges Scoring Manager

Assign Reading Challenges to your class and track results of both individual students and entire classes. You'll know how much your students understand and which topics need reinforcement.

Assessment Creator

Build customized assessments for your class. This tool lets you add, delete, edit, and sort questions and answers.

Lesson Tips from the TCI Community

Get ideas, engage in professional exchanges with teachers around the country, and share your own best practices. Our discussion groups are organized by program and chapter.

Enrichment Resources

Enhance student learning with chapter-related Web links and in-depth essays on selected topics.

Customized State Correlations

See how the content you are teaching aligns to your state standards in easy-to-read chart form.

Enhancing Engagement with LearnTCI

LearnTCI allows students to interact with *History Alive! The Medieval World and Beyond* on any computer with Internet access. With a LearnTCI subscription, students have access to the following online tools and resources.

Student Edition Text and Images

Students can read their Student Edition anywhere they have access to a computer with an Internet connection. They can zoom in on any image and sharpen their reading skills with a wealth of features.

Text-to-Audio Tool for Accessibility

Students can highlight the text and have it read to them. You decide which students have access to this feature, which is geared primarily toward English language learners and students reading below grade level.

Text Highlighting Tool

Students can highlight what they think are the main ideas of each section.

Main Idea Viewer

After using the Text Highlighting Tool, students can compare their answers to the main ideas identified by the program. Again, you decide which students have access to this feature. It is especially helpful for English language learners and students reading below grade level.

Reading Challenges

In Reading Challenges, students analyze videos, visuals, or primary sources related to the text and then respond to questions. To answer correctly, they need to read and understand the text as well as the multimedia element. Students receive immediate feedback, so if they didn't answer a question correctly, they can reread the passage to discover the correct answer.

Enrichment Resources

Students can gain deeper understanding by exploring links to other chapter-related Web sites and reading in-depth essays on selected topics.

Learn more about TeachTCI and LearnTCI at **www.teachtci.com/tech-demo**.

Growing Professionally

There is much, much more to learn about igniting students' interest in history and creating insightful and memorable classroom experiences. For a complete explanation of the TCI Approach, the Interactive Student Notebook, and how to create a cooperative, tolerant classroom, we encourage you to read *Bring Learning Alive!* This book covers every aspect of TCI's methodology for the middle and high school social studies classroom. Please visit **www.teachtci.com** or call Customer Service at **800-497-6138** for more information or to order.

TCI Academy Training

After you have taught a few TCI lessons and seen your students' active interest in learning about history, you may find that they have reignited your passion for teaching. Help your colleagues remember why they went into teaching by bringing TCI Academy training to your school or district.

Trainings are built around immersion lessons, in which teachers become students to experience the power of active, student-centered instruction. TCI Academy trainers are classroom teachers themselves and debrief activities to provide immediate feedback. You can mix and match TCI Academy sessions to build a course that best meets your needs. Please visit **www.tciacademy.com** or call us at **800-840-2698** to get started.

Europe During Medieval Times

Overview

This activity introduces the geographic information essential to Unit 1. Students read and interpret maps to learn about key physical and political features of medieval Europe. They annotate a map of medieval Europe and answer questions in their Interactive Student Notebooks, then discuss critical thinking questions. Students' comprehension of content and proficiency in map-reading and higher-order thinking skills will help you gauge their readiness for the unit. The pages that follow include a completed map, answers to questions, a scoring guide to inform your teaching, and suggestions for modifications to meet the needs of specific student.

Essential Geographic Understandings

1. Location of Europe, including an understanding of western and eastern Europe

2. Key physical features: the Atlantic Ocean, the Mediterranean Sea, the Black Sea, the Alps, the Pyrenees, the Carpathians

3. Key political features: Holy Roman Empire, Byzantine Empire, Constantinople

4. Importance of geographical features to the success of Europe as a whole and to the development of Constantinople

Procedures

1   **Introduce the unit.** Tell students that in this unit they will learn about medieval Europe. Explain that although the continent of Europe is small, it has had enormous influence on world history.

2   **Create a KWL chart with students.** Ask students to identify what they already know about the geography of Europe and what they want to learn. Use their responses to gauge how much additional background information your students will need as you progress through the unit. Students will return to the KWL chart at the end of the unit and add the key information they have learned.

3   **Have students read Unit 1 "Setting the Stage" in the Student Edition.**

4   **Have students complete the Geography Challenge.** Monitor students as they work. Use the guide on the next two pages to check their answers. You may wish to project the map from the Interactive Student Notebook and have students annotate it as the class works through the map-reading questions. Make sure students have grasped Essential Geographic Understandings 1 to 3.

5   **Discuss the "Critical Thinking" questions.** Help students understand the geographic relationships described in Essential Geographic Understanding 4.

Medieval Europe, About 1300

60°N

20°W   10°W   0°   10°E

N
W • E
S

20°E

NORWAY

SWEDEN

SCOTLAND

North Sea

Baltic Sea

TEUTONIC ORDER

IRELAND

50°N

Thames River

ENGLAND

DENMARK

London

Hamburg

LITHUANIA

ATLANTIC OCEAN

Elbe River

POLAND

HOLY ROMAN EMPIRE

Paris

Seine River

Orléans

Vienna

Danube River

CARPATHIAN MOUNTAINS

GASCONY (England)

FRANCE

NAVARRE

LEÓN

A L P S

VENAISSIN

Genoa

Venice

Budapest

HUNGARY

40°N

PORTUGAL

CASTILE

ARAGON

GENOA

Florence

Corsica

Tiber River

Rome

VENETIAN REPUBLIC

SERBIA

BULGARIA

30°E

Black Sea

Toledo

Lisbon

Sardinia

PAPAL STATES

Naples

NAPLES

Constantinople

BYZANTINE EMPIRE

Adriatic Sea

Aegean Sea

ASIA

GRANADA

KINGDOM OF MALLORCA

Tyrrhenian Sea

DUCHY OF ATHENS

PRINCIPALITY OF ACHAIA

Sicily

Crete

VENETIAN REPUBLIC

AFRICA

Mediterranean Sea

0   250   500 miles

0   250   500 kilometers

Lambert Azimuthal Equal-Area Projection

Geography Skills

Score 1 point for each correct answer. Use the map on the previous page to check shading and labeling.

1. The Carpathian Mountains lie between the Holy Roman Empire and the Byzantine Empire.

2. The Alps separate the Italian peninsula from the Holy Roman Empire.

3. Check students' maps for Constantinople.

4. Students should label the islands of England, Ireland, Corsica, Sicily, Sardinia, and Crete.

5. The Byzantine Empire included land in Europe and Asia.

6. The Carpathian Mountains extended through Poland and Hungary.

7. Large medieval cities were located along rivers because they provided a convenient transportation route and a method for shipping goods.

8. A trader from Constantinople would likely have traveled north on the Black Sea to the Danube River, sailed up the river to Vienna, traveled overland from Vienna to the Elbe River, and sailed up the Elbe to Hamburg.

Critical Thinking

Questions may have more than one correct answer. Score 1 to 3 points for each reasonable answer, depending on the strength of students' geographic reasoning. Possible answers are given here.

9. Europe has a long coastline with good harbors. This geographical factor would have made sea travel possible.

10. Invaders from northern Africa and the Middle East would have to cross the Mediterranean Sea to reach western Europe.

11. The Holy Roman Empire was contained within central Europe. It did not include lands in Asia or Africa, present-day Spain, France, or England, Italy, or Eastern Europe, as did the Roman Empire. However, it did extend further north than the Roman Empire.

Using Scores to Inform Instruction

Geography Skills A score of 5 out of 8 or better indicates that students have acquired sufficient geographic information to proceed with the unit.

Critical Thinking A score of 6 out of 9 or better indicates that students are beginning to understand the relationships between physical geography and the different ways in which people live.

Modifying Instruction

ELL or Learners with Special Education Needs Consider focusing on map-reading questions or limiting the number of "Critical Thinking" questions.

Students with Weak Map or Critical Thinking Skills Assign appropriate pages from the Social Studies Skills Toolkit in the back of the Lesson Masters.

The Legacy of the Roman Empire

To what extent have the contributions of ancient Rome influenced modern society?

Overview

In a Social Studies Skill Builder activity, students learn about the fall of the Roman Empire and the rise of the Byzantine Empire. They examine contributions of ancient Rome and assess their influences on modern society.

Objectives

In the course of reading this chapter and participating in the classroom activity, students will

Social Studies

- describe the internal weaknesses of the Roman Empire and identify reasons for the fall of the empire in the west.

- summarize the events that led to the establishment, by Constantine, of a new capital in the east and to the rise of the Byzantine Empire.

- identify some of the major lasting contributions of Rome and explain their influence on modern society.

- evaluate the relative extent to which the contributions of the Roman Empire influence society today.

Language Arts

- clarify word meanings through the use of definitions and examples.

- read expository text to connect essential ideas to prior knowledge.

- write persuasive compositions that state a clear position and describe the points in support of that position.

Social Studies Vocabulary

Key Content Terms Roman Empire, empire, corruption, decline, Constantine, mosaic, aqueduct, scribe, proverb, philosophy

Academic Vocabulary collapse, conflict, unique, document

Materials

History Alive! The Medieval World and Beyond

Interactive Student Notebooks

Visual 1

Placards 1A–1H (2 sets)

Lesson Masters

- Student Handout 1 (3–4 copies, cut apart)

- Information Master 1 (1 transparency)

- Vocabulary Development handout (1 per student, on colored paper)

Activity	Suggested Time	Materials
Preview	10 minutes	• Interactive Student Notebooks • Visual 1
Vocabulary Development	30–40 minutes	• *History Alive! The Medieval World and Beyond* • Interactive Student Notebooks • Vocabulary Development handout
Social Studies Skill Builder	75 minutes (2 regular periods) (1 block period)	• *History Alive! The Medieval World and Beyond* • Interactive Student Notebooks • Student Handout 1 (3–4 copies, cut apart) • Information Master 1 (1 transparency) • Placards 1A–1H
Processing	20 minutes	• Interactive Student Notebooks
Assessment	40 minutes	• Chapter 1 Assessment

Preview

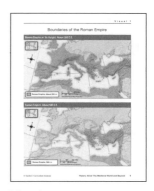

Visual 1

1   **Project the first map on *Visual 1: Boundaries of the Roman Empire* and have students complete Part 1 of the Preview activity in their Interactive Student Notebooks.** Ask students these questions in Part 1.

 • What do you notice about the Roman Empire in about 200 C.E.?

 • What might be some disadvantages to controlling such a large empire?

2   **Project the second map on Visual 1 and have students complete Part 2 of the Preview activity in their Interactive Student Notebooks.** Then ask students these questions in Part 2.

 • What do you notice about the second map compared to the first? What might have happened to cause these changes?

 • How might Roman culture continue to influence these territories today?

3   **Explain the connection between the Preview activity and the chapter.** Tell students that in this chapter, they will review why the Roman Empire fell, resulting in the changes between the maps. They will then look at the many legacies Rome left to the entire world.

Vocabulary Development

1   **Introduce the Key Content Terms.** Have students locate the Key Content Terms for the chapter in their Interactive Student Notebooks. These are important terms that will help them understand the main ideas of the chapter. Ask volunteers to identify familiar terms and use them in a sentence.

2   **Have students complete a Vocabulary Development handout.** Give each student a copy of the Vocabulary Development handout of your choice from the Reading Toolkit at the back of the Lesson Masters. These handouts provide extra Key Content Term practice and support, depending on your students' needs. Review the completed handout by asking volunteers to share one answer for each term.

Reading

1   **Introduce the Essential Question and have students read Section 1.1.** Have students identify the Essential Question on the first page of the chapter: *To what extent have the contributions of ancient Rome influenced modern society?* Then have students read Section 1.1 and do the following:

 • Describe the Roman Empire at its height.

 • Explain the meaning of the statement, "Rome perished, yet it lived on."

2   **Have students complete the Reading Notes for Chapter 1.** Assign Sections 1.2 to 1.6 during the activity as indicated in the procedures for the Social Studies Skill Builder. Remind students to use the Key Content Terms where appropriate as they complete their Reading Notes.

> ### Vocabulary Development: Idioms
>
> One legacy of Rome is linguistic: not only did Latin supply us with many roots and affixes, but it also gave us sayings. Introduce the saying "All roads lead to Rome." Explain that the saying is an *idiom* because the meanings of the individual words do not combine to create the meaning of the whole expression. Like many idioms, the saying had a meaning in the past (in Roman times, all roads actually did seem to radiate to and from Rome) but has a new meaning now—there are many ways to reach the same goal. Have students relate the old meaning to the new one.

Social Studies Skill Builder

1 **Prepare materials and arrange the classroom.** Before class, use www.
teachtci.com to create a second set of *Placards 1A–1H*. Post both sets on
the walls to create 16 stations. Cut apart the copies of *Student Handout 1:
Modern Images*. Consider making eight piles of like images and placing them
in an easily accessible location in your classroom, or placing each stack of
images in its own envelope labeled with the image letter.

2 **Have students read Section 1.2 and complete the Reading Notes for that
section.** Tell students that this section gives background on the internal
weakness that led to the fall of the Roman Empire. Consider having students
share their responses to that section with a partner or as a class.

3 **Distribute a modern image from Student Handout 1 to each pair and
introduce the activity.** Make sure that each pair of students gets one of the
eight images that have been cut from Student Handout 1. Explain to students
that this image shows a modern example of an ancient Roman influence.
With their partner, they must locate the corresponding placard image from
ancient Rome that clearly shows the influence on the modern example.

4 **Project *Information Master 1: Steps for Completing the Activity* and review
the steps listed there.** Remind students that they may be asked to read the
same section of text twice, but that they will look for different information
each time. (**Note:** You may wish students to raise their hands after matching
the first placard to verify that they are completing the activity correctly.)

5 **Conduct the activity and monitor students' work.** Use Guide to Reading
Notes 1 to occasionally check to see that groups have chosen the correct
placards for each section. Allow groups to continue until most have correctly
matched all eight images to placards and completed their Reading Notes.

6 **Review the connections between the modern images and the placards.**
Once most pairs have matched all eight images to placards, discuss as a class
which placards they matched to each image on Student Handout 1 and what
clues led them to each connection.

7 **Debrief the activity. Ask,**

- Were you surprised to learn that any of these influences actually came
  from the ancient Romans? In which instances?

- Which of these Roman influences most affects you personally? Least
  affects you personally?

- How have the contributions of ancient Rome influenced modern society?

Placards 1A–1H

Student Handout 1

Information Master 1

Processing

Have students complete the Processing activity in their Interactive Student Notebooks. Students evaluate the contributions they learned about in this lesson to determine which they think most affect modern society and which least affect it. Consider having students share their spectrums with the class, or create one class spectrum and have students debate the placement of certain Roman influences from this chapter.

Quicker Coverage

Eliminate the Placards from the Activity Instead of having students match the images on Student Handout 1 to placards, simply have them match the images in this chapter with the section of text that best connects to each modern image. Then have them read the section and complete the Reading Notes.

Have Students Complete the Reading for Homework Instead of having students read after each placard examination, have them complete only the Question 1 in Sections 1.3–1.6 in their Reading Notes in class as they match the modern examples of Roman influences to the placards. Then, as homework, have them read Sections 1.3–1.6 and complete the Reading Notes.

Deeper Coverage

Have Students Locate Examples of Roman Cultural Influences Have students find three examples of Roman influences, such as a building with a dome, a mosaic in a restaurant, or a sign containing a word or motto derived from or in Latin. Have students sketch or take a photograph of each example and write a caption for each. Captions should describe the example, state where it is located, and explain the connection to Roman legacies.

Assessment

Mastering the Content

1. B	5. A	9. C	13. C
2. B	6. C	10. D	14. A
3. C	7. D	11. D	15. A
4. A	8. A	12. B	16. D

Applying Social Studies Skills

17. Rhine River, Danube River, Carpathian Mountains, Black Sea

18. ship (boat, water)

19. Byzantium was at a crossroads between Europe and Asia, on both land and water routes. Its location made it an important trade city. It also was located on the end of a peninsula, which probably made it easier to defend.

Exploring the Essential Question

20. Answers should include all the elements requested in the prompt.

Scoring Rubric

Score	Description
3	Student draws and writes about three Roman influences on modern society. Writing is clear, accurate, and supported with descriptions, facts, or examples.
2	Student draws and writes about three influences, but with inaccuracies or unclear statements.
1	Student mentions three influences but does not write paragraphs describing or explaining them.
0	Response does not match the task or is incorrect.

English Language Learners

Eliminate the Activity Notes for Each Image Give students a copy of uncut Student Handout 1 and photocopies of the eight placards. At their desks, have students try to match each modern image on the Student Handout with its Roman counterpart on a placard. Using a marker, have them circle clues in each image that led them to make the match, such as similarities in each image or significant details that reveal the topic of the images. Then, have them read the indicated section and complete the Reading Notes.

Discuss the Preview Questions as a Class Before having students answer these questions in their Interactive Student Notebooks, project Visual 1 and discuss each map as an entire class. Encourage students to jot down their own and classmates' ideas as each question is answered.

Learners Reading and Writing Below Grade Level

Provide Support for the Processing Activity Provide students with the following prompts before they begin the Processing activity:

- I think the Roman influence that most affects today's society is
- One of the ways that this influence is important to today's society is
- A second way that this influence affects today's society is
- Other Roman influences such as _____ and _____ are important but do not affect society as much because
- In conclusion, I believe that the most important lasting contribution of the Romans is

Learners with Special Education Needs

Shorten the Reading Notes Reduce the amount of matching in the activity by having students focus on four of the eight modern images. Have them complete the Reading Notes for just those four images. Also, consider photocopying the four corresponding placards to allow them to match the modern images to them at their desks or later as homework.

Advanced Learners

Provide an Alternative to the Processing Activity Have students do the following:

- Assign groups of two or three students to the following contributions: language, law and justice, citizenship, road-building.
- In their groups, students should prepare to argue why their contribution has had the greatest impact on modern society. Their arguments should include:

  —a clear statement explaining why their contribution has most affected modern society

  —at least three specific examples of how their contribution is evident in today's society

  —counterarguments for why the other three contributions are NOT as significant

  —a closing sentence that re-states their position

- Allow students to present their final arguments. Then have the class vote on which contribution they think has had the greatest effect on modern society.

Enrichment Resources

Have students find out more about the legacy of the Roman Empire by exploring the following Enrichment Resources for *History Alive! The Medieval World and Beyond* at www.teachtci.com.

Enrichment Readings These in-depth readings encourage students to explore selected topics related to the chapter. You may also find readings that relate the chapter's content directly to your state's curriculum.

Internet Connections The recommended Web sites provide useful and engaging content that reinforces skills development and mastery of subjects within the chapter.

Literature Recommendations

The following books offer opportunities to extend the content in this chapter.

City: A Story of Roman Planning and Construction by David Macaulay (Boston: Houghton Mifflin Company, 1974)

Gladiatrix by Russell Whitfield (New York: St. Martin's Griffin: 2009)

How Rome Fell: Death of a Superpower by Adrian Goldsworthy (New Haven: Yale University Press, 2009)

Section 1.2

1. Political Instability: The transfer of power from one emperor to the next was often unpredictable. Often the army chose the next emperor.

   Economic Problems: Citizens, who paid high taxes to finance Rome's army, were often poor. Trade suffered and unemployment was a problem.

   Social Problems: Corruption and crime were common. The spirit of citizenship around the empire declined.

   Weakening Frontiers: The empire was so large, it was hard to defend. Communication throughout the empire was slow. Soldiers recruited from conquered tribes were sometimes disloyal.

2. First, in 330 C.E., Constantine decided to . . . move his capital east to Byzantium. He renamed the city New Rome. (Later named Constantinople.)

   Then, power in the empire was . . . divided between two emperors, one in Rome and one in Constantinople.

   In 410 C.E., . . . an invading Germanic tribe attacked Rome and looted it.

   In 476 C.E., . . . the last Roman emperor was driven out and the western half of the empire began to break apart.

   Finally, in the east… the Byzantine Empire continued for another 1,000 years.

Section 1.3

1. I think Modern Image D connects to Placard 1B because (Answers will vary but may include) both images are of elaborate paintings; both images show scenes painted on walls.

   I think Modern Image F connects to Placard 1D because (Answers will vary but may include) both images show a statue; both show a national leader.

2. Romans created realistic statues and colorful mosaics. They also painted frescoes that might show three-dimensional landscapes. Romans made decorative glass bottles, developed the arts of gem cutting and metalwork, and created cameos.

3. Some examples of Roman-influenced art forms today are murals in restaurants, banks, and other buildings; lifelike statues; cut gems; and cameos.

Section 1.4

1. I think Modern Image G connects to Placard 1C because (Answers will vary but may include) both images focus on roads.

   I think Modern Image B connects to Placard 1H because (Answers will vary but may include) both building have pillars; the buildings look very much alike.

2. arches, such as those used in the Roman Colosseum; vaults, arches used to support a ceiling; domes, roofs shaped like a half-globe, such as that found on the Pantheon

3. Roman-influenced architecture includes the Capitol in Washington, D.C., which has a dome and arches. The Arc de Triomphe in Paris is one huge triumphal arch.

4. aqueducts, which carried water from as far as 60 miles away; a system of 50,000 miles of roads that connected the Roman Empire

Section 1.5

1. I think Modern Image E connects to Placard 1A because (Answers will vary but may include) both images show Roman numerals.

   I think Modern Image A connects to Placard 1F because (Answers will vary but may include) both images focus on October; the modern calendar and the Roman calendar are similar.

2. Many modern European languages have developed from Latin, including Spanish, French, and Italian. English also borrows heavily from Latin. Many modern English words start with Latin prefixes or come from Latin roots. Even Latin proverbs are used in the United States.

3. The numbers 1, 10, 100, and 1,000 were written as I, X, C, and M.

Section 1.6

1. I think Modern Image H connects to Placard 1E because (Answers will vary but may include) both images involve documents made up of laws; both images show documents that are read by many people.

   I think Modern Image C connects to Placard 1G because (Answers will vary but may include) both images depict scenes involving what appears to be a judge; both images show a courtroom scene.

2. Stoicism is the belief that a divine intelligence rules all of nature and that a person's soul is a spark of that intelligence. Stoics wish to live in a way that agrees with nature and to have a good character.

3. The ideas of Roman law and justice live on in documents such as the Constitution and Declaration of Independence, as well as in modern-day courtrooms. People around the world share the Roman belief that humans have basic and natural rights.

4. In Rome, all free people were considered citizens and were subject to Roman law, enjoyed the rights of all Romans, and owed allegiance to the emperor. Today, in the United States, though most citizens are born in the country and immigrants can become citizens of the U.S., all citizens share basic rights and must follow the same laws.

The Development of Feudalism in Western Europe

How well did feudalism establish order in Europe in the Middle Ages?

Overview

In an Experiential Exercise, students assume the roles of serfs, knights, lords, and a monarch to understand the various inter-connections, responsibilities, and vassal-lord relationships that defined European feudal society.

Objectives

In the course of reading this chapter and participating in the classroom activity, students will

Social Studies

- describe the accomplishments of Charlemagne and explain how his cooperation with the pope fostered unity in western Europe.
- identify the factors that created a need for a new type of political system in Europe, leading to the development of feudalism.
- differentiate between the roles and responsibilities of the four main social classes in European feudal society.
- evaluate the extent to which feudalism brought political order, economic stability, prosperity, and opportunity to Europe in the Middle Ages.

Language Arts

- clarify word meanings through the use of definitions and examples.
- read expository text to connect essential ideas to prior knowledge.

Social Studies Vocabulary

Key Content Terms Christianity, Charlemagne, feudalism, fief, serf, chivalry

Academic Vocabulary reign, survive, function

Materials

History Alive! The Medieval World and Beyond

Interactive Student Notebooks

Lesson Masters

- Information Master 2 (1 transparency of each page)
- Student Handout 2A (1 copy, cut apart)
- Student Handout 2B (7 copies, cut apart to create 20 sets)
- Vocabulary Development handout (1 per student, on colored paper)

5 pieces of string or yarn, each about 40 feet long

masking tape (4 rolls)

several sheets of scrap paper crumpled into balls

snacks or a drink for one student

colored pencils or markers

Activity	Suggested Time	Materials
Preview	10 minutes	• *History Alive! The Medieval World and Beyond* • Interactive Student Notebooks
Vocabulary Development	30–40 minutes	• *History Alive! The Medieval World and Beyond* • Interactive Student Notebooks • Vocabulary Development handout
Experiential Exercise	90 minutes (2 regular periods) (1 block period)	• *History Alive! The Medieval World and Beyond* • Interactive Student Notebooks • Information Master 2 (1 transparency) • Student Handout 2A (1 copy, cut apart) • Student Handout 2B (7 copies, cut apart to create 20 sets) • 5 pieces of string or yarn, each about 40 feet long • masking tape (4 rolls) • several sheets of scrap paper crumpled into balls • colored pencils or markers • snacks or a drink for one student
Processing	15 minutes	• Interactive Student Notebooks
Assessment	40 minutes	• Chapter 2 Assessment

Preview

1 **Have students complete the Preview activity in their Interactive Student Notebooks.** Students write about a situation in which loyalty was important.

2 **Have students share their responses in pairs or with the class.**

3 **Connect the Preview activity to the chapter.** Explain to students that, just as loyalty can be important today among friends and family, in business, and in politics, promises of loyalty once helped to hold European society together after the fall of the Roman Empire. By creating the feudal system based on relationships, the western Europeans hoped to create political order and a stable form of leadership, as well as providing local protection and security from outside threats.

Vocabulary Development

1 **Introduce the Key Content Terms. Have students locate the Key Content Terms for the chapter in their Interactive Student Notebooks.** These are important terms that will help them understand the main ideas of the chapter. Ask volunteers to identify any familiar terms and suggest how they might be used in a sentence.

2 **Have students complete a Vocabulary Development handout.** Give each student a copy of the Vocabulary Development handout of your choice from the Reading Toolkit at the back of the Lesson Masters. These handouts provide extra Key Content Term practice and support, depending on your students' needs. Review the completed handout by asking volunteers to share one answer for each term.

Reading

1 **Introduce the Essential Question and have students read Section 2.1.** Have students identify the Essential Question on the first page of the chapter: *How well did feudalism establish order in Europe in the Middle Ages?* Then have students read Section 2.1. Afterward, have students use information from Section 2.1 and from the chapter opener image to propose some possible answers to the Essential Question.

2 **Have students read Section 2.2 and complete the corresponding Reading Notes.** Tell students that this section supplies information about Europe after the fall of Rome and discusses the factors that encouraged the development of feudalism. Use Guide to Reading Notes 2 to review the answers as a class.

3 **Have students complete the Reading Notes for Chapter 2.** Assign Sections 2.3 to 2.7 during the activity as indicated in the procedures for the Experiential Exercise. Remind students to use the Key Content Terms where appropriate as they complete their Reading Notes.

> **Reading: Structural Features of Informational Material**
>
> Before students read, have them identify structural features of their book, and review ways that these features organize the text and help telegraph and emphasize key information. Help students compare and contrast the text's structural features with those found in newspapers, instruction manuals, and signs.

Experiential Exercise

1 Before class, set up your classroom to resemble a feudal kingdom.

- Place one desk at the front of the class to be the throne. Create a "castle" around the throne by wrapping a length of string around four desks, leaving the throne in an open area in the center. Place snacks or a drink on the throne; these items represent the high privileges enjoyed by a monarch during the Middle Ages.

- Create four manors by placing four desks together in four areas of the room. Place a length of string, a roll of masking tape, and some markers at each manor.

- Move the remaining desks to the periphery of the room.

- Label the throne and the four manors as follows: *Throne, Auburn Manor, Bayhall Manor, Copshorn Manor,* and *Ditton Manor.* Also label an area at the back of the room *Cemetery.*

- Make one copy of *Student Handout 2A: Role Cards* and cut apart the role cards. Make seven copies of *Student Handout 2B: Food Tokens* and cut out the sets of food tokens to create at least twenty sets of ten cards. (**Note:** This activity requires one monarch, four lords, and five knights. For larger classes, increase the number of serfs. For smaller classes, decrease the number of knights and serfs.)

2 Distribute roles and introduce the activity. As students enter the classroom, randomly hand each student a role card from Student Handout 2A, making sure to hand each serf a set of ten food tokens. Explain to all students that they are members of European society during the 11th century. During this time, people were born into different classes and serfs were peasants who did not have the freedom to leave their lords' land without permission. Have students stand around the periphery of the room and silently read their cards.

3 Project *Information Master 2: Steps for Experiencing European Feudalism.* This outlines the seven steps of the activity. Beginning with the first page, reveal only one step at a time. Let students read what actions they need to take, and then give them the time to carry out the actions. Follow these guidelines to help the activity unfold smoothly:

- *During Step 2:* Explain to the serfs that holding onto a desk leg represents their lack of freedom. The "food" they produce for the kingdom is represented by tokens they must work to color in.

- *During Step 3:* Insist that the monarch take the hands of each lord while dictating the oath of loyalty (fealty). Circulate to make sure serfs are producing sufficient food tokens (at least three per serf).

- *During Step 4:* Remind serfs that if they refuse to provide food tokens to their lord, they will lose all points for the activity, and the lord will "execute" them.

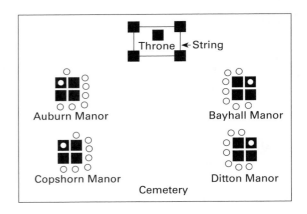

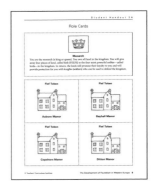

Student Handout 2A

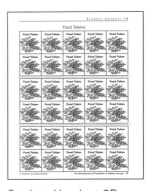

Student Handout 2B

Information Master 2

- *During Step 5:* Allow knights and lords only three minutes to negotiate. Make sure knights accept payment from only one lord. (**Note:** If a lord is having trouble attracting knights, suggest that he or she offer more pay.) Once all knights have reached an agreement with a lord, tell the lords to speak the oath.

- *During Step 6:* Tell students they must now protect their manors from an "attack" by using the four desks and the string to create a castle with four walls, similar to the monarch's. Explain that they will "survive" the attack if, while seated in the center of their castles, you (representing the invaders) cannot hit them with gently tossed balls of paper (representing weapons, such as a sword). Explain that knights—and only knights—may use a book (representing a shield) to deflect the balls of paper. Tell the monarch that he or she may request that two knights come to help defend the castle. Allow students three minutes to construct their castles and position their knights.

- *During Step 7:* To enhance the mood of the "attack," turn off the lights. Then assume the role of a fierce invader by grunting and walking toward a manor in a menacing fashion. *Gently* lob a few balls of paper inside the castle. If one strikes a student, have that student move to the cemetery, and gently admonish the knight who failed to protect the student. Continue this process with the remaining manors.

4   **Debrief the experience.** Center the discussion on these questions:

- How did it feel to be a monarch? A lord? A knight? A serf?

- In what ways were the lords, knights, and serfs interdependent?

- Do you think loyalty oaths were necessary? What do you think would happen if someone broke a loyalty oath?

- What are the benefits of this type of society? The challenges or drawbacks?

- How well did feudalism establish order in Europe in the Middle Ages?

5   **Have students read Sections 2.3 through 2.7 and complete the Reading Notes for those sections.** Use Guide to Reading Notes 2 to review the answers as a class.

Processing

Have students complete the Processing activity in their Interactive Student Notebooks. Students "grade" feudalism on how well it brought political order, economic stability, prosperity, and opportunity to medieval Europe. Consider having students share their responses with the class or with a partner.

Quicker Coverage

Break up the Reading After all students have read Sections 2.2 and 2.3, divide students into expert groups of four and assign each group to read and complete the Reading Notes for one of Sections 2.4 to 2.7. Then, give expert groups a few minutes to discuss the definitions and clarify any information they may have found confusing. Ask students to then number off within their expert groups. Form new jigsaw groups by having all number 1s meet, all number 2s meet, etc. In each jigsaw group, have students share the information from their section.

Deeper Coverage

Have Students Research Their Roles Before Completing the Activity Assign students to their roles the day before you plan to conduct the Experiential Exercise. Working with other members who have been assigned to their same role, have students read the section of text that applies to them, and use the Internet to learn such things as what their particular character might wear, what props they might carry, and what they might talk about as the simulation takes place. Encourage students to make simple costumes or bring in props to make the exercise more lifelike.

Assessment

Mastering the Content

1. B	5. C	9. C	13. B
2. D	6. A	10. A	14. D
3. B	7. A	11. C	15. D
4. D	8. A	12. A	16. B

Applying Social Studies Skills

17. William of Normandy conquers England

18. five years

19. He reigned in the Early Middle Ages. He took the title Holy Roman emperor; the title includes the words *Roman* and *emperor,* suggesting a link to the Roman Empire.

Exploring the Essential Question

20. Answers should include all the elements requested in the prompt.

Scoring Rubric

Score	Description
3	Student completes all three parts of the task. Interview responses are clearly stated and respond to both parts of the question: How is order established for this person (for example, by protection in return for loyalty) and how well does it work for this person? Responses are consistent with information learned in this chapter.
2	Student completes two parts of the task. The third part is missing or wrong. OR Student does all three parts of the task but incompletely.
1	Student completes one part of the task. The other two parts are missing or wrong. OR Student completes two or three parts of the task but minimally.
0	Response does not match the task or is incorrect or missing.

English Language Learners

Provide Students with a List of Key Vocabulary
Encourage them to find definitions and make simple illustrations for each term ahead of time. For some students, it may be helpful to reduce the number of key terms they must define to only those essential for understanding the main points of this lesson.

Learners Reading and Writing Below Grade Level

Provide Support for the Reading Notes Give some students a copy of Guide to Reading Notes 2 with only partial answers to each question revealed. Allow them to fill in the blanks or complete the unfinished sentences as they read each section.

Learners with Special Education Needs

Prepare Students for the Experiential Exercise Explain to students what will happen in the activity the day before you plan to execute it. Allow students who may be uncomfortable with the roles of this activity to choose to be observers or reporters. Provide them with a copy of Information Master 2 to use as a checklist. During the activity, have them check off items that they observe.

Allow for Additional Roles Assign the role of monarch to students who may find the physical aspects of this activity challenging. This will allow these students to remain in a central location where nobles, knights, and serfs will have to approach them. Or, assign these students the role of "invader." They can assist you in "attacking" various manors during Step 7 of the Experiential Exercise. Prior to this step, they can act as observers to the exchanges of fealty throughout the activity, and comment on these interactions during the debriefing.

Advanced Learners

Provide an Alternative to the Processing Activity Challenge students to compare feudalism to modern society. Encourage students to think about which individuals or groups in our society most resemble the various social classes in European feudal society. Next to each level of feudal society, have students list those modern groups, and draw symbols to represent them. Then have students list the similarities and differences between the modern groups and the feudal groups.

Enrichment Resources

Have students find out more about the development of the medieval feudal system in Western Europe by exploring the following Enrichment Resources for *History Alive! The Medieval World and Beyond* at www.teachtci.com.

Enrichment Readings These in-depth readings encourage students to explore selected topics related to the chapter. You may also find readings that relate the chapter's content directly to your state's curriculum.

Internet Connections The recommended Web sites provide useful and engaging content that reinforces skills development and mastery of subjects within the chapter.

Literature Recommendations

The following books offer opportunities to extend the content in this chapter.

The Door in the Wall by Marguerite De Angeli (New York: Bantam Doubleday Dell, 1998)

The Middle Ages: An Illustrated History by Barbara A. Hanawalt (New York: Oxford University Press, 1999)

A Proud Taste for Scarlet and Miniver by E.L. Konigsburg (New York: Atheneum, 2001)

Section 2.2

1. Answers will vary. Sample answer: After ruling the Franks for more than 40 years, Charlemagne, called the "King Father of Europe," has passed away. A six-foot-four-inch giant, he loved having scholarly works read to him and made his court a center of culture. Most importantly, he unified most Christian lands of Europe into a single empire. Crowned as the Holy Roman emperor in 800 C.E. by Pope Leo III, this great king will be sorely missed.

2. Pope Leo III helped Charlemagne by giving him the blessing of the Church (the Church was a central part of society) and by crowning him Holy Roman emperor in 800 C.E. In return, Leo gained the support of a strong leader with an army.

3. The rulers who came to power after Charlemagne failed to defend the empire. In addition, Europe was threatened by Muslims, Magyars, and Vikings in the 9th and 10th centuries.

Section 2.3

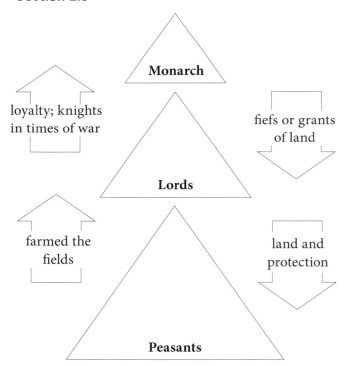

Monarch

loyalty; knights in times of war

fiefs or grants of land

Lords

farmed the fields

land and protection

Peasants

Section 2.4

1. Monarchs believed in the "divine right of kings," which meant that God gave them the right to rule.

2. William defeated his cousin Harold and established a line of Norman kings in England, bringing feudalism with him. Feudalism brought stability and order to England.

Section 2.5

1. Houses should be stone or wood, surrounded by gardens and outbuildings like stables. Students may include high walls or a moat as well.

2. Lords were responsible for managing and defending their manors and acting as judges. They fought for their own lords in times of war, and supplied soldiers. They also appointed officials.

3. Noblewomen were responsible for raising and training their children and sometimes the children of other noble families. They were also responsible for overseeing their large households.

Section 2.6

1. A boy started training for knighthood by becoming a page, where he learned skills, such as horseback riding and singing. After seven years, he became a squire and learned how to fight as a warrior. A deserving squire was made a knight in his early 20s at a special ceremony.

2. Knights were the mounted soldiers in the feudal system and were expected to be loyal to their Church and lord, to be fair, and to protect the helpless.

3. Answers will vary. Sample answer: I promise to be loyal to the Church and my lord. I will be just and fair and protect the helpless. When possible, I will perform acts of gallantry and I will show respect to women.

Section 2.7

1. Most peasants worked at raising crops and tending livestock. Some worked as carpenters, shoemakers, and smiths. Peasants paid taxes to lords.

2. The daily lives of peasants revolved around work. They had to pay numerous taxes. They were required to grind their grain at the lord's mill and the miller kept grain for the lord and for himself. They lived in small homes with few possessions. Serfs were bound to the manor and couldn't leave without permission.

The Roman Catholic Church in Medieval Europe

How influential was the Roman Catholic Church in medieval Europe?

Overview

In an Experiential Exercise students "visit" five medieval sites, such as Chartres Cathedral in France and the University of Bologna in Italy, to analyze the influence of the Roman Catholic Church in medieval Europe.

Objectives

In the course of reading this chapter and participating in the classroom activity, students will

Social Studies

- describe the structure and role of the Roman Catholic Church in medieval Europe.
- explain the conflict between Pope Gregory VII and Emperor Henry IV.
- analyze the Roman Catholic Church's role as a political, intellectual, and aesthetic institution.
- evaluate the extent to which the Roman Catholic Church influenced life in medieval Europe.

Language Arts

- write a poem that unifies important ideas by means of a coherent organizational structure
- include facts and examples to support implied or stated claims.

Social Studies Vocabulary

Key Content Terms religion, persecute, Roman Catholic Church, clergy, sacrament, pilgrimage, natural law, religious order

Academic Vocabulary widespread, hierarchy, authority, technique

Materials

History Alive! The Medieval World and Beyond

Interactive Student Notebooks

Placards 3A–3F (2 sets)

Visual 3

Lesson Masters

- Station Materials 3A–3B, 3D (2 copies of each)
- Station Materials 3C (1 copy)
- Student Handout 3 (1 per student)
- Vocabulary Development handout (1 per student on colored paper)

4 envelopes

4 sets of colored pencils

Activity	Suggested Time	Materials
Preview	10 minutes	• *History Alive! The Medieval World and Beyond* • Interactive Student Notebooks
Vocabulary Development	30–40 minutes	• *History Alive! The Medieval World and Beyond* • Interactive Student Notebooks • Vocabulary Development handout
Experiential Exercise	150–180 minutes (3 regular periods) (1.5 block periods)	• *History Alive! The Medieval World and Beyond* • Interactive Student Notebooks • Visual 3 • Placards 3A–3F (2 sets; original plus 1 copy) • 4 envelopes • 4 sets of colored pencils • Station Materials 3A (2 copies, cut apart and put into two envelopes) • Station Materials 3B (2 copies, cut apart and put into two envelopes) • Station Materials 3C (1 copy, hung on wall) • Station Materials 3D (2 copies) • Student Handout 3 (1 per student)
Processing	20 minutes	• Interactive Student Notebooks
Assessment	40 minutes	• Chapter 3 Assessment

Preview

1   **Have students complete the Preview activity for Chapter 3 in their Interactive Student Notebooks.**

2   **Have students share their responses in pairs or with the class.** Briefly discuss their choices.

3   **Connect the Preview activity to the chapter.** Explain that the most important building in a medieval European town was usually the church, which reflected its importance in people's daily lives during the Middle Ages. In the chapter and activity, students will learn more about the Roman Catholic Church and its influence in the daily life of medieval Europeans.

Vocabulary Development

1   **Introduce the Key Content Terms.** Have students locate the Key Content Terms for the chapter in their Interactive Student Notebooks. These are important terms that will help them understand the main ideas of the chapter. Ask volunteers to identify any familiar terms and how they might be used in a sentence.

2   **Have students complete a Vocabulary Development handout.** Give each student a copy of the Vocabulary Development handout of your choice from the Reading Toolkit at the back of the Lesson Masters. These handouts provide extra Key Content Term practice and support, depending on your students' needs. Review the completed handout by asking volunteers to share one answer for each term.

Reading

1   **Introduce the Essential Question and have students read Section 3.1.** Afterwards, have students use information from Section 3.1 and from the chapter opener image to propose possible answers to the Essential Question: *How influential was the Roman Catholic Church in medieval Europe?*

2   **Have students complete the Reading Notes for Chapter 3.** Assign Sections 3.2 to 3.8 during the activity as indicated in the procedures for the Experiential Exercise, below. Remind students to use the Key Content Terms where appropriate as they complete their Reading Notes.

Experiential Exercise

1 **Before class, prepare the materials and the classroom.** Follow these steps:

- Make one copy of *Student Handout 3: Site Research* for each student.

- Use www.teachtci.com to create a second set of Placards 3A–3F.

- Arrange the desks around the edge of the classroom to create five sites. At each site, set up two stations of three desks each, as shown on the classroom map below.

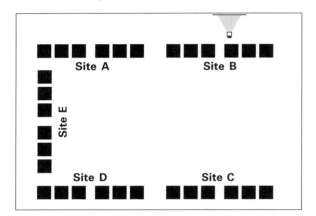

- For Site A, make two copies of *Station Materials 3A: Object and Description Cards.* Cut the Object Cards and Description Cards apart and place one set of each together in an envelope. Put one envelope at each station for Site A.

- For Site B, make two copies of *Station Materials 3B: Role Cards.* Cut the Role Cards apart and place one set in each envelope. (**Note:** Two groups will complete this station together and will need only one set of role cards. The other set is in case additional groups need to work on this site at the same time.) Make one copy of *Station Materials 3C: Pilgrimage Stops* and hang each in a different corner, or on a different wall, around the room. (**Note:** You may want to set those signs up in the hallway outside your classroom if there is another adult who can monitor students there.)

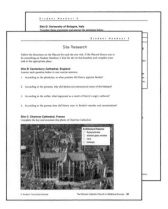

Student Handout 3

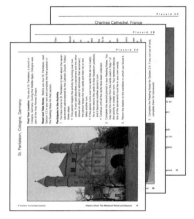

Placards 3A–3F

Station Materials 3A

Station Materials 3B

Station Materials 3C

- For Site C, place one set of colored pencils at each station.

- For Site D, make two copies of *Station Materials 3D: Latin Dictionary* and place one at each station.

- For Site E, place one set of colored pencils at each station.

- Put one copy of Placard A at each station at Site A, one copy of Placard B at each station at Site B, and so on for each site. Placard F will be hung at Site B, with Placard B. (**Note:** Directions for setting up each site are located on the back of each placard for easy reference during set-up.)

Note: If after completing the activity you put the materials for each station in labeled, resealable bags or in manila folders, the only preparation necessary for repeating this activity with other classes, or in future years, will be to recopy Student Handout 3 for each student.

Station Materials 3D

2 **Introduce the activity.** Have students sit on the floor at the center of the room. Explain to students that they are gathering information on the Roman Catholic Church's influence on medieval life. They will take a "walking tour" of five sites in medieval Europe. They will use the information they gather at each site to create an acrostic poem about the Church's influence in this era.

3 **Have students read and complete the Reading Notes for Section 3.2.** Before students read, explain that this section describes the organization and responsibilities of the Roman Catholic Church in medieval times.

4 **Project *Visual 3: Influence of the Roman Catholic Church in Medieval Europe*** and have students analyze the map. Ask,

- What do you see here?

- What cities or towns are labeled on the map?

- In what nations are the cities located?

- What does this map tell you about the influence of the Roman Catholic Church in the Middle Ages?

Visual 3

Explain to students that as they complete their walking tour, they will visit these five cities to gather information about the Church's influence on life in medieval Europe. You may want to continue to project this image as students complete their walking tour (Steps 5 and 6, below).

5 **Put students in groups of three and explain the activity.** Distribute one copy of Student Handout 3 to each student. Tell students that as they visit each site they will do the following:

- follow the directions on the placard

- read the appropriate section of their text and complete Reading Notes

- complete an activity for that site; in some cases, they will need to use Student Handout 3 to do this.

6 **Have students complete the walking tour.** Have each group begin at a different site. Each site has two stations, so two groups may work concurrently at each site. At each site, students will be directed to read a section of the text and complete their Reading Notes before completing an activity for that site. When a group finishes at a site, you may want to check their work and Reading Notes, and (optionally) award points, before having them move to another site. Continue until most groups have visited all sites.

7 **Debrief the activity.** Ask students, *During the Middle Ages, which role of the Roman Catholic Church do you think was most important to people spiritually? Socially? Intellectually? Artistically?*

Processing

Have students complete the Processing activity on a separate sheet of paper in their notebooks. Students will create an acrostic poem highlighting the influence of the Church in medieval Europe.

Quicker Coverage

Include Fewer Sites on the Walking Tour Use only Sites A–D on the walking tour. If you have a large class, you may want to set up three stations at each site.

Assign the Reading for Homework After conducting the Preview, Reading, and Reading Notes for Sections 3.1–3.2 in class, assign students to read Sections 3.3 through 3.5 and complete the Reading Notes for homework. The following day in class, have students visit Sites A–C. For homework that night, have students read Sections 3.6 through 3.8. The following day in class, have students visit Sites D–E. If you do only two or three sites per day, you might consider setting up an extra station at each site to accommodate additional groups.

Deeper Coverage

Create a Detailed Illuminated Manuscript Have students create an illuminated manuscript by adding the following requirements to the Processing activity:

- The first letter of the poem, a *T,* must be illuminated. Students will decorate the letter with designs, pictures, or symbols that represent medieval society.
- The poem must include at least four pictures. These can be placed in the margins, in the background, or within the poem itself. The pictures should relate to the poem and help illustrate students' ideas.

Assessment

Mastering the Content

1. C	5. D	9. B	13. B
2. A	6. A	10. C	14. D
3. B	7. B	11. C	15. A
4. D	8. C	12. B	16. D

Applying Social Studies Skills

17. Normally, monks may have one main meal or a breakfast and supper. They are allowed vegetables and fruit, when it is available. They are given one pound of bread per day.

18. Monks who have done a great deal of work may receive extra food; the sick and old may eat red meat.

19. Possible response: Benedict says it is not right for a Christian to eat too much, as the Lord said in the Bible. For younger boys, Benedict probably wants them to learn moderation, so that they will not overeat and become gluttons.

Exploring the Essential Question

20. Answers should include all the elements requested in the prompt.

Scoring Rubric

Score	Description
3	Student completes all five ratings and five explanations. Explanations are clearly stated, supported by details, and demonstrate command of standard English conventions.
2	Student responds to most or all parts of the task, but explanations may lack details or not be clearly stated.
1	Student responds to at least one part of the task. Explanations may contain factual and/or grammatical errors and may lack details.
0	Response does not match the task or is incorrect.

English Language Learners

Model the Task to Be Completed Before beginning the walking tour of the five medieval sites, consider doing the following with the whole class at one site:

- Review the directions at each station.
- Model each task to be completed.
- Ask students to explain the directions in their own words, to ensure that they understand the station directions and tasks.

Learners Reading and Writing Below Grade Level

Assist Students with Reading Notes Provide students with a copy of Guide to Reading Notes for Chapter 3 with occasional words in each section omitted (white out a portion of each answer before photocopying). Students can fill in the blanks as they read the text at each site.

Learners with Special Education Needs

Adapt the Processing Activity Make the following modifications to the acrostic poems students write:

- Reduce the number of stanzas from nine to six by requiring the first letters of the stanzas to spell out only the word CHURCH.
- Decrease the number of required words from the Key Content Terms from five to two or three.

Advanced Learners

Draw Parallels Between History and Today Have students explore the power of the Roman Catholic Church in medieval Europe by comparing and contrasting the role of the Church in medieval Europe to the role of government in the United States by doing the following:

- After they read Section 3.2, ask students to create a graphic organizer showing similarities and differences between the medieval Roman Catholic Church and the present-day U.S. government.
- When brainstorming ideas, students should consider including information on such topics as the following:
  - how these two organizations are structured
  - individuals or groups who hold various positions of power within each organization
  - the powers of these organizations over the people they serve
  - the responsibilities of these organizations toward the people they serve

Enrichment Resources

Have students find out more about the influence of the Roman Catholic Church in medieval Europe by exploring the following Enrichment Resources for *History Alive! The Medieval World and Beyond* at www.teachtci.com.

Enrichment Readings These in-depth readings encourage students to explore selected topics related to the chapter. You may also find readings that relate the chapter's content directly to your state's curriculum.

Internet Connections The recommended Web sites provide useful and engaging content that reinforces skills development and mastery of subjects within the chapter.

Literature Recommendations

The following books offer opportunities to extend the content in this chapter.

Cathedral by David Macaulay (Boston: Houghton Mifflin Company, 1974)

Francis: The Poor Man of Assisi by Tomie dePaola (New York: Holiday House, 1990)

Peregrine by Joan E. Goodman (Boston: Houghton Mifflin Company, 2000)

Section 3.2

1. The Roman emperor Constantine issued a decree in 313 C.E. allowing Christians to practice their religion freely. Prior to that, Christians had been persecuted by the Romans.

2. Answers will vary, but should include two of the following: provided leadership, at times organized the distribution of food, provided hospitality to refugees and travelers, copied and preserved old texts to help keep learning alive, and helped bring new converts to the Christian faith.

3. Illustrations will vary. One-sentence explanations may be similar to the ones below:

   Cardinals were high-ranking clergymen who assisted and counseled the pope.

   Archbishops oversaw large or important areas called archdioceses.

   Bishops governed areas called dioceses from great cathedrals.

   Priests oversaw local communities called parishes.

4. Pope Gregory VII banned the practice whereby kings (instead of the pope) could <u>appoint</u> members of the clergy. Henry IV considered it his <u>duty</u>, and privilege, to appoint Church officials. He declared that Gregory was no longer pope, so Gregory <u>excommunicated</u> Henry. Henry had to beg forgiveness, thereby recognizing the pope's <u>authority</u>, even over an emperor.

Section 3.3

1. Receiving the sacraments was an essential part of gaining salvation.

2. Symbols will vary. One sentence explanations should resemble the following:

   - Baptism is when a person is cleansed of sin and admitted to the Church.

   - Confirmation is when a person declares his or her belief in God and the Church.

   - The Eucharist is part of the Mass in which the bread and wine are consecrated.

   - Matrimony is the formal union of a couple by the Church.

   - Holy Orders is the ritual during which a man becomes a priest.

   - Penance is when sins are confessed to a priest to receive God's forgiveness.

   - Extreme Unction is the anointing of a person near death with holy oil by a priest.

Section 3.4

1. People went on pilgrimages to show their devotion to God, as an act of penance for their sins, or in hope of being cured of an illness. Some popular pilgrimage destinations were Jerusalem, Rome, and Canterbury.

2. Travel was difficult and sometimes dangerous. Pilgrims often traveled on foot. Robbery was a constant threat.

3. The Crusades were military expeditions to the Holy Land that attempted to recover Jerusalem and other sites of pilgrimage from Muslims.

Section 3.5

1. Most art was made for religious purposes. Paintings and sculptures in churches helped people to worship. Since most people couldn't read, art helped to tell the story of Jesus's life or Bible stories in a way everyone could understand.

2. Sketches will vary. Definitions should be similar to the following:

   nave: the long central section of a cathedral

   transept: the shorter side sections of a cathedral

   gargoyle: a decorative stone sculpture in the form of a mythical beast

   stained-glass window: a large window made from pieces of colored glass arranged in a design to form a picture (usually about the Bible)

   flying buttress: an exterior stone arch that helped spread the weight of the roof and walls

Section 3.6

1. A new form of writing with both upper- and lowercase letters made reading easier. Also, universities were created for advanced study.

2. Thomas Aquinas was an Italian scholar of philosophy and theology. He tried to bridge the gap between reason and faith by writing logical arguments to show how reason and religious belief worked together.

Section 3.7

1. holy day; Christian holidays celebrated Christian saints, events in the life of Jesus, and important religious ideas.

2. They attended Church services, and then celebrated with feasts and entertainments including bonfires, acrobats and jugglers, dancing bears, and plays.

3. Students should label the figure as "Thomas Aquinas" and label the land on each side of the bridge "faith" and "reason," respectively.

Section 3.8

	Benedictine Monks	Franciscan Friars
Where did they live?	in monasteries (communities devoted to prayer and service to fellow Christians)	traveled among ordinary people to preach and to care for the poor and sick
What promises or sacrifices did they make to join the order?	Benedict's Rule: poverty, chastity, and obedience	had to live in complete poverty and had to work or beg for food for themselves and the poor
How did they spend their time?	prayer, study, and work; attended Church services, cared for poor and sick, taught, and farmed	cared for the poor and sick; traveled; prayed

Life in Medieval Towns

What was life like in medieval European towns?

Overview

In a Problem Solving Groupwork activity, students create six dramatizations to learn about aspects of life in medieval European towns.

Objectives

In the course of reading this chapter and participating in the classroom activity, students will

Social Studies

- explain how geographic factors affected the development of towns in medieval Europe.
- discuss the relationship between trade and the growth of medieval towns.
- examine several aspects of daily life in medieval towns.
- describe the typical day of a townsperson in medieval Europe.

Language Arts

- clarify word meanings through the use of definitions and examples.
- read expository text to connect essential ideas to prior knowledge.
- deliver oral summaries that convey an understanding of sources, use the student's own words, and include the main ideas and most significant details.

Social Studies Vocabulary

Key Content Terms charter, guild, apprentice, common law

Academic Vocabulary surplus, resident, dominate, isolate

Materials

History Alive! The Medieval World and Beyond

Interactive Student Notebooks

Visuals 4A–4G

Lesson Masters

- Student Handout 4 (1 per student)
- Vocabulary Development handout (1 per student, on colored paper)

Activity	Suggested Time	Materials
Preview	10 minutes	• *History Alive! The Medieval World and Beyond* • Interactive Student Notebooks • Visual 4A
Vocabulary Development	30–40 minutes	• *History Alive! The Medieval World and Beyond* • Interactive Student Notebooks • Vocabulary Development handout
Problem Solving Groupwork	*Phase 1* 90-minutes (2 regular periods) (1 block period) • Prepare for Dramatizations (Steps 1–5) *Phase 2* 90-minutes (2 regular periods) (1 block period) • Perform Dramatizations (Steps 6–13)	• *History Alive! The Medieval World and Beyond* • Interactive Student Notebooks • Visuals 4B–4G • Student Handout 4 (1 per student)
Processing	20 minutes	• Interactive Student Notebooks
Assessment	40 minutes	• Chapter 4 Assessment

Preview

1 **Project *Visual 4A: Scenes of Medieval Life: A Medieval Marketplace*.** Tell students that this is a marketplace in a 13th-century European town. Have them carefully analyze the image to determine what it might have been like to live in a town in medieval Europe. Ask,

Visual 4A

- What interesting or important details can you identify? (Consider inviting volunteers to the screen to point out details.)

- This image has clues about how people lived in medieval European towns. What hypotheses can you make about what living conditions were like, based on those clues?

- This image has clues about job opportunities available to people living in medieval European towns. What hypotheses can you make about job opportunities, based on those clues?

- This image has clues about entertainment in medieval European towns. What hypotheses can you make about what entertainment was like, based on those clues?

2 **Have students complete the Preview activity for Chapter 4 in their Interactive Student Notebooks.**

3 **Connect the Preview activity to the chapter.** Explain to students that they will be exploring more aspects of medieval towns, like the one they just saw in the image. By the 12th century, towns had begun to sprout up around castles and monasteries and along trade routes. More and more people were leaving the countryside to find work or to trade in these towns. As these towns grew, a new way of living developed in Europe, too.

Vocabulary Development

1 **Introduce the Key Content Terms.** Have students locate the Key Content Terms for the chapter in their Interactive Student Notebooks. These are important terms that will help them understand the main ideas of the chapter. Ask volunteers to identify any familiar terms and how they might be used in a sentence.

2 **Have students complete a Vocabulary Development handout.** Give each student a copy of the Vocabulary Development handout of your choice from the Reading Toolkit at the back of the Lesson Masters. These handouts provide extra Key Content Term practice and support, depending on your students' needs. Review the completed handout by asking volunteers to share one answer for each term.

Reading

1 Introduce the Essential Question and have students read Section 4.1.
Have students identify the Essential Question on the first page of the chapter: *What was life like in medieval European towns?* Then have students read Section 4.1. Afterward, have students carefully analyze the chapter opener image. Then ask them to find words, phrases, or sentences in the text of Section 4.1 and connect them to visual details in the chapter opener image. Have several volunteers share with the class the connections they found.

2 Have students complete the Reading Notes for Chapter 4. Assign Sections 4.2 to 4.8 during the activity, as indicated in the procedures for the Problem Solving Groupwork activity. Remind students to use the Key Content Terms where appropriate as they complete their Reading Notes.

Problem Solving Groupwork

1 Arrange students in groups of four. You may wish to prepare a transparency that shows students with whom they will work and where they will sit.

2 Introduce the activity. Tell students that each group will create an interactive dramatization about one aspect of life in medieval European towns. Each dramatization will re-create historical conditions for the class to experience, and will involve four audience members. Pass out *Visuals 4B–4G: Scenes of Medieval Life,* one per group, and a corresponding copy of *Student Handout 4: Preparing an Interactive Dramatization About [Chosen Topic].* Tell students that they will be using these materials to create their dramatizations.

3 Have students read and complete the Reading Notes for Section 4.2. Tell students that this section provides an overview of the growth of medieval European towns. After students have completed this section of Reading Notes in their Interactive Student Notebooks, use Guide to Reading Notes for Chapter 4 to review the answers to these questions as a class.

4 Review the steps for creating interactive dramatizations. Read about and explain the four roles—Historian, Director, Props Master, and Host—listed on Student Handout 4. Assign each student a role for the activity. Tell students they will be responsible for leading the group through one of the steps to prepare their dramatizations. Then review Steps 2–5 on Student Handout 4 with students and answer any questions.

5 Monitor groups as they create their dramatizations. Allow adequate time—at least two class periods—for preparation. (**Note:** You may want to pair groups of students for the rehearsal of the dramatizations, with each group acting as audience members for the other.)

Visuals 4B–4G

Student Handout 4

6 **Arrange the classroom for presentations.** When students are ready, arrange the classroom with a stage area in front and the projector centrally located, as shown in the diagram.

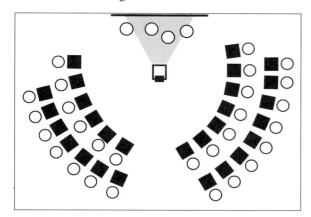

7 **Have students read Sections 4.3–4.5 and complete the corresponding Reading Notes.** This will provide them with background for the first three dramatizations. Consider assigning these sections for homework the night before students present the dramatizations for these topics.

8 **Have the first group select four participants from the audience and perform their dramatization.** Remind performers to speak loud enough to be heard clearly by all students in the room. Encourage all students in the audience to be supportive, respectful, and attentive.

9 **Debrief the dramatization and encourage students to ask questions.** Ask audience members the following question, *What did you learn about life in medieval European towns from this presentation?* Have the Host invite audience members to ask questions of the group.

10 **Repeat Steps 8 and 9 for the two dramatizations corresponding to Sections 4.4 and 4.5.**

11 **Have student read Sections 4.6–4.8 and complete the corresponding Reading Notes.** This will provide them with background for the final three dramatizations. Consider assigning these sections for homework the night before students present the dramatizations for these topics.

12 **Repeat Steps 8 and 9 for the three remaining dramatizations.**

13 **Hold a class discussion. Center the discussion on these questions:**

- What did you learn about life in medieval European towns?

- Do you think you would have enjoyed living in a town in medieval Europe? Why or why not?

- In what ways were these dramatizations unable to realistically portray various aspects of life in medieval European towns?

- How was life in medieval European towns different from life in modern towns? How was it similar?

Listening and Speaking: Effects on the Viewer

Ask the class to consider what effects the images, sound(s), and text have on them, including both logical and emotional responses. Have students identify how these effects were achieved. Also, ask them to offer feedback on ways the effects were exactly right, or might be intensified, decreased, or otherwise altered to make them more consistent with the purpose of the presentation.

Processing

Have students complete the Processing activity on a separate sheet of paper in their notebooks. Students will create a diary that describes a typical day for someone living in a medieval European town.

Quicker Coverage

Streamline the Activity Assign each group a section to read along with the corresponding visual from the list below:

- Section 4.3, Visual 4B
- Section 4.4, Visual 4C
- Section 4.5, Visual 4D
- Section 4.6, Visual 4E
- Section 4.7, Visual 4F
- Section 4.8, Visual 4G

With their groups, students should read their assigned section and complete the corresponding Reading Notes. Then, ask groups to annotate their visuals with information from their reading, making sure to focus on information needed to complete the Reading Notes for that section. Have each group select a presenter who, when called, will lead the class through an examination of the visual and will share the information that the class needs to complete their Reading Notes.

Deeper Coverage

Have Students do Additional Research for the Dramatizations Have students use the Internet or library resources to learn more about their aspect of daily life and then include what they learn in their presentations. The Enrichment Resources provided at www.teachtci.com for this chapter are excellent sources of additional information. Also, consider having students do Internet research to locate recipes from medieval Europe to share—as either a recipe itself or, if time and resources allow, the cooked item—with audience members during or after their presentations.

Assessment

Mastering the Content

1. C	5. D	9. A	13. B
2. B	6. D	10. B	14. C
3. D	7. B	11. B	15. C
4. C	8. A	12. A	16. A

Applying Social Studies Skills

17. Marseille, Genoa, Venice, Tunis, Constantinople (accept any four of these)

18. oceans, or bodies of water

19. Tunis

Exploring the Essential Question

20. Answers should include all the elements requested in the prompt.

Scoring Rubric

Score	Description
3	Student writes a persuasive paragraph for each of the four topics, as directed in the four bulleted points in the instructions. Taken as a group, the paragraphs state a position, give details in support of the position, and address potential reader concerns. Student includes details in support of the position.
2	Student responds to most or all parts of the task, but paragraphs may lack supporting details or not be clearly stated.
1	Student responds to at least one part of the task. Paragraphs may contain factual and/or grammatical errors and may lack details.
0	Response does not match the task or is incorrect.

English Language Learners

Add Support to the Preview Activity Distribute incomplete cue cards that students can use as prompts to help them participate in the analysis of Visual 4A. Prepare several identical cue cards for each spiral question. Here are some examples of cue cards for this image:

- An interesting detail I see in this image is . . .
- I think that living conditions in medieval towns can be described as _____ because _____.
- Jobs available to people in medieval towns might include _____ because_____.
- In medieval towns, people spent their free time . . .

Learners Reading and Writing Below Grade Level

Provide Additional Support for the Processing Activity Give students the following prompts:

10:30 AM	Stopped at grocers. Bought . . .
11:30 AM	For lunch, visited . . .
12:30 PM	Stopped by doctor's for . . .
1:30 PM	On the way home, passed by the stocks and noticeed . . .
2:30 PM	Outside my home, noticed children playing . . .
3:30 PM	Returned home. Gathered with the family in the solar to . . .
5:30 PM	Ate dinner with family. Afterward, helped the servants to clean up by . . .

Learners with Special Education Needs

Provide an Alternate Role Assign some students the role of Host, and prepare a short checklist for them to use when completing Step 5 on Student Handout 4. A checklist for the Host to use during rehearsal might include the following:

- Each group member is actively involved in the dramatization.
- Actors speak their lines loudly, clearly, and at the right time.
- Actors use costumes and props appropriately.
- Actors know when and how visitors will participate.

Provide Students with the Guide to Reading Notes Allow them to highlight their copy as they read the section prior to each dramatization. It may be helpful to model for some students how to highlight only those select words and phrases that will help them better process the material.

Create Larger Groups for Dramatizations Consider creating groups of five to accommodate students who may need additional help fulfilling the requirements of their roles as given in Step 1 of Student Handout 4.

Advanced Learners

Provide an Alternative to the Processing Activity Have students write a more elaborate set of diary entries of someone living in a medieval town. Instruct them to add details about each aspect of their day and to describe one of the following in their entry:

- an experience as a guild member
- an exchange with a family member in the solar
- a situation that involved medical treatment
- a description of events during a festival day in town

Allow students the opportunity to present this Processing activity in a creative format, such as a medieval manuscript, and to include illustrations.

Enrichment Resources

Have students find out more about life in medieval European towns by exploring the following Enrichment Resources for *History Alive! The Medieval World and Beyond* at www.teachtci.com.

Enrichment Readings These in-depth readings encourage students to explore selected topics related to the chapter. You may also find readings that relate the chapter's content directly to your state's curriculum.

Internet Connections The recommended Web sites provide useful and engaging content that reinforces skills development and mastery of subjects within the chapter.

Literature Recommendations

The following books offer opportunities to extend the content in this chapter.

Catherine, Called Birdy by Karen Cushman (New York: HarperCollins, 1995)

Daily Life in the Middle Ages by Paul B. Newman (Jefferson, NC: McFarland, 2001)

Life in a Medieval City by Joseph Gies and Frances Gies (New York: Harper Perennial, 1981)

Section 4.2

1. Towns were often located next to rivers, which made trade easier.

2. Improved farming methods and the revival of trade contributed to the growth of towns.

3. In some places, towns struggled violently to become independent. In others, the town leaders purchased a charter which gave them the right to govern themselves.

Section 4.3

1. Guilds were organizations of people who practiced the same craft or trade. They were set up to make sure their members were treated fairly and produced quality goods.

2. Guilds provided them with money and food in times of need.

3. Answers will vary. Sample answer:

Dear Sophie,

Guess what? My parents have just signed an agreement with a stonemason. I am going to become his apprentice! For the next few years, I will live and work in his home. My parents have agreed to pay him a small bit of money, but I don't know how much. I won't get paid, but in seven years, the master will examine a sample of my work. If I meet his standards, I will get to become a stonemason, too. I really hope I can do this.

Sincerely,

James

Section 4.4

1. Early in the Middle Ages, people traded in luxury goods, which only the wealthy could afford. Later, more local people were trading more and more kinds of goods, including everyday items such as food and clothing.

2. Merchants became wealthy and powerful by selling a variety of goods from faraway lands, dominating the town's business life, and joining town councils.

3. Because of religious prejudice and hostility, Jews found it hard to earn a living by farming, and sometimes they were the victims of violence. Rulers took their property at will. One opportunity open to Jews was banking and money lending.

Section 4.5

1. Most homes in medieval towns were small, crowded, and built of wood. The homes of the wealthy were much larger.

2. Almost half of all children died. Those who survived began preparing for their adult roles at age seven.

3. Most girls were educated at home in cooking, cloth making, and others skills for running a home. They typically married young and began raising children soon after. Only girls from wealthy families had an opportunity to learn how to paint or read music.

Section 4.6

1. Towns were very dirty places with no running water. Garbage and wastes were tossed in the streets. People lived in small crowded spaces. Rats and fleas were common and carried diseases.

2. Some common diseases in medieval Europe were measles, cholera, scarlet fever, and bubonic plague.

3. Medieval doctors used prayer, magic, and herbal medicines. Bloodletting, including the use of leeches, was also popular.

Section 4.7

1. Two methods were trial by ordeal, in which the accused had to pass a dangerous test, and trial by combat, in which the accused had to fight to prove his or her innocence, or could have someone fight for him or her.

2. Fines and the stocks were used to punish those found guilty of minor crimes. Those convicted of more serious crimes could be hanged or burned at the stake.

3. Monarchs began setting up a system of royal courts. This contributed to a growing body of common law. Both the independent judiciary and the new laws became a safeguard of individual rights and replaced trial by ordeal and combat.

Section 4.8

1. Children played with dolls and toys, such as wooden swords and hobbyhorses. They also rolled hoops and played badminton, lawn bowling, and blind man's bluff.

2. Adults liked games such as chess, checkers, and backgammon. Card games and dancing were also popular.

3. Mystery plays re-created stories from the Bible. Miracle plays dramatized the lives of saints.

The Decline of Feudalism

How did events in Europe contribute to the decline of feudalism and the rise of democratic thought?

Overview

In a Visual Discovery activity, students analyze key events in Europe between the 12th and 15th centuries to understand contributing factors to the decline of feudalism and the rise of democratic thought.

Objectives

In the course of reading this chapter and participating in the classroom activity, students will

Social Studies

- describe significant medieval English legal and constitutional developments, such as Magna Carta and the establishment of Parliament, and their impact on feudalism.

- analyze how the bubonic plague spread from Central Asia to Europe, and evaluate the impact it had on the population of Europe and on feudalism.

- summarize the impact of the Hundred Years' War on feudalism in Europe.

Language Arts

- clarify word meanings through the use of definitions and examples.

- deliver a narrative presentation that establishes a major or minor character and uses a range of appropriate strategies, including dialogue.

- write summaries that include the main idea and most significant details

Social Studies Vocabulary

Key Content Terms Magna Carta, habeas corpus, Model Parliament, bubonic plague, Hundred Years' War, heretic

Academic Vocabulary traditional, foundation, democratic, estimate, momentum

Materials

History Alive! The Medieval World and Beyond

Interactive Student Notebooks

Visuals 5A–5C

Lesson Masters

- Student Handout 5A (1 copy for every four students)
- Student Handout 5B (2 copies, cut apart)
- Student Handout 5C (2 copies, cut apart)
- Student Handout 5D (1 copy for every four students)
- Vocabulary Development handout (1 per student, on colored paper)

4 envelopes

Activity	Suggested Time	Materials
Preview	10 minutes	• *History Alive! The Medieval World and Beyond* • Interactive Student Notebooks
Vocabulary Development	30–40 minutes	• *History Alive! The Medieval World and Beyond* • Interactive Student Notebooks • Vocabulary Development handout
Visual Discovery	120 minutes (3 regular periods) (1.5 block periods)	• *History Alive! The Medieval World and Beyond* • Interactive Student Notebooks • Visuals 5A–5C • Student Handout 5A (1 copy for every four students) • Student Handout 5B (2 copies, cut apart) • Student Handout 5C (2 copies, cut apart) • Student Handout 5D (1 copy for every four students) • 4 envelopes
Processing	20 minutes	• Interactive Student Notebooks
Assessment	40 minutes	• Chapter 5 Assessment

Preview

1 **Have students complete the Preview activity for this chapter in their Interactive Student Notebooks.** Students write about an event that changed their lives.

2 **Have students share their responses in pairs or with the class.**

3 **Connect the Preview activity to the chapter.** Tell students that, just as the event they wrote about in the Preview activity changed their lives, several events in medieval Europe dramatically changed the way people lived. Students will reenact two of these events to discover how they led to the decline of feudalism and the rise of democratic thought.

Vocabulary Development

1 **Introduce the Key Content Terms.** Have students locate the Key Content Terms for the chapter in their Interactive Student Notebooks. These are important terms that will help them understand the main ideas of the chapter. Ask volunteers to identify any familiar terms and how they might be used in a sentence.

2 **Have students complete a Vocabulary Development handout.** Give each student a copy of the Vocabulary Development handout of your choice from the Reading Toolkit at the back of the Lesson Masters. These handouts provide extra Key Content Term practice and support, depending on your students' needs. Review the completed handout by asking volunteers to share one answer for each term.

Reading

1 **Introduce the Essential Question and have students read Section 5.1.** Have students identify the Essential Question on the first page of the chapter: *How did events in Europe contribute to the decline of feudalism and the rise of democratic thought?* Then have students read Section 5.1. Afterward, have students use information from Section 5.1 and from the chapter opener image to propose some possible answers to the Essential Question.

2 **Have students complete the Reading Notes for Chapter 5.** Assign Sections 5.2 to 5.4 during the activity as indicated in the procedures for the Visual Discovery. Remind students to use the Key Content Terms where appropriate as they complete their Reading Notes.

Writing: Written English Language Conventions

Use the chapter Key Concept Terms and other key vocabulary to teach or review some rules of capitalization:

1. Capitalize the names of important documents (Magna Carta).

2. Capitalize the names of government bodies (Model Parliament).

3. Capitalize the names of historical events, including wars and battles (Hundred Years' War, Battle of Crécy).

Visual Discovery

1 **Prepare materials and arrange the classroom.** Before class, cut apart two copies of *Student Handout 5B: Fate Cards,* and place each set of 10 cards in an envelope. Also cut apart two copies of *Student Handout 5C: Plague Cards.* Designate four areas of the classroom to be four different cities. Label the cities Constantinople, Paris, Venice, and London. Put one envelope of Fate Cards at each city. Keep the Plague Cards with you. Designate an area of your room to be the graveyard, and label it as such.

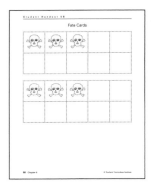

Student Handout 5B

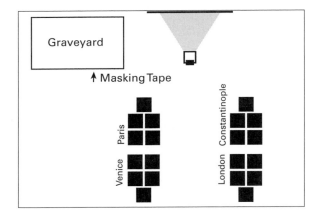

2 **Introduce the activity.** Explain that students will examine images showing three different events that affected medieval Europe. For each event, students will answer questions about an image and then discuss how the event pictured led to the decline of feudalism and the rise of democratic thought. Students will conduct two act-it-outs to gain insight into how two of these events affected Europe.

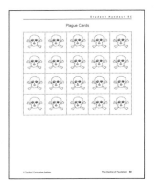

Student Handout 5C

3 **Project *Visual 5A: King John at Runnymede* and have students analyze the image.** Ask,

- What do you see here?

- Who do you think these men are?

- These angry nobles forced King John to meet with them to discuss their rights. What is the document they are presenting to him? What do you think it might contain?

- This is a charter outlining an agreement between King John and the English nobles. How might a charter like this affect the men standing around the table? How might it affect King John?

- How might this charter contribute to the decline of feudalism and the rise of democratic thought?

Visual 5A

4   Have students read Section 5.2 and complete the corresponding Reading Notes. Have them share their responses, and then review the main points with the class.

5   Distribute one copy of *Student Handout 5A: Creating an Act-It-Out of the Meeting at Runnymede* to each group, and have students prepare for and perform the act-it-out.

- Assign each group of students to be one of the following characters: King John, a noble, or a bishop.

- Tell students they will have ten minutes to prepare an act-it-out to bring to life this scene where King John puts his seal on Magna Carta. Make sure that students understand that they are only responsible for portraying their assigned character.

- Review the guidelines on the handout with students.

- When the class is ready, randomly select one student from each group to "step into" the projected image and take on the various roles. Have King John be seated while a noble presents him with a mock Magna Carta. A bishop and a second noble should stand behind them.

- During the act-it-out, interview the characters, using the questions from the handout.

6   Project *Visual 5B: An Outbreak of the Plague* and have students analyze the image. Ask,

- What do you see here?

- How might the person being carried off have died? What details in the image lead you to believe that?

- What does the group of people in the center of the image seem to be doing?

- How do you think the outbreak of the plague affected people living in towns like this?

- How might the spread of the bubonic plague have contributed to the decline of feudalism?

7   Have students read Section 5.3 and complete the Reading Notes.

8   Conduct the act-it-out of the spread of the bubonic plague. Distribute *Student Handout 5D: Creating an Act-It-Out of the Spread of Bubonic Plague* and follow the steps on the handout to conduct the reenactment. Use these tips to facilitate the reenactment:

- **Step 1:** Randomly divide students into four groups, or families, and have each "family" sit at one of the four cities. (**Note:** You may wish to offer bonus points to the group with the most family members surviving at the end of the activity.) This will help "families" feel more connected, and upset when one of them "dies" from the plague.

Student Handout 5A

Visual 5B

Student Handout 5D

- **Step 2:** When students come to you with Fate Cards showing a skull and crossbones, give them each a Plague Card and tell them they have contracted the plague. Tell them to return the Fate Card to the envelope at their city and to hold onto the Plague Card. (**Note:** These actions are intended to ensure that the "plague" spreads to other cities.)

- **Step 3:** Have families move clockwise to the next city and sit down.

- **Step 4:** Continue the process until students have visited all four cities or until approximately one-fourth have "died" from the plague. Then ask, *How did the plague spread so quickly throughout Europe?*

9 **Project *Visual 5C: The Battle of Crécy* and have students analyze the image.** Ask,

Visual 5C

- What do you see here?

- What do these people seem to be doing?

- What kinds of weapons are these soldiers carrying? Which weapons do you think will be the most successful in battle? Why?

- How would the more advanced military technology (such as the longbows used by the English in this painting) affect the usefulness of knights and castles?

- How might continuous war have contributed to the decline of feudalism and the rise of democratic thought?

10 **Have students read Section 5.4 and complete the corresponding Reading Notes.** Have them share their responses and then review the main points with the class.

Processing

Have students complete the Processing activity in their Interactive Student Notebooks. Students will describe the events leading to the decline of feudalism from the perspectives of three individuals from medieval Europe and predict how their roles in medieval society might change. Consider having students share their thought bubbles in pairs or with the class.

Quicker Coverage

Eliminate One or Both of the Act-It Outs Instead of having students conduct both the act-it-out of the meeting between King John and his nobles and the reenactment of the spread of the bubonic plague, have students simply analyze the images and complete the Reading Notes for those sections.

Deeper Coverage

Have Students Conduct an Act-It-Out for the Battle of Crécy Follow these steps to conduct the simulation.

1 **Arrange the classroom and gather materials.** Move all desks to the periphery of the room to create a rectangular battlefield. Use masking tape to mark a line 3 feet in front of where the English archers will stand. The location of this line should force the French knights to advance as far as possible before firing their crossbows. Also, make sure that you have one die to roll during the act-it-out.

2 **Create an Information Master with the following steps for conducting an act-it-out that simulates the Battle of Crécy.** Project the directions, revealing one step at a time.

- **Step 1:** Randomly select 24 students to act as French knights and 8 to act as English archers. (**Note:** Whatever the class size, assign students to be French or English in an approximately 3:1 ratio.) Have the two forces stand at opposite ends of the battlefield.

- **Step 2:** Project Visual 5C again for students to see how to hold a crossbow and a longbow.

- **Step 3:** Tell the French knights that they must "advance" across the battlefield and fire their crossbows at the English. Explain that, because of their limited range, the French cannot fire until they reach the firing line. Allow the French to take any size step they wish when advancing toward the English.

- **Step 4:** Tell the English archers that, because of the extensive range of their weapons, they may fire their longbows at any time. Once the English have "fired" their weapons, roll the die. If you roll a 1, announce that the French knight closest to the English has been wounded. If you roll a 2, announce that the two French knights closest to the English have been wounded, and so on.

- **Step 5:** Each time the French advance, simulate the increasing accuracy of the English archers. Thus, for the second advance, if you roll a 1, have the two knights closest to the English sit down. For the third advance, if you roll a 1, have three knights sit down, and so on.

- **Step 6:** Continue to implement the odds as in Step 5 until the French knights all are wounded or surrender. You may wish to allow the French to retreat, as many actually did at the Battle of Crécy. (**Note:** If no French knights are able to reach the English, skip Step 6 and declare the battle an immediate English victory.)

Assessment

Mastering the Content

1. A	5. A	9. C	13. B
2. C	6. B	10. D	14. C
3. D	7. B	11. D	15. D
4. B	8. C	12. A	16. A

Applying Social Studies Skills

17. witnesses (or credible witnesses)

18. lawful judgment of his peers

19. Sample answer: This means that all people are guaranteed justice under the law.

Exploring the Essential Question

20. Answers should include all the elements requested in the prompt.

Scoring Rubric

Score	Description
3	Student completes a letter or journal entry that addresses all five bulleted points with historical accuracy. Information is clearly stated, supported by details, and demonstrates command of standard English conventions.
2	Student responds to most or all parts of the task, but the letter or journal entry may be vague or unclear, or may contain minor inaccuracies.
1	Student responds to at least one part of the task. Letter or journal entry may contain factual and/or grammatical errors and may lack details.
0	Response does not match the task or is incorrect.

The Trials of Joan of Arc

1   **Read aloud the introduction to the Chapter 5 Reading Further in the Student Edition.** Ask students what they know about Joan of Arc. As the students discuss what they know, write their responses on the board.

2   **Have students read the rest of the Reading Further.** Ask: *What did the article add to your knowledge of Joan of Arc? What were her key accomplishments? Why did the French people admire her so much? How did Joan's life show that attitudes during feudal Europe were beginning to change?*

3   **Have students complete the Reading Further in their Interactive Student Notebooks.** Explain that students will prepare a television interview with Joan of Arc. Their interview questions will summarize Joan of Arc's attitudes and accomplishments.

4   **Have students read aloud their interview questions in front of the class.**

English Language Learners

Provide an Alternative to the Preview Activity Allow students to use illustrations to complete the Preview activity. Instruct them to draw the event that they believe changed the way they lived and then write short, bulleted phrases explaining how their lives were changed.

Prepare Students for the Visual Discovery Provide students with copies of the questions you will ask about each visual. Give students these questions the night before, along with copies of the visuals, so that students can be prepared to take part in the discussions the following day.

Learners Reading and Writing Below Grade Level

Modify the Processing Activity Provide students with the following prompts before they begin the Processing activity:

- As a noble, present at King John's acceptance of Magna Carta, I saw . . .

  I felt . . .

  The decline of feudalism will change my life because . . .

- As a common person who lived through the bubonic plague, I saw . . .

  I felt . . .

  The decline of feudalism will change my life because . . .

- As a soldier at the Battle of Crécy, I saw . . .

  I felt . . .

  The decline of feudalism will change my life because . . .

Learners with Special Education Needs

Provide Added Support for the Assessment Several days before the lesson assessment, photocopy and cut apart the multiple-choice questions. Give students a set of these strips, and allow them to work with an aide or parent to prepare for the assessment they will take in class.

Offer Support for the Visual Discovery Make paper copies of the visuals and allow students to annotate the images. As the class is discussing and analyzing the images, encourage students to write some of their classmates' comments and ideas directly on the images. This may help them connect the image to the reading and to their Reading Notes.

Advanced Learners

Assign an Alternative to the Processing Activity Have students do the following:

- Assume the perspective of one of the three individuals featured in the Processing activity.
- From that perspective, write a letter to a friend predicting the future of Europe. Letters should include
  - a proper greeting.
  - a brief summary of the changes that Europe has undergone in the recent past.
  - a look at how these changes have affected your own life, as well as the lives of other Europeans.
  - a discussion of what Europe will be like in the coming years and your concerns about the future.
  - a proper closing and signature.

Enrichment Resources

Find out more about the decline of feudalism by exploring the following Enrichment Resources for *History Alive! The Medieval World and Beyond* at www.teachtci.com.

Enrichment Readings These in-depth readings encourage students to explore selected topics related to the chapter. You may also find readings that relate the chapter's content directly to your state's curriculum.

Internet Connections These recommended Web sites provide useful and engaging content that reinforces skills development and mastery of subjects within the chapter.

Literature Recommendations

The following books offer opportunities to extend the content in this chapter.

1215: The Year of Magna Carta by Danny Danziger and John Gillingham (New York: Touchstone, 2005)

In the Wake of the Plague: The Black Death and the World It Made by Norman Cantor (New York: Harper Perennial, 2002)

Joan of Arc: The Lily Maid by Margaret Hodges (New York: Little Brown & Co., 1990)

Section 5.2

1. He insisted that a jury formally accuse a person of a serious crime. People were tried by royal judges and had to have a court trial. By strengthening the royal courts, he weakened the power of the feudal lords.

2. A monarch could no longer collect special taxes without the consent of nobles and Church officials. No "free man" could be jailed except by the lawful judgment of his peers or by the law of the land. It also introduced the idea that not even the monarch was above the law.

3. It was an English governing body created by Edward I that included commoners, lower-ranking clergy, Church officials, and nobles. It was intended to include more people in government.

4. Political Events: Magna Carta limited the power of English monarchs and affirmed that monarchs should rule with the advice of the governed; Henry II's legal reforms strengthened common law, judges, and juries; and Edward I's Model Parliament gave a voice to some common people.

Section 5.3

1.

| 1. Central Asia | Travels along trade route to | 2. The Black Sea | Carried on a ship to |
| 3. Italy | Spreads north and west to | 4. England, Germany, France | |

Students should write the numerals 1 to 4 on the map in the correct locations.

2. The term probably came from the black-and-blue spots, or buboes, that appeared on the skin of many victims. Symptoms included fever, vomiting, coughing and sneezing, and swelling.

3. The bacteria that caused the plague were spread by fleas. The dirty conditions of the time significantly contributed to the spread of the disease.

4. Bubonic Plague: Power shifted a bit from nobles to common people because, since so many workers had died, the few who remained could demand higher pay and more rights; serfs abandoned feudal manors and moved to towns and cities, seeking better opportunities; peasant revolts also occurred when nobles tried to return things to the way they had been.

Section 5.4

1. The war began when the king of France challenged England's claim to French fiefs.

2. The English army relied on archers armed with longbows. Arrows fired from longbows flew farther, faster, and more accurately than those fired from French crossbows.

3. Joan of Arc was a 17-year-old peasant girl who claimed she heard the voices of saints urging her to save France. She led a French army to victory in a battle. Her actions inspired many French people to feel more strongly about their king and nation.

4. Hundred Years' War: The war shifted power from lords to monarchs and common people; military technology used in the war made knights and castles less important; a new feeling of nationalism helped to shift power away from lords and toward monarchs and commoners; peasants who survived the war were more in demand as soldiers and workers and therefore had greater power.

The Byzantine Empire

How did the Byzantine Empire develop and form its own distinctive church?

Overview

In a Visual Discovery activity, students act out images that represent Constantinople, Justinian's rule, the development of the Eastern Orthodox Church, and the schism between Roman Catholic and Eastern Orthodox Christians in 1054.

Objectives

In the course of reading this chapter and participating in the classroom activity, students will

Social Studies

- demonstrate the importance of Constantinople as a trading hub and explain how it emerged as the capital of the Byzantine Empire.
- describe the reign of Justinian I, including his contributions to public works and his creation of a code of law.
- discuss the relationship between religion and government in the Byzantine Empire.
- trace the development of the Eastern Orthodox Church and its relations with the west.

Language Arts

- clarify word meanings through the use of definitions and examples.
- read expository text to connect essential ideas to prior knowledge.

Social Studies Vocabulary

Key Content Terms Constantinople, Byzantine Empire, Eastern Orthodox Church, patriarch

Academic Vocabulary distinctive, revolt, emerge

Materials

History Alive! The Medieval World and Beyond

Interactive Student Notebooks

Visuals 6A–6E

Lesson Masters

- Student Handout 6 (1 per group of 4)
- Information Master 6
- Vocabulary Development handout (1 per student, on colored paper)

construction paper (in 7 colors)

Activity	Suggested Time	Materials
Preview	45 minutes	• *History Alive! The Medieval World and Beyond* • Interactive Student Notebooks • Visual 6A • Information Master 6 • masking tape • construction paper (in 7 colors)
Vocabulary Development	30–40 minutes	• *History Alive! The Medieval World and Beyond* • Interactive Student Notebooks • Vocabulary Development handout
Visual Discovery	90 minutes (2 regular periods) (1 block period)	• *History Alive! The Medieval World and Beyond* • Interactive Student Notebooks • Student Handout 6 (1 per group of 4) • Visuals 6B–6E
Processing	20 minutes	• Interactive Student Notebooks
Assessment	40 minutes	• Chapter 6 Assessment

Preview

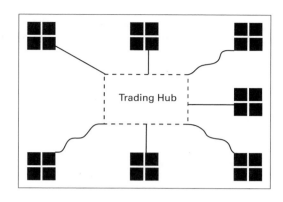

1   **Prepare the classroom and materials for the activity.** Follow these steps:

- Cut construction paper into 2-inch squares to create 7 sets of 28 trading tokens, each set a different color. (**Note:** You can collect these tokens at the conclusion of the activity and save for reuse each period and each succeeding year.)

- Arrange desks as shown in the diagram to represent different regions of the world. In the center of the room, place a set of desks or a table labeled "Trading Hub."

- Use masking tape on the floor to create seven trade routes as shown in the diagram. (**Note:** Consider placing some groups of desks farther from the center than others to represent the varying distances traders traveled and the fact that some traveled by land and others by water.)

- Place a set of tokens at each group of desks.

2   **Project** *Information Master 6: Rules to Complete the Trading Activity* **and introduce the trading activity.** Review the intent of the activity and the rules found on Information Master 6. Answer any questions from students.

3   **Have students trade.** Divide the class into seven groups. Have each group go to a trade region. Remind them to trade for as many different-color tokens as possible as they work through the activity. Make sure students trade for only one color of token while in the trading hub. Continue the activity until at least one group has accumulated all seven colors.

4   **Debrief the activity.** Have each group tally their tokens. Ask a representative from each group to share how many of each color they acquired. (**Note:** Consider offering a reward such as bonus points to groups who acquired all seven colors.) Then hold a class discussion centering on these questions:

- What did you like about trading? What was difficult about it?

- Was it easy to acquire different colors once you reached the trading hub? Explain.

5   **Project** *Visual 6A: The Byzantine Empire and Trade* **and analyze the map shown.** Ask,

- What does this map show?

- What do the red and blue lines represent? The lists of items in black?

- Where do many of the trade routes seem to intersect?

- What does this tell us about Constantinople?

Information Master 6

Visual 6A

6 **Have students complete the Preview activity in their Interactive Student Notebooks.** Guide them by using details from the map on Visual 6A, and the chart below.

Historical Connection	Classroom Experience
• Traders came from various regions of the world, such as Africa, France, and China.	• Students came from different groups to trade.
• Various goods were traded, such as ivory, wool, and silk.	• Students traded different-color tokens.
• Many traders came to Constantinople to trade.	• Tokens had to be traded in the trading hub.
• Traders traveled to Constantinople by land and water routes.	• Students walked along strips of tape to trade.
• Traders brought new products to their homelands after trading in Constantinople.	• Groups finished the activity with a variety of colored tokens.

7 **Connect the Preview activity to the chapter.** Explain to students that just as the trading hub became the center of successful trade in the classroom, Constantinople became a very successful, wealthy city due to its location at the crossroads of Europe and Asia. As it grew, so did the Byzantine Empire. In this chapter, students will learn how the Byzantine Empire developed and how it formed the Eastern Orthodox Church, a Church with distinctively different traditions than the Roman Catholic Church in the west.

Vocabulary Development

1 **Introduce the Key Content Terms.** Have students locate the Key Content Terms for the chapter in their Interactive Student Notebooks. These are important terms that will help them understand the main ideas of the chapter. Ask volunteers to identify any familiar terms and suggest how they might be used in a sentence.

2 **Have students complete a Vocabulary Development handout.** Give each student a copy of the Vocabulary Development handout of your choice from the Reading Toolkit at the back of the Lesson Masters. These handouts provide extra Key Content Term practice and support, depending on your students' needs. Review the completed handout by asking volunteers to share one answer for each term.

Reading

1 **Introduce the Essential Question and have students read Section 6.1.** Have students identify the Essential Question on the first page of the chapter: *How did the Byzantine Empire develop and form its own distinctive church?* Then have students read Section 6.1. Afterward, have students respond to these questions:

- Where was the Byzantine Empire located?

- How did a split in the Roman Empire eventually lead to a new and distinctive church?

2 **Have students complete the Reading Notes for Chapter 6.** Assign Sections 6.2 to 6.5 during the activity, as indicated in the procedures for the Visual Discovery. Remind students to use the Key Content Terms where appropriate as they complete their Reading Notes.

Visual Discovery

1 **Introduce the activity.** Put students in groups of four. Explain that students will examine images that represent Constantinople, Justinian's rule, the development of the Eastern Orthodox Church, and the schism between Roman Catholics and Eastern Orthodox Christians in 1054.

2 **Project *Visual 6B: Constantinople* and have students analyze the image.** Ask,

- What interesting details do you see here? (You might have volunteers point out details.)

- What buildings stand out? What do you think they are used for?

- What features might protect the city from invaders?

- What features might allow people to reach this city easily?

- What details in this image might lead you to believe this is a wealthy city?

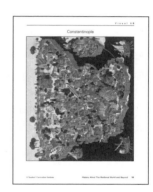

Visual 6B

3 **Have students read Section 6.2 and complete the corresponding Reading Notes.** Have them share their responses, and then review the main points with the class.

4 **Project *Visual 6C: The Court of Justinian* and have students analyze the image.** Ask,

- What interesting details do you see here?

- Who stands out in this image? Why?

- In the center of the image is Justinian, a famous Byzantine ruler. What do you notice about the figures standing next to him?

- What roles do you think they played in his court?

- What does this image say about Justinian's power?

Visual 6C

5   Have students read Section 6.3 and complete the corresponding Reading Notes. Have them share their responses, and then review the main points with the class.

6   Pass out *Student Handout 6: Creating an Act-It-Out About Justinian* to each group and have students prepare for and perform an act-it-out.

Student Handout 6

- Assign each group one of these characters: Church official, general, Justinian, legal advisor, Procopius, or Theodora. (**Note:** With larger classes, assign some roles to more than one group.)

- Tell students they will have 10 minutes to prepare an act-it-out to bring to life a scene in Justinian's palace. Make sure they understand that they are responsible for portraying only their assigned historical figure.

- Explain that because Procopius and Theodora are not pictured, actors representing those characters will stand to the far left and right of the projected image during the act-it-out. The class will pretend these characters are speaking from another room in Justinian's palace.

- Review the guidelines on the handout with students.

- When the class is ready, randomly select one student from each group to "step into" the projected image and take on the various roles, with Procopius and Theodora standing to the far left and right.

- During the act-it-out, interview the characters, using one or two questions for each character from Student Handout 6.

7   Project *Visual 6D: Interior of Hagia Sophia* and have students analyze the image. Remind them that this structure was first built during the reign of Justinian. Play CD Track 5 as background music and ask a few students to stand in front of the image as though they have just entered Hagia Sophia. Prompt them to think about the feelings such a structure inspires, by asking,

Visual 6D

- What interesting details do you see here? (Encourage them to touch items they mention.)

- What is the mood like in this building?

- What types of activities might take place here?

- What aspects of the architecture strike you as interesting?

- How high do you think the dome is? (It reaches 180 feet, or 12 stories above the floor.)

- How does the building's size make you feel?

- What do you notice about the lighting? Why do you think light might be important in a church?

8   Have students read Section 6.4 and complete the corresponding Reading Notes. Have them share their responses, and then review the main points with them.

9 Project *Visual 6E: Patriarch Athenagoras and Pope Paul VI* and have students analyze the image. Ask,

- What interesting details do you see here?

- Who are these two men?

- What do they seem to be doing?

- In what ways are they alike?

- In what ways are they different?

Visual 6E

10 **Have students read Section 6.5 and complete the corresponding Reading Notes.** Have them share their responses, and then review the main points with them.

Processing

Have students complete the Processing activity in their Interactive Student Notebooks. Students create a real-estate advertisement to encourage people to move to Constantinople.

Quicker Coverage

Eliminate the Act-It-Out Instead of having students participate in the act-it-out, simply analyze Visual 6C and have them complete the Reading Notes for that section.

Modify the Preview Activity Instead of having students participate in the trading activity, project Visual 6A and have students answer the following questions for discussion.

- From what regions of the world were traders coming to Constantinople?
- What kinds of goods were being traded?
- Why was Constantinople so ideally located as a trading hub?

Deeper Coverage

Have Students Conduct an Act-It-Out for Pope Paul VI and Patriarch Athenagoras After students have read Section 6.5 in Step 10 of the Visual Discovery directions, assign two groups to represent the two men pictured. Assign the other four groups to act as reporters who will create at least two questions to ask each of the men in the image. Tell the groups acting as reporters that at least one of their questions must use the word *excommunication*. As the reporters prepare their questions, instruct the groups who are representing Pope Paul VI and Patriarch Athenagoras to prepare to answer the following questions: *How do you feel about this meeting today? What do you believe caused this schism between the two churches?* If possible, encourage students to use the Internet to do further research about the meeting in 1964 that undid the excommunications of 1054.

Assessment

Mastering the Content

1. B	5. A	9. D	13. C
2. A	6. A	10. D	14. D
3. B	7. B	11. C	15. A
4. C	8. C	12. D	16. B

Applying Social Studies Skills

17. Charlemagne was crowned Holy Roman emperor.

18. 146 years (330–476)

19. 324 years (476–800)

Exploring the Essential Question

20. Answers should include all the elements requested in the prompt.

Scoring Rubric

Score	Description
3	Student writes a sentence in each of the three boxes, on the stated topic, using the word shown in the drawing. The three sentences are clearly stated, accurate, supported by details, and demonstrate command of standard English conventions. Student's summary accurately summarizes the causes of the schism.
2	Student responds to most or all parts of the task, but the sentences may lack details or not be clearly stated. Summaries are not complete or include inaccuracies.
1	Student responds to at least one part of the task. Sentences may contain factual and/or grammatical errors and may lack details. Summaries are incomplete or not present.
0	Response does not match the task or is incorrect.

English Language Learners

Provide Support for the Act-It-Out Give students copies of Student Handout 6 and Visual 6C the day before this activity is scheduled to take place. Assign each student to a particular character, and encourage students to read Section 6.3 of *History Alive! The Medieval World and Beyond* as they consider the questions on Student Handout 6. It may also help some students to write down ahead of time the answers to the act-it-out.

Learners Reading and Writing Below Grade Level

Modify the Processing Activity Use the following as a model for creating writing prompts to help students add some of the required information:

- *Constantinople is a great place for the capital of the Byzantine Empire because . . .*
- *One special thing about Constantinople's geography is . . .*
- *During the day, people in Constantinople . . .*
- *Others spend time . . .*

Learners with Special Education Needs

Adapt the Preview Activity Allow students who may find the physical aspects of the Preview activity challenging to station themselves at the trading hub in the center of the room as natives of Constantinople. Assign these students the responsibility for tallying their groups' collection of tokens.

Offer Additional Help for the Preview Activity Using the chart in Step 6 of the Preview activity, provide students with a list of the classroom experiences, in random order, for the Preview activity. Students can then match the historical connections from the list in the Interactive Student Notebook with the various classroom experiences.

Advanced Learners

Assign a Culminating Project Have students research achievements and contributions of the Byzantine Empire and design a mobile or collage as a culminating project. Encourage them to use the Enrichment Resources provided at www.teachtci.com as a starting point in their research on achievements and contributions of the Byzantine Empire. Include the following basic criteria for them to follow when completing the project:

- Detail four achievements or contributions of the Byzantine Empire, including those in the fields of architecture, art, education, religion, politics, medicine, science, or economics.
- Include an image of each achievement or contribution from the past, or a related image from the present.
- Write a paragraph describing each achievement or contribution, how it affected the lives of people during the Byzantine Empire, and two ways it has affected people's lives in modern times. (For example, how it might have affected further innovations or inventions.)

Enrichment Resources

Have students find out more about the Byzantine Empire by exploring the following Enrichment Resources for *History Alive! The Medieval World and Beyond* at www.teachtci.com.

Enrichment Readings These in-depth readings encourage students to explore selected topics related to the chapter. You may also find readings that relate the chapter's content directly to your state's curriculum.

Internet Connections The recommended Web sites provide useful and engaging content that reinforces skills development, as well as mastery of subjects within the chapter.

Literature Recommendations

The following books offer opportunities to extend the content in this chapter.

Anna of Byzantium by Tracy Barrett (New York: Bantam Doubleday Dell, 2000)

Daily Life in the Byzantine Empire by Marcus Rautman (Westport: Greenwood Press, 2006)

A Travel Guide to Medieval Constantinople by James Barter (Farmington Hills, MI: Lucent Books, 2003)

Section 6.2

1. Constantinople was easy to defend, being surrounded by water on three sides, and it lay at the crossroads of many sea and overland trade routes linking east and west.

2. Answers will vary. Sample answer: Dear Habib, Constantinople is like nothing you have ever seen! The marketplace here overflows with ivory and silk. Traders walk the streets speaking every language imaginable. There is even a sewer system! Many in the city are very rich. Even the poor are given jobs sweeping the streets and weeding the gardens in exchange for bread. It is a beautiful city, Habib. Your friend, Kalim

Section 6.3

1. Large parts of the city were ruined when fighting in the Hippodrome between the Blues and Greens escalated into a rebellion.

2. New bridges, public baths, parks, roads, and hospitals were built. In addition, Hagia Sophia was built.

3. Under Justinian's direction, a committee studied thousands of laws inherited from the Roman Empire and revised those that were outdated or confusing. They also made some revisions, such as expanding women's property rights. By doing so, they created a code that served as the basis for many legal codes in the western world.

Section 6.4

1. Religion and government were closely linked. The emperor was both the head of the government and the living representative of Jesus Christ.

2. A. Possible answers: Many Orthodox Christians believe icons such as this bring them closer to God. St. Cyril helped create the Cyrillic alphabet, which allowed scholars to translate the Bible for people in the Byzantine Empire.

   B. Possible answers: Many Orthodox Christians believe icons such as this bring them closer to God. Jesus, or the Pantocrator, holding a Gospel and giving a blessing, rules over everything, according to Eastern Orthodox belief.

Section 6.5

See chart below.

Date	People Involved	Event That Led to the Disagreement	Result of the Disagreement
730 C.E.	Emperor Leo III and Pope Gregory III	Leo III bans the use of all religious images in Christian churches and homes, leading to a policy of iconoclasm.	The pope, angered by Leo's ban, excommunicates the emperor.
800 C.E.	Pope Leo III, Empress Irene, and Charlemagne	Pope Leo III refuses to recognize Empress Irene as the ruler of the Byzantine Empire because she is a woman; he crowns Charlemagne as Holy Roman emperor.	The pope's action outrages the Byzantines who feel their empress is the rightful ruler of the Roman Empire.
1054 C.E.	Cerularius, Pope Leo IX, Cardinal Humbert	Patriarch Cerularius closes all churches that worship with western rites. In response, Cardinal Humbert, on the pope's orders, excommunicates Cerularius, who in return, excommunicates the cardinal.	The schism is final, and future attempts to heal the division are ineffective.

Europe During Medieval Times

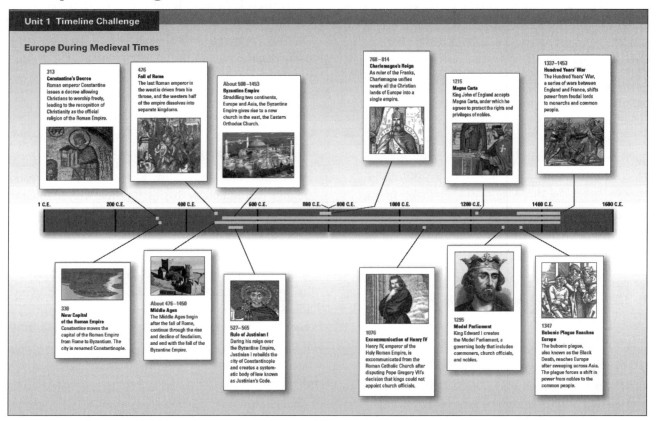

Overview

This Timeline Challenge helps students review the main events and ideas of this unit while providing practice in reading and interpreting timelines. You can vary and expand the activity according to students' needs and the amount of time available.

Basic Procedure

1 **Introduce the timeline in the Student Edition.** Direct students to the Europe During Medieval Times Timeline at the end of Unit 1 in the Student Edition. You may wish to have students read aloud and discuss the timeline entries.

2 **Introduce the Timeline Challenge in the Interactive Student Notebook.** Direct students to the Unit 1 Timeline Challenge. Point out the two types of questions, "Timeline Skills" and "Critical Thinking," and model how to answer each type.

3 **Have students complete the Timeline Challenge.** Monitor students as they work. Use the Guide to Unit 1 Timeline Challenge to check their answers. You may wish to project a transparency of this page as you work through the questions with the class and conduct a discussion of the "Critical Thinking" questions.

4 **Complete the KWL chart.** Return to the KWL chart created at the beginning of the unit, and ask students to list the key information they have learned.

Classroom Timeline

1   **Prepare the Timeline Challenge Cards.** Copy and cut the cards from *Student Handout TC1: Unit 1 Timeline Challenge Cards.* You may wish to laminate the cards for future use.

2   **Create a timeline on a classroom wall.** On an empty wall or a large bulletin board, make a timeline with masking tape or colored paper. Mark off the time intervals in advance, or ask students to do so in class.

3   **Have students place the Timeline Challenge Cards.** Distribute cards to individual students or pairs and have them tape the cards to the timeline in the correct locations. Call on students to provide more information on the timeline topics to review main events and issues.

Internet Research

1   **Review students' suggestions for additional timeline entries.** Have students share their answers to the last question of the Timeline Challenge.

2   **Have students conduct Internet research.** Ask students to choose and research one of their suggested events.

3   **Have students create additional Timeline Challenge Cards.** Direct students to research an appropriate image for their cards and then use the computer to create an illustrated card, complete with timeline entry.

Student Handout TC4

Timeline Skills

Score 1 point for each correct answer.

1. Europe, Asia, and Africa

2. Constantine's decree allowing Christians to worship freely led eventually to the recognition of Christianity as the religion of the Roman Empire.

3. Byzantium

4. the fall of the Roman Empire

5. the Eastern Orthodox Church

6. 38 years

7. Charlemagne unified most of the Christian lands of Europe into a single empire.

8. Henry IV was excommunicated for disputing the pope's decision that kings could not appoint church officials.

9. 16 years longer than 100 years

Critical Thinking

Score 1 to 3 points for each answer, depending on the thoroughness of the response.

10. The political instability that occurred because no real system existed for choosing the next empire allowed ineffective rulers to come to power. Many economic and social problems, such as high taxes, unemployment and growing crime and corruption, further weakened the empire. The empire's weakening frontiers made it very hard to defend.

11. Charlemagne's relationship with Pope Leo III is an example of cooperation between the church and the monarchy in that the pope's blessing gave Charlemagne more power in the empire, while Leo III received the support of a strong leader with an army. The conflict between the Church and the monarchy, however, was exemplified in the disagreement between Pope Gregory VII and Henry IV over the king's power to appoint church officials.

12. Three major events led to the decline of feudalism. First, many political reforms, including the court system gave more authority to monarchs, while also shifting power to commoners. Second, the bubonic plague reduced the population of Europe, giving the workers who remained the power to demand more money and more rights, and encouraging others to leave the manors and move to towns and cities for better opportunities. Finally, the Hundred Years' War shifted power to the common people.

13. Answers will vary. Students must explain why the events they chose merit inclusion.

Using Scores to Inform Instruction

Timeline Skills A score of 6 out of 9 indicates that students understand most of the key events in the unit.

Critical Thinking A score of 8 out of 12 indicates that students are able to think critically about most of the key issues in this unit.

If students score below these levels, consider reviewing timeline and critical thinking skills.

Islam in Medieval Times

Geography Challenge

Chapter 7: The Origins and Spread of Islam
How did Islam originate and spread?
Writing for Understanding

Chapter 8: Learning About World Religions: Islam
How do the beliefs and practices of Islam shape Muslims' lives?
Problem Solving Groupwork

Chapter 9: Muslim Innovations and Adaptations
What important innovations and adaptations did medieval Muslims make?
Social Studies Skill Builder

Chapter 10: From the Crusades to New Muslim Empires
How did the Crusades affect the lives of Christians, Muslims, and Jews?
Experiential Exercise

Timeline Challenge

Islam in Medieval Times

Overview

This activity introduces geographic information essential to Unit 2. Students read and interpret maps to learn key physical features of the Arabian Peninsula and how those features contributed to the development of the region. They annotate a map of the Arabian Peninsula and answer questions in their Interactive Student Notebooks, and then discuss critical thinking questions. Students' comprehension of content and proficiency in map-reading and higher-order thinking skills will help you gauge their readiness for the unit. The pages that follow include a completed map, answers to questions, a scoring guide to inform your teaching, and suggestions for modifications to meet specific student needs.

Essential Geographic Understandings

1. Location of the Arabian Peninsula

2. Key physical features: the Mediterranean Sea, the Red Sea, the Persian Gulf, Makkah

3. Relative location of the Arabian Peninsula, specifically its proximity to the continents of Africa, Asia, and Europe

4. Impact of location on the Arabian Peninsula as a trading center and on the spread of Islam

Procedures

1 **Introduce the unit.** Tell students that in this unit they will learn about the peninsula in the Middle East known in medieval times as Arabia. Explain that this area of the world played key economic and cultural roles in history.

2 **Create a KWL chart with students.** Ask students to identify what they already know about the geography of the Arabian Peninsula and what they want to learn. Use their responses to gauge how much additional background information your students will need as you progress through the unit. Students will return to the KWL chart at the end of the unit and add the key information they have learned.

3 **Have students read Unit 2 "Setting the Stage" in the Student Edition.**

4 **Have students complete the Geography Challenge.** Monitor students as they work. Use the guide on the next two pages to check their answers. You may wish to project the map from the Interactive Student Notebook and have students annotate it as the class works through the map-reading questions. Make sure students have grasped Essential Geographic Understandings 1 to 3.

5 **Discuss the "Critical Thinking" questions.** Help students understand the geographic relationships described in Essential Geographic Understanding 4.

The Arabian Peninsula and Surrounding Lands

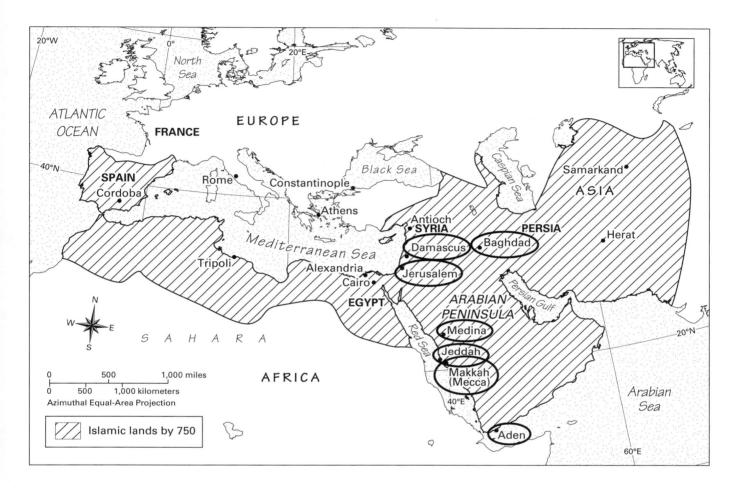

Geography Skills

Score 1 point for each correct answer. Use the map on the previous page to check shading and labeling.

1. Students should label Europe, Africa, and Asia.

2. Students should label the Mediterranean Sea.

3. Students should label the Atlantic Ocean, the North Sea, the Black Sea, the Caspian Sea, the Red Sea, the Arabian Sea, and the Persian Gulf.

4. The cities of Aden, Makkah, Jedda, Jerusalem, Damascus, and Baghdad would have been important trading centers, due to their locations on the coasts of the Red Sea and the Mediterranean Sea, and due also to their proximity to the continents of Africa, Asia, and Europe.

5. A trader traveling from Makkah to Cairo would likely have traveled by sea, while a trader from Makkah to Baghdad would likely have traveled overland.

6. They would have been slowed by the Pyrenees Mountains.

7. Jerusalem is closest to Cairo. Because of this proximity, it is likely that these two cities traded frequently.

8. The Sahara formed the southern boundary of Islamic lands in Africa. The empire stopped at this physical barrier because traders and armies would have found it difficult to survive in the desert.

Critical Thinking

Questions may have more than one correct answer. Score 1 to 3 points for each reasonable answer, depending on the strength of students' geographic reasoning. Possible answers are given here.

9. The Arabian Peninsula is located between Africa, Asia, and Europe, which brought its people into contact with outsiders from these places. This contact helped to spread Islam.

10. Medieval Europe was largely Christian. In addition, it was strong economically. Geographically, its many mountain ranges would have made conquest more difficult.

11. The location of the Arabian Peninsula was close to lands in Europe, Asia, and Africa.

Using Scores to Inform Instruction

Geography Skills A score of 5 out of 8 or better indicates that students have acquired sufficient geographic information to proceed with the unit.

Critical Thinking A score of 6 out of 9 or better indicates that students are beginning to understand the relationships between physical geography and the different ways in which people live.

Modifying Instruction

ELL or Learners with Special Education Needs
Consider focusing on map-reading questions or limiting the number of "Critical Thinking" questions.

Students with Weak Map or Critical Thinking Skills
Assign appropriate pages from the Social Studies Skills Toolkit in the back of the Lesson Masters.

The Origins and Spread of Islam

How did Islam originate and spread?

Overview

In a Writing for Understanding activity, students explore the origins and spread of Islam by taking on the role of Arab nomads, listening to a recording about the origins of Islam, and creating an illuminated manuscript retelling the story of the origins of Islam.

Objectives

In the course of reading this chapter and participating in the classroom activity, students will

Social Studies

- analyze the origins of Islam and the life and teachings of Muhammad, including Islamic teachings about Judaism and Christianity.
- explain the importance of the Arabic language and Islamic religion in unifying the diverse groups of the region.
- summarize the spread of Islam from Muhammad's time to the mid 700s C.E.

Language Arts

- organize ideas for an illuminated manuscript that summarizes the reading material.
- express ideas clearly, demonstrating an understanding of spelling, grammar, and sentence structure.

Social Studies Vocabulary

Key Content Terms Islam, Muhammad, polytheism, prophet, monotheism, Muslim, boycott, siege

Academic Vocabulary prosperous, proclaim, credibility, unification

Materials

History Alive! The Medieval World and Beyond

Interactive Student Notebooks

Visuals 7A–7B

CD Tracks 1–4

Lesson Masters

- Information Masters 7A–7D (1 copy of each)
- Information Master 7E (1 transparency)
- Vocabulary Development handout (1 per student, on colored paper)

construction paper (in 7 colors)

masking tape

Activity	Suggested Time	Materials
Preview	10 minutes	• *History Alive! The Medieval World and Beyond* • Interactive Student Notebooks • Visual 7A
Vocabulary Development	30–40 minutes	• *History Alive! The Medieval World and Beyond* • Interactive Student Notebooks • Vocabulary Development handout
Writing for Understanding	180 minutes (2 regular periods) (1 block period)	• *History Alive! The Medieval World and Beyond* • Interactive Student Notebooks • Information Masters 7A–7D (1 copy of each, posted around the room) • CD tracks 1–4 • Visual 7B • Information Master 7E (1 transparency)
Processing (optional)	30 minutes	Illuminated manuscript serves as the Processing activity
Assessment	40 minutes	• Chapter 7 Assessment

Preview

1 **Project *Visual 7A: Muslim Population*.** Tell students that in the 7th century, a religion called Islam was founded. This map shows the modern-day distribution of the followers of Islam, called Muslims, all around the world.

2 **Have students complete the Preview activity.** Give students a minute to look at the map and then ask them the following questions. As you discuss these questions as a class, students should record answers in their Interactive Student Notebooks.

Visual 7A

   • Which colors on the map represent the highest concentration of Muslims? The lowest?

   • In what regions of the world do most Muslims live? The least?

   • Based on this map, in what region of the world do you think the Islamic faith may have originated? Why?

   Tell students that the Muslim prophet Muhammad founded the Islamic faith on the Arabian Peninsula. Point out that the Arabian Peninsula is located in the Middle East. From the Arabian Peninsula, Islam spread across the Middle East, North Africa, and into Europe and Asia. Today, followers of Islam, called Muslims, live in every part of the world.

3 **Explain the connection between the Preview activity and Chapter 7.** Remind students that in the Preview activity they looked at a map showing the population distribution of Muslims. In this chapter, students will learn more about the life of the prophet Muhammad, the origins of Islam, and how Islam spread throughout the Middle East, southern Asia, northern Africa, and parts of Europe in the 7th and 8th centuries.

Vocabulary Development

1 **Introduce the Key Content Terms.** Have students locate the Key Content Terms for the chapter in their Interactive Student Notebooks. These are important terms that will help them understand the main ideas of the chapter. Ask volunteers to identify any familiar terms and suggest how they might be used in a sentence.

2 **Have students complete a Vocabulary Development handout.** Give each student a copy of the Vocabulary Development handout of your choice from the Reading Toolkit at the back of the Lesson Masters. These handouts provide extra Key Content Term practice and support, depending on your students' needs. Review the completed handout by asking volunteers to share one answer for each term.

Reading

1 **Introduce the Essential Question and have students read Section 7.1.** Have students identify the Essential Question on the first page of the chapter. Then have students read Section 7.1 Afterward, have students use information from Section 7.1 and from the chapter opener image to propose some possible answers to the Essential Question: *How did Islam originate and spread?*

2 **Have students complete the Reading Notes for the chapter.** Assign Sections 7.2 through 7.8 during the activity, as indicated in the procedures for the Writing for Understanding activity. Remind students to use the Key Content Terms where appropriate as they complete their Reading Notes.

Writing for Understanding

1 **Prepare the materials and classroom.** Before class, do the following:

- Make one copy of *Information Masters 7A–7D: Arabic Words* and post them on the walls around the classroom. Post all four pages of Information Master 7A on one wall, all four of Information Master 7B on a second wall, and so on.

- Cue CD Track 1, *"The Origins of Islam: Part 1."*

- Push students' desks against the walls of the classroom so they can be used as writing surfaces during the activity.

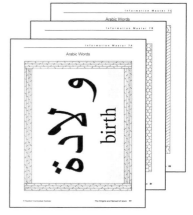

Information Masters 7A–7D

2 **Have students complete the Reading Notes for Section 7.2.** Tell students that this section provides background information on Muhammad's life before he founded Islam. Have them read Section 7.2 and complete the corresponding Reading Notes in their Interactive Student Notebooks. Then ask,

- Why was Makkah already important in Muhammad's time?

- What was Arabia like when Muhammad was young?

3 **Have students form pairs, and then explain the activity.** Create an atmosphere of the oral storytelling tradition by asking pairs to sit on the floor with their Interactive Student Notebooks and textbook. Point out the Arabic words on the walls and explain that Arabic is sacred to Muslims. The Qur'an, or Muslim scripture, is most commonly printed and memorized in Arabic. Although portions of the Qur'an were written down in Muhammad's time, a single written compilation was prepared about 15 years after Muhammad's death. During Muhammad's lifetime, the Qur'an was preserved through an oral tradition. Tell students that they will act as nomads in a desert in Arabia and will listen to a recording of the story of the origins of Islam. They will need to listen carefully to the story, just as the people of the Arabian Peninsula did before the Qur'an was written down.

4 **Play CD Track 6.** You may want students to read along with the recording in *History Alive! The Medieval World and Beyond* beginning with Section 7.3, which corresponds closely to CD Track 1. After students have listened to the recording, pause the CD.

5 Have students complete Reading Notes for Section 7.3. Tell students to follow the directions in the Reading Notes for Section 7.3. Then:

- Review the Reading Notes with students to make sure that they understand the directions.

- Send pairs to the walls of the classroom to complete the first part of their Reading Notes. One word on each wall matches each part of the story, for a total of four per story. Students may want to refer to their books as they make their matches.

- After pairs have found the four words pertaining to this story, have them come back to the center of the room to complete their Reading Notes for that section.

- The words that best match Part 1 of the Origins of Islam are: *birth, orphan, trader,* and *marriage.*

6 Repeat Steps 3 and 4 for the next three CD tracks. Repeat the procedure for CD Tracks 2–4, "*The Origins of Islam: Parts 2–4,*" which correspond to Sections 7.4 to 7.6. Have students complete the corresponding Reading Notes after each recording. Use this key, if needed:

- CD Track 2/Section 7.4: *cave, Gabriel, Allah, Qur'an*

- CD Track 3/Section 7.5: *reject, followers, boycott, Night Journey*

- CD Track 4/Section 7.6: *Madinah, People of the Book, battles, Last Sermon*

7 Project *Visual 7B: Arabic Calligraphy.* Ask students,

- What do you see?

- What decorative touches has the artist used to make this page beautiful?

Tell students that in medieval times, Muslim artists created beautifully detailed illuminated manuscripts. Prohibited from depicting human or animal forms, artists concentrated their attention on geometric shapes, plant life, and elaborate writing, called calligraphy.

8 Review the directions for the writing assignment. Project *Information Master 7E: Creating an Illuminated Manuscript* and review the directions with students. Then have students create their own illuminated manuscripts.

9 Have students read Sections 7.7 and 7.8 and complete the Reading Notes. These sections cover the rapid spread of Islam in the century after Muhammad's death.

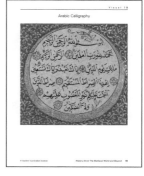

Visual 7B

Information Master 7E

Processing (Optional)

The illuminated manuscript functions as a Processing activity for this lesson. If students are not doing the activity, they will write a short letter from the viewpoint of a 7th-century Arab merchant. The letter will tell about meeting Muhammad, and will explain who Muhammad is and what he is teaching.

Quicker Coverage

Have Students Complete Reading Notes at Home Have students complete the first part of the Reading Notes for Section 7.3 where they visit the walls of the classroom to find the words that correspond to what they listened to in class. Then, instead of having them complete the rest of the Reading Notes in class, tell them to finish them for homework. Repeat this process for Sections 7.4 to 7.6.

Deeper Coverage

Have Students Use Arabic Words During the activity, have students record the Arabic words that correspond to the English words they select for each part of the story. When they work on their illuminated manuscripts, have students include some of the Arabic words as art in the appropriate places.

Use Video with the Lesson Consider incorporating clips from the film "The Message," starring Anthony Quinn, to enhance lesson content on Muhammad.

> **Listening and Speaking: Narrative Presentation**
>
> Another alternative for deeper coverage is to have students create a narrative presentation about Muhammad as prophet from the point of view of someone living at the time. Remind students to locate their character in a definite setting and to relate their narrative using appropriate movement, gestures, and expression.

Assessment

Mastering the Content

1. B	5. A	9. D	13. A
2. C	6. A	10. D	14. C
3. C	7. B	11. A	15. D
4. D	8. C	12. B	16. B

Applying Social Studies Skills

17. Baghdad

18. Red Sea, Mediterranean Sea, Persian Gulf (any order)

19. Tours, France

Exploring the Essential Question

20. Answers should include all the elements requested in the prompt.

Scoring Rubric

Score	Description
3	Student completes all six parts of the task. Sentences demonstrate accurate understanding of events or developments and their importance. Sentences show command of standard English conventions.
2	Student responds to most or all parts of the task, but sentences may not be clearly stated.
1	Student responds to at least some parts of the task. Answers may not be complete sentences or may contain factual and/or grammatical errors.
0	Response does not match the task or is incorrect.

English Language Learners

Have Students Work with a Peer on Reading Notes Pair these students with more proficient readers for this activity. Have them record all the information together on one copy of the Reading Notes. After the activity, photocopy the Reading Notes so that each student has a copy.

Create a Class Outline for the Writing Assignment Have the class work together to create an outline (on the board or an overhead transparency) that tells them where they might find the relevant information for each part of their illuminated manuscript. An outline might look like the following:

Page 1: Cover with title and illustrations

Page 2: Muhammad's early life (Section 7.3)

- key words: *birth, orphan, trader, marriage*

Page 3: The Prophet of Islam (Section 7.4)

- key words: *cave, Gabriel, Allah, Qur'an*

And so on for the rest of the writing assignment.

Learners Reading and Writing Below Grade Level

Adapt the Reading Notes Provide students with copies of Sections 7.3 through 7.6 of *History Alive! The Medieval World and Beyond,* as well as a list of the 12 words or terms that are posted around the room. As students listen to the recording and follow along in the text, have them highlight the four words that they come across in their reading, as well as the sentences in which those words appear. This will help them complete the Reading Notes for these sections.

Adapt the Writing Assignment When creating the illuminated manuscripts, require students to include only one or two words from Step 1 in each section of the Reading Notes, rather than all the words.

Learners with Special Education Needs

Simplify the Writing Assignment Modify the directions on Information Master 7E for the illuminated manuscript, as follows:

1. Create a cover page with the title *The Origins of Islam.* Add designs that include colorful geometric shapes.

2. Create four pages about the life of Muhammad. Each page should include

   - one of the following sentences that best matches the topic for that page:
     - Muhammad was born poor, but he grew up to become a trader.
     - For more than 20 years, Muhammad listened to the messages the angel Gabriel brought from God, whom Muslims call Allah.
     - Muhammad preached his ideas but was rejected by most Makkans.
     - Muhammad created a Muslim community in Madinah that respected Christians and Jews; later he captured Makkah and forgave his enemies.

   - colorful and appropriate illustrations (no human or animal figures)

3. Add creative touches to make the manuscript look authentic.

Advanced Learners

Have Students Research Islam Using the Web sites suggested in the Internet Connections at www.teachtci.com, assign students to research Islam in medieval times. Consider altering the writing assignment in this lesson to incorporate their research. You may wish to have them include information on some or all of the following:

- Muhammad's teachings about Allah, women, or other religions

- the various ways Islam was spread during and after Muhammad's death (e.g., treaties, conquests)

- Islam in medieval Europe (particularly the cultural influence of Muslim rule in modern-day Spain)

Enrichment Resources

Have students find out more about the origins and spread of Islam by exploring the following Enrichment Resources for *History Alive! The Medieval World and Beyond* at www.teachtci.com.

Enrichment Readings These in-depth readings encourage students to explore selected topics related to the chapter. You may also find readings that relate the chapter's content directly to your state's curriculum.

Internet Connections The recommended Web sites provide useful and engaging content that reinforces skills development and mastery of subjects within the chapter.

Literature Recommendations

The following books offer opportunities to extend the content in this chapter.

The Essential Koran: The Heart of Islam by Thomas Cleary, trans. (New York: Book Sales, Inc., 1998)

Islam by Matthew S. Gordon (New York: Chelsea House Publications, 2009)

The Life of the Prophet Muhammad by Leila Azzam (Cambridge, UK: Islamic Texts Society, 1999)

Section 7.2

1. Possible answer: Around the time of Muhammad's birth, Makkah was a <u>prosperous desert trading city</u> on the Arabian Peninsula where many <u>merchants</u> had become wealthy. Makkah was also a <u>religious center</u>, and pilgrims from all over Arabia came to worship at the Ka'bah.

2. The Ka'bah was built by Abraham, for God, centuries before Muhammad's birth. In Muhammad's time, most Arabs were polytheists and the Ka'bah housed statues of many different gods.

3. Possible answer: Though there was no central <u>government</u> uniting Arabs during this time, they shared ties of <u>culture</u>, particularly <u>language</u>.

Section 7.3

1. birth, orphan, trader, marriage

2. Possible answer: Few people noticed Muhammad's birth. His family was not very wealthy, and his mother sent him to live with a family of nomads in the desert. He later returned to the city and his mother, before becoming an orphan. In time, Muhammad became a trader who was known for his honesty. When he was 25, a widow named Khadijah proposed marriage. She and Muhammad had several children, including a daughter named Fatima.

Section 7.4

1. cave, Gabriel, Allah, Qur'an

2. Muhammad was praying in a cave in the mountains when he was visited by the angel Gabriel.

3. *Muslim* means "one who surrenders to God."

4. The holy book of Islam is the Qur'an. It contains the messages from God that Muhammad received from Gabriel.

Section 7.5

1. reject, followers, boycott, Night Journey

2. Muhammad taught that people must worship one God, that all believers in God were equal, and that the rich should share their wealth with the poor. He urged Makkans to take care of orphans and the poor, and to improve the status of women.

3. Makkah's leaders did not want to share their wealth, and they feared that if Muhammad became too powerful he would seize political power.

4. Jerusalem is the site of Muhammad's Night Journey where he met and prayed with earlier prophets, such as Abraham, Moses, and Jesus, before being guided through the seven levels of heaven and meeting God (Allah).

Section 7.6

1. Madinah, People of the Book, battles, Last Sermon

2. See completed timeline below.

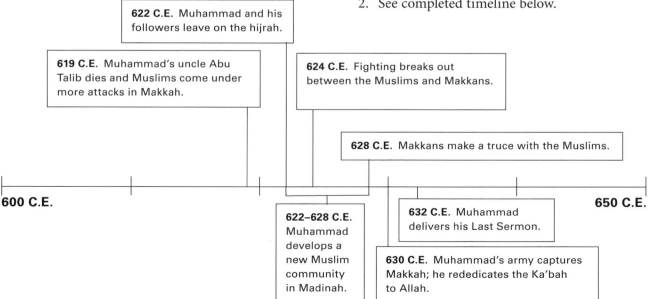

622 C.E. Muhammad and his followers leave on the hijrah.

619 C.E. Muhammad's uncle Abu Talib dies and Muslims come under more attacks in Makkah.

624 C.E. Fighting breaks out between the Muslims and Makkans.

628 C.E. Makkans make a truce with the Muslims.

600 C.E.

650 C.E.

622–628 C.E. Muhammad develops a new Muslim community in Madinah.

632 C.E. Muhammad delivers his Last Sermon.

630 C.E. Muhammad's army captures Makkah; he rededicates the Ka'bah to Allah.

7.7 and 7.8

1. See completed map below.

2. Possible answer: Most of Arabia was under Muslim control by the time Muhammad died. After his death, later caliphs unified Arabia and expanded Islamic territory across the Middle East and North Africa. The fourth caliph was Muhammad's son-in-law, Ali. After his death, Sunnis and Shi'ah split in a dispute over who should be the next caliph.

This division continues today. In 661, the Umayyad caliphs moved the Muslim capital to Damascus. Muslims expanded into India, Central Asia, and Europe. A Muslim defeat at the Battle of Tours in France in 732 ended expansion into Europe, but Muslims kept control of Spain.

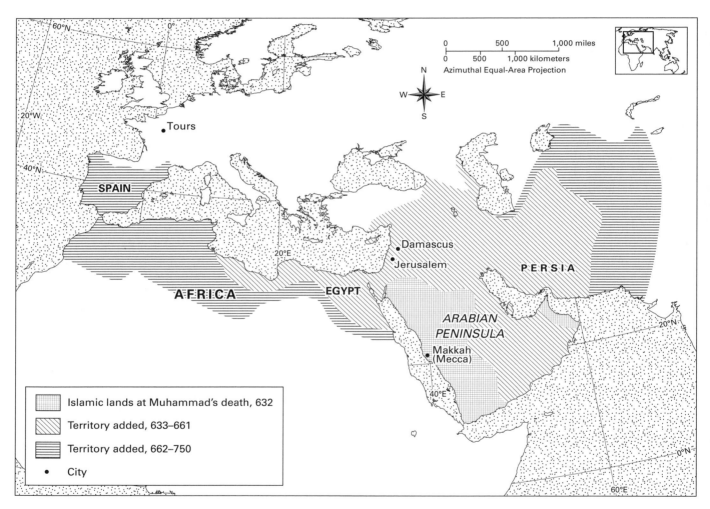

Islamic lands at Muhammad's death, 632

Territory added, 633–661

Territory added, 662–750

• City

Learning About World Religions: Islam

How do the beliefs and practices of Islam shape Muslims' lives?

Overview

In a Problem Solving Groupwork activity, students read, create illustrations, and make presentations to demonstrate an understanding of eight main beliefs and practices of Islam.

Objectives

In the course of reading this chapter and participating in the classroom activity, students will

Social Studies

- understand key beliefs and practices of Islam.
- explain the significance of the Qur'an and the Sunnah and their influence on Muslims' beliefs, practices, laws, and daily life.
- describe the Five Pillars of Islam.
- explain the meaning of *jihad* and the role of *shari'ah* in Islam.

Language Arts

- practice effective presentation skills by providing supporting details, descriptions, and examples effectively and persuasively.
- practice effective speaking techniques, including voice modulation, enunciation, and eye contact.

Social Studies Vocabulary

Key Content Terms Qur'an, Sunnah, Five Pillars of Islam, mosque, Ramadan, jihad, shari'ah

Academic Terms reveal, edition, identify, distribute, contradict

Materials

History Alive! The Medieval World and Beyond

Interactive Student Notebooks

Visual 8

Lesson Masters

- Information Master 8 (1 transparency)
- Student Handout 8 (1 per group)
- Vocabulary Development handout (1 per student, on colored paper)

butcher paper or poster board (1 large sheet per group)

index cards (1 per student)

Activity	Suggested Time	Materials
Preview	10 minutes	• Interactive Student Notebooks • Visual 8
Vocabulary Development	30–40 minutes	• *History Alive! The Medieval World and Beyond* • Interactive Student Notebooks • Vocabulary Development handout
Problem Solving Groupwork	180 minutes (4–5 regular periods) (2–2.5 block periods)	• *History Alive! The Medieval World and Beyond* • Interactive Student Notebooks • Student Handout 8 (1 per group) • Information Master 8 (1 transparency) • butcher paper or poster board (1 large sheet per group) • index cards (1 per student)
Processing	30 minutes	• Interactive Student Notebooks
Assessment	40 minutes	• Chapter 8 Assessment

Preview

1 **Project *Visual 8: Islamic Beliefs and Practices* and have students complete the Preview activity in their Interactive Student Notebooks.** Students analyze images depicting practices of Islam and develop questions about those practices.

2 **Have students share their questions in pairs or with the class.** For example, they might ask, *Why are these men sitting on the sidewalk?* (They are preparing to pray; Muslims often stop their daily activities to pray wherever they are.) Or, *Why are all these people moving around in a circle?* (This ritual is one way Muslims honor God.)

3 **Explain the connection between the Preview activity and Chapter 8.** Tell students that the images they looked at in the Preview activity illustrate aspects of Islamic beliefs, practices, laws, and daily life that they will learn about in this lesson. As they read the chapter and participate in the activity, students will learn about the Five Pillars of Islam, jihad, and shari'ah and how they influence Muslims' lives.

Visual 8

Vocabulary Development

1 **Introduce the Key Content Terms.** Have students locate the Key Content Terms for the chapter in their Interactive Student Notebooks. These are important terms that will help them understand the main ideas of the chapter. Ask volunteers to identify any familiar terms and suggest how they might be used in a sentence.

2 **Have students complete a Vocabulary Development handout.** Give each student a copy of the Vocabulary Development handout of your choice from the Reading Toolkit at the back of the Lesson Masters. These handouts provide extra Key Content Term practice and support, depending on your students' needs. Review the completed handout by asking volunteers to share one answer for each term.

Reading

1 **Introduce the Essential Question and have students read Section 8.1.** Have students identify the Essential Question on the first page of the chapter. Then have students read Section 8.1. Afterward, have students use information from Section 8.1 and from the chapter opener image to propose some answers to the Essential Question: *How do the beliefs and practices of Islam shape Muslims' lives?*

2 **Have students complete the Reading Notes for Chapter 8.** Assign Sections 8.2 to 8.10 during the activity, as indicated in the procedures for the Problem Solving Groupwork activity. Remind students to use the Key Content Terms where appropriate as they complete their Reading Notes.

Problem Solving Groupwork

1   **Before class, prepare the materials and the classroom.** Arrange the desks
    into eight groups of equal size (3–4 desks per group, depending on your class
    size). At each group of desks, place the following materials:

    - index cards (1 per student)

    - a large sheet of poster board or butcher paper

    - scissors

    - glue

    - colored pencils or markers

    Make one copy of *Student Handout 8: Creating a Presentation on Islamic
    Beliefs and Practices* for each group. You may also want to collect images
    related to Islam from library and Internet sources before beginning this
    activity. Providing photocopies of pages from books, printouts from the
    Internet, and other materials will reduce research time and may enhance the
    end product.

Student Handout 8

2   **Have students complete the Reading Notes for Section 8.2.** Tell students
    that this section provides background information on Islam. Have them
    read Section 8.2 and complete the corresponding Reading Notes in their
    Interactive Student Notebooks.

3   **Arrange students in eight groups of equal size and introduce the activity.**
    Tell students that they will work in groups to create a visual presentation
    on one of eight key beliefs and practices of Islam. Their visuals will be used
    to create a poster in the shape of a large, 8-pointed star that represents the
    eight beliefs and practices of Islam. Tell students that stars are used often in
    Islamic art because the Qur'an discourages the depiction of human or animal
    figures (because worship of human and animal idols was a common practice
    among polytheists before Muhammad's time). Each of the eight sections of
    the class star will represent a key belief or practice of Islam.

4   **Distribute materials and review steps for creating visuals about Islam.**
    Distribute one copy of Student Handout 8 to each group.

5   **Have students complete Step 1.** Assign each student a role within his or her
    group (or let students choose roles based on their individual strengths). If
    you have groups with fewer than four students, consider eliminating the role
    of Production Supervisor and making all group members responsible for
    assembling the visuals for the presentation.

6   **Have students complete Steps 2–5.** Assign each group one of Sections 8.3
    to 8.10 in *History Alive! The Medieval World and Beyond*. Before having
    students complete the steps, check that they understand their responsibilities.
    Check their work and initial Student Handout 8 as they complete each step.
    Also, consider the following tips:

    - For Step 3, you may want to offer students the option of creating their
      presentations on transparencies or using presentation software.

- When groups reach Step 5 on the handout, project *Information Master 8: Eight-Pointed Star* onto a wall. Have volunteers from each group come up to trace a section of the star onto their sheet of butcher paper. Assign each group a different color for outlining their section of the star. Make sure that the projector will not move during this process, as each section of the star needs to be the same size.

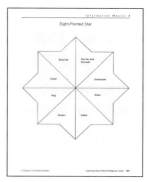

Information Master 8

7   **Have students complete Steps 6–7.** Allow students adequate time to complete their visuals. Also, consider the following tips:

- When groups have completed Step 6, collect their quiz questions and make sure they are organized by topic for the quiz game.

- Before groups present, have them cut out their section of the star so that it can be assembled with the other sections of the star during the presentations. Make sure tape is available at the front of the room where groups will present, so that each group can hang its section after they finish their presentation.

8   **Conduct the presentations and quiz game.** Have one group post their star section and summary on the wall and make their presentation. Make sure students in the audience take notes in the appropriate section of their Reading Notes during each presentation. Conduct a quiz game as follows:

- Assign all members in each group a letter: A, B, C, or D.

- Randomly choose one of the four letters, and have students with that letter stand up.

- Select one quiz question written by the presenting group, and read it to these "contestants." Depending on the time available, you may want to ask more than one question.

- Have contestants write their answers in large print on scrap paper.

- Have contestants hold up their answers simultaneously. Award points to groups accordingly.

9   **Debrief the activity.** Ask students,

- What aspects of Islam will you most remember from this activity?

- For those of you who did not know much about Islam before this activity, how is Islam like what you thought before? Unlike what you thought?

- Why might Islam have been a unifying force in medieval times? Why might it be a unifying force today?

- How are Muslims' lives shaped by the beliefs and practices of Islam?

Processing

Have students complete the Processing activity in their Interactive Student Notebooks. Students illustrate and annotate an eight-pointed star to explain the eight key beliefs and practices of Islam.

Quicker Coverage

Conduct a Gallery Walk Have each group complete Steps 1–5 on Student Handout 8. Create eight stations by having groups post their illustrated section of the star and their presentation outline around the room. Then have groups rotate to each station to view the illustrations, read the presentation outlines, and complete their Reading Notes.

Deeper Coverage

Host a Visiting Scholar Consider inviting an Islamic scholar to talk to students and answer questions about Islam. This person should be an academic, rather than a clergy member. If possible, you may wish to have this person in class during the presentations to answer additional questions students may have.

Assessment

Mastering the Content

1. B	5. D	9. A	13. D
2. A	6. D	10. C	14. A
3. C	7. C	11. D	15. A
4. B	8. B	12. B	16. C

Applying Social Studies Skills

17. worship only God; be kind to one's parents

18. took care of them when they were little

19. Answers will vary; leading them to treat their aging parents well

Exploring the Essential Question

20. Answers should include all the elements requested in the prompt.

Scoring Rubric

Score	Description
3	Student completes all five parts of the task. Outlines include Arabic and English names, important details, and information about the effect(s) of the item on Muslim life, and demonstrate command of standard English conventions.
2	Student responds to most or all parts of the task, but outlines may describe an item without an effect or influence or without important details, or not be clearly stated.
1	Student responds to at least one part of the task. Outlines may contain factual and/or grammatical errors and may lack details.
0	Response does not match the task or is incorrect.

English Language Learners

Provide Hints for the Preview Activity For each image used in the Preview activity, provide annotated hints that might guide students to ask thoughtful questions. Give students a copy of Visual 8 with hints that ask them to consider various aspects of each image. For example, for the image in the upper left, one hint might be, "When you create your question, think about what position the people are in, where they are, and how many there are."

Learners Reading and Writing Below Grade Level

Provide Answers to Reading Notes Once each group has been assigned a specific section of this chapter to read and present, provide some students with a copy of Guide to Reading Notes 8 with all answers provided, except those for his or her group's assigned section. Students can fill in their assigned section with their groups. For the other seven sections, they should check off each answer once it has been addressed in the student presentations, then highlight no more than five key words per section that they believe summarize the most important details of that topic.

Learners with Special Education Needs

Have Students Choose Roles In Step 1 on Student Handout 8, have students choose the role in which they feel they would be most successful. Then help these students closely examine Student Handout 8 to highlight any key directions pertaining to that role. For example, if a student were to choose the role of Writing Supervisor, he or she would need to highlight Step 3, as well as Steps 2 and 6, which apply to all group members.

Advanced Learners

Have Students Create a Diagram Have students use the information provided in their Reading Notes, as well as additional research, to create a triple Venn diagram comparing Islam to Judaism and Christianity.

Encourage students to research the following:

- statistics concerning the prevalence of each religion in the modern world
- the countries where each religion is most predominant
- the holy books each religion follows
- the origins of each religion
- the manner in which followers of each religion practice their faith

Enrichment Resources

Have students find out more about the beliefs and practices of Islam by exploring the following Enrichment Resources for *History Alive! The Medieval World and Beyond* at www.teachtci.com.

Enrichment Readings These in-depth readings encourage students to explore selected topics related to the chapter. You may also find readings that relate the chapter's content directly to your state's curriculum.

Internet Connections The recommended Web sites provide useful and engaging content that reinforces skills development and mastery of subjects within the chapter.

Literature Recommendations

The following books offer opportunities to extend the content in this chapter.

Mosque by David Macaulay (Boston: Houghton Mifflin Company, 2003)

Muslim Child: Understanind Islam Through Stories and Poems by Rukhsana Khan (Morton Grove, IL: Albert Whitman & Company, 2002)

What Do Muslims Believe? by Ziauddin Sardar (New York: Walker & Company, 2007)

Section 8.2

1. the Middle East, North Africa, Asia, and in nearly every country of the world

2. Similarities: monotheistic; trace their origins to the prophet Abraham; scriptures include such figures as Adam, Abraham, and Moses; consider the Torah/New Testament to be a holy books which came from God. Differences: Muslims believe the Qur'an contains God's final revelations.

Section 8.3

1. The Qur'an is Islam's sacred book and is considered to be the words of God. In the Qur'an, God describes his laws and moral teachings. The Sunnah, or "practice," is the example set by Muhammad during his lifetime.

2. The Sunnah contains precedents of behavior set by Muhammad. Hadith are written accounts of Muhammad's actions that illustrate the Sunnah.

3. The Qur'an provides general commands to perform these five duties, and the Sunnah explains how, using Muhammad's example.

Section 8.4

1. "There is no god but God" illustrates the idea of monotheism; and "Muhammad is the messenger of God" identifies Muhammad as God's messenger or prophet.

2. Muslims believe Allah is the one, all-powerful God who created the universe.

3. Muslims believe that angels do Allah's work throughout the universe. They believe that everyone will face God's judgment; those who properly follow Islam will go to paradise and those who have done evil will go to hell.

Section 8.5

1. Salat is the Muslim daily prayer ritual that emphasizes religious discipline, spirituality, and closeness to God.

2. Muslims pray five times a day, wherever they are (though praying in a mosque is preferable).

3. Answers should include at least three of the following: perform a ritual washing of hands, face, arms, and feet; form lines behind a prayer leader called an imam (if in a mosque); face in the direction of Makkah; proclaim "Allahu akbar!" ("God is most great!"); recite verses from the Qur'an; and kneel before God.

Section 8.6

1. Zakat is the practice of charity. Muslims believe that wealth is purified by giving some of it away, that sharing helps control greed, and that giving reminds people of God's gifts.

2. They are expected to give about one-fortieth (2.5%) of their wealth and possessions, but are encouraged to give more.

3. Zakat pays for orphanages, hospitals, soup kitchens, and clothing and shelter for the poor. It pays debts for the poor and helps stranded travelers.

Section 8.7

1. Siyam is daily fasting. It is performed during Ramadan, the ninth month of the Islamic calendar.

2. During Ramadan, observant Muslims do not eat or drink between sunrise and sunset.

3. Ramadan encourages generosity, equality, and charity. Fasting teaches self-control, and helps Muslims realize what it would be like to be poor and hungry. Muslims are also encouraged to avoid arguments and bad deeds, to give thanks, and to practice forgiveness.

Section 8.8

1. The hajj is the pilgrimage to Makkah that all Muslims are expected to make at least once. It promotes fellowship and equality by bringing Muslims of many cultures and places together.

2. They dress in simple white clothing and visit the Great Mosque, which houses the Ka'bah. They circle the Ka'bah seven times, which is a ritual outlined in the Qur'an.

3. They travel along a passage between two small hills, as Hagar did when she searched for water, and drink from the Zamzam spring. They camp in tents at Mina, pray at the plain of Arafat, and some climb Mount Arafat.

Section 8.9

1. Sample response: Jihad means "to strive." Originally, jihad meant "physical struggle that is important for spiritual reasons." The Qur'an tells Muslims to fight to protect themselves from anyone who wants to hurt them or to fix a terrible injustice.

2. The Qur'an tells Muslims to fight to protect themselves from those who would do them harm or to right a terrible wrong. Early Muslims considered their efforts to protect their territory and extend their rule over other regions to be a form of jihad.

3. Jihad represents the human struggle to overcome difficulties and do things that would be pleasing to God. Jihad encourages Muslims to strive to respond positively to personal difficulties (the "greater jihad") as well as to worldly challenges.

Section 8.10

1. Shari'ah is the body of Islamic law based on the Qur'an and the Sunnah. It guides Muslims in their behavior. It was developed by caliphs and scholars who used the Qur'an and the Sunnah to solve problems that arose after Muhammad's death.

2. Islamic law guides Muslim life by placing actions into one of five categories: forbidden, discouraged, allowed, recommended, and obligatory (required). For example, it forbids Muslims to eat pork.

3. Western codes of law have replaced or supplemented shari'ah in many Muslim countries. However, shari'ah continues to develop in response to modern ways of life, and is in force in different ways in different nations.

Muslim Innovations and Adaptations

What important innovations and adaptations did medieval Muslims make?

Overview

In a Social Studies Skill Builder students visit nine stations where they read and learn about Muslim innovations and adaptations in fields such as science, geography, mathematics, philosophy, medicine, art, and literature.

Objectives

In the course of reading this chapter and participating in the classroom activity, students will

Social Studies

- explain the conditions that led to cultural blending in Islamic civilization.
- trace the growth of cities and the establishment of trade routes in the Muslim world.
- describe Muslim adaptations and innovations in learning and scholarship, science and technology, mathematics, medicine, the arts, and recreation.

Language Arts

- support evaluative statements with descriptions, facts, and specific examples.

Social Studies Vocabulary

Key Content Terms adaptation, innovation, cultural diffusion, philosopher, immortal, evolution

Academic Vocabulary diverse, logic, equation, illuminated, intellectual

Materials

History Alive! The Medieval World and Beyond

Interactive Student Notebooks

Placards 9A–9I (print additional sets from TeachTCI)

Lesson Masters

- Information Master 9 (1 transparency)
- Vocabulary Development handout (1 per student, on colored paper)

masking tape

Activity	Suggested Time	Materials
Preview	10 minutes	• Interactive Student Notebooks
Vocabulary Development	30–40 minutes	• *History Alive! The Medieval World and Beyond* • Interactive Student Notebooks • Vocabulary Development handout
Social Studies Skill Builder	90–120 minutes (2–3 regular periods) (1–1.5 block periods)	• *History Alive! The Medieval World and Beyond* • Interactive Student Notebooks • Placards 9A–9I • Information Master 9 (1 transparency) • masking tape
Processing	20–30 minutes	• Interactive Student Notebooks
Assessment	40 minutes	• Chapter 9 Assessment

Preview

1 **Have students complete the Preview activity in their Interactive Student Notebooks.** After students have completed the Preview activity, ask several students to share examples for each category.

2 **Connect the Preview activity to the chapter.** Tell students that they regularly experience and even benefit from something called *cultural diffusion*. Cultural diffusion is the spread of cultural elements, such as food, art, music, sports, language, and ideas, from one culture to another. Cultural diffusion occurs as different societies interact with each other through trade, travel, or even conflict. Often these cultural elements are changed, or adapted, in the regions where they spread. In this chapter students will learn how medieval Muslims participated in cultural diffusion. Muslims during this time developed new innovations and made adaptations to existing technology, scholarship, art, music, and so forth, and helped spread this knowledge to different areas of the world.

Vocabulary Development

1 **Introduce the Key Content Terms.** Have students locate the Key Content Terms for the chapter in their Interactive Student Notebooks. These are important terms that will help them understand the main ideas of the chapter. Ask volunteers to identify any familiar terms and suggest how they might be used in a sentence.

2 **Have students complete a Vocabulary Development handout.** Give each student a copy of the Vocabulary Development handout of your choice from the Reading Toolkit at the back of the Lesson Masters. These handouts provide extra Key Content Term practice and support, depending on your students' needs. Review the completed handout by asking volunteers to share one answer for each term.

Reading

1 **Introduce the Essential Question and have students read Section 9.1.** Have students identify the Essential Question on the first page of the chapter: *What important innovations and adaptations did medieval Muslims make?* Then have students read Section 9.1. Afterward, have students respond to these questions:

   • What made the Islamic world rich, diverse, and creative?

   • What are some examples of Muslim influence that remain today?

2 **Have students complete the Reading Notes for Chapter 9.** Assign Sections 9.2 to 9.11 during the activity, as indicated in the procedures for the Social Studies Skill Builder. Remind students to use the Key Content Terms where appropriate as they complete their Reading Notes.

Social Studies Skill Builder

1 Before class, prepare the materials and the classroom. Make a transparency of *Information Master 9: Activity Directions*. Post *Placards 9A–9I: Muslim Innovations or Adaptations* on the walls to create nine stations. (If you have a large class, you might want to print an extra set of the placards from www. teachtci.com, and post one set on each side of the classroom.)

2 Have students complete the Reading Notes for Section 9.2. Tell students that this section provides information about how medieval Muslims participated in the cultural diffusion of ideas and inventions. Have students read Section 9.2 and complete the corresponding Reading Notes in their Interactive Student Notebooks.

3 Place students in pairs and review the directions for the activity. Tell students that they will be working with their partners to learn about some of the innovations and adaptations made by medieval Muslims. Project a transparency of Information Master 9. Have students open their Interactive Student Notebooks to the Reading Notes. Point out that the first question for each section asks students to identify the letter of the matching placard. On Information Master 9, review the steps students will follow to learn about nine Muslim innovations and adaptations. Consider modeling the activity, using one of the placards.

4 Monitor students' work. Keep Information Master 9 posted so that students can reference the activity steps, if necessary. After partners have examined the placard at a station, have them return to their desks and complete the Reading Notes for the applicable section before moving to another station. You might consider checking their work after the first couple of stations before letting them progress from station to station independently. Allow students to continue working until most pairs have had a chance to visit most of the stations.

5 Review the innovations and adaptations. Place pairs in groups of four. Remove the placards from the wall, and assign one to two placards to each group. Explain that groups will present their placard(s) to the class by describing the Muslim innovation or adaptation shown on the placard and explaining how the details from the image correspond to the topic. Give groups a few minutes to prepare, and then have students in each group stand up and present their placard(s). Have students take notes during the presentations on any placards they did not visit, and instruct them to complete the Reading Notes for that section for homework.

Processing

Have students complete the Processing activity. Students create an illustrated and annotated spectrum evaluating the impact of medieval Muslim adaptations and innovations.

Information Master 9

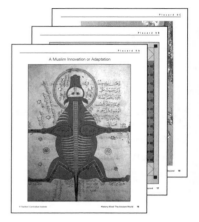

Placards 9A–9I

Listening and Speaking: Oral Summaries

Remind students that their presentations should clearly state a main idea as well as all the most significant details. Students should use their own words and convey a comprehensive understanding of the contribution, not just superficial details.

Quicker Coverage

Assign One Placard per Group Instead of conducting the Social Studies Skill Builder by having each pair go to each station to learn about the adaptations and innovations, put students into nine groups of roughly equal size. Assign each group one section of Sections 9.3 to 9.11 of the text, and give them the corresponding placard. Have groups complete their Reading Notes for their section, and prepare a brief explanation for the class about their placard. Then have each group present its placard. Have students complete the section-specific portions of their Reading Notes for homework.

Deeper Coverage

Create a Human Spectrum After students have completed Step 4 of the Social Studies Skill Builder, debrief the activity as follows:

- Create a spectrum by placing a 10- to 15-foot strip of masking tape across the floor in the front of the room. On the board above either end of the spectrum, write "Least Significant Impact" and "Most Significant Impact."

- Explain the purpose of a spectrum, and tell students they will now rank the Muslim adaptations and innovations according to what students think their impact is on the world today.

- Give groups two to three minutes to discuss where on the spectrum they would place their innovation or adaptation, and why. Then have each group choose a student representative for each of their placards. Those students should stand on the spectrum where the group thinks their innovation or adaptation belongs. Have students hold their placards in front of their chests.

- Encourage discussion among the "audience" about where the contributions should be placed, challenging students to identify contributions they believe are misplaced. The purpose of this activity is not to find the "correct" locations, but to have students support their opinions with good evidence.

Assessment

Mastering the Content

1. B	5. C	9. C	13. C
2. D	6. D	10. A	14. B
3. B	7. A	11. D	15. C
4. A	8. D	12. A	16. C

Applying Social Studies Skills

17. secondary source; Sample response: The book was published in 1886, long after the time described. The author quoted another writer instead of using personal knowledge.

18. The writer compares Cordoba to a woman dressed in fancy clothes.

19. Answers will vary but should be facts, not opinions. Sample answers: Cordoba has been ruled by a long line of Muslim rulers. The city has many poets. The city is known for learning and science. The city has skilled artists and craftspeople.

Exploring the Essential Question

20. Answers should include all the elements requested in the prompt.

Scoring Rubric

Score	Description
3	Student completes all four parts of the task. Text for the plaque is clearly stated, is supported by details, and demonstrates command of standard English conventions.
2	Student responds to most or all parts of the task, but text for the plaque may lack details or not be clearly stated.
1	Student responds to at least one part of the task. Text for the plaque may contain factual and/or grammatical errors and may lack details.
0	Response does not match the task or is incorrect.

History at the Dinner Table

1 **Discuss with students some of their favorite or least-favorite foods.** Ask students to suggest some of their favorite or least-favorite foods. List the responses on the board. Then ask students to offer descriptive words, or adjectives, that tell what each food is like. Encourage students to be creative and to consider all their senses—taste, touch/texture, smell, sight, and hearing, if applicable.

2 **Have students read the Chapter 9 Reading Further.** Direct students to pay special attention to descriptive words or phrases relating to food as they read.

3 **Have students define the process of *cultural diffusion*.** Based on what they have read, ask students to define, in their own words, the term *cultural diffusion*. Discuss the reasons why the Middle East provided a rich environment for cultural diffusion to occur. Ask students for examples of foods in the United States that might have come from other countries or cultures.

4 **Have students complete the Reading Further activity in their Interactive Student Notebooks.** Tell students to choose six foods mentioned in the Reading Further. Students may be familiar with the foods or they might imagine what the foods are like based on the images in the selection.

5 **Invite students to share their descriptive paragraphs with the class.** Which foods did students most often describe? Did the same descriptive words appear in several students' paragraphs? Explore with students why food is one of the cultural features that people exchange most often. Ask, *Why do you think people so often enjoy eating foods from different cultures?*

English Language Learners

Review the Topics for the Activity After students read Section 9.1, ask them to identify the nine categories that will be covered in the text and the activity. Then consider listing the categories on the board or an overhead transparency and brainstorming as a class one or two achievements that might fall under each category. For example, for "city building and architecture," students might list a sewer system, columns and arches, and streets.

Learners Reading and Writing Below Grade Level

Guide Students During the Reading Provide students with photocopies of Sections 9.3 through 9.11 of the textbook. After copying one set and before making classroom copies, do the following:

- Write corresponding placard letters next to the sections or subsections that describe the images on the placards.
- Circle locations in each section that might later guide students.
- Prompt students as they read to highlight key words and phrases that they might use in the Reading Notes.

Learners with Special Education Needs

Provide Guidance for Activity Give students the placard letter that corresponds to each section number and title before they begin the activity.

Modify the Processing Activity Modify the Processing activity as follows:

- Allow students to place four contributions on the spectrum rather than six.
- Have students justify only their "least significant" and "most significant" contributions by writing one sentence in support for each.

Advanced Learners

Assign an Alternative Processing Activity Have students imagine that they are on a committee that must select the one Muslim figure from history who, in their opinion, has made the most significant contribution to the world. The nominees might include:

- Caliph al-Ma'mun
- Ibn Sina
- al-Khwarizmi
- Rabi'a
- Ziryab

Have students locate these historical figures in the chapter and do additional research about each one, using the Internet or the library. Then have each student select the person he or she considers to have made the greatest impact on the modern world. Students should then each write a letter to the "selection committee," making a case for his or her choice and giving at least three examples of the candidate's lasting contributions.

Enrichment Resources

Have students find out more about Muslim adaptations and innovations by exploring the following Enrichment Resources for *History Alive! The Medieval World and Beyond* at www.teachtci.com.

Enrichment Readings These in-depth readings encourage students to explore selected topics related to the chapter. You may also find readings that relate the chapter's content directly to your state's curriculum.

Internet Connections The recommended Web sites provide useful and engaging content that reinforces skills development and mastery of subjects within the chapter.

Literature Recommendations

The following books offer opportunities to extend the content in this chapter.

The Arabian Nights by Husain Haddawy (trans.) (New York: W. W. Norton & Co., 2008)

The House of Wisdom by Florence P. Heide and Judith Gilliland (London: Dorling Kindersley, 1999)

Um El Madayan: An Islamic City Through the Ages by Abderrahaman Ayoub (Boston: Houghton Mifflin Company, 1994)

Section 9.2

1. Muslim rulers built great cities where scholars and artists made great innovations and adaptions and cultural diffusion could take place.

2. the spread of cultural elements from one society to another

3. Muslim lands were located at the crossroads of important trade routes from Asia, North Africa, and Europe.

4. Answers will vary. Sample answer: Wherever people travel to trade goods, they also exchange elements of their culture. Examples of this in Muslim lands include: the compass from China, the astrolabe from Greece, the concept of zero from India, and paper making from China.

Section 9.3

1. Placard: 9C

   Answers will vary but may include:

   • city with different styles of buildings

   • minaret (at mosque)

   • thick wall surrounding the city

2. Answers will vary but may include:

   • new Abbasid capital at the crossroads of trade routes, connecting distant parts of the empire

   • took 100,000 architects, workers, and craftspeople four years to build the new capital

   • "round city"—caliph's palace and the grand mosque at the center, city spread around it

   • many bridges, palaces, and gardens added to its splendor

3. Answers will vary but may include:

   • usually have a minaret for the call to prayer

   • a walled courtyard outside with a fountain for washing before prayers

   • inside is the prayer room

   • many design styles reflect diversity of Muslim lands

Section 9.4

1. Placard: 9E

   Answers will vary but may include:

   • men reading (and, possibly, discussing) books

   • books on shelves in background, looks like a library

   • globe on table in foreground

2. A shared (Arabic) language and a love of learning allowed Muslim scholars in Europe, North Africa, and the Middle East to exchange ideas and build on one another's work. At the same time, Muslim rulers built schools, colleges, libraries, and other centers of learning where scholars could research and work together.

3. They used reason and logic to try to prove important truths. They also tried to make reason and logical proof agree with their religious faith.

Section 9.5

1. Placard: 9A

   aerial view of animal (cow); diagram of animal's bones; Arabic annotations around animal's body

2.

Zoology	Astronomy
Answers will vary but may include two of the following:	Answers will vary but may include two of the following:
• wrote books describing the structure of animals' bodies • explained how to make medicine from animal parts • established zoological gardens	• used compasses and astrolabes to locate Makkah • realized that Earth rotated • questioned the idea that Earth was the center of the universe

3. They built canals and waterwheels to bring water where it was needed.

Section 9.6

1. Placard: 9G

   diagram of a round map showing mountains and rivers

2. Answers will vary, but may include:

   - divided the world into climate zones
   - calculated Earth's circumference within nine miles of its correct value
   - created extremely accurate maps and atlases
   - adapted and perfected the compass and astrolabe

3. The compass (from the Chinese) allows people to identify the direction in which they are traveling; with the astrolabe (from the Greeks), sailors could use the position of objects in the sky to pinpoint their location.

Section 9.7

1. Placard: 9B

   mathematical equation; variables: x and y

2. His famous book on algebra became the most important mathematics text in European universities. Another of his books helped popularize Arabic numerals in Europe, which was a big help to business and trade, and is still used today.

3. Zero is important in calculations. It also makes it easier to write large numbers, and to distinguish between numbers (for example, 123 and 1,230).

Section 9.8

1. Placard: 9D

   patients in beds; man carrying vials; man examining patient's heart/body

2. Answers will vary but may include:

   - Hospitals: established the world's first hospitals, which served as teaching centers for doctors; anyone could get treatment

   - Medication: gave patients remedies from plants, animals, and minerals; drugs, antiseptics, and ointments were used for a variety of purposes

   - Surgery: used opium and hemlock to put patients to sleep before operations; amputated limbs, took out tumors, and removed cataracts; stitched up wounds with animal gut

   - Disease: understood that infections were caused by bacteria; studied deadly diseases, such as smallpox and measles, to determine how to diagnose and treat them

3. The book was considered a classic in the field of medicine. It explored the treatment of diseases and was used as a textbook in European medical schools.

Section 9.9

1. Placard: 9H

   handwritten (in Arabic) book; miniature paintings within text

2. Answers will vary but may include:

   - learned the art of paper making from the Chinese; soon were making books with leather bindings and miniature paintings

   - bookshops opened; sold copies of the Qur'an, volumes of poetry and prose

3. *A Thousand and One Nights,* also called *Arabian Nights,* is one of the most famous examples of Muslim literature. It is a collection of stories that originally came from many places, including India, Persia, and the Middle East. The stories spread to Europe, where they were translated and new stories were added.

Section 9.10

1. Placard: 9I

   Students should provide two of the following: geometric designs; arabesque; Arabic calligraphy

2. Muslim artists turned shapes and patterns found in nature and geometry into marvelous designs and decorations. Using a type of design called arabesque, borrowed from nature, artists crafted stems, leaves, flowers, and tendrils into elegant patterns. They also used geometric shapes to form complex patterns. Calligraphy, the art of beautiful handwriting, was another highly valued art form.

3. Textiles were important to the Arab people as practical items (clothing, for example, could show rank and status) and as trade goods.

4. The music that developed in Cordoba, Spain, blended elements of Arab and native Spanish cultures.

Section 9.11

1. Placard: 9F

   two men playing a chess

2.

Polo	Chess
• Polo is a sport in which teams on horseback use mallets to strike a ball through a goal. • Muslims viewed horses as status symbols, and polo quickly became popular among the wealthy.	• Chess is a battle of wits in which players move pieces on a board according to complex rules. • Chess quickly gained popularity because players enjoyed the intellectual challenge the game presented.

From the Crusades to New Muslim Empires

How did the Crusades affect the lives of Christians, Muslims, and Jews?

Overview

In an Experiential Exercise, students experience the challenges facing various groups as they compete to acquire and control the same territory, and compare their experience to the competition over Jerusalem during the Middle Ages.

Objectives

In the course of reading this chapter and participating in the classroom activity, students will

Social Studies

- explain the causes of the religious Crusades.
- describe the course of the religious Crusades.
- evaluate the effects of the Crusades on Christian, Muslim, and Jewish populations.
- describe the larger effects and aftermath of the Crusades, including the Reconquista and the rise of the Ottoman Turks and other Muslim empires in the 1500s.

Language Arts

- pose relevant and tightly drawn questions, and convey clear, accurate, and varied perspectives in response.

Social Studies Vocabulary

Key Content Terms Crusades, sultan, Holy Land, Inquisition, anti-Semitism, segregation, shah

Academic Terms response, cooperation, economic, dramatically

Materials

History Alive! The Medieval World and Beyond

Interactive Student Notebooks

Visual 10

Lesson Masters

- Information Masters 10A–10B (1 transparency each)
- Student Handout 10A (1 copy for every 3 students) (optional)
- Student Handout 10B (1 copy for every 3 students) (optional)
- Vocabulary Development handout (1 per student, on colored paper)

red, blue, and green stickers (1 for every 3 students) (optional)

colored poster board or cardboard (7)

white poster board or cardboard (1)

Activity	Suggested Time	Materials
Experiential Exercise	40–50 minutes (1 regular period) (.5 block period)	• *History Alive! The Medieval World and Beyond* • Interactive Student Notebooks • Visual 10 • Information Masters 10A and 10B (1 transparency each) • colored poster board or cardboard (7) • white poster board or cardboard (1) • red, blue, and green stickers (1 for every 3 students)
Vocabulary Development	30–40 minutes	• *History Alive! The Medieval World and Beyond* • Interactive Student Notebooks • Vocabulary Development handout
Processing	20–30 minutes	• Interactive Student Notebooks
Assessment	40 minutes	• Chapter 10 Assessment

Preview (Optional)

1 **Understand the intent of the Preview activity.** The Experiential Exercise serves as the Preview activity for this lesson. In the event that you do not choose to do the activity, directions for an optional Preview are as follows:

2 **Project *Visual 10: Jerusalem's "Old City."*** Lead a class discussion by asking the questions, below. Have students complete the Preview activity in their Interactive Student Notebooks by recording answers to these questions as the class discusses them.

- How is the area on the map divided?

- What religions are represented in the different quarters?

- What important landmarks do you see? With which religion is each affiliated?

- What do you think makes this an important or special city?

- Why might people fight over this city?

3 **Connect the Preview activity to the chapter.** Tell students that this is a modern-day map of the historical part (the "Old City") of Jerusalem. Explain that today Jerusalem is located in the nation of Israel in the Middle East. Historically, followers of the Christian, Muslim, and Jewish faiths fought for control of Jerusalem because of its historical and religious significance for each religion. During the 7th century, Jerusalem became part of the expanding Muslim empire. For centuries, Jews and Christians were allowed to live there and practice their faiths. However, growing tension between Muslims and Christians in the 11th century led Christian Crusaders to attempt to seize control of the Holy Land, including Jerusalem. In the chapter, students will learn about the causes of the Crusades, how the Crusades affected Jews, Christians, and Muslims in Europe and the Middle East, and how new Muslim empires rose to power following the Crusades.

Visual 10

Experiential Exercise

1 **Use the Experiential Exercise in place of a Preview activity.** After you complete the Experiential Exercise, proceed with the rest of the lesson.

2 **Understand the intent of the activity.** This activity is designed to help students experience some of the challenges facing groups competing for control of the same territory. As the activity progresses, the territory representing Jerusalem becomes increasingly valuable. This is intended to model the importance of Jerusalem to Christians, Muslims, and Jews. As Christianity and Islam developed, competition over Jerusalem led to conflict among the three groups.

3 **Prepare the classroom and materials.** Do the following:

- Scatter eight pieces of poster board or cardboard on the classroom floor or on the ground outside. Seven pieces should be colored and one should be white. The pieces of poster board represent territory in the Middle East.

- Place some pieces close enough to enable a student to reach two pieces with two parts of his or her body (as in the mat game Twister™).

- The white piece of poster board represents Jerusalem. Place it in a central location.

- Secure the pieces of poster board so that they cannot move.

- Make one transparency of *Information Master 10A: Rules and Scoring* and, if you have not already done so, one transparency of *Information Master 10B: Connecting the Activity and Reading*

4 **Place students into three groups of equal size.** The three teams represent the three groups who competed for territory in the Middle East during the Crusades. As an optional approach, have students affix a red, blue, or green sticker to their shirts to indicate their team affiliation. Teams must have an equal number of students. Have extra students alternate during the next round of play, or assign them to be your scorekeepers during the activity. If you have a large class and are concerned about classroom management issues, consider having only six students from each group compete during each round. You can alternate the players in each round so that all students have a chance to play, and the students not playing can help their team members strategize from the sidelines.

5 **Explain the rules of the game.** Tell students that they will play a game in which teams compete to acquire "territory" represented by the pieces of poster board on the floor. The territories are worth different amounts, and their values may change in each round of the game. Project Information Master 10A and review the rules with students, but cover up and do not display the table with the directions and scoring guide for each round. Tell students that teams will receive points for each piece of territory where they have members at the end of a round. Emphasize that students may not push, shove, or grab each other. Also, tell students that they may not move any of the territories.

6 **Conduct Rounds 1–3 of the game.** Use the following procedures for each round of the game:

- Before each round, have teams line up along the sides of the classroom.

- Reveal the appropriate row on Information Master 10A, and review the directions and scoring guide for that round.

- Make sure students understand that in the first round, the white territory is worth 1 point, but Blue team members on the white territory will earn 5 points. In the second round, both Blue and Red team members earn 5 points for being on the white territory; and in the third round, all group members earn 5 points for being on the white territory.

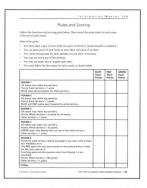

Information Master 10A

Information Master 10B

- Answer any questions students may have about that round.

- During each round of play, audibly signal the end of the round. Consider playing 20 to 30 seconds of high-energy music and then turning it off to signal the end of the round.

- After each round, tally the scores for each team and record the total in the appropriate row on Information Master 10A.

7 **Conduct Round 4 of the game.** Reveal the appropriate row on Information Master 10A, and review the directions and scoring guide. Make sure students understand that the Green team members on the white territory will be able to determine if members of any other groups will also be allowed to claim white territory.

8 **Conduct Round 5 of the game.** Reveal the appropriate row on Information Master 10A, and review the directions and scoring guide. Have each team discuss its strategy and write down its plan for claiming territory. Have each group read its plan aloud, and then announce that Round 5 will not be played for safety reasons.

9 **Debrief the game.** Ask students,

- Blue team, how did it feel to earn more points for the white territory first?

- In Rounds 2 and 3, why did competition over the white territory increase?

- Green team, how did you feel about deciding who should occupy the white territory in Round 4? Blue and Red teams, how did you feel about this?

- Were the plans you all developed in Round 5 justified? Why?

- Can you think of any time in history when a single territory has been considered more important or more desirable than any other and has caused competition and conflict?

10 **Discuss the conflict over Jerusalem.** Project *Visual 10: Jerusalem's "Old City."* Lead a classroom discussion by asking the following questions:

- How is the area on the map divided?

- What religions are represented in the different quarters?

- What important landmarks do you see? With which religion is each affiliated?

- What do you think makes this an important or special city?

- Why might people have conflicts over this city?

Tell students that the visual shows a modern-day map of the historical part of Jerusalem known as "the Old City." Today, Jerusalem is located in the nation of Israel in the Middle East. Explain that throughout history, Jerusalem has been fought over by followers of the Christian, Muslim, and Jewish faiths because of its historical and religious significance to each group.

11 **Connect the activity to the chapter.** In the activity, students experienced increasing competition to control a single piece of territory. Explain to students that during the 7th century, Jerusalem became part of the expanding Muslim empire. For centuries, Jews and Christians were still allowed to live there and practice their faiths. However, growing tension between Muslims and Christians in the 11th century led Christian Crusaders to attempt to seize control of the Holy Land, including Jerusalem. In the reading that follows, students will learn about the causes of the Crusades, how the Crusades affected Jews, Christians, and Muslims in Europe and the Middle East, and how new Muslim empires rose to power following the Crusades.

Vocabulary Development

1 **Introduce the Key Content Terms.** Have students locate the Key Content Terms for the chapter in their Interactive Student Notebooks. These are important terms that will help them understand the main ideas of the chapter. Ask volunteers to identify any familiar terms and suggest how they might be used in a sentence.

2 **Have students complete a Vocabulary Development handout.** Give each student a copy of the Vocabulary Development handout of your choice from the Reading Toolkit at the back of the Lesson Masters. These handouts provide extra Key Content Term practice and support, depending on your students' needs. Review the completed handout by asking volunteers to share one answer for each term.

Reading

1 **Introduce the Essential Question and have students read Section 10.1.** Have students identify the Essential Question on the first page of the chapter: *How did the Crusades affect the lives of Christians, Muslims, and Jews?* Then have students read Section 10.1. Afterward, have students respond to these questions:

- What caused the Crusades?

- What was the purpose of the Crusades?

- How long did the Crusades last?

- What groups were affected by the Crusades?

2 **Have students read and complete the Reading Notes for Section 10.2.**

3 **Connect Section 10.2 to the Experiential Exercise.** Project Information Master 10B, but cover the bulleted points in the T-chart. Have students create a T-chart in their notebooks and copy the headers from the Information Master. Then do the following:

> **Writing: Written English Language Conventions**
>
> Use the chapter vocabulary term *anti-Semitism* to help students identify one instance of correct hyphen use—when a prefix comes before a proper noun, as in *un-American* or *trans-Saharan*. When a prefix does not come before a proper noun, as in *displace* or *antibiotic*, there is usually no hyphen.

- Reveal the first bullet point under "Classroom Competition" and have students copy the sentence onto their T-charts. Then have the class discuss the historic connection to that part of the classroom activity. Record an appropriate connection on the Information Master, and have students write it in their notebooks.

- Repeat the process for the rest of the bullet points. Answers can be found in the table below.

Classroom Competition Over Territory	Historic Competition Over Jerusalem and Holy Land
• Three teams took part in the game. • One piece of territory was more valuable than others were to the groups. • By Round 4, the Green team was able to decide who could have the most valuable piece of territory. • In Round 5, the Red team developed a plan to ensure they would control the most valuable piece of territory, while other teams tried to remain there.	• Members of three faiths lived in the Holy Land: Jews, Christians, and Muslims. • One city, Jerusalem, was very important to people of all three faiths. • Before the start of the Crusades, Muslim leaders controlled the Holy Land and were able to control access to Jerusalem. • European Christians tried to seize control of Jerusalem and the rest of the Holy Land, which led to a series of religious wars called the Crusades.

- Lead a class discussion about the religious group each team represented. Make sure that students can support their choices. The Blue team represented the Jews, for whom Jerusalem was a holy city before Christianity and Islam existed. The Red team represented Christians, whose religion developed out of Judaism. The Green team represented Muslims, whose religion developed hundreds of years after Christianity and who controlled Jerusalem, beginning in the 7th century.

- Ask students, Do you think the religious and historical significance of Jerusalem and the Holy Land to Jews, Christians, and Muslims made conflict in this area inevitable? Why or why not?

4 Have students complete the Reading Notes for Chapter 10. Assign students to read Sections 10.3–10.8 and complete the corresponding Reading Notes. Remind students to use the Key Content Terms where appropriate.

Processing

Have students complete the Processing activity in their Interactive Student Notebooks. Students "interview" three medieval figures to discover how they were affected by the Crusades.

Quicker Coverage

Abbreviate the Activity Skip the competition over the territory entirely. Have students complete only Steps 10 and 11 where they analyze the image of the Old City of Jerusalem. Then skip Step 3 under the Reading directions.

Deeper Coverage

Conduct a Talk-It-Out After they complete the reading and Reading Notes for Sections 10.4–10.6, place students in groups of three and do the following:

1. Have each student choose one role: Richard I of England (Christian); Salah al-Din (Muslim); or Eliezer ben Nathan (Jew). Give each student the appropriate pages of the optional Student Handouts 10A and 10B, based on his or her role.

2. After students have read about their historical figure and completed the prompts at the end of their Student Handouts, have them share the description of their historical figure with their groups.

3. Have students cut out the mask of their historical figure from Student Handout 10B to wear, or tape to their chest, in preparation for the talk-it-out.

4. Then give the class each of the discussion prompts below, one at a time, and have groups discuss the prompt by doing the following:

   • Each student has 30 seconds to respond to the prompt from the point of view of his or her historical figure.

   • After all group members have responded, groups have 30 seconds more to ask questions of each other or to challenge each other's perspective.

Discussion Prompts:

1. Who is responsible for starting the Crusades?

2. Which group gained the most from the Crusades, and why?

3. Which group suffered the most from the Crusades, and why?

Assessment

Mastering the Content

1. D	5. B	9. D	13. B
2. A	6. C	10. C	14. A
3. A	7. B	11. A	15. D
4. C	8. A	12. B	16. C

Applying Social Studies Skills

17. 358 years

18. The Jews were expelled from England.

19. Success: Mongols destroy Baghdad, 1258; Failure: Mongols stopped by Mamluks in Palestine, 1260

Exploring the Essential Question

20. Answers should include all the elements requested in the prompt.

Scoring Rubric

Score	Description
3	Student completes all three ratings and three explanations. Explanations are clearly stated, supported by details, and demonstrate command of standard English conventions.
2	Student responds to most or all parts of the task, but explanations may lack details or not be clearly stated.
1	Student responds to at least one part of the task. Explanations may contain factual and/or grammatical errors and may lack details.
0	Response does not match the task or is incorrect.

English Language Learners

Provide Support for Connecting the Reading and Activity Assist students with Step 3 of the Reading directions, as follows:

- Copy the chart in Information Master 10B and write out the correct answers for the T-chart under "Historic Competition Over Jerusalem and Holy Land." Make copies and cut them into strips so that each student gets a strip with the three correct answers.

- Have students work together or independently to match the "Historic Competition" answer with each appropriate step on the "Classroom Competition" side of the T-chart.

Learners Reading and Writing Below Grade Level

Provide Support for the Processing Activity Give students additional support in the Processing activity by providing them with the interview questions listed below. You could allow students to use these as inspiration for writing their own questions or allow them to use these questions and require only that they provide the Muslim, Christian, and Jewish responses.

1. In your opinion, why did the Crusades happen?
2. Did the Crusades hurt or help the followers of your religion? How?
3. Do you think different religious groups will keep fighting over Jerusalem? Why or why not?

Learners with Special Education Needs

Assign a Scorekeeper for the Activity Assign students who may be uncomfortable with the game, or who might find it physically challenging, to keep score. Have them add up the actual points for each team and record the scores on Information Master 10A at the end of each round. If there are multiple students unable to do the activity, you may want to assign each student one team to monitor.

Advanced Learners

Have Students Create a Crusades Museum Assign each student to represent one medieval group affected by the Crusades: Christians, Jews, or Muslims. Have students do additional research on their group. Students should find out information such as:

- approximate number of people involved in or affected by the Crusades
- clothing, weapons, or supplies used by this group
- major events of the Crusades that involved or affected this group

Students should then create a museum exhibit that includes the following:

- wall plaque summarizing the effect of the Crusades on this group
- appropriate data demonstrating how this group was affected by the Crusades
- images/illustrations of clothing, weapons, or supplies used by this group
- timeline showing major events that involved or affected this group

Hang exhibits for each group on a different wall. The entire class can do a gallery walk to learn more about the impact of the Crusades.

Enrichment Resources

Have students find out more about the Crusades and Muslim empires by exploring the following Enrichment Resources for *History Alive! The Medieval World and Beyond* at www.teachtci.com.

Enrichment Readings These in-depth readings encourage students to explore selected topics related to the chapter. You may also find readings that relate the chapter's content directly to your state's curriculum.

Internet Connections The recommended Web sites provide useful and engaging content that reinforces skills development and mastery of subjects within the chapter.

Literature Recommendations

The following books offer opportunities to extend the content in this chapter.

The Book of the Lion by Michael Cadnum (New York: Viking, 2001)

The Crusades by John Child (New York: McGraw Hill, 1996)

Rock: A Tale of Seventh-Century Jerusalem by Kanan Makiya (New York: Pantheon Books, 2001)

Section 10.2

1. Answers will vary, but may include:

   - The Seljuk Turks expanded their empire westward, overrunning much of Anatolia, which was part of the Byzantine Empire.

   - Christians in Europe were alarmed by the Seljuk advance and concerned about the safety and property of Christians living to the east.

   - Christians were worried about the fate of the Holy Land, especially Jerusalem.

   - After the Seljuks took control of Palestine, political turmoil made travel unsafe and tales reached Europe of highway robbers attacking and even killing Christian pilgrims.

   - Christians feared they would no longer be able to visit Jerusalem and other holy sites in the Holy Land.

2. Jerusalem was the city where Jesus was crucified and rose from the dead.

3. Jerusalem was the place where Muhammad rose to heaven during his Night Journey.

4. Jerusalem was the spiritual capital of the Jews; it was where their great Temple once stood.

Section 10.3

Flow charts will vary. Sample answers:

Causes: By 1095, the Muslim Seljuk Turks had advanced to within 100 miles of Byzantine capital, Constantinople. The emperor appealed to Pope Urban II. The pope called for a European Crusade to drive the Muslims from the Holy Land.

First Crusade: In 1098, the Crusaders laid siege to the city of Antioch in Syria for nine months before it fell to them. The following year they surrounded Jerusalem and fought their way into the city. Some of the Crusaders stayed in the Holy Land to establish four Crusader kingdoms.

Second Crusade: As Muslims banded together, they fought against the Crusader kingdoms, which led Christians to call for a Second Crusade. The Crusade ended in failure after German and French armies were defeated in Anatolia and Damascus.

Third Crusade: Richard I of England led the Third Crusade to retake the Holy Land from the Muslim leader Salah al-Din, who had recaptured much of Palestine. After forcing the surrender of the Palestinian town of Acre, Richard's troops fought their way toward Jerusalem, but his army was not strong enough to attack the city. In 1192, the two leaders signed a peace treaty allowing the Crusaders to keep some territory, and allowing Christian pilgrims to enter Jerusalem.

Later Crusades: Later Crusades, such as the "Childen's Crusade," tended to be popular movements of poor people, and seldom reached the Holy Land. In Europe, Christians launched the Reconquista to retake the Iberian Peninsula. Both Portugal and Spain became independent Catholic countries. Queen Isabella and King Ferdinand of Spain used a Church court, called the Inquisition, to root out Muslims and Jews who were still practicing their old religion. Eventually Jews and Muslims were expelled from Spain.

Sections 10.4–10.6

Impact of the Crusades on Christians

Positive

- Crusaders' need to pay for supplies increased the use of money in Europe.

- Some knights began performing banking functions, such as making loans or investments.

- Monarchs grew more powerful, which weakened feudalism.

- Christians were introduced to new foods and clothing, and some European merchants made enormous profits trading for these new goods.

Negative

- Many Crusaders were wounded or killed in battle.

- Many Crusaders died from disease and the hardships of travel.

Impact of the Crusades on Muslims

Positive

- Gained exposure to some new weapons and military ideas and began to adopt standing, or permanent, armies.
- Muslim merchants earned wealth from trade with Europe, which helped to fund new mosques and religious schools.
- Muslims united to fight their common foe.

Negative

- An unknown number of Muslims lost their lives in battles and massacres.
- Muslim property was destroyed by Crusaders.

Impact of the Crusades on Jews

Negative

- Crusaders in the Holy Land killed some Jews, and others became slaves.
- The lives of Jews in Europe were dramatically worsened as they suffered a series of persecutions.
- Anti-Semitism spread among non-Crusaders as well, and riots and massacres broke out throughout Europe.
- European Jews' place in society worsened. They could not hold public office, some Jewish businesses were seized, and some countries expelled all Jews.
- In the 14th and 15th centuries, Jews were forced to live in ghettos in many European cities.

Section 10.7

1. The Mongols were a nomadic people from north of China. Led by Genghis Khan, they began wars of conquest in which they took over part of China and then swept across Central Asia.

2. Islam helped bring unity to the Mongol Empire. Mongols made Persian the language of government, rebuilt the cities they had destroyed, and encouraged learning, the arts, and trade.

3. The Mongol Empire suffered from fighting among rivals because local rulers controlled different regions.

Section 10.8

Ottoman Empire: Arose in Anatolia and eventually conquered Constantinople (renaming it Istanbul), bringing an end to the Byzantine Empire. The empire then conquered large parts of the Middle East, as well as parts of southeastern Europe, North Africa, Persia, and Turkey. Although Muslim, the Ottomans allowed their Jewish and Christian subjects considerable freedoms within millets.

Safavid Empire: Founded by Muslims in Persia and spread east. The Safavids were Shi'ah Muslims, unlike the Ottomans who were Sunnis. The two groups fought a number of wars.

Mughal Empire: Founded by a descendant of Genghis Khan and Timur Lang, the Mughals invaded India and ruled there until sometime after 1700, which left Muslims as a significant minority of India's population.

Islam in Medieval Times

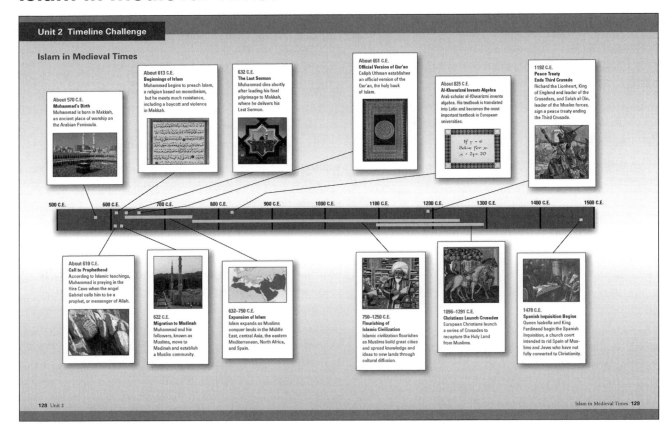

Overview

This Timeline Challenge helps students review the main events and ideas of this unit while providing practice in reading and interpreting timelines. You can vary and expand the activity according to students' needs and the amount of time available.

Basic Procedure

1 **Introduce the timeline in the Student Edition.** Direct students to the Islam in Medieval Times Timeline at the end of Unit 2 in the Student Edition. You may wish to have students read aloud and discuss the timeline entries.

2 **Introduce the Timeline Challenge in the Interactive Student Notebook.** Direct students to the Unit 2 Timeline Challenge in their notebooks. Point out the two types of questions, "Timeline Skills" and "Critical Thinking," and model how to answer each type.

3 **Have students complete the Timeline Challenge.** Monitor students as they work. Use the Guide to Unit 2 Timeline Challenge to check their answers. You may wish to project a transparency of this page as you work through the questions with the class and conduct a discussion of the "Critical Thinking" questions.

4 **Complete the KWL chart.** Return to the KWL chart created at the beginning of the unit, and ask students to list the key information they have learned.

Classroom Timeline

1   **Prepare the Timeline Challenge Cards.** Copy and cut the cards from *Student Handout TC2: Unit 2 Timeline Challenge Cards.* You may wish to laminate the cards for future use.

2   **Create a timeline on a classroom wall.** On an empty wall or a large bulletin board, make a timeline with masking tape or colored paper. Mark off the time intervals in advance, or ask students to do so in class.

3   **Have students place the Timeline Challenge Cards.** Distribute cards to individual students or pairs and have them tape the cards to the timeline in the correct locations. Call on students to provide more information on the timeline topics to review main events and issues.

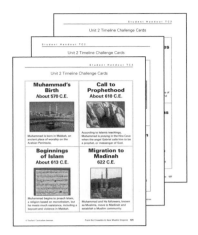

Student Handout TC2

Internet Research

1   **Review students' suggestions for additional timeline entries.** Have students share their answers to the last question of the Timeline Challenge.

2   **Have students conduct Internet research.** Ask students to choose and research one of their suggested events.

3   **Have students create additional Timeline Challenge Cards.** Direct students to research an appropriate image for their cards and then use the computer to create an illustrated card, complete with timeline entry.

Timeline Skills

Score 1 point for each correct answer.

1. According to Islamic teachings, the angel Gabriel called Muhammad to be a prophet for Allah.

2. nine years

3. Muhammad and his followers moved to Madinah because of the resistance and violence they experienced in Makkah.

4. Shortly before his death, Muhammad made his last pilgrimage to Makkah and delivered his Last Sermon.

5. Islam expanded to the Middle East, Central Asia, the eastern Mediterranean, North Africa, and Spain.

6. The official version of the Qur'an was created in 651 and helped to unify Muslims.

7. Islamic civilization flourished as Muslims built great cities and spread knowledge and ideas to new lands through cultural diffusion.

8. 195 years

9. Christians launched the Crusades to recapture the Holy Land from Muslims.

10. The Spanish Inquisition was a Church court intended to rid Spain of Muslims and Jews who had not fully converted to Christianity.

Critical Thinking

Score 1 to 3 points for each answer, depending on the thoroughness of the response.

11. Answers will vary, but students will likely say that Christians benefited the most because their contact with eastern cultures had a major impact on their lives, including introducing them to new foods and goods. European merchants also earned enor-mous profits by trading for these goods. Students may say that Jews lost the most as a result of the Crusades, because not only were Jews living in Palestine attacked by Crusaders, but European Jews also faced increasing discrimination at home. Alteratively, students may say that Muslims lost the most because most of the fighting took place in Muslim lands, untold numbers of Muslims lost their lives in battles or massacres, and much of their property was destroyed by Crusaders.

12. Answers will vary. Students should support their choices with concrete reasons.

13. Answers will vary. Students must explain why the events they chose merit inclusion.

Using Scores to Inform Instruction

Timeline Skills A score of 7 out of 10 indicates that students understand most of the key events in the unit.

Critical Thinking A score of 6 out of 9 indicates that students are able to think critically about most of the key issues in this unit.

If students score below these levels, consider reviewing timeline and critical thinking skills.

The Culture and Kingdoms of West Africa

Geography Challenge

Timeline Challenge

The Culture and Kingdoms of West Africa

Overview

This activity introduces geographic information essential to Unit 3. Students read and interpret maps to learn key physical features of the African continent and West Africa in particular, and to discover how these features affected trade, religion, and the growth of West African kingdoms. They annotate a map of Africa and answer questions in their Interactive Student Notebooks, and then discuss critical thinking questions. Students' comprehension of content and proficiency in map-reading and higher-order thinking skills will help you gauge their readiness for the unit. The pages that follow include a completed map, answers to questions, a scoring guide to inform your teaching, and suggestions for modifications to meet specific student needs.

Essential Geographic Understandings

1. Location of the continent of Africa

2. Location of West Africa

3. Key physical features: the Atlantic Ocean, the Mediterranean Sea, the Red Sea, the Senegal and Niger rivers, Timbuktu, the Sahara

4. The Sahara as a barrier to trade and cultural diffusion and the eventual triumph over that barrier

5. Impact of location on the development of West Africa

Procedures

1 **Introduce the unit.** Tell students that in this unit they will learn about the history and culture of West Africa. Explain that geography greatly influenced the development of this region.

2 **Create a KWL chart with students.** Ask students to identify what they already know about the geography of Africa and what they want to learn. Use their responses to gauge how much additional background information they will need as you progress through the unit. Students will return to the KWL chart at the end of the unit and add the key information they have learned.

3 **Have students read Unit 3 "Setting the Stage" in the Student Edition.**

4 **Have students complete the Geography Challenge.** Monitor students as they work. Use the guide on the next two pages to check their answers. You may wish to project the map from the Interactive Student Notebook and have students annotate it as the class works through the map-reading questions. Make sure students have grasped Essential Geographic Understandings 1 to 3.

5 **Discuss the "Critical Thinking" questions.** Help students understand the geographic relationships described in Essential Geographic Understandings 4 and 5.

Africa

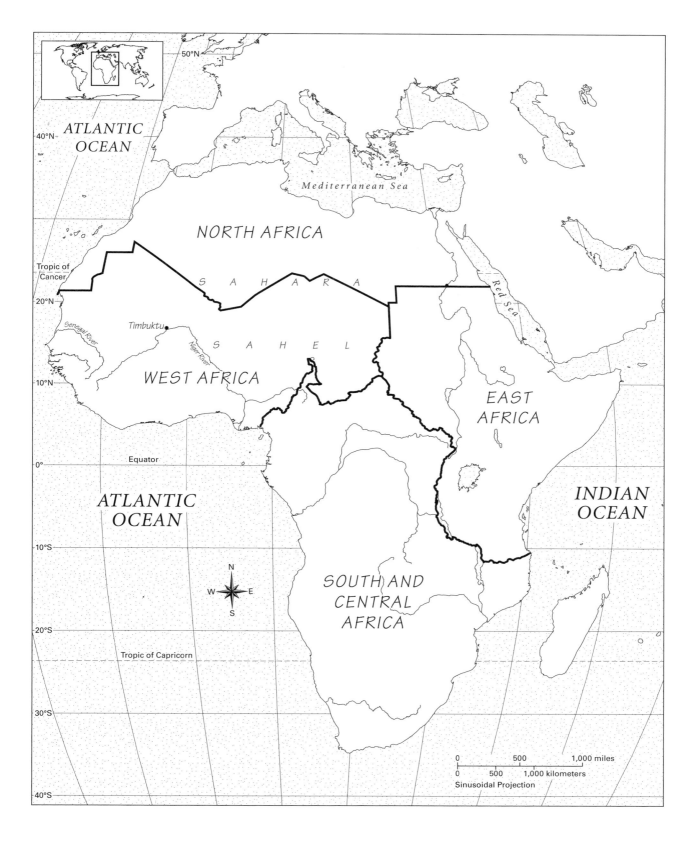

ATLANTIC
OCEAN

50°N

40°N

Mediterranean Sea

NORTH AFRICA

Tropic of
Cancer

S A H A R A

Red Sea

20°N

Senegal River

Timbuktu

S A H E L

Niger River

WEST AFRICA

10°N

EAST
AFRICA

Equator

0°

ATLANTIC
OCEAN

INDIAN
OCEAN

10°S

N

W   E

S

SOUTH AND
CENTRAL
AFRICA

20°S

Tropic of Capricorn

30°S

0   500   1,000 miles

0   500   1,000 kilometers

Sinusoidal Projection

40°S

Geography Skills

Score 1 point for each correct answer. Use the map on the previous page to check shading and labeling.

1. Students should label the Atlantic Ocean, the Indian Ocean, and the Mediterranean Sea.

2. Students should label North Africa, West Africa, East Africa, and South and Central Africa.

3. Students should label the Sahara and the Sahel.

4. People were least likely to settle in desert and desert scrub zones. The climate there is too hot and dry to be hospitable to life. Necessities such as food and water are too scarce in the desert.

5. The kingdoms of Ghana, Mali, and Songhai were located in West Africa. The vegetation zones in this region are desert, desert scrub, temperate grassland, and tropical grassland (or savanna).

6. The Niger River extended through the Mali and Songhai kingdoms.

7. The West African kingdom of Songhai was the largest.

8. Timbuktu is located on the Niger River.

9. Timbuktu was part of both the Mali and Songhai kingdoms.

Critical Thinking

Questions may have more than one correct answer. Score 1 to 3 points for each reasonable answer, depending on the strength of students' geographic reasoning. Possible answers are given here.

10. The Niger and Senegal rivers helped make the land fertile and provided fish. Also, traders traveled along the rivers.

11. Islam likely spread first to North Africa, from its origins on the Arabian Peninsula, because few geographical features would have interfered with its expansion there.

Using Scores to Inform Instruction

Geography Skills A score of 5 out of 8 or better indicates that students have acquired sufficient geographic information to proceed with the unit.

Critical Thinking A score of 4 out of 6 or better indicates that students are beginning to understand the relationships between physical geography and the different ways in which people live.

Modifying Instruction

ELL or Learners with Special Education Needs
Consider focusing on map-reading questions or limiting the number of "Critical Thinking" questions.

Students with Weak Map or Critical Thinking Skills
Assign appropriate pages from the Social Studies Skills Toolkit in the back of the Lesson Masters.

Early Societies in West Africa

What was the most significant factor in the development of early societies in West Africa?

Overview

In a Response Group activity, students respond to three possible situations faced by early West African societies, and then read to learn what really happened in each situation.

Objectives

In the course of reading this chapter and participating in the classroom activity, students will

Social Studies

- describe the relationship between the Niger River, trade, and growth of settlements in West Africa.
- distinguish between the vegetation zones of forest, savanna, Sahel, and desert.
- trace how early societies in West Africa evolved into kingdoms.
- analyze the importance of family, labor specialization, and regional commerce in the development of cities and kingdoms in West Africa.

Language Arts

- read expository text to connect essential ideas to prior knowledge.
- write persuasive compositions that state a clear position, and support that position with well-articulated evidence.

Social Studies Vocabulary

Key Content Terms Sahara, Sahel, savanna, Niger River, Nok, artifact, smelting, Jenne-jeno, tribute

Academic Vocabulary efficient, process, predict

Materials

History Alive! The Medieval World and Beyond

Interactive Student Notebooks

Visuals 11A–11D

Lesson Masters

- Vocabulary Development handout (1 per student, on colored paper)

Activity	Suggested Time	Materials
Preview	20 minutes	• *History Alive! The Medieval World and Beyond* • Interactive Student Notebooks • Visual 11A
Vocabulary Development	30–40 minutes	• *History Alive! The Medieval World and Beyond* • Interactive Student Notebooks • Vocabulary Development handout
Response Group	90 minutes (1 regular period) (.5 block period)	• *History Alive! The Medieval World and Beyond* • Interactive Student Notebooks • Visuals 11B–11D
Processing	20 minutes	• Interactive Student Notebooks
Assessment	40 minutes	• Chapter 11 Assessment

Preview

Visual 11A

1 Have students analyze images to make a prediction about where cities develop. Project *Visual 11A: Vegetation Zones in West Africa* and have students complete the Preview activity in their Interactive Student Notebooks. Students analyze the images to determine where they think a city would be most likely to develop.

2 Have students share their responses in pairs or with the class.

3 Connect the Preview activity to the chapter. Explain to students that in this lesson they will examine four West African vegetation zones: the savanna and forest they just saw pictured, as well as the desert and the Sahel. They will learn the effects of geography on the development of West African settlements, cities, and kingdoms. They will also study the significant role that the Niger River played in trade and in the growth of settlements in the region.

Vocabulary Development

1 Introduce the Key Content Terms. Have students locate the Key Content Terms for the chapter in their Interactive Student Notebooks. These are important terms that will help them understand the main ideas of the chapter. Ask volunteers to identify any familiar terms and suggest how they might be used in a sentence.

2 Have students complete a Vocabulary Development handout. Give each student a copy of the Vocabulary Development handout of your choice from the Reading Toolkit at the back of the Lesson Masters. These handouts provide extra Key Content Term practice and support, depending on your students' needs. Review the completed handout by asking volunteers to share one answer for each term.

Reading

1 Introduce the Essential Question and have students read Section 11.1. Have students identify the Essential Question on the first page of the chapter: *What was the most significant factor in the development of early societies in West Africa?* Then have students read Section 11.1. Afterward, have students respond to these questions:

- When did Muslim scholars begin writing about Ghana? At least how many years old was the kingdom at that point? *(in the 800s; Ghana was at least 300 years old by then, and possibly older.)*

- What do historians and archaeologists study to learn about a place when they do not have written records? *(They study geography, evidence from ancient settlements, and artifacts.)*

2 Have students complete the Reading Notes for Chapter 11. Assign Sections
11.2 to 11.5 during the activity, as indicated in the procedures that follow.
Remind students to use the Key Content Terms where appropriate as they
complete their Reading Notes.

Response Group

1 Arrange students in groups of three and introduce the activity. Explain
that students will place themselves in three situations faced by people living
in early societies in West Africa:

- responding to an attack on a settlement

- effectively managing a system of trade for a village

- establishing a powerful kingdom

For each situation, they will decide as a group on the best response from
among the available choices. Then they will share their choice with the class
and try to reach a consensus about the best way to handle each situation.
Finally, they will read about early societies in West Africa and compare their
choices to historical reality.

**2 Have students read Section 11.2 and complete the corresponding Reading
Notes in their Interactive Student Notebooks.** Tell students that this sec-
tion provides background information about the geography of West Africa.
Students should read carefully. They should also examine the maps in
Setting the Stage for this unit to label the map in their Reading Notes. (**Note:**
Consider assigning this step as homework the night before you intend to do
the Response Group activity.) Have students discuss their answers with a
partner or as a class.

3 Have students develop a response to the threat of attack. Project *Visual
11B: The Threat of Attack*. Tell students to suppose that they are the leaders
of a small settlement along the Niger River. Review the details of Problem A
on Visual 11B as a class. Give groups several minutes to discuss the three
options listed after Critical Thinking Question A on the visual, and to rank
the options from best to worst, based on what they think will be best for their
settlement over the long term.

4 Have groups share their answers. Appoint a Presenter for each group. The
Presenter will share the group's answer to Critical Thinking Question A with
the class when called upon. Have the class try to reach a consensus.

Visual 11B

**5 Have students read Section 11.3 and complete the corresponding Reading
Notes.** Connect the reading to the activity by asking, Based on your reading,
how did West Africans solve the problem of the threat of attack?

6 **Have students develop a response for managing a system of trade.** Repeat Steps 3–5 for Problem B. Make the following modifications:

- Project *Visual 11C: Effectively Controlling Trade* and have students suppose that 4,000 thousand years have passed. They are now leaders of the same village, but it has grown and now has several thousand residents.

- Have groups review the details of Problem B on Visual 11C and discuss the three options.

- Rotate the role of Presenter to a new student in each group.

- After the discussion, have students read Section 11.4 and complete the corresponding Reading Notes.

- Then ask, Based on your reading, how did West Africans control trade?

Visual 11C

7 **Have students develop a response for establishing a powerful kingdom.** Repeat Steps 3–5 for Problem C. Make the following modifications:

- Project *Visual 11D: Establishing a Powerful Kingdom,* and have students suppose that 500 more years have passed. They are now leaders of the same city, which has grown even larger and wealthier, thanks to its location as a busy trading center on the river.

- Have groups review the details of Problem C on Visual 11D and discuss the three options.

- Rotate the role of Presenter to a new student in each group.

- After the discussion, have students read Section 11.5 and complete the corresponding Reading Notes.

- Then ask, Based on your reading, how did West Africans establish powerful kingdoms?

Visual 11D

8 **Hold a class discussion about the three responses.** Ask,

- As villages continued to grow and trade with one another, why did some develop into successful cities?

- As cities grew wealthy by taxing goods, how did this affect their power in the region?

- What were some factors that led to the development of early societies in West Africa?

- What do you think was the most significant factor in the development of early societies in West Africa?

Processing

Have students complete the Processing activity in their Interactive Student Notebooks. Students evaluate which factor had the most impact on the development of early societies in West Africa. Have students share their choices in pairs or with the class.

Quicker Coverage

Shorten the Activity Rather than conducting the entire Response Group activity, have students discuss just Problem A (Steps 3–5 in the activity directions) or have them discuss Problem A and Problem B (Steps 3–6 in the activity directions). For those problems you choose not to discuss in class, have students read and complete the Reading Notes for the corresponding sections.

Conduct the Activity as a Class Instead of having groups discuss each problem in advance, project each visual and open the discussion to the whole class. Invite individual volunteers to share their opinions on the best choice for each critical thinking question. Then have the whole class decide, either by vote or general consensus, which option is best.

Deeper Coverage

Make Picture Books Once students have completed the four-panel storyboards in their Reading Notes, have them exchange their storyboards with partners to check for accuracy, concise language, and sufficient detail. Then give students a few sheets of blank white paper that they can fold or staple into a book. Have them create titles for their stories, an illustrated cover and title page, and then turn their four-panel storyboards into illustrated picture books. Encourage students to add pages as needed, but to keep their stories simple and accurate. If possible, coordinate with a teacher of a third- or fourth-grade class and have students share their books with small groups of younger students.

Assessment

Mastering the Content

1. C	5. A	9. C	13. D
2. B	6. B	10. C	14. A
3. A	7. B	11. C	15. D
4. D	8. A	12. D	16. B

Applying Social Studies Skills

17. savanna

18. the Sahara or the desert

19. its location on the Niger River (Also accept other plausible answers that draw on information in the map, such as "its location near the border of two vegetation zones." Do not accept "on major trade routes" without further explanation, as it is non-specific and does not use the map.)

Exploring the Essential Question

20. Answers should include all the elements requested in the prompt.

Scoring Rubric

Score	Description
3	Student completes all five parts of the task (writing on four wall layers and the floor of the pit). Comments are clearly stated, list both a factor and an explanation, and demonstrate command of standard English conventions.
2	Student responds to most or all parts of the task, but some comments may omit an explanation or not be clearly stated.
1	Student responds to at least one part of the task. Comment(s) may contain factual and/or grammatical errors.
0	Response does not match the task or is incorrect.

English Language Learners

Prepare in Advance for the Response Group Activity
The night before you conduct the Response Group activity, give students photocopies of Visuals 11B–11D. Encourage students to read through the problems and critical thinking questions the night before and think about which option is best, so that they will be prepared to share their opinions with their groups the following day.

Learners Reading and Writing Below Grade Level

Provide Extra Support for the Reading Notes
Give students the following four captions written on separate strips of paper as they begin the four-panel storyboard in their Reading Notes. Have them glue them in the lower areas of the panels in the correct order, and then illustrate each caption.

- Early communities in West Africa were made up of extended families who worked together to survive.

- Sometimes extended families banded together in villages for defense, to trade, or to control a flooding river.

- As more and more villages traded surplus goods, some villages became trading sites and grew wealthy. These sites attracted more people and became cities and towns.

- Over time, the wealthiest cities in West Africa raised large armies. Then, they could conquer nearby areas and collect tribute from them. Gradually, as cities conquered more territory, kingdoms, and then empires, formed.

Learners with Special Education Needs

Provide an Alternative Processing Activity Instead of having students write the paragraph, have students complete the following prompt for each of the four factors listed in the instructions: geography, knowledge of ironworking, specialization of labor, and increased local trade.

Geography was important to the development of settlements in West Africa because . . .

Then ask students to think about which of the four factors they wrote about was the most important to the development of settlements. Have them place a star next to that statement.

Modify the Reading Notes Give students the option of telling their stories in a different format than the one described in the Reading Notes. For example, they may choose to create illustrations, but explain them orally to a peer helper, an aide, or to you. Or consider providing students with the simple flowchart shown below. Have them add two details around each box to explain each step and how it led to the next step. Again, it may help to allow students to explain their thoughts orally, rather than to write each explanation.

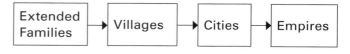

Advanced Learners

Extend the Storyboard Activity in the Reading Notes Suggest that students write their stories in the first person. Encourage them to think about the four steps of their stories from the perspective of a senior-male who loses authority as his extended family unites with others to form villages. How might leaders from early West Africa feel about these changes? Prompt students to look at both the advantages and disadvantages of this development, as well as the later stages, as villages formed cities and then kingdoms.

Enrichment Resources

Have students find out more about early societies in West Africa by exploring the following Enrichment Resources for *History Alive! The Medieval World and Beyond* at www.teachtci.com.

Enrichment Readings These in-depth readings encourage students to explore selected topics related to the chapter. You may also find readings that relate the chapter's content directly to your state's curriculum.

Internet Connections The recommended Web sites provide useful and engaging content that reinforces skills development and mastery of subjects within the chapter.

Literature Recommendations

The following books offer opportunities to extend the content in this chapter.

History of West Africa by the Diagram Group (New York: Facts on File, 2003)

The Penguin Atlas of African History by Colin McEvedy (New York: Penguin, 1996)

The Sahara Desert by Megan Lappi (New York: Weigl Publishers, 2006)

Section 11.2

1. Use the completed map below to check that students have labeled the Sahara, the Sahel, the savanna, the forest, and the Niger River. For vegetation drawings, students might indicate that short grasses, small bushes, and trees grow in the Sahel; tall grasses, trees, and grains grow on the savanna; and that trees and shrubs, including oil palms, yams, kola trees, mahogany, and teak, grow in the forest.

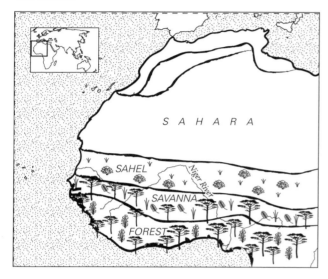

2. Because different types of food grew in different vegetation zones, people had to trade to get things they could not produce themselves.

Section 11.3

1. Possible answer for Panel 1: Early communities in West Africa were made up of extended families that worked together to survive.

2. Possible answer for Panel 2: Sometimes extended-family communities banded together in villages to control flooding rivers, to mine for iron or gold, or for defense.

Section 11.4

1. Possible answer for Panel 3: Villages located along rivers or other trade routes became trading sites. By taxing trade, villages became wealthy. Wealth led to an increase in population, and villages often grew into towns and cities.

2. The Nok used enormous amounts of charcoal to fuel the furnaces that would melt ore to extract the iron. Once the iron was red-hot, it was then hammered and bent into shape by skilled workers called blacksmiths.

3. With iron tools, farmers cleared land and grew crops more efficiently. Abundant food supported larger villages where more people were free to take up other jobs, such as weaving, metalworking, and making pottery.

4. Jenne-jeno was located at the intersection of the Niger and Bani rivers. Its ideal location allowed for farming, fishing, and trade, which helped it to become a large city.

Section 11.5

1. Possible answer for Panel 4: Rulers taxed goods that were traded in their cities, and then used this wealth to raise large armies. With these armies, they could conquer other cities and become even wealthier. Gradually, as kings conquered more territory, kingdoms formed.

2. *Tribute* is a payment from a conquered group collected by the conquering ruler. It meant that the conquered people accepted the ruler's authority.

3. Possible answer: Advantages—Armies made sure that trade routes were safe. They kept out foreign armies and raiders. Wars between small cities ended. Disadvantages—People living in conquered areas had to pay tribute, and the men had to serve in the army.

Ghana: A West African Trading Empire

To what extent did trans-Saharan trade lead to Ghana's wealth and success?

Overview

In an Experiential Exercise, students role-play trans-Saharan trade in gold and salt, using the silent-barter system to explore how it helped to make Ghana a powerful empire.

Objectives

In the course of reading this chapter and participating in the classroom activity, students will

Social Studies

- explain how trade in gold and salt led to the growth of Ghana and Mali.
- model the system of silent barter used by Wangarans and North African traders.
- describe the government of Ghana.
- evaluate how trans-Saharan trade affected different groups in West African, both culturally and religiously.

Language Arts

- clarify word meanings through the use of definitions and examples.
- write a summary of reading materials that conveys the perspective of a historical character; include a main idea and the most significant details.

Social Studies Vocabulary

Key Content Terms Ghana, matrilineal, trans-Saharan trade

Academic Vocabulary maintain, require, evaporation

Materials

History Alive! The Medieval World and Beyond

Interactive Student Notebooks

Lesson Masters

- Information Masters 12A and 12B (1 transparency of each)
- Student Handout 12A (copied onto yellow paper; 1 for every 2 students, plus 1 extra)
- Student Handout 12B (copied onto white paper; 1 for every 2 students)
- Vocabulary Development handout (1 per student, on colored paper)

Activity	Suggested Time	Materials
Preview	10 minutes	• Interactive Student Notebooks
Vocabulary Development	30–40 minutes	• *History Alive! The Medieval World and Beyond* • Interactive Student Notebooks • Vocabulary Development handout
Experiential Exercise	90 minutes (2 regular periods) (1 block period)	• *History Alive! The Medieval World and Beyond* • Interactive Student Notebooks • Information Master 12A and 12B (1 transparency of each) • Student Handout 12A (copied onto yellow paper; 1 for every 2 students, plus 1 extra) • Student Handout 12B (copied onto white paper; 1 for every 2 students)
Processing	15 minutes	• Interactive Student Notebooks
Assessment	40 minutes	• Chapter 12 Assessment

Preview

1 **Have students rank items for trade.** Have students complete the first part of the Preview activity in their Interactive Student Notebooks. Students suppose they are traveling to Ghana with cattle to trade. Students rank a list of trade goods from 1 to 5, as most desirable to least desirable. Have students share their responses with the class. Discuss the factors students considered when ranking their items.

2 **Have students re-rank the items based on a new scenario.** Now have students complete the next part of the Preview activity. First, present *Scenario 1:* You live in a hot climate where food spoils easily. Have students copy the scenario in the appropriate place in the Preview activity in their Interactive Student Notebooks. Then have students re-rank the five items based on Scenario 1. When all students have completed this step, ask,

- Now what item did you most want to trade for? Least want to trade for?

- How do your new rankings differ from your previous rankings?

- Why did your rankings change?

3 **Change the scenario and have students re-rank the items.** Have students complete the third part of the Preview activity. First, give students *Scenario 2:* You live in a cold climate where you need shelter and warm clothing. Have students copy this information in the appropriate place in the Preview activity. Then have them re-rank the five items in the box below it. When all students have completed this step, ask,

- Now what item did you most want to trade for? Least want to trade for?

- How do your new rankings differ from your previous rankings?

- Why did your rankings change?

Help students see that the value of a product is based partly on demand, or on how many people want it, as well as local conditions and resources.

4 **Connect the Preview activity to the chapter.** Remind students that in the Preview activity they learned how such factors as living conditions and demand can affect the value of trade goods. Explain that in this chapter they will learn why West Africans in the medieval period found more value in some goods than in others. For example, salt was as valuable to medieval people living in West Africa as gold is to people today. Students will learn how the trade in salt and gold led to the growth of powerful kingdoms in West Africa.

Vocabulary Development

1 **Introduce the Key Content Terms.** Have students locate the Key Content Terms for the chapter in their Interactive Student Notebooks. These are important terms that will help them understand the main ideas of the chapter. Ask volunteers to identify any familiar terms and suggest how they might be used in a sentence.

2 **Have students complete a Vocabulary Development handout.** Give each student a copy of the Vocabulary Development handout of your choice from the Reading Toolkit at the back of the Lesson Masters. These handouts provide extra Key Content Term practice and support, depending on your students' needs. Review the completed handout by asking volunteers to share one answer for each term.

Reading

1 **Introduce the Essential Question and have students read Section 12.1.** Have students identify the Essential Question on the first page of the chapter: *To what extent did trans-Saharan trade lead to Ghana's wealth and success?* Then have students read Section 12.1. Afterward, have students respond to these questions:

• Where was the kingdom of Ghana? How long did it last?

• How are historians able to learn about the kingdom of Ghana?

• How might Ghana have become a kingdom? What led to Ghana's wealth?

2 **Have students complete the Reading Notes for Chapter 12.** Assign Sections 12.2 to 12.6 during the activity, as indicated in the procedures for the Experiential Exercise. Remind students to use the Key Content Terms where appropriate as they complete their Reading Notes.

Experiential Exercise

1 **Prepare for the activity.** Before class, prepare materials and the classroom for the activity. Follow these steps:

• Copy *Student Handout 12A: Gold Tokens* and *Student Handout 12B: Salt Tokens,* as directed in the Planning Guide.

• Cut enough gold tokens from one copy of Student Handout 12A to distribute one token to half the students in the class.

• Divide the room into four areas, as shown at right.

• Tape five labels—North Africa, Sahara, Taghaza, Ghana, and Wangara—in the appropriate places.

• Place two desks in Ghana and two near Taghaza.

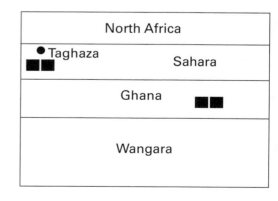

2 **Assign roles. Follow these steps:**

- Assign two students to be salt miners in Taghaza, a city in the Sahara, and two students to be Ghana government officials. Have them sit at the appropriate desks.

- Divide the remaining students into two equal-size groups.

- Designate one of the groups as "North African traders" and the other as "Wangaran gold miners." Have each group sit on the floor in its assigned area. Explain that Wangara is a gold-rich region south of Ghana. (**Note:** Historically, the salt miners in Taghaza were slaves of Arab merchants. In this activity, they will be referred to as salt miners.)

3 **Prepare students for the game. Follow these steps:**

- Distribute a copy of Student Handout 12A to each of the Wangaran gold miners. Distribute a copy of Student Handout 12B to each of the North African traders. Have students cut or tear out their tokens.

- Have each of the North African traders keep three of their salt tokens. They should write their names on the others and give those labeled tokens to the Taghaza salt miners. Explain that the tokens given to the salt miners represent salt that they will "mine" during the game. The tokens kept by the traders represent salt they have already acquired in Taghaza.

- Give each North African trader one of the gold tokens you have prepared.

- Give the Wangaran gold miners each a sheet of paper and ask them to place these on the floor before them.

Student Handout 12A

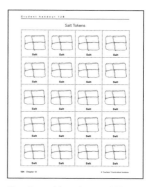
Student Handout 12B

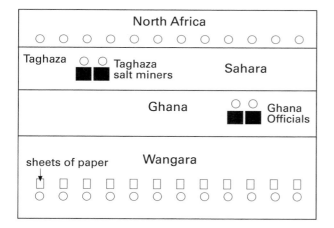

4 **Guide students through a practice round.** Project *Information Master 12A: Practicing How to Trade in West Africa.* Follow the steps on Information Master 12A to guide students through a practice round. The tips listed below will help the practice round proceed smoothly and help you understand the historical analogies. (**Note:** Historical analogies for each step are also provided below. Do not reveal the historical analogies to students now.)

Information Master 12A

Tips for Step 1

- Remind students that this is a practice round.

- For this practice round, make sure that each trader is paired with a Wangaran miner.

Historical Analogy

- Crawling across the desert represents the difficulty of trans-Saharan trade.

- Payment of the gold token to the Ghana official represents the tax Ghana charged on goods coming into and going out of Ghana.

- Turning their backs represents the system of silent barter used by the North African traders and Wangarans.

Tips for Step 2

- Emphasize that students may not talk during the trading.

- They must turn their backs after an offer has been made.

- They must clap to indicate that some decision has been reached.

- Remind students that gold and salt tokens will be returned after this practice round.

Historical Analogy

Clapping represents the beating of drums announcing a trade offer.

Tips for Step 3

- Explain that if either the North African trader or the Wangaran gold miner is unhappy with the first offer made by the other, he or she can make a counteroffer.

- For this practice round, state that the North African trader is not happy with the Wangaran's offer. Have students practice the options listed. When they understand how to make a counteroffer, have them return the tokens they have traded.

Historical Analogy

Although the game allows only one counteroffer per trade, silent barter, historically, might have continued for many rounds over several days.

Tip for Step 4

Explain that after North African traders have traded their three tokens, they can get more salt tokens for trading by going to Taghaza, but on the way they must pay taxes to Ghana officials.

Historical Analogy

This step is analogous to how traders paid Ghana a tax whenever they moved goods through Ghana.

5   **Have students play the game independently.** Project *Information Master 12B: Conducting Trade in West Africa* and read through the steps and rules listed there. Ask if students have any questions. Then allow them to play for 20 minutes or until a few students have no tokens left with which to trade.

If students have difficulty distinguishing who is clapping, have students whisper their names when they clap. Also, you may wish to have the Taghaza salt miners write "receipts" for salt, which traders must show to the Ghana officials for tax purposes as they travel through Ghana. This will prevent students from trying to "smuggle" salt through Ghana.

Information Master 12B

6   **Declare the winners.** Have the traders count their gold tokens and the gold miners count their salt tokens. Declare the winners to be the North African trader and the Wangaran miner who have the most of their required tokens. Also ask the Ghana officials to report how many gold tokens they collected.

7   **Debrief the activity.** Ask,

- What problems did you encounter when you could not talk with the person with whom you wished to trade?

- Why might North African traders and Wangaran gold miners have used a method of trading that involved silent communication?

- How were the students who represented Ghana able to get gold?

- Why were traders willing to pay this tax to Ghana?

8   **Prepare students to read Sections 12.2–12.6 by connecting the reading to the Experiential Exercise.** Ask,

- What did the tokens in the game represent? *(gold and salt)*

- How were the hardships of crossing the Sahara shown? *(by having students crawl)*

- Why do you think students were not allowed to talk to each other? *(to represent the practice of silent trading)*

- What did the clapping represent? *(Clapping represented the beating of the drums announcing that a trade offer had been made.)*

- How did Ghana became wealthy? *(Ghana gained wealth by taxing goods going into and out of the empire.)*

- How was this shown in the game? *(by having to give gold tokens to the "Ghana officials" for goods traded)*

9   **Assign Sections 12.2–12.6 and have students complete the corresponding Reading Notes.** Use the Guide to Reading Notes to check their answers. (**Note:** Most of this lesson focuses on the benefits of West African participation in trans-Saharan trade. After students complete the last section of Reading Notes, consider examining the costs involved, as well. Students might discuss how Ghana's accessibility to outsiders also brought invaders or how Ghana's increasing wealth stimulated the population growth that depleted the kingdom's natural resources.)

Processing

Have students complete the Processing activity in their Interactive Student Notebooks. Here are examples of statements they might include:

- North African trader: "I reap huge profits by trading gold for just some salt. I don't have to fear bandits because Ghana secures the trade routes."

- Wangaran: "I'm really happy to exchange my gold, which is of little value to me, for salt that I need to survive. Silent bartering allows us to trade with people who speak a different language. It also protects the secret of where our gold mines are located."

- King of Ghana: "I have become wealthy because I demand gold from North African traders when they enter and leave my territory. I use this gold to build up my army, which protects me and allows me to conquer other territories."

Quicker Coverage

Complete Only Steps 1 Through 4 on Information Master 12A Instead of conducting the entire trading game, just have students do the practice round to see how the silent barter system worked and to experience Ghana's role in trans-Saharan trade.

Jigsaw the Reading After all students have read Section 12.2, divide the class into expert groups of four. Assign each group to read and complete the Reading Notes for one of Sections 12.3 to 12.6. Then give expert groups a few minutes to discuss the definitions and clarify any information they may have found confusing. Ask students to then number off within their expert groups. Form new jigsaw groups by having all number 1s meet, all number 2s meet, and so on. In each jigsaw group, have students share the information from their section.

Deeper Coverage

Have Students Take on the Roles of the Figures in the Processing Activity After students have completed their speech bubbles for each figure, assign every student to be one of the three figures in the Processing activity: a North African trader, a Wangaran gold miner, or the King of Ghana. Create a mock talk-show set in your room by placing three chairs in the front of the room. Invite volunteers to come forward and take the roles of each of the three characters. Then, acting as the host of the talk show, ask the following questions of your "guests":

- Who are you and what is your relationship to our two other guests?

- How does trans-Saharan trade benefit you?

- How has the use of camels affected your life?

- How do you feel about Ghana's role in controlling trans-Saharan trade?

Consider providing students with these questions beforehand. Also, consider allowing audience members to ask questions of the guests.

> **Writing: Autobiographical Narrative**
>
> An alternative activity for processing or enrichment is an autobiographical narrative, in which students retell and elaborate on their trading experience by adopting the viewpoint of the trader or miner they represented in the role-play. Require the establishment of a definite setting; a plot line that develops rising action and conflict as trade is initiated and accomplished; and internal dialogue, as well as its accompanying body language.

Assessment

Mastering the Content

1. A	5. B	9. B	13. C
2. A	6. C	10. C	14. A
3. C	7. D	11. D	15. D
4. B	8. D	12. A	16. A

Applying Social Studies Skills

17. its location in central West Africa and near three major rivers

18. Atlas Mountains

19. North of Kumbi is the Sahara, so camels were the best transportation method across that type of land. South of Kumbi was thick forest, so humans on foot—porters—were probably the best way to transport goods over that type of land.

Exploring the Essential Question

20. Answers should include all the elements requested in the prompt.

Scoring Rubric

Score	Description
3	Student completes all four journal entries, complying with all the bulleted points. Entries are clearly stated, supported by details, and demonstrate command of standard English conventions.
2	Student responds to most or all parts of the task, but entries may lack details or not be clearly stated.
1	Student responds to at least one part of the task. Entries may contain factual and/or grammatical errors and may lack details.
0	Response does not match the task or is incorrect.

English Language Learners

Provide Support During the Experiential Exercise
Give students their own copies of Information Masters 12A and 12B. Highlight the key points on the handout that might help students better follow the directions of the game. Also take a moment to discuss with these students each step of the trading process to make sure they understand what to do.

Learners Reading and Writing Below Grade Level

Help Students Make Connections to History After the activity, provide students with the three focus questions, below. Also consider giving students photocopies of Sections 12.3, 12.4, and 12.5 and encouraging them to highlight any information that would help them answer these questions.

- Section 12.3: What did the tokens in the game represent? How were the hardships of crossing the Sahara shown?

- Section 12.4: How do you think Ghana became wealthy? How was this shown in the game?

- Section 12.5: Why do you think students were not allowed to talk to each other? What did the clapping mean?

Learners with Special Education Needs

Make Adaptations to the Activity Address the physical limitations of some students by doing the following, if necessary:

- Have students tap each other on the back or shoulder, instead of clapping, to indicate that a trade offer has been made.

- Place the sheet of paper in front of each Wangaran on a desk or stool so that it is more accessible.

- Substitute crawling across the Sahara with having students count to ten slowly each time they cross through that part of the room.

Modify the Processing Activity Create three sample statements for the Processing activity, and provide students with three strips of paper, with one statement on each. Have students match each statement to the figure most likely to have said it, and either glue the strip of paper into the matching speech bubble, or write it in.

Advanced Learners

Provide an Alternative Processing Activity Have students create a political cartoon about the role of the rulers of Ghana in the trade between Taghaza and Wangara. Remind students that political cartoons often use satire to make a point about a political situation. The cartoons should have one to three illustrations. Each illustration should have a speech bubble or a caption that explains the illustration and tells how the king is using the situation to his advantage.

Enrichment Resources

Have students find out more about the growth of Ghana as a trading empire by exploring the following Enrichment Resources for *History Alive! The Medieval World and Beyond* at www.teachtci.com.

Enrichment Readings These in-depth readings encourage students to explore selected topics related to the chapter. You may also find readings that relate the chapter's content directly to your state's curriculum.

Internet Connections The recommended Web sites provide useful and engaging content that reinforces skills development and mastery of subjects within the chapter.

Literature Recommendations

The following books offer opportunities to extend the content in this chapter.

Ancient Ghana: The Land of Gold by Philip Koslow (New York: Chelsea House, 1995)

Empires of Medieval West Africa by David C. Conrad (New York: Chelsea House, 2009)

Golden Trade of the Moors: West African Kingdoms in the Fourteenth Century by Edward William Bovill (Princeton, NJ: Marcus Wiener, 1994)

Section 12.2

1. Possible answers: The king of Ghana was the head of the army and had the final say in matters of justice. The king was very wealthy, since he controlled the supply of gold. The king held court with his people daily.

2. Officials helped the king govern different parts of society, such as the armed forces and industry. Governors helped him rule different parts of the empire.

3. Because the royal succession was matrilineal, the son of the king's sister, his nephew, took the throne when the king died.

Section 12.3

1. For the North African camel, students might draw or write *copper, cowrie shells*, and *salt*. For the Wangaran, students might draw or write *kola nuts, hides, leather goods, ivory, slaves*, or *gold*.

2. Travel across the Sahara was challenging because the journey was long and travelers could lose their way or be unable to find water.

3. The two factors that led to the growth of trans-Saharan trade were the introduction of the camel and the spread of Islam.

Section 12.4

1. Use the completed chart to check student answers.

	Gold	**Salt**
Why it was valuable to West Africans	Gold was important because it was used to make coins and to purchase silk and porcelain from China.	Salt was needed to replace body salt lost through perspiration. It also kept food from spoiling, the people liked its taste, and cattle needed it.
Where it came from	Wangara	Taghaza

2. Trade made Ghana wealthy because Ghana taxed goods coming into and out of the empire. Taxes helped pay for armies to protect the kingdom and to conquer other territories.

Section 12.5

1. Possible answers: North African trader—I spread my goods out along the river. I beat a drum to tell the Wangaran I am making an offer, and then I leave. If the Wangaran leaves enough gold dust, I take it and leave. If not, I leave my goods there until he makes an offer I can accept. Wangaran gold miner—When I see the goods left by the North African trader, I leave what I think is a fair amount of gold dust. If the trader does not accept my offer, I add to the gold dust until both of us think we have a fair deal.

2. Two advantages of the silent-barter system were that it allowed people who spoke different languages to conduct trade and it allowed the Wangarans to guard the secret location of their gold mines.

Section 12.6

Two reasons why the kingdom of Ghana declined were that Muslim warriors, called Almoravids, attacked Ghana and seized its capital city and that Ghana was further weakened by the loss of natural resources.

The Influence of Islam on West Africa

In what ways did Islam influence West African society?

Overview

In a Social Studies Skill Builder, students learn about various Islamic influences and use this knowledge to identify Islamic influences on West Africa.

Objectives

In the course of reading this chapter and participating in the classroom activity, students will

Social Studies

- trace the growth of the Mali empire.
- discuss the role of trans-Saharan trade in spreading Islam in West Africa.
- describe the growth of the Arabic language in government, trade, and Islamic scholarship in West Africa.
- analyze contemporary photographs from West Africa to identify influences of Islamic culture.

Language Arts

- clarify word meanings through the use of definitions and examples.
- read expository text to connect essential ideas to prior knowledge.

Social Studies Vocabulary

Key Content Terms Mali, Mansa Musa, Songhai, patrilineal, textile

Academic Vocabulary convert, tolerance, devoted, geometric

Materials

History Alive! The Medieval World and Beyond

Interactive Student Notebooks

Visual 13

Placards 13A–13H

Lesson Masters

- Information Master 13A (8–10 copies, on card stock)
- Information Master 13B (1 transparency)
- Vocabulary Development handout (1 per student, on colored paper)

Activity	Suggested Time	Materials
Preview	15 minutes	• *History Alive! The Medieval World and Beyond* • Interactive Student Notebooks • Visual 13
Vocabulary Development	30–40 minutes	• *History Alive! The Medieval World and Beyond* • Interactive Student Notebooks • Vocabulary Development handout
Social Studies Skill Builder	90 minutes (2 regular periods) (1 block period)	• *History Alive! The Medieval World and Beyond* • Interactive Student Notebooks • Placards 13A–13H • Information Master 13A (8–10 copies on card stock) • Information Master 13B (1 transparency)
Processing	20 minutes	• Interactive Student Notebooks
Assessment	40 minutes	• Chapter 13 Assessment

Preview

Visual 13

1 **Analyze an image to examine Islamic influences.** Project *Visual 13: Islamic Influences in West Africa* and analyze the image as a class. Ask,

- What are these people doing?

- What is the building in the background?

- Where might this photo have been taken? *(northern Nigeria)*

2 **Have students complete the Preview activity in their Interactive Student Notebooks.** Review the directions with students, and answer any questions students may have.

3 **Have students share their responses in pairs or with the class.**

4 **Connect the Preview activity to the chapter.** Explain to students that, as they have observed in the image, Islamic culture and beliefs influenced West Africa in many ways. Theses influences can still be seen in the areas of government, religion, education, language, and architecture. In this chapter, students will examine images of modern West Africa to identify the variety of ways that Islam continues to influence society and culture there.

Vocabulary Development

1 **Introduce the Key Content Terms.** Have students locate the Key Content Terms for the chapter in their Interactive Student Notebooks. These are important terms that will help them understand the main ideas of the chapter. Ask volunteers to identify any familiar terms and suggest how they might be used in a sentence.

2 **Have students complete a Vocabulary Development handout.** Give each student a copy of the Vocabulary Development handout of your choice from the Reading Toolkit at the back of the Lesson Masters. These handouts provide extra Key Content Term practice and support, depending on your students' needs. Review the completed handout by asking volunteers to share one answer for each term.

Reading

1 **Introduce the Essential Question and have students read Section 13.1.** Have students identify the Essential Question on the first page of the chapter: *In what ways did Islam influence West African society?* Then have students read Section 13.1. Afterward, have students use information from Section 13.1 and from the chapter opener image to propose some answers to the Essential Question.

2 **Have students complete the Reading Notes for Chapter 13.** Assign Sections 13.2 to 13.8 during the activity, as indicated in the procedures for the Social Studies Skill Builder. Remind students to use the Key Content Terms where appropriate as they complete their Reading Notes.

Social Studies Skill Builder

1 **Prepare the classroom for the activity.** Post *Placards 13A–13H: Contemporary Photographs of West Africa* along the walls of the classroom. Create 8–10 dice for the activity using *Information Master 13A: Die Template.* Place the dice in a central location.

2 **Put students in pairs and introduce the activity.** Tell students that they will be learning about ways in which Islam has influenced, and continues to influence, West Africa. In this activity, they will analyze a gallery of contemporary photographs from West Africa, which are posted on the walls of the classroom, and will identify Islamic influences represented in the images.

3 **Have pairs complete the Reading Notes for Section 13.2.** Tell students that this section explains how Islam spread into West Africa. Have them read Section 13.2 and complete the corresponding Reading Notes in their Interactive Student Notebooks.

4 **Review the activity.** Have students open their Interactive Student Notebooks to the Reading Notes for Chapter 13. Project *Information Master 13B: Analyzing Photographs of West Africa,* and review the steps for completing the activity.

5 **As a class, practice the steps for analyzing the photographs.** Ask students to read Section 13.3. Have pairs complete steps 3–5 on Information Master 13B. Encourage students to find as many photographs as possible that show examples of this Islamic influence—religious practices—on West Africa. Then have volunteers share their ideas from their Reading Notes with the class. You may want to consult Guide to Reading Notes 13.

6 **Conduct the Social Studies Skill Builder activity.** Continue projecting Information Master 13B during the activity. Have pairs come to you to have their work checked for the first section or two of the Reading Notes. If they are following directions accurately, consider circulating around the room to spot-check work rather than checking each pair's work for every section.

7 **Conduct a wrap-up activity.** Follow these steps to have students create a human bar graph:

   • Write the six topics of Islamic influence in West Africa—religious practices, government and law, education, language, architectural styles, and decorative arts—spaced part, along the board. Clear some space in front of the board.

   • Ask pairs to analyze their Reading Notes and discuss which of these areas of West African life they think have been most influenced by Islam. Make sure that students can support their opinions with at least two or three concrete examples.

   • Have each pair send one partner to stand in front of the topic they think was most influenced by Islam. As students come up to the board, have them stand in a single-file line—like bars on a graph—in front of their chosen topic.

Placards 13A–13H

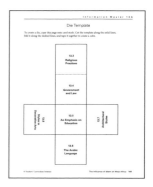

Information Master 13A

Information Master 13B

- As students remain standing in the bar graph, ask,

  According to our human bar graph, which topics were most influenced by Islam? (**Note:** Religious practices will likely be one of the top two topics.)

  According to our bar graph, which topics were least influenced by Islam?

  What evidence can you identify to support your topic as the most influenced by Islam? (**Note:** Have seated students answer this question.)

  What reasons might explain why the class selected the topics it did as most influenced by Islam? (**Note:** Consider dismissing the human bar graph before asking this question and having students discuss it with their partners before you call on volunteers. Answers might include that religious practices were most influenced because, in Islamic culture, religious practices and beliefs have a very strong influence on almost all aspects of life, including law, art, and education.)

Processing

Review the instructions for completing the Processing activity. When students have finished their sensory figures, have several share their answers with the class. For each sensory sentence shared, have the class identify the related topic of Islamic influence.

Quicker Coverage

Reduce the Number of Islamic Influences Students Examine Instead of having students look for all six Islamic influences in the images, assign each group just one or two influences on which to focus. Then, as a whole class, focus on one influence at a time, and have those groups share what they found with the class. At that time, students can fill in the Reading Notes for the influences they did not already examine.

Omit the Human Bar Graph Instead of having students come to the front of the class in Step 7, write each influence down the left side of a transparency, and have students raise their hands to show which area they thought was most influenced by Islam. For each hand raised, make an X next to that influence to make a quick bar graph. Follow up with the four questions provided in Step 7.

Deeper Coverage

Have Students Find Additional Images That Reveal Islamic Influences Have students work with a partner to use the Internet or the library to find at least two additional images that show Islamic influences in West Africa. Have them print or copy their images and annotate them to explain what influences are pictured. Then have them pair up with another group and share their images.

Assessment

Mastering the Content

1. D	5. C	9. D	13. C
2. C	6. B	10. B	14. A
3. B	7. D	11. A	15. C
4. D	8. A	12. B	16. A

Applying Social Studies Skills

17. Mali

18. 680 years or about 700 years

19. Mansa Musa's hajj (c. 1324) and the visit of Ibn Battuta (1352) probably contributed to the fact that by 1375, Europeans were showing Mali on their maps.

Exploring the Essential Question

20. Answers should include all the elements requested in the prompt.

Scoring Rubric

Score	Description
3	Student completes comments for all three sites, including at least one Islamic influence for each. Tour guide comments are clearly stated and demonstrate command of standard English conventions.
2	Student responds to most or all parts of the task, but tour guide comments may lack true Islamic influence or may not be clearly stated.
1	Student responds to at least one part of the task. Tour guide comments may contain factual and/or grammatical errors and may lack Islamic influences.
0	Response does not match the task or is incorrect.

English Language Learners

Assign the Reading Before the Activity Prior to conducting the class activity, suggest that students read Sections 13.3 through 13.8 and complete the third column of the chart in their Reading Notes. As they read, have them focus on Islamic influences on West Africa by writing specific examples from their reading in a chart like the one shown below. This may help students analyze and classify the photographs during the Social Studies Skill Builder and complete the Processing assignment as well.

	Examples of Influences in This Area
Religious Practices	
Government and Law	
Education	
Language	
Architecture	
Decorative Arts	

Learners Reading and Writing Below Grade Level

Add Structure to the Processing Activity Provide some or all of the following sentences for students to complete with the correct words:

- With my mouth, I say that _____ is the language of religion, learning, commerce, and government in West Africa.

- With my hands, I touch the walls of the _____ where I worship. Its walls are made of _____ and _____, while some even have a _____, or tower.

- With my eyes, I see the _____ patterns that decorate the textiles and containers in the marketplace. Since drawings of humans and animals are forbidden, these simple designs have become common in West Africa.

- With my eyes, I see a person facing the judges, or _____, in a court for having broken the _____, or Islamic law.

- With my ears, I hear students studying the Qur'an, law, and literature at the University of _____. I also hear the voices of the scholars, or _____, who run the smaller schools of the university.

Learners with Special Education Needs

Make Modifications to the Activity Post the placards at a height that will allow all students to access them easily. Also, consider creating a separate packet of photographs that some students can analyze at their desks, instead of having to move around the room.

Advanced Learners

Add to the Processing Activity Challenge advanced learners to find out more about one of the topics listed below. Using the resources found at www.teachtci.com or other resources at local libraries, have students research one of the following topics and add new information to one or more of the sensory boxes in the Processing activity:

- Eid al-Fitr
- Ibn Battuta
- shari'ah
- University of Sankore
- Djingareyber
- calligraphy

Enrichment Resources

Have students find out more about the influence of Islam on West Africa by exploring the following Enrichment Resources for *History Alive! The Medieval World and Beyond* at www.teachtci.com.

Enrichment Readings These in-depth readings encourage students to explore selected topics related to the chapter. You may also find readings that relate the chapter's content directly to your state's curriculum.

Internet Connections The recommended Web sites provide useful and engaging content that reinforces skills development and mastery of subjects within the chapter.

Literature Recommendations

The following books offer opportunities to extend the content in this chapter.

Daily Life in Ancient and Modern Timbuktu by Larry Brooks (Minneapolis: Lerner, 1999)

The Royal Kingdoms of Ghana, Mali, and Songhay by Patricia McKissack and Frederick McKissack (New York: Henry Holt and Co., 1995)

Traveling Man: The Journey of Ibn Battuta by James Ruford (Boston: Houghton Mifflin Company, 2001)

Section 13.2

Timelines will vary. Possible answers:

1076: Almoravids capture Kumbi. Under their rule Islam becomes more widespread in Ghana.

1240: Mande capture Kumbi and build the empire of Mali. Mande leaders accept Islam.

1312: Mansa Musa takes over Mali. He is the first ruler to practice Islam devoutly.

1323–1324: Mansa Musa makes a hajj to Makkah.

1490s: Muslims in Songhai rebel and place a devout Muslim on the throne.

Sections 13.3–13.8

Use the completed charts to check student answers. Simple illustrations will vary.

Section 13.3 Influence of Islam on Religious Practices	
Letter of Placard and Explanation	Questions for this Section
D shows a mosque with minarets. A shows two children in front of a mosque. B shows a child studying the Qur'an, the holy book of Islam. C shows Muslims praying. E shows the celebration of an Islamic festival. F shows a man studying the Qur'an. H shows people praying.	List two ways that West Africans adopted Islamic religious practices. • *They learned the Five Pillars of Islam.* • *They fasted, worshipped in mosques, and went on pilgrimages.* List two ways that West Africans preserved their own religious practices. • *They showed respect for dead ancestors.* • *They kept their beliefs in spirits and used amulets to protect themselves from harm.*

Section 13.4 Influence of Islam on Government and Law	
Letter of Placard and Explanation	Questions for this Section
C shows an emir, the title of a ruler in Islamic lands. E shows the emir's horsemen, soldiers of the Islamic ruler. G shows a shari'ah court. Shari'ah was the law of Islam	How did the line of succession change with the arrival of Islam? *Before, succession to the throne had been matrilineal. After the arrival of Islam, succession became patrilineal, or passed from father to son.* How did the structure of government change under Islamic influence? *Government became more centralized and kings exercised more control over local leaders.* Give one example of how shari'ah was different from customary law. *Customary law was often not written down, but shari'ah was written law.*

Section 13.5 Influence of Islam on Education	
Letter of Placard and Explanation	Questions for this Section
A shows a tablet used by students to study the Qur'an. B shows a Qur'anic school. F shows a love a books and the importance of education at all ages.	List three ways that Islamic love of learning influenced West Africa. • *Timbuktu became a center of learning with many universities.* • *Local schools were set up where children could learn the Qur'an.* • *Muslims' love of books led to the development of large libraries.*

Section 13.6 Influence of Islam on Language	
Letter of Placard and Explanation	Questions for this Section
A shows Arabic writing on a tablet. B shows Arabic writing on a tablet. F shows Arabic writing on a book.	Though West Africans still used their native language in everyday speech, in what aspects of society did Arabic become the primary language? *Arabic became the language of religion, learning, commerce and government.* How did the use of Arabic in West Africa become an important tool for historians? *Scholars used Arabic to write about the history and culture of West Africa.*

Section 13.7 Influence of Islam on Architectural Styles	
Letter of Placard and Explanation	Questions for this Section
A shows the use of mud and projecting beams, as in the architecture introduced by al-Saheli. D shows a mosque with minarets, a necessary element of all mosques. H shows a rectangular building with a flat roof at the far right, a style introduced by al-Saheli.	What two new architectural changes were influenced by Islam? *People designed mosques and brick, flat-roofed houses.* How were the homes built by al-Saheli different from traditional West African houses? *Traditional homes were round with a cone-shaped, thatched roof. Al-Saheli built rectangular homes made of brick with flat roofs, no windows and a single door*

Section 13.8 Influence of Islam on Decorative Arts	
Letter of Placard and Explanation	Questions for this Section
B shows geometric designs on textiles. C shows geometric designs on walls and men in Arabic dress. D shows geometric designs on clothes and Arabic robes. E shows Arabic robes. F shows an Arabic robe. G shows Arabic dress. H shows Arabic robes	List and describe two new decorative arts or styles that West Africans adopted from Muslims. *West Africans adopted calligraphy, or decorative writing, and geometric patterns for their art and textiles.* How did West African clothing change with the arrival of Islam? *West Africans adopted the flowing Arabic robes worn by Muslims.*

The Cultural Legacy of West Africa

In what ways do the cultural achievements of West Africa influence our culture today?

Overview

In a Problem Solving Groupwork activity, students listen to a griot tell the story of Sundjata and create a griot performance of scenes from the story.

Objectives

In the course of reading this chapter and participating in the classroom activity, students will

Social Studies

- describe the importance of written and oral traditions in the transmission of African history and culture.

- discuss various cultural achievements of West Africa and analyze the function of each in West African society.

- explain how African cultural achievements of the past continue to shape the world today.

Language Arts

- clarify word meanings through the use of definitions and examples.

- use speaking techniques, including voice modulation, inflection, tempo, and eye contact, to communicate meaning to an audience.

Social Studies Vocabulary

Key Content Terms oral tradition, griot, genealogy, folktale, call and response, terra-cotta, appliqué, kente

Academic Vocabulary transmit, verbal, communicate, evolve

Materials

History Alive! The Medieval World and Beyond

Interactive Student Notebooks

CD Tracks 5–7

Lesson Masters
- Information Master 14
- Student Handout 14A (6 copies of each scene)
- Student Handout 14B (1 per student)
- Vocabulary Development handout (1 per student, on colored paper)

Activity	Suggested Time	Materials
Preview	25 minutes	• *History Alive! The Medieval World and Beyond* • Interactive Student Notebooks • CD Tracks 5–6
Vocabulary Development	30–40 minutes	• *History Alive! The Medieval World and Beyond* • Interactive Student Notebooks • Vocabulary Development handout
Problem Solving Groupwork	120 minutes (3 regular periods) (1.5 block periods)	• *History Alive! The Medieval World and Beyond* • Interactive Student Notebooks • CD Track 7 • Information Master 14 • Student Handout 14A (6 copies of each scene) • Student Handout 14B (1 per student)
Processing	30 minutes	• Interactive Student Notebooks
Assessment	40 minutes	• Chapter 14 Assessment

Preview

1 Introduce the concept of music as an example of a cultural legacy. Tell students that music is an important part of life in West Africa. Prepare to play CD Track 5, "Kpatsa/Toke." Before playing the song, explain to students that this is an example of a call-and-response song. The piece is performed by Obo Addy, a master drummer of Ghana. Play the song. After students have listened to the recording, ask,

- How difficult was it to identify the call and the response? *(The call can be heard in the solo voice; the response follows, by a group of singers.)*

- What kinds of emotions does this song evoke?

- For what kind of events or occasions do you think the song was created? *(It is often performed at ceremonies, including the initiation ceremony for a young woman about to get married. The portion of the song on the recording means, "Come on, let's play and have fun.")*

2 Recite a call-and-response song as a class. Divide the class into two large groups, and have them gather on either side of the classroom. Assign one group to sing the call and the other to sing the response. Have students open their Interactive Student Notebooks to the Preview activity and practice reciting the appropriate part to the first verse of the song "Everybody Ought to Know."

"Everybody Ought to Know"

Call: Everybody ought to know

Response: Everybody ought to know

Call: Everybody ought to know

Response: Everybody ought to know

Together: Everybody ought to know

Call: What freedom is

Response: What freedom is

For verses 2–5, replace the word *freedom* with *justice, friendship, happiness,* and then repeat *freedom*.

3 Perform a call-and-response song as a class. Play CD Track 6, *"Everybody Ought to Know,"* and have students perform the call and response. First have students just listen to the song. Then play the track a second time and have them perform the call and response they recited in Step 2. Afterward, explain that this song is performed by Sweet Honey in the Rock, a quintet of African American singers whose sound is rooted in the 18th- and 19th-century singing traditions.

4 Have students complete the Preview activity in their Interactive Student Notebooks. Once all students are finished, have them share their responses in pairs or with the class. (**Note:** You may wish to share with students that "Everybody Ought to Know" was meant to be a song of protest.)

5 Connect the Preview activity to the chapter. Tell students that call-and-response songs are one of West Africa's cultural legacies to the world. Today, they can be heard in the vocals and instrumentation of contemporary pop, gospel, blues, rock, and jazz. Explain that music is just one example of West Africa's cultural legacy. Other examples include oral and written traditions, sculpture, dance, and everyday objects. Tell students that in this chapter, they will learn about notable West African cultural achievements and how they continue to influence the world.

Vocabulary Development

1 Introduce the Key Content Terms. Have students locate the Key Content Terms for the chapter in their Interactive Student Notebooks. These are important terms that will help them understand the main ideas of the chapter. Ask volunteers to identify any familiar terms and suggest how they might be used in a sentence.

2 Have students complete a Vocabulary Development handout. Give each student a copy of the Vocabulary Development handout of your choice from the Reading Toolkit at the back of the Lesson Masters. These handouts provide extra Key Content Term practice and support, depending on your students' needs. Review the completed handout by asking volunteers to share one answer for each term.

Reading

1 Introduce the Essential Question and have students read Section 14.1. Have students identify the Essential Question on the first page of the chapter: *In what ways do the cultural achievements of West Africa influence our culture today?* Have students read Section 14.1. Then ask,

- What are *oral traditions?*

- Why were they so important to early West African culture?

- What are *griots?*

- Why were they important to West African history and culture?

2 Have students complete the Reading Notes for Chapter 14. Assign Sections 14.2 to 14.4 during the activity, as indicated in the procedures for the Problem Solving Groupwork activity. Remind students to use the Key Content Terms where appropriate as they complete their Reading Notes.

> **Vocabulary Development: Clarify Word Meanings**
>
> Guide students to identify the types of context clues in the text that clarify the meanings of the Key Content Terms. Students should identify not only definitions, but also examples—such as examples of call and response—and contrast and restatement, where those clues are present. Students might also brainstorm their own examples, restatements, or contrasts, such as the contrast of oral tradition with written literature.

Problem Solving Groupwork

1 **Have students complete the Reading Notes for Section 14.2.**

2 **Organize students for the activity.** Place students in six groups of about equal size. This activity requires six groups to perform the six scenes in the griot tale, with two griots. For small classes, consider having two griots, one rhythm maker, and one performance artist per group. For larger classes, assign up to four rhythm makers and four performance artists per group.

3 **Display *Information Master 14: Performing the Story of Sundjata*, and introduce the activity.** Tell students that they will now hear a portion of the most famous tale of West Africa and then perform their own version of it. This story centers on a king named Sundjata who founded Mali's empire in the 13th century. (**Note:** There is no definitive version of this story. Content and performance traditions vary, yet there are more similarities among the versions than differences. This version was adapted from *Sundiata: An Epic of Old Mali,* by D. T. Niane.)

Information Master 14

4 **Play CD Track 7, "Sunyetta."** You may want to warn students that the recording is difficult to understand, but that they should listen carefully to capture the feel of what a real griot sounds like. Before playing the CD track, share the following with students:

This recording of the Sundjata story was recited by Abdoulie Samba, a griot whose people lived in West Africa, between the Senegal and Gambia rivers, in what is now Senegal. Samba also plays the musical accompaniment on the halam, the direct ancestor of the five-string banjo.

5 **Have students work as a class or with a partner to analyze the griot's retelling of Sundjata.** Once the recording is finished, ask,

- What was the pattern of the griot's voice?

- What types of instruments do you think he was using?

- Do you recognize any words in the griot's tale?

Student Handout 14A

6 **Pass out materials and review the directions for the activity with students.** Give each group a different copy of the six scripts on *Student Handout 14A: Story of Sundjata,* and each student a copy of *Student Handout 14B: Notes on the Story of Sundjata.* Review the three roles—Griot, Rhythm Maker, Performance Artist—listed on Information Master 14. Assign each student a role for the activity. Then review Steps 2 through 4 on Information Master 14 with students and answer any questions.

7 **Monitor groups as they create their performances.** Allow adequate time for preparation. Consider having Performance Artists make name tags to show which characters they are portraying.

Student Handout 14B

8 **Arrange the classroom and have the first group perform Scene 1.** When students are ready, arrange the classroom with a stage area in front. You may want to introduce this first scene by reading the following aloud:

Listen, children of (your school), and hear the story of Sundjata, the king who founded Mali, the most powerful empire in all West Africa. The words I speak are those of my teacher and her teachers before her, pure and full of truth. For we are griots. Centuries of history and learning reside within our minds. Thus, we serve our community with wisdom, bringing to life the lessons of the past so that the future may grow and do well. Listen, then, to the story of Sundjata.

9 **Have groups complete Student Handout 14B for Scene 1.** Students should identify the scene with a brief description, draw an important element of the scene they just saw performed, and annotate their drawings.

10 **Repeat Steps 8–9 for the remaining five scenes.**

11 **Have students complete the Reading Notes for Sections 14.3 and 14.4.**

Processing

Have students complete the Processing activity on a separate sheet of paper in their notebooks. Students create a museum display that highlights West African cultural achievements and their impact on modern society.

Quicker Coverage

Streamline the Activity Complete Steps 1–5 of the activity directions. Then, instead of having students create performances of the story in Steps 6–10, read the griot tale from Student Handout 14A aloud as a class and complete Student Handout 14B together.

Deeper Coverage

Have Students Create a Call and Response After They Read Section 14.3
Replay CD Tracks 5 and 6, if necessary, to review call-and-response songs. Then, assign each group of six students one of the following occasions and have them write, practice, and perform an appropriate call-and-response song.

- celebrating a friend's 13th birthday
- celebrating a student's graduation from middle school
- celebrating the birth of a baby
- protesting an injustice
- mourning the end of summer vacation
- inspiring a school team before an important game

Explain that each song should be two minutes in length, have clear lyrics so that the audience can join in the response, and include rhythm and sounds created by "instruments," such as books, desktops, rulers, pens, pencils, and voices.

Assessment

Mastering the Content

1. D	5. A	9. C	13. B
2. D	6. A	10. B	14. A
3. D	7. B	11. A	15. B
4. C	8. B	12. C	16. C

Applying Social Studies Skills

17. It was preserved by being passed down through oral tradition.

18. He drops water on them to trick them into thinking it is raining. Then he invites them to go into the gourd to keep dry.

19. Answers will vary but should recognize that Anansi has the character traits of a trickster—clever, fools others, uses trickery to achieve his goals, and so on.

Exploring the Essential Question

20. Answers should include all the elements requested in the prompt.

Scoring Rubric

Score	Description
3	Student completes all three parts of the task. Responses to literature are clearly stated, supported by details, and demonstrate command of standard English conventions.
2	Student responds to most or all parts of the task, but responses to literature may lack details or not be clearly stated.
1	Student responds to at least one part of the task. Responses to literature may contain factual and/or grammatical errors and may lack details.
0	Response does not match the task or is incorrect.

Youssou D'Nour: A Modern-Day Griot

1 **Elicit students' ideas about the role of music and musicians in the modern world.** Ask, *How can songs help support traditions and values or teach lessons about life?* Ask students to name examples of songs with lessons, or that celebrate a cause or support traditions and values. Remind students about the role of griots in medieval West African society. Tell them that they will now learn about a modern-day griot named Youssou D'Nour.

2 **Have students read the Chapter 14 Reading Further.**

3 **Have students compare and contrast medieval griots with modern-day griots.** Ask, *What makes Youssou D'Nour a modern-day griot? How are the activities of today's griots different from those in the past?* Draw a Venn diagram on the board. Label one side "Medieval Griots," the other side "Modern-Day Griots," and the middle section "Both." Have students use the Venn diagram to compare and contrast the two groups.

4 **Have students complete the Chapter 14 Reading Further in their Interactive Student Notebooks.** To prepare for the activity, have students make a class list of topics. Students can then choose a topic from the list or choose one of their own. For the second part of the activity, if students are having trouble getting started, suggest that they select a tune to a traditional song they already know and then write their lyrics to it.

5 **Have students share their song lyrics with the class.** Encourage volunteers to read or sing their songs. Alternatively, you may want to give students time to rehearse their songs with a partner or in a small group, accompanied by instruments.

English Language Learners

Prepare Students for the Activity Provide students with a copy of the entire Sundjata story (taken from Student Handout 14A) the night before you plan to introduce this activity. Allow students to take note of parts that they didn't understand and ask questions before forming groups the following day.

Learners Reading and Writing Below Grade Level

Provide Support for the Reading Notes Give students a copy of Guide to Reading Notes 14, with key words omitted in each answer for them to fill in as they read each section.

Shorten the Processing Activity Reduce from three to one or two the number of achievements that students must highlight in their museum displays.

Learners with Special Education Needs

Offer an Alternative to the Problem Solving Groupwork Activity Allow some students to participate just as observers during the performances of Sundjata. If appropriate, have them act as judges to rate their peers in the following categories:

- how clearly and loudly the griots speak
- the use of musical instruments during the performance
- how well the drumming matches the mood and tone of what is happening in the story
- the use of simple pantomime movements that illustrate the major actions in the story

Modify the Problem Solving Groupwork Activity Have students work with a peer, who has been assigned a similar role, to develop and practice their roles on Student Handout 14A.

Advanced Learners

Expand the Processing Activity Suggest that students do a bit more research in one of the following areas and include these examples in their museum displays:

- the Brer Rabbit stories by Joel Chandler Harris or other African trickster tales
- the influence of West African traditions on American gospel, jazz, blues, rock and roll, and rap
- West African dance
- basket making

Enrichment Resources

Have students find out more about cultural legacy of West Africa by exploring the following Enrichment Resources for *History Alive! The Medieval World and Beyond* at www.teachtci.com.

Enrichment Readings These in-depth readings encourage students to explore selected topics related to the chapter. You may also find readings that relate the chapter's content directly to your state's curriculum.

Internet Connections The recommended Web sites provide useful and engaging content that reinforces skills development and mastery of subjects within the chapter.

Literature Recommendations

The following books offer opportunities to extend the content in this chapter.

Orphan Girl and Other Stories: West African Folktales by Buchi Offodile (Northampton, MA: Interlink Books, 2001)

Mali: Crossroads of Africa by Philip Koslow (New York: Chelsea House, 1995)

Sundiata: Lion King of Mali by David Wisniewski (Boston: Houghton Mifflin Company, 1999)

Section 14.2

1. For a long time, there was no written tradition in West Africa. The oral tradition was used to pass down important information and history.

2. A griot is a verbal artist responsible for memorizing and retelling the history and traditions of West Africa. Griots also helped advise rulers.

3. Many traditional folktales were brought to the Americas by African slaves, which they then spread among the other slaves and their descendants.

4. Preserved writings tell us about West African heritage and culture. Some modern West African writers build on medieval written and oral traditions.

Section 14.3

1. Music communicated ideas, values, and feelings and marked important events, such as weddings and funerals.

2. Call and response is a style of singing in which a leader plays or sings a call and a chorus sings a response.

3. (a) ngoni; (b) kora; (c) balafon

4. People still perform traditional West African dance. West African music has influenced gospel, jazz, blues, rock, and rap. West African and Afro-Cuban drum music are popular features of modern world music.

Section 14.4

1. Some visual art, such as fabrics and baskets, served everyday needs. Other art was used in rituals and ceremonies to honor spirits, ancestors, and royalty.

2. They created sculptures, masks, textiles, and everyday objects.

3. Modern artists, such as Pablo Picasso, were inspired by West African art. Kente cloth is worn around the world. West African basket-making techniques are still used in the American South.

The Culture and Kingdoms of West Africa

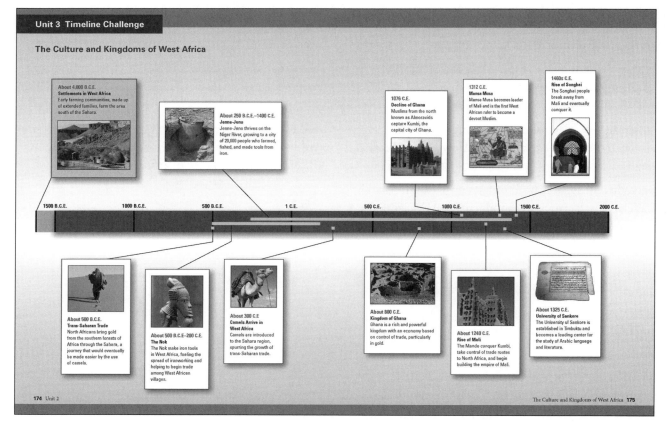

Unit 3 Timeline Challenge

The Culture and Kingdoms of West Africa

About 4,000 B.C.E.
Settlements in West Africa
Early farming communities, made up of extended families, farm the area south of the Sahara.

About 250 B.C.E.–1400 C.E.
Jenne-Jeno
Jenne-Jeno thrives on the Niger River, growing to a city of 20,000 people who farmed, fished, and made tools from iron.

1076 C.E.
Decline of Ghana
Muslims from the north known as Almoravids capture Kumbi, the capital city of Ghana.

1312 C.E.
Mansa Musa
Mansa Musa becomes leader of Mali and is the first West African ruler to become a devout Muslim.

1460s C.E.
Rise of Songhai
The Songhai people break away from Mali and eventually conquer it.

1500 B.C.E.　1000 B.C.E.　500 B.C.E.　1 C.E.　500 C.E.　1000 C.E.　1500 C.E.　2000 C.E.

About 500 B.C.E.
Trans-Saharan Trade
North Africans bring gold from the southern forests of Africa through the Sahara, a journey that would eventually be made easier by the use of camels.

About 500 B.C.E.–200 C.E.
The Nok
The Nok make iron tools in West Africa, fueling the spread of ironworking and helping to begin trade among West African villages.

About 300 C.E.
Camels Arrive in West Africa
Camels are introduced to the Sahara region, spurring the growth of trans-Saharan trade.

About 800 C.E.
Kingdom of Ghana
Ghana is a rich and powerful kingdom with an economy based on control of trade, particularly in gold.

About 1240 C.E.
Rise of Mali
The Mande conquer Kumbi, take control of trade routes to North Africa, and begin building the empire of Mali.

About 1325 C.E.
University of Sankore
The University of Sankore is established in Timbuktu and becomes a leading center for the study of Arabic language and literature.

174 Unit 2　　The Culture and Kingdoms of West Africa 175

Overview

This Timeline Challenge helps students review the main events and ideas of this unit while providing practice in reading and interpreting timelines. You can vary and expand the activity according to students' needs and the amount of time available.

Basic Procedure

1 **Introduce the timeline in the Student Edition.** Direct students to The Culture and Kingdoms of West Africa Timeline at the end of Unit 3 in the Student Edition. You may wish to have students read aloud and discuss the timeline entries.

2 **Introduce the Timeline Challenge in the Interactive Student Notebook.** Direct students to the Unit 3 Timeline Challenge in their notebooks. Point out the two types of questions, "Timeline Skills" and "Critical Thinking," and model how to answer each type.

3 **Have students complete the Timeline Challenge.** Monitor students as they work. Use the Guide to Unit 3 Timeline Challenge to check their answers. You may wish to project a transparency of this page as you work through the questions with the class and conduct a discussion of the "Critical Thinking" questions.

4 Complete the KWL chart. Return to the KWL chart created at the beginning of the unit, and ask students to list the key information they have learned.

Classroom Timeline

1 Prepare the Timeline Challenge Cards. Copy and cut the cards from *Student Handout TC3: Unit 3 Timeline Challenge Cards.* You may wish to laminate the cards for future use.

2 Create a timeline on a classroom wall. On an empty wall or a large bulletin board, make a timeline with masking tape or colored paper. Mark off the time intervals in advance, or ask students to do so in class.

3 Have students place the Timeline Challenge Cards. Distribute cards to individual students or pairs and have them tape the cards to the timeline in the correct locations. Call on students to provide more information on the timeline topics to review main events and issues.

Student Handout TC3

Internet Research

1 Review students' suggestions for additional timeline entries. Have students share their answers to the last question of the Timeline Challenge.

2 Have students conduct Internet research. Ask students to choose and research one of their suggested events.

3 Have students create additional Timeline Challenge Cards. Direct students to research an appropriate image for their cards and then use the computer to create an illustrated card, complete with timeline entry.

Timeline Skills

Score 1 point for each correct answer.

1. The first West African settlements were small farming communities of extended families.

2. gold

3. about 700 years

4. About 800 years after trans-Saharan trade began, camels were introduced to the region.

5. farming, fishing, and iron making

6. Ghana's economy was based on control of trade, particularly in gold.

7. Muslims from the north known as Almoravids captured Kumbi, the capital city of Ghana.

8. Mansa Musa

9. Songhai

10. Timbuktu

Critical Thinking

Score 1 to 3 points for each answer, depending on the thoroughness of the response.

11. With iron tools, crops could be planted and harvested more efficiently. More food meant that more people were free to work at other trades, which led villages to produce a surplus of goods. These goods were then traded at key villages along the Niger, allowing the villages to prosper and grow into sizable towns and cities.

12. Trans-Saharan trade developed from the introduction of the camel and the spread of Islam. The camel allowed traders to more easily travel across the Sahara in caravans. When Muslims invaded Ghana's empire in the 7th century, they hoped to spread their beliefs throughout the region, as well as to control trade routes, which led to an even greater need to establish routes across the Sahara.

13. With the arrival of Islam in West Africa, succession of rulers changed from matrilineal to patrilineal. Arabic became the language of learning, religion, trade, and government. Muslims began to emphasize education in West Africa and built universities where people could study the Qur'an, as well as other subjects.

14. Answers will vary. Students must explain why the events they chose merit inclusion.

Using Scores to Inform Instruction

Timeline Skills A score of 7 out of 10 indicates that students understand most of the key events in the unit.

Critical Thinking A score of 8 out of 12 indicates that students are able to think critically about most of the key issues in this unit.

If students score below these levels, consider reviewing timeline and critical thinking skills.

Imperial China

Europe During Medieval Times

Overview

This activity introduces geographic information essential to Unit 4. Students read and interpret maps to learn about key physical features of China and how these features affected Chinese medieval history. They annotate a map and answer questions in their Interactive Student Notebooks, and then discuss critical thinking questions. Students' comprehension of content and proficiency in map-reading and higher-order thinking skills will help you gauge their readiness for the unit. The pages that follow include a completed map, answers to questions, a scoring guide to inform your teaching, and suggestions for modifications to meet specific student needs.

Essential Geographic Understandings

1. Location of China.

2. Key physical features: Huang He (Yellow River), Chang Jiang (Yangtze River), Plateau of Tibet, Himalayas, Taklimakan Desert, Gobi Desert, Tian Shan

3. Importance of the Huang He (Yellow River) and Chang Jiang (Yangtze River) to the development of Chinese civilization

4. Impact of location on the diffusion of ideas to and from China

Procedures

1 **Introduce the unit.** Tell students that in this unit they will learn about the history and culture of imperial China.

2 **Create a KWL chart.** Ask students to identify what they already know about the geography of China and what they want to learn. Use their responses to gauge how much additional background information they will need as you progress through the unit. Students will return to the KWL chart at the end of the unit and add the key information they have learned.

3 **Have students read Unit 4 "Setting the Stage" in the Student Edition.**

4 **Have students complete the Geography Challenge.** Monitor students as they work. Use the guide on the next two pages to check their answers. You may wish to project the map from the Interactive Student Notebook and have students annotate it as the class works through the map-reading questions. Make sure students have grasped Essential Geographic Understandings 1 to 3.

5 **Discuss the "Critical Thinking" questions.** Help students understand the geographic relationships described in Essential Geographic Understanding 4.

Asia

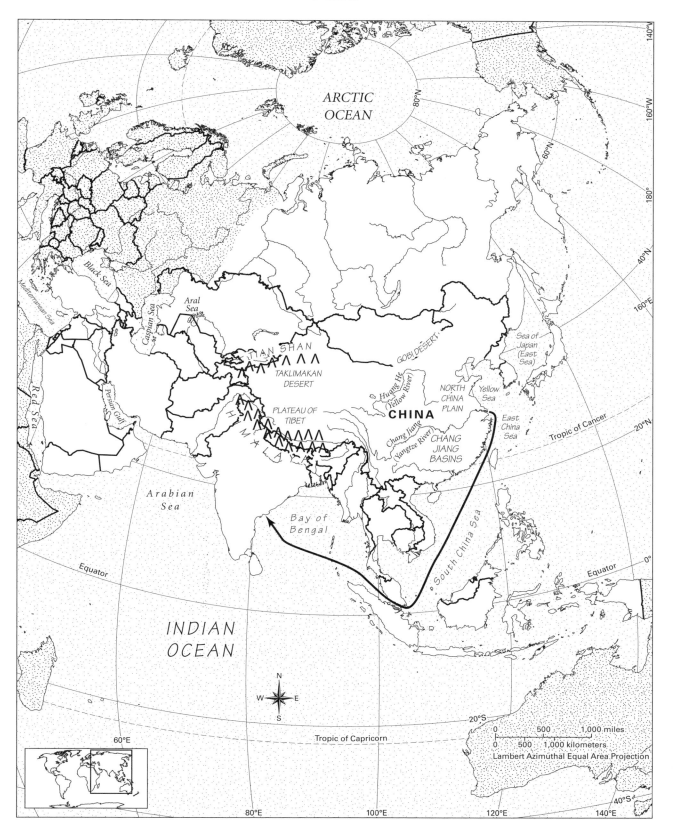

Geography Skills

Score 1 point for each correct answer. Use the map on the previous page to check shading and labeling.

1. The Sea of Japan (East Sea) lies farthest north.

2. Students should label the Taklimakan Desert and the Gobi Desert.

3. Traders would have had to cross the Gobi Desert, the Taklimakan Desert, and part of the Tian Shan mountains.

4. Check students' map for sea route to India. The compass allowed the Chinese to travel even when the sun and the stars were not visible. Thus, they could reach their destinations more quickly and accurately.

5. The northern border of China is not mountainous, as are its western and southwestern borders. Its eastern border is protected by the sea. China was open to attack from the north, which is why the Great Wall of China extends along this border.

6. Students should label the Huang He and the Chang Jiang rivers, the North China Plain, and the Chang Jiang Basins. The land near the Huang He and Chang Jiang was heavily populated because it was a flat, fertile region. The rivers provided water and a readily available transportation route.

7. Students should label the Plateau of Tibet, the Tian Shan, and the Himalayas. China's highlands are located in the western part of the country. These mountains would have to have been crossed by overland traders. This would have proven difficult because they are so high and the climate is very cold. Trade by way of the sea would have avoided these mountains.

Critical Thinking

Questions may have more than one correct answer. Score 1 to 3 points for each reasonable answer, depending on the strength of students' geographic reasoning. Possible answers are given here.

8. India is much closer to China than is Europe. In addition, it was easier for people and ideas to travel between India and China than between Europe and China. Although overland travel to India would have required passage through the Himalayas, the sea route was much safer. Sea travel to Europe was nearly impossible, since it required sailing around Africa. Overland travel was also extremely difficult, since the route was long and required crossing mountains and deserts.

9. The land to the north of the North China Plain is desert. People who lived in this region may have attacked the Chinese to obtain food from their farms or to gain control of the river.

10. Harsh physical features confined the expansion of China to the lowlands along the coast and to the plateau of central China. The mountains and deserts of surrounding areas prohibited expansion.

11. The flat, fertile land near the Huang He (Yellow River) and Chang Jiang (Yangtze River) allowed people to produce plenty of food. This meant they sometimes had extra food and had the free time to produce other goods. The rivers made transporting these goods possible, which caused trade to flourish. The growth in trade caused certain areas near the rivers to attract more and more people, which led to the growth of cities.

Using Scores to Inform Instruction

Geography Skills A score of 4 out of 7 or better indicates that students have acquired sufficient geographic information to proceed with the unit.

Critical Thinking A score of 8 out of 16 or better indicates that students are beginning to understand the relationships between physical geography and the different ways in which people live.

Modifying Instruction

ELL or Learners with Special Education Needs Consider focusing on map-reading questions or limiting the number of "Critical Thinking" questions.

Students with Weak Map or Critical Thinking Skills Assign appropriate pages from the Social Studies Skills Toolkit in the back of the Lesson Masters.

The Political Development of Imperial China

Which method of selecting officials led to the best leaders for China?

Overview

In an Experiential Exercise, students will role-play figures from medieval China as they debate the advantages and disadvantages of three methods used by rulers to select officials.

Objectives

In the course of reading this chapter and participating in the classroom activity, students will

Social Studies

- describe the reunification of China under the Sui and Tang dynasties.

- explain how the imperial state developed and describe the role of the scholar-official class.

- analyze the influence of Confucianism on how government officials were selected.

- compare and contrast approaches to Confucian thought during the Song and Mongol periods.

- evaluate the different methods of selecting officials in imperial China.

Language Arts

- write a persuasive composition stating a clear position and describing points in support of the position.

Social Studies Vocabulary

Key Content Terms emperor, imperial, dynasty, bureaucracy, warlord, aristocracy, civil service examination, meritocracy

Academic Vocabulary irrigation, sibling, rational, emphasize

Materials

History Alive! The Medieval World and Beyond

Interactive Student Notebooks

Lesson Masters

- Student Handout 15 (See Planning Guide for quantities.)

- Information Master 15 (1 transparency)

- Vocabulary Development handout (1 per student, on colored paper)

masking tape

Activity	Suggested Time	Materials
Preview	10 minutes	• Interactive Student Notebooks
Vocabulary Development	30–40 minutes	• *History Alive! The Medieval World and Beyond* • Interactive Student Notebooks • Vocabulary Development Handout
Experiential Exercise	50–75 minutes (1–2 regular periods) (.5–1 block period)	• *History Alive! The Medieval World and Beyond* • Interactive Student Notebooks • Student Handout 15 (1 for Emperor; 5 for Chancellors; equal number of Aristocrats, Foreigners, and Scholars for remaining students) • Information Master 15 (1 transparency)
Processing	15–20 minutes	• Interactive Student Notebooks
Assessment	40 minutes	• Chapter 15 Assessment

Preview

1 **Have students complete the Preview activity in their Interactive Student Notebooks.** Students choose the type of person they would trust to make decisions on their behalf. After students have recorded their responses, allow several of them to share their ideas.

2 **Connect the Preview activity to the chapter.** Tell students that, just as different students had different ideas about whom they would trust to make decisions for them, medieval Chinese emperors sometimes disagreed about the types of officials suited to help them govern. In this lesson, students will learn about three methods Chinese emperors used to select people to help them rule a vast and diverse country.

Vocabulary Development

1 **Introduce the Key Content Terms.** Have students locate the Key Content Terms for the chapter in their Interactive Student Notebooks. These are important terms that will help them understand the main ideas of the chapter. Ask volunteers to identify any familiar terms and suggest how they might be used in a sentence.

2 **Have students complete a Vocabulary Development handout.** Give each student a copy of the Vocabulary Development handout of your choice from the Reading Toolkit at the back of the Lesson Masters. These handouts provide extra Key Content Term practice and support, depending on your students' needs. Review the completed handout by asking volunteers to share one answer for each term.

Reading

1 **Introduce the Essential Question and have students read Section 15.1.** Have students identify the Essential Question on the first page of the chapter: *Which method of selecting officials led to the best leaders for China?* Then have students read Section 15.1. Afterward, have students use information from Section 15.1 and from the chapter opener image to propose some possible answers to the Essential Question.

2 **Have students complete the Reading Notes for Chapter 15.** Assign Sections 15.2 to 15.6 during the activity, as indicated in the procedures for the Experiential Exercise. Remind students to use the Key Content Terms where appropriate as they complete their Reading Notes.

> **Vocabulary Development: Greek and Latin Roots**
>
> Point out the Greek root *crat/cracy*, which means "rule by" or "supporter of a rule by." Note how all three words with this root refer to government. Explain that *bureau* comes from the French word meaning "office" (and, that word, in turn, came from Latin); *aristo* comes from a Greek word meaning "best"; and *merito* comes from a Latin word meaning "to deserve." Relate these root meanings to the meanings we give to each whole word today.

Experiential Exercise

1 Arrange the classroom and prepare materials. Do the following:

- On unlined paper, make six signs with large writing. Label them "Province A," "Province B," "Province C," "Province D," "Province E," and "Throne."

- Using the classroom map below as a guide, create five stations of seven desks each and use a single desk to create a throne. Put the "Throne" sign above the single desk. Post one "Province" sign at each group of desks.

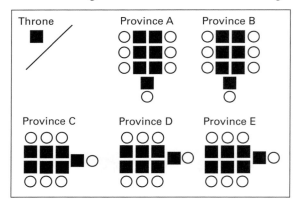

- Make copies of *Student Handout 15: Roles in Imperial China* in these quantities: one Emperor, five Chancellors, and, for the remaining students, an equal number of Aristocrats, Foreigners, and Scholars.

- Make a transparency of *Information Master 15: Directions for Choosing Chinese Leaders.*

2 Have students read Section 15.2 and complete the corresponding Reading Notes. Tell students that this section supplies background information on the history of early governments in China.

3 Introduce the activity. Tell students that throughout Chinese history, emperors have appointed different types of people to help them govern. During different eras, they have chosen aristocrats, or wealthy members of society, they have selected scholars, and they have appointed foreigners. Tell students that in this activity, they will each be assigned a role and will debate the advantages and disadvantages of appointing various groups of people as government officials.

4 Assign roles and distribute materials. Randomly distribute the roles from Student Handout 15. Tell students that in this activity the role of the Emperor may be played by either a boy or a girl. Have students read the background information on their handouts to familiarize themselves with their roles. Later, they will complete the blank at the top of the page.

Student Handout 15

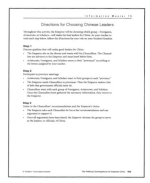

Information Master 15

5 Project Information Master 15 and guide students through the activity.
Use a sheet of paper to cover the steps listed on Information Master 15. Then do the following:

- **Reveal Step 1.** Assign each student in the Aristocrat, Foreigner, and Scholar groups a letter from A to E to represent the provinces to which they will move in Step 2. Have students write their assigned letter at the top of their role cards. You may also want students to prepare name tags for each role. (**Note:** Alternatively, you can write the letters on the handouts before distributing them to students.) Have students move to the appropriate places in the classroom—their provinces—as described on the Information Master. As students are working on this step, assign each Chancellor a letter from A to E (to represent the provinces from which they will gather information).

- **Reveal Step 2.** Allow students time to complete the province meetings. In large classes, you will likely send two students from each role group and one Chancellor to each province.

- **Reveal Step 3.** Then have the Emperor follow the directions on Student Handout 15 for gaining information from each Chancellor.

6 Debrief the experience. Ask students,

- Which argument do you think was strongest for choosing the Aristocrats? Against choosing this group?

- Which argument do you think was strongest for choosing the Foreigners? Against choosing this group?

- Which argument do you think was strongest for choosing the Scholars? Against choosing this group?

- How do you feel about the Emperor's decision?

- Which group do you think should be most eligible for government positions? Why?

7 Have students read and complete the Reading Notes. Assign students to read Sections 15.3 to 15.6 and complete the related Reading Notes.

Processing

Have students complete the Processing activity on a separate sheet of paper in their notebooks. Students will determine the method of selecting Chinese officials they think resulted in the best leaders. Then they will create a sensory figure for that type of official.

Quicker Coverage

Alter the Experiential Exercise Instead of having role groups meet with the Chancellors in each province (Step 2 on the Student Handout and Information Master) and then having the Chancellors present that information to the Emperor (Step 3), have each role group prepare a 30- to 60-second presentation for the Emperor and his or her Chancellors explaining why their group is the best choice to help govern China, and why the other groups are not good choices. After each group has presented, have the Emperor consult his or her Chancellors before making a decision.

Deeper Coverage

Debate the Fairest Way to Select Government Officials Begin by having students rank the following list of qualifications from most important to least important:

- not a member of any political party
- social class
- level of education
- experience
- ethnicity, gender, or age

Then have students create written justifications for the three qualifications they believe are most important. Finally, facilitate a class discussion in which students debate which should be the top three qualifications to consider when selecting government officials.

Assessment

Mastering the Content

1. B	5. A	9. C	13. B
2. B	6. D	10. D	14. B
3. C	7. A	11. C	15. D
4. D	8. A	12. C	16. A

Applying Social Studies Skills

17. Yuan

18. Tang, Song

19. vase

Exploring the Essential Question

20. Answers should include all the elements requested in the prompt.

Scoring Rubric

Score	Description
3	Student circles word at top and completes all four parts of the job application form. Entries on the form are clearly stated, supported by details, and demonstrate command of standard English conventions.
2	Student responds to most or all parts of the task, but entries on the form may lack details or not be clearly stated.
1	Student responds to at least one part of the task. Entries on the form may contain factual and/or grammatical errors and may lack details.
0	Response does not match the task or is incorrect.

English Language Learners

Have Students Read Ahead Before beginning the activity, tell these students what role they will be assigned—Aristocrat (Section 15.3), Scholar (Section 15.4), or Foreigner (Section 15.5) —and then have them read the section of the book that relates to their group before participating in the activity. You might consider giving them Student Handout 15 ahead of time as well, and allowing them to complete Step 2 before meeting with their group during the activity.

Learners Reading and Writing Below Grade Level

Provide Additional Support for the Reading Notes Using the Guide to Reading Notes, complete a copy of the Reading Notes. Leave a key word or phrase blank in each answer. Give copies of these partially completed Reading Notes to students and have them complete the unfinished sentences as they read.

Learners with Special Education Needs

Explain the Activity in Advance Explain the Experiential Exercise to students at least one day in advance. Allow them to select their roles or to act as observers. During the Experiential Exercise, place observers near the Emperor and provide them with a copy of a handout that explains what they are observing and asks them simplified versions of the questions that you have prepared ahead to check understanding.

Advanced Learners

Compare Methods for Selecting Leaders Have students compare the methods of selecting leaders in imperial China to the way leaders are chosen in China today. Have students research three examples of appointed officials, either at the national or at the provincial level, and the qualifications for holding each office.

Enrichment Resources

Find out more about the political development of imperial China by exploring the following Enrichment Resources for *History Alive! The Medieval World and Beyond* at www.teachtci.com.

Enrichment Readings These in-depth readings encourage students to explore selected topics related to the chapter. You may also find readings that relate the chapter's content directly to your state's curriculum.

Internet Connections The recommended Web sites provide useful and engaging content that reinforces skills development and mastery of subjects within the chapter.

Literature Recommendations

The following books offer opportunities to extend the content in this chapter.

Ancient China by Tony Allan (New York: Chelsea House, 2007)

Ancient Chinese Dynasties by Eleanor J. Hall (Farmington Hills, MI: Gale Group, 1999)

The Examination by Malcolm J. Bosse (New York: Straus & Giroux, 1996)

Section 15.2

1. People can overthrow an emperor when he rules badly.

2. A bureaucracy is an organized group of government officials. When the bureaucracy became corrupt, people suffered from high taxes, forced labor, and attacks by bandits. Warlords who opposed the emperor fought with one another. The government grew weak and was not able to protect people.

3. When the Han dynasty fell, China broke into separate kingdoms. It was reunited by the Sui dynasty.

4. Symbols will vary.

Section 15.3

1. Scholar-officials were scholars who were given government jobs only after passing a civil service examination to prove they were qualified.

2. The examination was mainly based on the teachings of Confucius.

3. Only the wealthy could afford the tutors, books, and study time needed to prepare for the exams.

4. Symbols will vary.

Section 15.4

1. Government officials who had studied Confucius would be rational, moral, and able to maintain order.

2. People from lower classes were also allowed to become government officials by attending state-supported local schools and could go on to the university to become scholars.

3. People wanted these jobs because government officials were respected and enjoyed privileges, such as being excused from taxes and military service.

4. Symbols will vary.

Section 15.5

1. He did not believe that Confucian learning was needed for government jobs, and he did not want to rely on the Chinese to run his government.

2. He appointed relatives, other Mongols, and trusted foreigners.

3. Chinese scholars worked only as teachers and minor government officials.

4. Symbols will vary.

Section 15.6

Hiring Scholar-Officials Helped China

- provided a well-organized government
- education of scholar-officials emphasized rational, moral behavior, justice, kindness, loyalty to the emperor, proper conduct, and the importance of family
- values helped unify China
- gave poor men who were ambitious and hardworking the chance to be government officials
- ensured that officials were trained and talented, not merely rich, or related to the emperor

Hiring Scholar-Officials Hurt China

- stood in the way of progress by not teaching and testing knowledge of science, mathematics, or engineering
- Confucian scholars had little respect for merchants, business, and trade; trade and business were not encouraged.
- bureaucrats became set in their ways

China Develops a New Economy

How did the Chinese improve their economy during the Tang and Song dynasties?

Overview

In a Visual Discovery activity, students analyze images of advancements in agriculture and trade and commerce in medieval China, and evaluate their influence on China's economy.

Objectives

In the course of reading this chapter and participating in the classroom activity, students will

Social Studies

- describe the agricultural changes that occurred under the Tang and Song.
- explain the causes and effects of the growth of trade and commerce and the development of a money economy.
- explain the causes and effects of urbanization.
- evaluate the impact of the changes in agriculture, commerce, and urbanization during this period.

Language Arts

- clarify word meanings through the use of definition, example, and restatement.

Social Studies Vocabulary

Key Content Terms economy, commerce, currency, urbanization

Academic Vocabulary elaborate, restriction, circulation, stimulate

Materials

History Alive! The Medieval World and Beyond

Interactive Student Notebooks

Visuals 16A–16C

Lesson Masters
- Information Master 16 (1 transparency)
- Student Handout 16 (1 copy, cut in half)
- Vocabulary Development handout (1 per student, on colored paper)

masking tape

white poster board

Activity	Suggested Time	Materials
Preview	10 minutes	• Interactive Student Notebooks
Vocabulary Development	30–40 minutes	• *History Alive! The Medieval World and Beyond* • Interactive Student Notebooks • Vocabulary Development handout (1 per student, on colored paper)

Visual Discovery	*Phase 1*
	60-90 minutes
	  (2 regular periods)
	  (1 block period)
	
	Phase 2
	30 minutes
	  (1 regular period)
	  (.5 block period)
		• *History Alive! The Medieval World and Beyond*
		• Interactive Student Notebooks
		• Visuals 16A–16C
		• Student Handout 16 (cut in half)
		• Information Master 16 (transparency)

Processing	20 minutes	• Interactive Student Notebooks
Assessment	40 minutes	• Chapter 16 Assessment

Preview

1 **Have students complete the Preview activity in their Interactive Student Notebooks.** Explain that a *characteristic* is a feature that describes a person, object, place, or event. Some characteristics are unique. For example, if you were giving the characteristics of a particular flower, you might say, "It has thorns and a nice smell." You would not say, "It has petals and a green stem," because most flowers have those features. To describe this flower—a rose— you would want to tell the characteristics of this particular kind of flower. (**Note:** To encourage students to think of characteristics that are unique, you might offer students a prize or extra credit if they think of a characteristic no one else does.)

2 **Have students share their responses in pairs or with the class.**

3 **Connect the Preview activity to the chapter.** Remind students that in the Preview activity they identified four characteristics of a classroom. These characteristics were things that distinguished a classroom from other types of rooms. Similarly, in the chapter and activity, they will identify the characteristics of Chinese agriculture, commerce, and urbanization to examine the growth of medieval China's economy.

Vocabulary Development

1 **Introduce the Key Content Terms.** Have students locate the Key Content Terms for the chapter in their Interactive Student Notebooks. These are important terms that will help them understand the main ideas of the chapter. Ask volunteers to identify any familiar terms and suggest how they might be used in a sentence.

2 **Have students complete a Vocabulary Development handout.** Give each student a copy of the Vocabulary Development handout of your choice from the Reading Toolkit at the back of the Lesson Masters. These handouts provide extra Key Content Term practice and support, depending on your students' needs. Review the completed handout by asking volunteers to share one answer for each term.

Reading

1 **Introduce the Essential Question and have students read Section 16.1.** Have students identify the Essential Question on the first page of the chapter: *How did the Chinese improve their economy during the Tang and Song dynasties?* Then have students read Section 16.1. Afterward, have students respond to this question: *How did China change during the Song dynasty?*

2 **Have students complete the Reading Notes for Chapter 16.** Assign Sections 16.2 to 16.6 during the activity, as indicated in the procedures for the Visual Discovery activity. Remind students to use the Key Content Terms where appropriate as they complete their Reading Notes.

> **Reading: Cause-and-Effect Pattern**
>
> Review cause and effect as a pattern of organization. Guide students to compile a list of words and phrases that signal causes and effects, such as *one reason why, as a result, therefore, because, so, since, due to,* and so on. Have students identify various causes and effects as they read. Then, at the close of the chapter, review cause and effect as a pattern of organization in expository text.

Visual Discovery

1. **Prepare materials and arrange the classroom.** Before class, place student desks in pairs angled toward the projection screen. Make one copy of *Student Handout 16: Preparing for an Act-It-Out on Life in a Song City*. Cut the pages in half so the questions for each of the eight groups are on one half-sheet of paper. Make a transparency of *Information Master 16: Conducting an Act-It-Out on Life in a Song City*.

2. **Introduce the activity.** Place students in pairs. Tell students they will now analyze images of medieval China and read to learn about changes that occurred in Chinese agriculture, commerce, and urbanization during the Tang and Song dynasties.

3. **Project *Visual 16A: Chinese Agriculture* and have students analyze the images.** Follow these steps to help them analyze the images:

   • Tell pairs to identify as many characteristics of Chinese agriculture as they can find in the images. Remind them that a *characteristic* is something special about a subject—in this case, agriculture. Encourage them to find unique characteristics by telling them that in the next step they will need to identify and describe at least one characteristic that no one else lists. For example, a student might say, "People planted rice seedlings by hand," or "Rice plants are grown in flooded fields."

   • Have one student from each pair come to the front of the room. Have students form a line along the front wall of the classroom with the head of the line near the projection screen. Show students the sheet of white poster board ("magic paper"). Explain that the "magic paper" can be held about a foot in front of the projection screen to enlarge a detail of the image. (**Note:** If you've never used "magic paper" with your students, you may want to demonstrate how this works.)

   • Give the first student in line the piece of "magic paper." Have that student hold the "magic paper" in front of the screen so that one characteristic is projected onto it. He or she should then identify and describe that characteristic. Have this student return to his or her seat when finished.

   • The next student in line should step forward and use the "magic paper" to identify and describe a different characteristic. Continue this process until all the characteristics of agriculture in the images have been identified.

4. **Have students read and complete Reading Notes for Section 16.2.**

5. **Debrief the image.** When students have finished reading the corresponding section, project Visual 16A again. Ask,

   • What characteristics of farming shown in these images were mentioned in the reading?

   • What characteristics of farming were mentioned in the reading, but are not shown in these images?

Student Handout 16

Information Master 16

Visual 16A

6 Repeat Steps 3–5 for *Visual 16B: Commerce in a Song City.* Make the following adaptations:

- In Step 4, have students read and complete the Reading Notes for Section 16.3.

- In Step 5, ask students about the characteristics of commerce shown in the transparency that were or were not mentioned in the section.

7 Repeat Steps 3–5 for *Visual 16C: Urbanization Under the Song.* Make the following adaptations:

- In Step 4, have students read and complete the Reading Notes for Section 16.4.

- In Step 5, ask students about the characteristics of urbanization shown in the transparency that were or were not mentioned in the section.

8 Prepare for an act-it-out using Visual 16C. Arrange students in eight groups. Explain that each group will represent one of the urban people shown in the last image they analyzed. Then help students prepare for the act-it-out by doing the following:

- To each group, distribute one of the eight sets of directions cut from Student Handout 16.

- Give each group a long strip of masking tape (for attaching their personal act-it-out questions to their clothing).

- Project Information Master 16 and review the directions with the class.

9 Conduct the act-it-out. Depending upon how in-depth you would like to make this part of the activity, you may want to adjust the length of time for students to act out their characters.

Visual 16B

Visual 16C

Processing

Have students complete the Processing activity on a separate sheet of paper or other appropriate material. Students will create an advertisement promoting the aspect of society they believe most improved the economy of medieval China.

Quicker Coverage

Eliminate the Act-It-Out After conducting the Visual Discovery activity for the three images on Visuals 16A–16C (Steps 1–7), skip the act-it-out (Steps 8–9).

Abbreviate the Image Analysis In Step 3 of the Visual Discovery activity, do not have pairs come to the front of the room to point out characteristics on each image. Instead, call on four to five pairs and ask them to tell you what characteristic they see. You can then use the "magic paper" to highlight each characteristic for the class.

Deeper Coverage

Have Students Create Skits After conducting Steps 1–7 of the Visual Discovery activity, divide the class into six groups of equal size (three groups if you have a smaller class). Assign two groups to represent agriculture, two to represent commerce, and two to represent urbanization. Have students create a 30-second skit that:

- explains at least two reasons for change in their aspect of society
- demonstrates at least three characteristics of their aspect of society
- explains at least two of the results of change in their aspect of society

Assessment

Mastering the Content

1. C	5. B	9. A	13. A
2. B	6. B	10. A	14. D
3. C	7. D	11. D	15. B
4. A	8. D	12. C	16. C

Applying Social Studies Skills

17. The number of copper coins made each year increased sharply, especially between the Tang and Song dynasties.

18. Trade and commerce increased greatly during the Song dynasty, so people needed coins for all that buying and selling.

19. By 1080 or 1085, so many copper coins were being made that there was a copper shortage. As a result, paper money was sometimes used instead.

Exploring the Essential Question

20. Answers should include all the elements requested in the prompt.

Scoring Rubric

Score	Description
3	Student identifies an appropriate person to interview for the three topics and lists two interview questions for each topic. Questions are clearly stated, worded to elicit relevant information, and demonstrate command of standard English conventions.
2	Student responds to most or all parts of the task, but interviewees may be inappropriate and questions may have only marginal relevance or not be clearly stated.
1	Student responds to at least one part of the task. Questions may contain grammatical errors and may lack relevance.
0	Response does not match the task or is incorrect.

English Language Learners

Add Roles for the Act-It-Out When conducting the act-it-out at the end of the Visual Discovery activity, consider adding nonspeaking roles for some students. Have these students act in the roles their groups have been assigned, but do not interview them.

Learners Reading and Writing Below Grade Level

Provide Assistance on the Reading Notes Make a photocopy of Sections 16.2 to 16.4 of the chapter. On the photocopy, circle the subheadings. Each of the three subheadings in each section corresponds to the three parts of the graphic organizer in the Reading Notes. On their copies, have students underline the reasons for change, the characteristics of that change, and the results of that change. Then have them copy that information into the graphic organizer in their Reading Notes.

Students with Special Needs

Provide Copies of Visuals The day before you begin the activity, give students photocopies of the images on the visuals (or just direct them to the images in Sections 16.2 to 16.4 in the text). Label Visual A "Agriculture," Visual B "Commerce," and Visual C "Urbanization." Explain to students that, in the activity, they will need to analyze these images to find characteristics of agriculture, commerce, and urbanization. Review with students what a characteristic is. Have them study the images that night for homework and find at least two characteristics for each. This will help ensure that they are prepared to contribute to the discussion during the Visual Discovery.

Modify the Act-It-Out Questions Modify the questions on Student Handout 16 to make them more direct. For example, for Group 1, Peasant Selling Homemade Silk, you might rewrite the questions in the following way:

- Do you grow crops and make silk, too? What is one crop you grow?
- Do you think more people drink more tea these days? Why?
- Do you make any other goods at home that you can sell in the city? What is one of those other goods?
- Have there been any discoveries that have made growing rice easier? Tell about one of them.

Advanced Learners

Make Connections Among Reading Notes Tell students to draw an arrow between details on the graphic organizers that represent a cause-and-effect relationship. For example, an arrow might be drawn from "Peasants could take time away from farming to make products to sell or trade" (Section 16.2 on the graphic organizer) to "Peasants sold surplus crops, animals, and goods they made at home" (Section 16.3). Have students draw each arrow in a different color to make the cause/effect relationships easier to trace. Then have students meet in groups of four to compare the connections they found.

Create an Alternative Processing Activity In place of the current Processing activity, have students create a journal of a person who moves from a rural area to a city in medieval China. The journal should include:

- an entry summarizing the changes the person experienced in rural China
- an entry explaining why the person moved to the urban area
- an entry describing how the city is different from the country
- historical details from Chapter 16 to make the story come alive
- at least one appropriate illustration

Enrichment Resources

Find out more about the development of a new economy in medieval China under the Tang and Song by exploring the following Enrichment Resources for *History Alive! The Medieval World and Beyond* at www.teachtci.com.

Enrichment Readings These in-depth readings encourage students to explore selected topics related to the chapter. You may also find readings that relate the chapter's content directly to your state's curriculum.

Internet Connections The recommended Web sites provide useful and engaging content that reinforces skills development and mastery of subjects within the chapter.

Literature Recommendations

The following books offer opportunities to extend the content in this chapter.

A Grain of Rice by Helena C. Pittman (New York: Skylark, 1996)

Marco Polo: A Journey Through China by Fiona MacDonald and Mark Bergin (Danbury, CT: Franklin Watts, 1998)

The Silk Route: 7,000 Miles of History by John S. Major (New York: HarperCollins, 1995)

Section 16.2

Answers will vary. Possible reasons for agricultural changes: farmers moved to the south, a good region for growing rice; a new type of rice was introduced; an improved plow and harrow were developed; and farmers fertilized their crops.

Possible characteristics of the new agriculture: crops were grown on terraced hillsides; chain pumps were used for irrigation; water buffaloes pulled plows; rice plants began to be grown in seedbeds; rice growing took a lot of work by many people; rice was transplanted to paddies; cotton, sugar, tea, and mulberry trees were grown; a new kind of fast-growing, drought-resistant rice was grown; improved plows and harrows were used.

Results of agricultural changes: increased food production; abundance of food helped support a larger population; peasants could take time away from farming to make products to sell or trade; rich landowners could buy luxury items; and these changes encouraged the growth of trade and commerce.

Section 16.3

Answers will vary. Possible reasons commerce developed: there was a vast system of rivers and canals; improvements in navigation made long sea voyages easier; wealthy landowners demanded more goods; and paper currency helped trade.

Possible characteristics of China's commercial growth: goods were moved along canals on barges; junks were used for trade with foreign countries; peasants sold surplus crops, animals, and goods they made at home; oxcarts and pack animals moved products along roads; small shops lined streets and bridges; people used paper money and traded in copper coins at deposit shops; indigo, spices, silver, ivory, and coral were imported.

Results of growth in trade and commerce: growth of the merchant class; increased prosperity gave China the highest standard of living in the world; and commercial centers grew into big cities.

Section 16.4

Answers will vary. Possible reasons for urbanization: people came to the cities to trade as commerce increased; and large landowners moved to cities because they preferred the shops and social life there.

Possible characteristics of cities: cities were crowded and exciting; many types of people lived in the cities; signs identified the many goods being sold; there were theaters and outdoor entertainers; urban women had less status than rural women; Chinese cities were the largest in the world; restaurants, wine shops, and teahouses provided food and drink; vendors sold food from trays carried on their heads; silk and many other items were for sale.

Results of urbanization: vibrant centers of activity changed the way many ordinary Chinese lived; public works projects provided employment; and artists gained a wealthy audience, encouraging the growth of arts and culture

Chinese Discoveries and Inventions

How have medieval Chinese discoveries and inventions influenced the modern world?

Overview

In a Social Studies Skill Builder, students investigate Chinese discoveries and inventions to determine their influence on the modern world.

Objectives

In the course of reading this chapter and participating in the classroom activity, students will

Social Studies

- describe Chinese technological developments from about 200 to 1400 C.E., especially during the Tang and Song dynasties.

- analyze the ways in which such Chinese inventions such as gunpowder, the compass, and printing, affected China and the rest of the world.

Language Arts

- arrange supporting details, reasons, descriptions, and examples effectively and persuasively in relation to an audience.

Social Studies Vocabulary

Key Content Terms movable type, mass-produce, gunpowder, inoculate

Academic Vocabulary magnetic, segment, fundamental

Materials

History Alive! The Medieval World and Beyond

Interactive Student Notebooks

Placards 17A–17J

Lesson Masters

- Information Master 17 (1 transparency)
- Vocabulary Development handout (1 per student, on colored paper)

masking tape

Activity	Suggested Time	Materials
Preview	15–20 minutes	• *History Alive! The Medieval World and Beyond* • Interactive Student Notebooks
Vocabulary Development	30–40 minutes	• *History Alive! The Medieval World and Beyond* • Interactive Student Notebook • Vocabulary Development handout
Social Studies Skill Builder	60-90 minutes (2 regular periods) (1 block period)	• *History Alive! The Medieval World and Beyond* • Interactive Student Notebooks • Placards 17A–17J • Information Master 17
Processing	20–30 minutes	• Interactive Student Notebooks
Assessment	40 minutes	• Chapter 17 Assessment

Preview

1 **Introduce the Preview activity.** Explain that in this lesson, students will examine Chinese discoveries and inventions that affected both China and the rest of the world. As they take notes on these achievements, they will write the Chinese character for each. First, they will learn the proper method of forming Chinese characters.

2 **Practice drawing Chinese characters.** On a whiteboard or overhead transparency, review the guidelines for drawing the strokes of Chinese characters on the Preview page. Then, have students follow along by tracing the strokes for *day* with a finger, as you say the stroke number aloud and draw it on the whiteboard or overhead. Next, have students follow the diagram to create the character for *day* in the Preview activity in their Interactive Student Notebooks. Ask students to write the character at least twice. Have them repeat this process for *wood* and *mountain.*

3 **Connect the Preview activity to the chapter.** In the Preview activity, students learned how to create Chinese characters, and practiced a few simple ones. Tell students that in the chapter, they will read about various Chinese discoveries and inventions, such as tea, paper, woodblock printing, the compass, and gunpowder. During the activity, they will analyze images of each discovery or invention, determine the impact of the discovery or invention, and reproduce the Chinese character for each.

Vocabulary Development

1 **Introduce the Key Content Terms**. Have students locate the Key Content Terms for the chapter in their Interactive Student Notebooks. These are important terms that will help them understand the main ideas of the chapter. Ask volunteers to identify any familiar terms and suggest how they might be used in a sentence.

2 **Have students complete a Vocabulary Development handout.** Give each student a copy of the Vocabulary Development handout of your choice from the Reading Toolkit at the back of the Lesson Masters. These handouts provide extra Key Content Term practice and support, depending on your students' needs. Review the completed handout by asking volunteers to share one answer for each term.

Reading

1 Introduce the Essential Question and have students read Section 17.1.
Have students identify the Essential Question on the first page of the chapter:
How have medieval Chinese discoveries and inventions influenced the modern world? Then have students read Section 17.1. Afterward, have students use information from Section 17.1 and from the chapter opener image to propose some possible answers to the Essential Question.

2 Have students complete the Reading Notes for Chapter 17. Assign Sections 17.2 to 17.6 during the activity, as indicated in the procedures for the Social Studies Skill Builder. Remind students to use the Key Content Terms where appropriate as they complete their Reading Notes.

Social Studies Skill Builder

1 Before class, prepare the classroom. Post *Placards 17A–17J: Chinese Discoveries and Inventions* on the walls around the classroom to create ten separate stations. Either place two student books at each station, or have students carry theirs with them during the activity.

2 Place students in pairs and introduce the activity. Tell students that in this activity they will visit ten stations, each one highlighting a medieval Chinese discovery or invention. Project *Information Master 17: Learning About Chinese Discoveries and Inventions* and review the steps with students.

3 Monitor students' work. Have pairs go to a station and begin working.

- Depending on class size, you will probably have more than one pair at each station. If you have a large class, consider creating additional copies of the placards.

- Check students' work as they finish at a station before sending them on to a new station. You may want to do this for just the first one or two placards until you are confident that students understand the process and are following the instructions correctly.

- Once students have finished analyzing all the placards, have them move to Step 5 on Information Master 17. If necessary, remind students of the purpose of a spectrum.

4 Debrief the activity. Wrap up the activity by doing the following:

- Create a spectrum by placing a 10- to 15-foot strip of masking tape along the floor at the front of the room. On the board above opposite ends of the spectrum, write "Least Influential to the Modern World" and "Most Influential to the Modern World."

- Group pairs together to form ten groups. Remove the placards from the wall and assign one to each group.

- Tell students that based on their reading and Reading Notes, they should determine where on the spectrum they would place their placards.

Placards 17A–17J

Information Master 17

- Have one student from each group come forward to stand on the spectrum where the group thinks their contribution belongs. Tell students to hold their placards in front of them.

- Challenge the other students to identify contributions they believe are misplaced. Encourage discussion about where the contributions should be placed. The purpose of this activity is not to find "correct" locations, but to have students support their evaluations and opinions.

5 **Assign the Reading Notes for Sections 17.2–17.6 (Part 2).** Students review Sections 17.2 through 17.6 and complete a scroll in their Reading Notes to list additional discoveries and inventions that were not pictured on the placards.

Processing

Have students complete the Processing activity on a separate sheet of paper in their notebooks. Students create a scroll that celebrates the four Chinese discoveries or inventions that they believe have had the greatest effect on the world.

Quicker Coverage

Skip the Activity Debrief After having students complete Steps 1–3 of the Social Studies Skill Builder activity, do not have the class create the spectrum with the placards (Step 4). Instead, you may want to hold a quick discussion of the spectrum they completed in their Reading Notes, or just skip this step entirely.

Deeper Coverage

Expand the Activity Debrief Conduct Steps 1–3 of the Social Studies Skill Builder, as written above. Then assign Step 5, where students complete the Reading Notes for Sections 17.2–17.6. Finally, assign Step 4, the activity debrief, with these modifications:

- Assign each of the ten groups a placard to represent; also assign them one or two of the inventions or discoveries covered in the Reading Notes for Sections 17.2–17.6. Groups should make a sign with the name of their additional invention or discovery, and draw a quick illustration of it.

- Have groups come up with a one-sentence explanation of where they would place each of their inventions or discoveries on the spectrum.

- Have students come up to the spectrum, one at a time, as you say the name of each invention or discovery. Students should explain why their group has placed the invention or discovery at a certain point on the spectrum.

- Allow students to debate the placement of the invention or discovery, if necessary, before having the next student come up to the spectrum. Repeat this process for all inventions and discoveries.

> **Listening and Speaking: Ask Questions**
>
> As students present their group's choice, put the accent on listening, as well as speaking, by encouraging listeners to ask questions to learn more, including the reasons and evidence that support the choice. As needed, model questions that probe specific pieces of information, as well as the position on the spectrum.

Assessment

Mastering the Content

1. C	5. B	9. C	13. C
2. A	6. D	10. D	14. D
3. B	7. D	11. B	15. C
4. C	8. A	12. D	16. A

Applying Social Studies Skills

17. The lock would be most useful where the ground slopes steeply and the barge or boat would be very hard to move upstream.

18. Answers will vary. Sample answer: A. I open the lower gate so the boat can enter the lock. B. I close both gates and wait for the lock to fill with water, raising the boat to the upper level. C. I open the upper gate so the boat can leave the lock and continue upstream.

19. Students should circle answer choice B, gravity. Sample explanation: The lock fills and empties because the water flows downstream. When the upper gate is closed, the water flows out to the lower level. When the lower gate is closed, water flows in from above. Gravity makes the water flow downhill.

Exploring the Essential Question

20. Answers should include all the elements requested in the prompt.

Scoring Rubric

Score	Description
3	Student completes top and bottom of all four hourglasses. Entries are clearly stated, supported by details, and demonstrate command of standard English conventions.
2	Student responds to most or all parts of the task, but entries may lack details or not be clearly stated.
1	Student responds to at least one part of the task. Entries may contain factual and/or grammatical errors and may lack details.
0	Response does not match the task or is incorrect.

English Language Learners

Create Focused Reading Sheets Instead of having students skim Sections 17.2–17.6 after examining each placard during the activity, create focused reading sheets to accompany each placard. Photocopy the page(s) of *History Alive! The Medieval World and Beyond* that relate to each placard. Focus the amount of text that students will read by highlighting key sentences or passages that pertain to the invention or discovery on that placard. Place these focused reading sheets in envelopes next to their corresponding placards. Have students consult these sheets, rather than their books, to complete the Reading Notes.

Learners Reading and Writing Below Grade Level

Model the Activity Model the steps of the Social Studies Skill Builder by exploring one Chinese invention as a class. Make a transparency of Placard 17A. Then go through the steps on Information Master 17. Have volunteers share answers aloud, and write them on a transparency of the Reading Notes. Once students have a general understanding of the assignment, have pairs begin working on their own.

Demonstrate Step 2 on Information Master 17 Show students how they can use the section titles and subsection headings of Chapter 17 as clues to help find the section of Chapter 17 that corresponds to each placard. For example, for Placard 17A, students can quickly review the section titles and recognize that the compass is probably described in Section 17.2, in the subsection "Improving Travel by Sea."

Learners with Special Education Needs

Select Mixed-Ability Pairs Support students who may have difficulty with the Social Studies Skill Builder by pairing them with students who can help them. For students who may have difficulty writing, have their partners record their joint answers on one copy of the Reading Notes, which can later be photocopied. Pair up students who may struggle with reading with proficient readers who can read the sections aloud.

Simplify the Processing Activity Have these students select only three (or fewer) Chinese discoveries or inventions. Also, instead of having students write a paragraph for Step 2, allow them to explain their selections orally.

Advanced Learners

Create an Alternative Processing Activity Instead of the current Processing activity, challenge students to compare the discoveries and inventions of the last century with the Chinese inventions from Chapter 17. Begin by having the class brainstorm inventions of the last century under the categories discussed in Chapter 17: exploration and travel, industry, military technology, everyday objects, and disease prevention. Possible modern-day inventions could include airplanes, robotics, nuclear weapons, computers, and anti-bacterial hand sanitizer. Then have students create a "Best Discoveries and Inventions" poster that showcases the discoveries and inventions of both China, between 200 and 1400 C.E., and the modern world. The poster should include the following:

- a title
- the names of the five categories of competition: exploration and travel, industry, military technology, everyday objects, and disease prevention
- labeled drawings of a Chinese invention and a modern invention under each category
- a blue ribbon next to the most important invention in each category
- a short description of why the invention in each category was awarded a blue ribbon

Enrichment Resources

Find out more about Chinese discoveries and inventions by exploring the following Enrichment Resources for *History Alive! The Medieval World and Beyond* at www.teachtci.com.

Enrichment Readings These in-depth readings encourage students to explore selected topics related to the chapter. You may also find readings that relate the chapter's content directly to your state's curriculum.

Internet Connections The recommended Web sites provide useful and engaging content that reinforces skills development and mastery of subjects within the chapter.

Literature Recommendations

The following books offer opportunities to extend the content in this chapter.

Legacies from Ancient China by Anita Ganeri (North Mankato, MN: Thameside Press, 2000)

Oracle Bones, Stars, and Wheelbarrows: Ancient Chinese Science and Technology by Frank Ross, Jr. (Boston: Houghton Mifflin Company, 1989)

Science in Ancient China by George W. Beshore (Danbury, CT: Grolier Publishing, 1998)

Sections 17.2 to 17.6 (Part 1)

Answers will vary. Possible answers include:

A: Compass
Section 17.2: Exploration and Travel

Summary of invention: Early Chinese compasses were made of a magnetic ore called lodestone, but later it was replaced by a steel needle. Summary of influence: The compass still helps travelers navigate.

B: Smallpox Inoculation
Section 17.6: Disease Prevention

Summary of invention: The Chinese inoculated people against smallpox by exposing them to a small amount of a virus. Summary of influence: Today there are vaccines for many diseases, such as smallpox and the flu.

C: Paper Money
Section 17.5: Everyday Objects

Summary of invention: Paper money was printed with wood blocks, using many colors on each bill. Summary of influence: Paper money is the most common form of currency today.

D: Mechanical Clock
Section 17.5: Everyday Objects

Summary of invention: The first mechanical clock had a wheel, turned by dripping water, that made one revolution every 24 hours. Every quarter hour, drums would beat; every hour, a bell would chime, so people knew what time it was. Summary of influence: Modern mechanical clocks are based on the same principles as early Chinese clocks.

E: Rocket
Section 17.4: Military Technology

Summary of invention: At first, rockets were used only in fireworks; later, as weapons to drop arrows over enemies. Summary of influence: The rockets we use to explore space are based on the same principles as ancient Chinese rockets.

F: Movable Type
Section 17.3: Industry

Summary of invention: Movable type used a separate block of baked clay for each character. Summary of influence: Until relatively recently, all newspapers, books, and magazines were printed using movable type.

G: Canal Lock
Section 17.2: Exploration and Travel

Summary of invention: The canal lock allowed boats to pass from one level to another in a canal, and could raise boats 100 feet above sea level. Summary of influence: Canal locks are still used on modern canals, such as the Panama Canal.

H: Porcelain
Section 17.3: Industry

Summary of invention: Porcelain is a form of beautiful pottery that was mass-produced in medieval China. Summary of influence: Fine dishes are still called "china," in reference to Chinese porcelain.

I: Gunpowder
Section 17.4: Military Technology

Summary of invention: Experiments with explosive saltpeter led to the manufacture of gunpowder and, eventually, to powerful weapons. Summary of influence: Gunpowder changed the way wars were conducted around the world.

J: Tea
Section 17.3: Industry

Summary of invention: The Chinese have been drinking tea—tea leaves steeped in boiling water—for thousands of years. Summary of influence: People around the world drink tea for enjoyment and for their health.

Sections 17.2 to 17.6 (Part 2)

Symbols will vary.

Section 17.2

Improved boat construction. watertight compartments

Made bridges flatter and stronger. segmental arch bridge

Section 17.3

Made from bark; became an important industry. papermaking

Led to the printing of modern-style books. woodblock printing

Stronger and lighter than iron. steel

Section 17.4

Made from gunpowder mixed with oil. flamethrower

Caused a loud sound when exploded. artillery shell

A slingshot-like war machine to shoot arrows. catapult

Small bomb thrown by hand. grenade

Section 17.5

Made from woodblock printing on thick paper. game cards

Section 17.6

Poisonous smoke used to kill germs. disinfectant

China's Contacts with the Outside World

How did the foreign-contact policies of three medieval Chinese dynasties affect China?

Overview

In a Response Group activity, students consider the benefits and drawbacks of foreign contact during three Chinese dynasties, and evaluate the effects on China of their foreign-contact policies.

Objectives

In the course of reading this chapter and participating in the classroom activity, students will

Social Studies

- explain the importance of overland trade and identify products that traveled along trade routes during the Tang and Yuan dynasties.
- describe the importance of maritime expeditions during the Ming dynasty.
- evaluate the benefits and drawbacks of foreign contact during each dynasty's rule.

Language Arts

- determine the speaker's attitude toward the subject.
- respond to persuasive messages with questions, challenges, or affirmations.
- write a persuasive composition that states a clear position and describes the points in support of the proposition.

Social Studies Vocabulary

Key Content Terms Mongols, maritime, Ming, tributary

Academic Vocabulary import, status, accumulate, astronomy

Materials

History Alive! The Medieval World and Beyond

Interactive Student Notebooks

Visuals 18A–18C

CD Tracks 8–10

Lesson Masters

- Student Handout 18 (1 per student–class set)
- Vocabulary Development handout (1 per student on colored paper)

transparency pens

Activity	Suggested Time	Materials
Preview	10 minutes	• Interactive Student Notebooks
Vocabulary Development	30–40 minutes	• *History Alive! The Medieval World and Beyond* • Interactive Student Notebooks • Vocabulary Development handout
Response Group	90–120 minutes (2–3 regular periods) (1–1.5 block periods)	• *History Alive! The Medieval World and Beyond* • Interactive Student Notebooks • Visuals 18A–18C • CD tracks 8–10 • Student Handout 18 • transparency pens
Processing	20–30 minutes	• Interactive Student Notebooks
Assessment	40 minutes	• Chapter 18 Assessment

Preview

1   **Place students in groups of three and have them complete the Preview activity in their Interactive Student Notebooks.** Read the situation from the Preview activity aloud and then review the directions with students. Have groups work together to determine the arguments for an open-door and for a closed-door policy. (**Note:** Students will stay in their groups of three during the activity).

2   **Have groups share their responses with the class.** Select some groups to share their responses for an open-door policy, and others to share their responses for a closed-door policy.

3   **Connect the Preview activity to the chapter.** Tell students that in the Preview activity they looked at the advantages and disadvantages of contact with neighbors. In this chapter and activity, they will learn that throughout China's history there has been much disagreement about whether to have an open- or closed-door policy toward foreigners. Sometimes, China opened its doors to foreign trade and visitors. At other times, it slammed them shut and tried to isolate itself from the rest of the world.

Vocabulary Development

1   **Introduce the Key Content Terms.** Have students locate the Key Content Terms for the chapter in their Interactive Student Notebooks. These are important terms that will help them understand the main ideas of the chapter. Ask volunteers to identify any familiar terms and suggest how they might be used in a sentence.

2   **Have students complete a Vocabulary Development handout.** Give each student a copy of the Vocabulary Development handout of your choice from the Reading Toolkit at the back of the Lesson Masters. These handouts provide extra Key Content Term practice and support, depending on your students' needs. Review the completed handout by asking volunteers to share one answer for each term.

Reading

1   **Introduce the Essential Question and have students read Section 18.1.** Have students identify the Essential Question on the first page of the chapter: *How did the foreign-contact policies of three medieval Chinese dynasties affect China?* Then have students read Section 18.1. Afterward, have students use information from Section 18.1 and from the chapter opener image to propose some possible answers to the Essential Question.

2   **Have students complete the Reading Notes for Chapter 18.** Assign Sections 18.2 to 18.4 during the activity as indicated in the procedures for the Response Group activity. Remind students to use the Key Content Terms where appropriate as they complete their Reading Notes.

Response Group

1 **Introduce the activity and distribute materials.** Explain to students that they will listen to three conversations about China's contact with foreigners during three periods of Chinese history: the Tang dynasty; the Yuan dynasty; and the Ming dynasty. Emphasize that the dialogues are fictional and represent opinions rather than facts. After listening to each dialogue, students will evaluate the government's decisions about foreign contact. Distribute one copy of *Student Handout 18: Three Dialogues About Foreign Contact* to each student. Tell students they will use this transcript as they listen to the dialogues about each dynasty. (**Note:** You can reuse these handouts with each class, so you may want to ask that students not write on them).

Student Handout 18

2 **Conduct the first dialogue.** Conduct the dialogue that takes place during the Tang dynasty by doing the following:

- Before beginning the dialogue, remind students that the Tang dynasty ruled China from 618 to 907. Have them examine the map of the Silk Road during the Tang dynasty, in Section 18.2 of *History Alive! The Medieval World and Beyond.* Explain that the Silk Road stretched from China to the eastern shore of the Mediterranean Sea. People, goods, and ideas traveled along this route. In addition, sea routes provided another way for China to interact with the outside world.

3 **Project *Visual 18A: In a Teahouse During the Tang Dynasty.*** Tell students they are about to hear a conversation between two Tang officials in a Chinese teahouse—one who supports an open-door policy and one who supports a closed-door policy. As students listen to the recording, they should read along with the first dialogue on Student Handout 18. Play CD Track 8, "A Conversation in a Tearoom."

Visual 18A

4 **Have students read Section 18.2 and complete the Reading Notes.**

5 **Have students participate in a Response Group discussion.** Have students share their responses to the questions in the Reading Notes for Section 18.2 by doing the following:

- Assign each group a number. Have one member of each group use a transparency pen to write the group's number above the spectrum on Visual 18A in the same location as the X on their group's Reading Notes.

- Have each group choose a presenter for this dialogue. Then select a few groups who chose different points on the spectrum to defend their choices.

- Encourage debate by asking other groups who may not have presented to provide alternative points of view about where they placed their numbers on the spectrum.

6 Repeat Steps 3–5 for the dialogue during the Yuan dynasty. Make the following modifications:

- Before beginning the dialogue, remind students that the Mongols were foreign invaders from north of China who named their dynasty the Yuan dynasty. They ruled China from 1279 to 1368. As in the previous period, people, ideas, and goods traveled along both the Silk Road and sea routes.

- Step 3: Project *Visual 18B: At the Khan's Court During the Yuan Dynasty.* Tell students that they will hear a conversation between two officials at the khan's court. You may need to explain that *khan* is the Mongolian title for a ruler. Play CD Track 9, "A Conversation in Khan's Court."

- Step 4: Read and complete the Reading Notes for Section 18.3.

- Step 5: Use the Step 3 question in the Reading Notes for Section 18.3.

Visual 18B

7 Repeat Steps 3–5 for the dialogue during the Ming dynasty. Make the following modifications:

- Before beginning the dialogue, tell students that the Ming dynasty followed the Mongol dynasty and ruled China from 1368 to 1644. Early Ming emperors were very interested in contact with foreign lands. Have students turn to the map of Zheng He's voyages in Section 18.4 in their books and name some of the countries he visited. Explain that later Ming officials stopped these expeditions and attempted to restrict trade.

- Step 3: Project *Visual 18C: On the Dock During the Ming Dynasty.* Tell students they are about to hear a conversation between two officials at the docks during the Ming dynasty. Play CD Track 10, "A Conversation on the Dock During the Ming Period."

- Step 4: Read and complete the Reading Notes for Section 18.4.

- Step 5: Use the Step 3 question in the Reading Notes for Section 18.4.

Visual 18C

8 Hold a class discussion. Ask,

- What are some of the strongest arguments in favor of China having foreign contacts? Against China having foreign contacts?

- What do you think would be the negative effects of China refusing all contacts with foreign countries at this time?

- What do you think would be the negative effects of China accepting all contacts with foreign countries at this time?

Processing

Have students complete the Processing activity. Students will write a proclamation from a Ming emperor regarding foreign contact. Explain to students, if necessary, that a proclamation is an official statement of law, usually made by a ruler. Students write five reasons to support their proclamation and add an illustration for each.

Quicker Coverage

Skip the Dialogues To more quickly accomplish the activity, skip Step 3 in the Response Group directions, and Step 1 in the Reading Notes directions. Students will still read each section, complete the Reading Notes, and debate the Reading Notes Step 3 question for each dynasty.

Skip the Response Group Discussion To more quickly accomplish the activity, skip Step 5 in the Response Group directions. Students will still listen to the dialogues, read each section and complete the Reading Notes, and respond to the Reading Notes Step 3 question for each section; but groups will not debate with the class.

Deeper Coverage

Add to the Dialogues After reading each section, have groups write additional conversation for each dialogue. Students should add to the dialogues by using facts from the reading to create one or two more arguments in favor of an open-door policy and one or two more arguments in favor of a closed-door policy.

Assessment

Mastering the Content

1. B	5. C	9. C	13. D
2. D	6. A	10. D	14. C
3. B	7. B	11. C	15. A
4. A	8. A	12. D	16. B

Applying Social Studies Skills

17. It was about halfway along the Silk Road; several different routes came together there.

18. the need to avoid the most difficult, dangerous parts of the desert and mountains; lack of water.

19. Answers will vary. Sample answer: Merchants who traveled the Silk Road wanted to sell goods to Europeans and others in the huge Mediterranean market. Land routes to Persia and India were blocked by mountains and rivers.

Exploring the Essential Question

20. Answers should include all the elements requested in the prompt.

Scoring Rubric

Score	Description
3	Student completes an editorial that addresses all five bulleted points. The editorial is clearly stated, supported by details, and demonstrates command of standard English conventions.
2	Student responds to most or all parts of the task, but the editorial may lack details or not be clearly stated.
1	Student responds to at least one part of the task. The editorial may contain factual and/or grammatical errors and may lack details.
0	Response does not match the task or is incorrect.

The Explorations of Admiral Zheng He

1   **Prepare students to read the Chapter 18 Reading Further.** Ask students to name famous explorers and summarize what they know about them. Explain that when they tell or read the story of an explorer's life, they are telling or reading a *narrative*. A narrative has a plot, or story line, with a beginning, a middle, and an end. Tell students that they will now read a narrative of the life of Chinese explorer Zheng He (JENG HAY).

2   **Have students read the Chapter 18 Reading Further.** Tell students to jot down important plot points as they read the narrative of Zheng He's life.

3   **Complete a story map to summarize the narrative of Zheng He's life.** When students have finished reading, complete a story map for Zheng He's life by writing the following items on the board, either in a list or in a chart: story title; setting; main character(s); and major events of the beginning, middle, and end of the story. Tell students that a story map helps to summarize the main parts of a narrative. It can also help when students are planning to write a new narrative.

4   **Have students complete the Reading Further activity in their Interactive Student Notebooks.** Students will write an autobiographical narrative telling about a fun or exciting experience they have had. Before students begin to work on the story maps and then on their narratives, review what an *autobiography* is. Remind students that "first person" means that a story is told from the narrator's—in this case the student's—point of view.

5   **Have volunteers read their autobiographical narratives to the class.** Encourage students to use an animated and lively voice to enhance the reading of their narratives.

English Language Learners

Break Conversations into Manageable Parts Make sure students understand the ideas being presented in the three CD conversations by breaking each conversation into manageable parts. Pause the CD after every two or four exchanges, and have groups identify one or two arguments from that part of the script in favor of welcoming foreigners, and one or two in favor of rejecting foreigners.

Add a Step to the Reading Notes Help students connect the dialogues on the CD by giving each student a copy of Chapter 18. Have students read the corresponding section of the chapter after they listen to each dialogue on Student Handout 18. Then have them underline any details in the dialogue that were also included in the chapter.

• Help students focus their reading by explaining that the first subsection generally corresponds to the open-door perspective and the second to the closed-door perspective.

• Have students read the first subsection and underline, in one color, the corresponding points on Student Handout 18. Then have them read the second subsection and underline the corresponding points in another color.

Learners Reading and Writing Below Grade Level

Simplify the Processing Activity Directions Provide students with the following simplified directions for the Processing activity.

Pretend you are a Ming emperor. You must decide what type of policy China should have with the outside world. Create a royal proclamation to explain your opinion. Your proclamation should:

• clearly state whether your policy welcomes or rejects contact with the outside world

• list three reasons why your policy is good for China. Each reason should begin, "This policy is good for China because . . ."

• include illustrations to help explain your three reasons

Learners with Special Education Needs

Preview the Activity Give students a copy of Student Handout 18 ahead of time. Tell them they will listen to a CD recording of these dialogues in class. When Chapter 18 is presented in class, these students will already be familiar with the arguments.

Shorten the Processing Activity To more appropriately challenge students, offer an alternate Processing activity. Have students complete this statement: "I proclaim that China will have an open-door/closed-door policy (circle one) that welcomes/rejects (circle one) contact with the outside world because . . . ." Have students provide two reasons for their choice, and illustrate at least one.

Advanced Learners

Create an Illustrated Map Provide students with a map of Asia, preferably one on which the countries are labeled. As students complete the Reading Notes, challenge them to do the following for each section:

• For countries that had contact with China, draw arrows from the country to China; where possible, put arrows over the land for countries that had overland trade routes to China, and put arrows over the water for countries that had maritime trade routes to China.

• Color the arrows to correspond to dynasties. For example, if Persia traded with China during the Tang dynasty, students might make that arrow green. Any other arrows representing trade during the Tang dynasty (Section 18.2) would also be green. Have students put the appropriate colors and labels in a key.

Enrichment Resources

Find out more about foreign contact during three Chinese dynasties by exploring the following Enrichment Resources for *History Alive! The Medieval World and Beyond* at www.teachtci.com.

Enrichment Readings These in-depth readings encourage students to explore selected topics related to the chapter. You may also find readings that relate the chapter's content directly to your state's curriculum.

Internet Connections The recommended Web sites provide useful and engaging content that reinforces skills development and mastery of subjects within the chapter.

Literature Recommendations

The following books offer opportunities to extend the content in this chapter.

China's Golden Age: Everyday Life in the Tang Dynasty by Charles Benn (New York: Oxford University Press, USA, 2004)

The Kite Rider by Geraldine Mccaughrean (New York: HarperTeen, 2002)

The Remarkable Journey of Prince Jen by Lloyd Alexander (New York: Dutton, 1991)

Section 18.2

1. Answers may include six of the following: the Central Asian kingdoms, Persia, the Byzantine Empire, Korea, Japan, Indonesia, India, Turkey, and Tibet.

2. Foreigners: Foreigners were less welcome, partly because of attacks on China by foreigners; restrictions were placed on foreigners and violence broke out against foreign merchants. Buddhists: Buddhism was attacked as a foreign religion; the government seized Buddhist property and monasteries, shrines, and temples were destroyed. Trade routes: Trade continued with other lands, but began to shift from the Silk Road to a flourishing sea trade with the countries of Southeast Asia.

Step 3: Answers will vary; accept all reasonable responses.

Section 18.3

1. Merchants were respected and trade along the Silk Road flourished; goods such as medicine, perfume, and ivory were brought to China. Maritime trade flourished and new goods, such as pearls, ginger, cotton, muslin, black pepper, white walnuts, and cloves were brought from various countries. Foreign visitors brought special skills, such as architecture, astronomy, mathematics, medicine, and water management. Skills, information, and inventions from China spread to other parts of the world.

2. During the Yuan dynasty, the Mongols awarded foreigners high status and special privileges. Many visiting foreigners were appointed to official government positions. Life was more pleasant for Mongols and foreigners than it was for the native Chinese, who were at the bottom of the social order. They resented the many restrictions placed on them and disliked being ruled by foreigners. Eventually, that resentment made the Chinese suspicious of further contact with foreigners.

Step 3: Answers will vary; accept all reasonable responses.

Section 18.4

1. The Ming saw China as the oldest, largest, most civilized, and most important country in the world. They felt other nations should acknowledge China's superiority by paying tribute.

2. Zheng He's expeditions were meant to parade China's power, give gifts, and collect tribute from foreign nations.

3. Later Ming rulers wanted to protect their people from foreign influences. They forbade travel outside China, and limited Chinese contact with foreigners. Their desire for a strongly unified state, based on a single ruler and traditional values, led to a huge government bureaucracy led by scholar-officials. This made it difficult for the government to respond to new conditions, and as the government became too rigid to adapt, peasants were able to bring down the government by rebelling.

Step 3: Answers will vary; accept all reasonable responses.

Imperial China

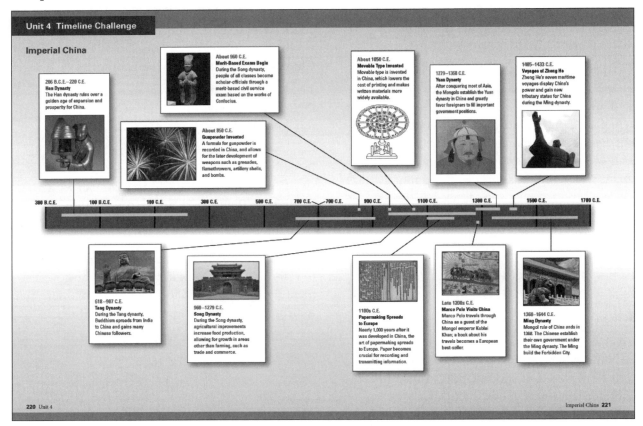

Unit 4 Timeline Challenge

Imperial China

206 B.C.E.–220 C.E.
Han Dynasty
The Han dynasty rules over a golden age of expansion and prosperity for China.

About 960 C.E.
Merit-Based Exams Begin
During the Song dynasty, people of all classes become scholar-officials through a merit-based civil service exam based on the works of Confucius.

About 850 C.E.
Gunpowder Invented
A formula for gunpowder is recorded in China, and allows for the later development of weapons such as grenades, flamethrowers, artillery shells, and bombs.

About 1050 C.E.
Movable Type Invented
Movable type is invented in China, which lowers the cost of printing and makes written materials more widely available.

1279–1368 C.E.
Yuan Dynasty
After conquering most of Asia, the Mongols establish the Yuan dynasty in China and greatly favor foreigners to fill important government positions.

1405–1433 C.E.
Voyages of Zheng He
Zheng He's seven maritime voyages display China's power and gain new tributary states for China during the Ming dynasty.

300 B.C.E.   100 B.C.E.   100 C.E.   300 C.E.   500 C.E.   700 C.E.   700 C.E.   900 C.E.   1100 C.E.   1300 C.E.   1500 C.E.   1700 C.E.

618–907 C.E.
Tang Dynasty
During the Tang dynasty, Buddhism spreads from India to China and gains many Chinese followers.

960–1279 C.E.
Song Dynasty
During the Song dynasty, agricultural improvements increase food production, allowing for growth in areas other than farming, such as trade and commerce.

1100s C.E.
Papermaking Spreads to Europe
Nearly 1,000 years after it was developed in China, the art of papermaking spreads to Europe. Paper becomes crucial for recording and transmitting information.

Late 1200s C.E.
Marco Polo Visits China
Marco Polo travels through China as a guest of the Mongol emperor Kublai Khan; a book about his travels becomes a European best-seller.

1368–1644 C.E.
Ming Dynasty
Mongol rule of China ends in 1368. The Chinese establish their own government under the Ming dynasty. The Ming build the Forbidden City.

220 Unit 4   Imperial China 221

Overview

This Timeline Challenge helps students review the main events and ideas of this unit while providing practice in reading and interpreting timelines. You can vary and expand the activity according to students' needs and the amount of time available.

Basic Procedure

1 **Introduce the timeline in the Student Edition.** Direct students to the Imperial China Timeline at the end of Unit 4 in the Student Edition. You may wish to have students read aloud and discuss the timeline entries.

2 **Introduce the Timeline Challenge in the Interactive Student Notebook.** Direct students to the Unit 4 Timeline Challenge. Point out the two types of questions, "Timeline Skills" and "Critical Thinking," and model how to answer each type.

3 **Have students complete the Timeline Challenge.** Monitor students as they work. Use the Guide to Unit 4 Timeline Challenge to check their answers. You may wish to project a transparency of this page as you work through the questions with the class and conduct a discussion of the "Critical Thinking" questions.

4 **Complete the KWL chart.** Return to the KWL chart created at the beginning of the unit, and ask students to list the key information they have learned.

Classroom Timeline

1 **Prepare the Timeline Challenge Cards.** Copy and cut the cards from *Student Handout TC4: Unit 4 Timeline Challenge Cards.* You may wish to laminate the cards for future use.

2 **Create a timeline on a classroom wall.** On an empty wall or a large bulletin board, make a timeline with masking tape or colored paper. Mark off the time intervals in advance, or ask students to do so in class.

3 **Have students place the Timeline Challenge Cards.** Distribute cards to individual students or pairs and have them tape the cards to the timeline in the correct locations. Call on students to provide more information on the timeline topics to review main events and issues.

Student Handout TC4

Internet Research

1 **Review students' suggestions for additional timeline entries.** Have students share their answers to the last question of the Timeline Challenge.

2 **Have students conduct Internet research.** Ask students to choose and research one of their suggested events.

3 **Have students create additional Timeline Challenge Cards.** Direct students to research an appropriate image for their cards and then use the computer to create an illustrated card, complete with timeline entry.

Timeline Skills

Score 1 point for each correct answer.

1. 426 years; also accept "about 500 years"

2. Buddhism; India

3. the Song dynasty

4. During the Song dynasty, increased food production resulted in growth in areas other than farming, such as trade and commerce.

5. the invention of movable type

6. The art of papermaking was developed in China around 100 C.E. Papermaking is crucial for recording and transmitting information.

7. 53 years; also accept "about 50 years"

8. the Mongols

9. Marco Polo travelled through China during the Yuan dynasty.

10. Zheng He made his seven maritime voyages during the Ming dynasty.

Critical Thinking

Score 1 to 3 points for each answer, depending on the thoroughness of the response.

11. Answers may vary, but students will likely say that agricultural change most contributed to a high quality of life because it allowed people to focus on trade and commerce, which provided new goods that improved the quality of life for many people. Whichever they choose, students should support their reasoning with facts.

12. Answers will vary. Students must explain why the two inventions they chose most affect life today.

13. During the Song dynasty, scholar-officials' appointments to govern were based on merit. Applicants had to pass a difficult civil service exam to become officials. During the Yuan dynasty, Mongols and other non-Chinese were appointed to fill important positions.

14. Answers will vary. Students must explain why the events they chose merit inclusion.

Using Scores to Inform Instruction

Timeline Skills A score of 7 out of 10 indicates that students understand most of the key events in the unit.

Critical Thinking A score of 8 out of 12 indicates that students are able to think critically about most of the key issues in this unit.

If students score below these levels, consider reviewing timeline and critical thinking skills.

Japan During Medieval Times

Japan During Medieval Times

Overview

This activity introduces geographic information essential to Unit 5. Students read and interpret maps to learn key geographical features of Japan and how these features affected Japanese medieval history. They annotate a map of Japan and answer questions in their Interactive Student Notebooks, and then discuss critical thinking questions. Students' comprehension of content and proficiency in map-reading and higher-order thinking skills will help you gauge their readiness for the unit. The pages that follow include a completed map, answers to questions, a scoring guide to inform your teaching, and suggestions for modifications to meet specific student needs.

Essential Geographic Understandings

1. Location of Japan

2. Key physical features: Sea of Japan (East Sea), East China Sea, Pacific Ocean, mountain ranges, Kanto Plain

3. Relative location of Japan and the countries of East Asia, particularly China and Korea

4. Influence of physical features, such as mountains and bodies of water, on historical and cultural development

Procedures

1   **Introduce the unit.** Tell students that in this unit they will learn about the history and culture of medieval Japan. Explain that the cultural identity of Japan developed in ways that were directly related to its physical geography.

2   **Create a KWL chart.** Ask students to identify what they already know about medieval Japan and what they want to learn. Use their responses to gauge how much additional background information they will need as you progress through the unit. Students will return to the KWL chart at the end of the unit and add the key information they have learned.

3   **Have students read Unit 5 "Setting the Stage" in the Student Edition.**

4   **Have students complete the Geography Challenge.** Monitor students as they work. Use the guide on the next two pages to check their answers. You may wish to project the map from the Interactive Student Notebook and have students annotate it as the class works through the map-reading questions. Make sure that students have grasped Essential Geographic Understandings 1 to 3.

5   **Discuss the "Critical Thinking" questions.** Help students understand the geographic relationships described in Essential Geographic Understanding 4.

Japan

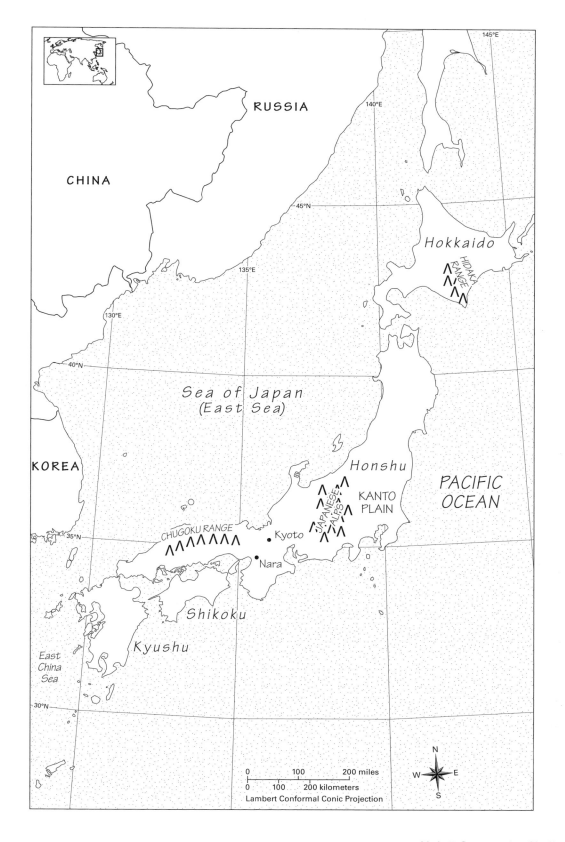

Geography Skills

Score 1 point for each correct answer. Use the map on the previous page to check shading and labeling.

1. Japan extends about 1,500 miles from north to south. At its widest point, it is about 150 miles wide (excluding peninsulas).

2. The distance from Japan to the Asian continent is shortest between Japan and Korea.

3. The Kanto Plain is located on the island of Honshu.

4. Students should label Nara and Kyoto.

5. 15 percent

6. The bodies of water surrounding Japan protected it from invasion by hostile countries. They also served as a plentiful food source. The oceans also served as transportation routes to other countries.

7. Students should label the Chugoku Range, the Japanese Alps, and the Hidaka Range.

8. The United States lies to the east of Japan, across the Pacific Ocean.

Critical Thinking

Questions may have more than one correct answer. Score 1 to 3 points for each reasonable answer, depending on the strength of students' geographic reasoning. Possible answers are given here.

9. It is likely that the island of Honshu became a center of power, because it is the largest of the Japanese islands, the most centrally located, and it has less mountainous territory than the other islands.

10. Advantages include the protection from attack provided by the oceans and the availability of food in the oceans. Disadvantages include volcanic eruptions and earthquakes and the lack of flat land for farming.

11. The Kanto Plain is the most populated area in Japan because it is the largest lowland area. In addition, its soil is fertile.

12. Possible answer: Mountains and oceans no longer are a significant barrier to the movement of people, goods, and ideas. Modern forms of transportation, including planes and ships, allow people and goods to move easily and rapidly. Technologies such as the Internet and cellular devices allow communication to take place immediately between any two places on Earth.

Using Scores to Inform Instruction

Geography Skills A score of 5 out of 8 or better indicates that students have acquired sufficient geographic information to proceed with the unit.

Critical Thinking A score of 8 out of 16 or better indicates that students are beginning to understand the relationships between physical geography and the different ways in which people live.

Modifying Instruction

ELL or Learners with Special Education Needs
Consider focusing on map-reading questions or limiting the number of "Critical Thinking" questions.

Students with Weak Map or Critical Thinking Skills
Assign appropriate pages from the Social Studies Skills Toolkit in the back of the Lesson Masters.

The Influence of Neighboring Cultures on Japan

In what ways did neighboring cultures influence Japan?

Overview

In a Social Studies Skill Builder activity, students create playing cards to study the influences of India, China, and Korea on the development of Japanese culture, and play a game to learn about cultural diffusion in medieval Japan.

Objectives

In the course of reading this chapter and participating in the classroom activity, students will

Social Studies

- describe how aspects of culture were transmitted from India, China, and Korea to Japan.

- explain the significance of Japan's proximity to China and Korea and the influences of those countries on Japan.

- discuss the influence of Prince Shotoku and the characteristics of Japanese society during his rule.

- summarize a distinctive form of Japanese Buddhism and explain how this form developed.

Language Arts

- clarify word meanings through the use of definitions and examples.

- write a letter that summarizes their reading and learning.

Social Studies Vocabulary

Key Content Terms Prince Shotoku, Shinto, meditation, pagoda

Academic Vocabulary rural, acquire, enlightenment, mythical

Materials

History Alive! The Medieval World and Beyond

Interactive Student Notebooks

Lesson Masters

- Information Master 19A (1 transparency)

- Information Master 19B (1 transparency)

- Student Handout 19 (1 per pair, ideally copied on heavy paper)

- Vocabulary Development handout (1 per student, on colored paper)

Activity	Suggested Time	Materials
Preview	15 minutes	• Interactive Student Notebooks
Vocabulary Development	30–40 minutes	• *History Alive! The Medieval World and Beyond* • Interactive Student Notebooks • Vocabulary Development handout
Social Studies Skill Builder	90 minutes (1–2 regular periods) (.5–1 block period)	• *History Alive! The Medieval World and Beyond* • Interactive Student Notebooks • Information Master 19A (1 transparency) • Information Master 19B (1 transparency) • Student Handout 19 (1 per pair, ideally copied on heavy paper) • colored pencils or marker
Processing	20 minutes	• Interactive Student Notebooks
Assessment	40 minutes	• Chapter 19 Assessment

Preview

1 **Have students complete the Preview activity in their Interactive Student Notebooks.** Students examine a list of items to decide if they are native to the United States or if they originated somewhere else. Review the directions with students, and answer any questions they may have.

2 **Have students share their responses in pairs and then explain each item's origin.**

Item	Aspect of Culture Represented	From the U.S. or Borrowed from Another Country?
piano	music	Borrowed from Italy
fire engine	government	Borrowed from Egypt
blue jeans	clothing	United States
ice cream	food	Borrowed from China
television	entertainment	United States

(**Note:** Students may include other aspects of culture than those provided in the chart above. Allow their ideas to prompt discussion about what defines an aspect of culture.)

3 **Connect the Preview activity to the chapter.** Explain that, in general, much of a country's culture is borrowed from other countries, rather than arising from within the country. As students may know, the spread of cultural elements is called *cultural diffusion*. In this lesson, students will learn how cultural diffusion helped shape the culture of medieval Japan.

Vocabulary Development

1 **Introduce the Key Content Terms.** Have students locate the Key Content Terms for the chapter in their Interactive Student Notebooks. These are important terms that will help them understand the main ideas of the chapter. Ask volunteers to identify any familiar terms and suggest how they might be used in a sentence.

2 **Have students complete a Vocabulary Development handout.** Give each student a copy of the Vocabulary Development handout of your choice from the Reading Toolkit at the back of the Lesson Masters. These handouts provide extra Key Content Term practice and support, depending on your students' needs. Review the completed handout by asking volunteers to share one of their answers for each term.

Reading

1   Introduce the Essential Question and have students read Section 19.1.
Have students identify the Essential Question on the first page of the chapter:
In what ways did neighboring cultures influence Japan? Then have students
read Section 19.1. Afterward, have students use information from Section
19.1 and the chapter opener image to propose some possible answers to the
Essential Question.

2   Have students complete the Reading Notes for Chapter 19. Assign Sections
19.2 to 19.10 during the activity, as indicated in the procedures for the Social
Studies Skill Builder. Remind students to use the Key Content Terms where
appropriate as they complete their Reading Notes.

Social Studies Skill Builder

1   Prepare the materials for the activity. Make transparencies of *Information
Master 19A: Preparing Game Cards* and *Information Master 19B: Instructions
for Playing the Cultural Matching Game.* Create four signs with the following
country names written in large letters: India, China, Korea, and Japan. Post
the signs around the room so that they approximate their geographical
relationship to each other as shown on the map in Section 19.2 of the book.

Information Master 19A

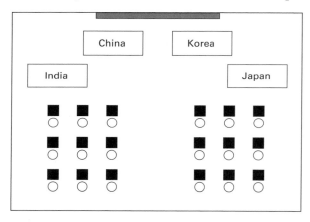

Information Master 19B

2   Put students in pairs and introduce the activity. Tell students that they will
be completing a set of cards to play a game with their partners. The object of
the game will be to match a card that shows a cultural aspect of Japan with
another card that represents its country of origin.

3   Have pairs complete the Reading Notes for Section 19.2. Tell students that
this section provides an overview of how aspects of Korean, Chinese, and
Indian cultures came to influence medieval Japan.

4   Review the procedures for preparing the game cards. Distribute both
pages of *Student Handout 19: Game Cards* to each pair of students. Project
Information Master 19A and review the directions. For Step 6, have students
turn to the Reading Notes in their Interactive Student Notebooks, and review
the directions with them.

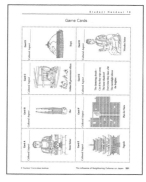

Student Handout 19

5 **Have students prepare their cards.** As each pair of students completes one set of cards, use the Guide to Reading Notes to verify that pairs have matched the cards correctly.

6 **Review the guidelines and play the game.** When all pairs have completed their Reading Notes, project Information Master 19B and explain the rules for the game, which is similar to Concentration. Then have students play the game with their partners. If time permits, let them switch partners and play the game a second time.

7 **Conduct a wrap-up activity.** Follow these steps:

- Assign each pair of students one set of Game Cards representing one cultural aspect listed below. (**Note:** You may have more than one pair assigned to the same cultural aspect.)

- Explain that each pair must be able to demonstrate how the idea for their cultural aspect reached Japan by moving through the correct labeled areas of your classroom. For example, a pair might start near the label that says "India," then move to "China," and finally move to "Japan."

- Students must then state what happened to that idea once it reached Japan. In other words, they must explain how the Japanese adapted the original idea to their culture.

- Once pairs have had a few minutes to prepare, randomly choose a cultural aspect from the following list and call on one of the pairs assigned to it to demonstrate how their idea reached Japan and what happened to it there. Continue until all cultural aspects have been shared.

Cultural Aspects

Government	City Design
Religion	Writing
Literature	Sculpture
Architecture	Music

Processing

Have students complete the Processing activity on a separate sheet of paper in their notebooks. Students will write a letter, as a visitor to Japan from a neighboring Asian country, in which they describe the similarities and differences between Japan and their home culture.

Writing: Outlining

Remind students that all forms of writing, including letters, need a clear pattern of organization. Discuss ways to group details in the letter, such as by category or from most important to least important. Require students to outline their letters (using a formal or informal method) before they draft or to outline their drafts before they revise to test whether their organization is logical.

Quicker Coverage

Omit the Cultural Matching Game Skip Step 6 in the procedures for the Social Studies Skill Builder and instead, after students have created their cards, have them move right into the wrap-up in Step 7.

Jigsaw the Reading and the Completion of the Game Cards Follow these steps:

- Assign each pair to a different cultural aspect (listed under Step 7 of the Social Studies Skill Builder). You may assign more than one pair of students to a cultural aspect.

- Have pairs locate the section in Chapter 19 that corresponds to the cultural aspect they have been assigned and read that section.

- Instruct students to label their pair of game cards with the cultural aspect they've been assigned.

- Have students complete the corresponding Reading Notes for that section.

- Make a transparency of Student Handout 19, and as you call each pair forward to share their cultural aspect, have them write in their cultural aspect on the correct cards for other students to copy.

- Have students share what they wrote in their Reading Notes for that section.

Deeper Coverage

Have Students Create Their Own Game Cards Instead of handing out Student Handout 19, give students two sheets of blank paper and have them create 16 cards (8 per sheet) on their own. Provide the following directions:

- Each set of cards must focus on a different cultural aspect of Japan. (**Note:** Consider providing the list from Step 7 of the Social Studies Skill Builder.)

- Each set of two cards must include an original idea from an Asian mainland country (China, Korea, or India) and, on the second card, the idea as it was adopted in Japan.

- Each card must include an illustration of the cultural aspect, a label explaining what is pictured, and the name of the cultural aspect.

Consider making a transparency of Cards C and P on Student Handout 19 to provide examples of what a matching pair of cards should look like.

Assessment

Mastering the Content

1. B	5. D	9. D	13. A
2. C	6. B	10. B	14. C
3. C	7. A	11. B	15. A
4. B	8. D	12. D	16. C

Applying Social Studies Skills

17. Sample answer: The relation between emperor and subject is like heaven and earth; if they are in their proper positions, all will work properly.

18. Sample answer: Behave properly, do not pull people away from agriculture for forced labor in the farming season, and consult others before making important decisions.

19. Sample answer: Order, harmony, and obedience are very important to maintain a happy nation.

Exploring the Essential Question

20. Answers should include all the elements requested in the prompt.

Scoring Rubric

Score	Description
3	Student completes all nine circles in the diagrams. Notations in the circles are clearly stated, supported by details, accurate, and demonstrate command of standard English conventions.
2	Student writes in most or all circles, but notations may lack details or not be clearly stated.
1	Student writes in at least one diagram. Notations may contain factual and/or grammatical errors and may lack details.
0	Response does not match the task or is incorrect.

English Language Learners

Provide Additional Support for the Processing Activity Provide the following template for students and have them complete the unfinished sentences.

Dear friend back in China,

Japan is really beautiful. Many aspects of its culture are similar to ours. For example, Japan's religion is similar because_____. Also, its _____ is a lot like ours. But some of its culture is different. Japan's capital city, Nara, is different from Chang'an because _____. There are Buddhist statues everywhere, but they are different from ours because _____.

Hope you can visit soon. Your friend,
(Name of student)

Learners Reading and Writing Below Grade Level

Reduce the Number of Reading Notes Have students annotate the maps in the Reading Notes to show the types and flow of ideas, instead of answering the questions in full sentences.

Change the Requirements in the Processing Activity Instead of having students find two similarities and two differences, have them write about just one of each in their letters.

Learners with Special Education Needs

Simplify the Preview Activity Provide the following answers for the "Aspect of Culture Represented" column:

- piano: music
- fire engine: government
- jeans: clothing
- ice cream: food
- television: entertainment

Then have students decide whether each item originated in the United States or was borrowed from another country.

Provide Additional Support During the Social Studies Skill Builder Before the activity, write the corresponding section of Chapter 19 on each of the cards on Student Handout 19. For example, write "19.8" on Card A. Make a copy of this and distribute it to pairs. Tell students to use these guides to locate the place in their books where they can find out more about each cultural aspect.

Advanced Learners

Expand the Preview Activity Challenge students to create their own world maps of cultural influences on the United States. Provide each student with a blank world map. Tell them to think about items or aspects of our culture that have diffused to the United States, to research where each originated, and to write each aspect on the country or region it came from. For example, students might write *lasagna* in Italy and *sushi* in Japan. Remind them to think about all aspects of culture, including language, religion, technology, government, entertainment, and clothing. Once they have labeled at least seven or eight items, have them answer these questions:

- Which countries or regions of the world seem to have had the most impact on American culture? Why do you think this is so?

- Which regions seem to have had little impact on American culture? Why might this be the case?

- Which regions do you think will have the most impact on American culture during your lifetime? Why?

Enrichment Resources

Find out more about influences on medieval Japanese culture by exploring the following Enrichment Resources for *History Alive! The Medieval World and Beyond* at www.teachtci.com.

Enrichment Readings These in-depth readings encourage students to explore selected topics related to the chapter. You may also find readings that relate the chapter's content directly to your state's curriculum.

Internet Connections These recommended Web sites provide useful and engaging content that reinforces skills development and mastery of subjects within the chapter.

Literature Recommendations

The following books offer opportunities to extend the content in this chapter.

The Cat Who Went to Heaven by Elizabeth Coatsworth (New York: Simon & Schuster, 1991)

Japan: The Culture by Bobbie Kalman (New York: Crabtree Publishing, 2001)

Shinto by Paula R. Hartz (New York: Chelsea House, 2009)

Section 19.2

1. Students' maps should have labels for Japan, India, China, and Korea. Each country should be a different color.

2. Prince Shotoku was a regent under the Empress Suiko. He came to power when his family became powerful enough to loosely control all of Japan.

3. Type of Society: agricultural society; Main Crop: rice; Family Life: centered around the mother; Government: power divided among uji

4. Knowledge of Asian mainland culture came to Japan from Japanese who traveled to China, through gifts sent from the mainland to Japan, and from Korean workers who settled in Japan.

Section 19.3

1.

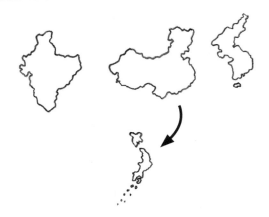

Letters of the Matching Cards	C	P
Country the Card Represents	Japan	China

2. Before it was influenced by countries on the mainland, Japan's government was ruled by an emperor who had loose control over semi-independent clans called uji. Each uji controlled the land but often struggled with other uji for power.

3. The Japanese adopted the idea of a strong emperor when Prince Shotoku issued the Seventeen Article Constitution based upon Chinese ideas. However, Japan did not accept the idea of government officials being appointed based on ability. By the ninth century, nobles held all high government positions.

Section 19.4

1.

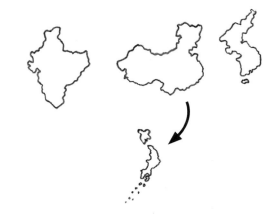

Letters of the Matching Cards	F	I
Country the Card Represents	Japan	China

2. The design of the new capital city of Nara resembled the design of the Chinese capital, Chang'an. Its streets were laid out in an orderly pattern and a wide boulevard ran down the center.

3. Nara was smaller and did not have a wall.

Section 19.5

1.

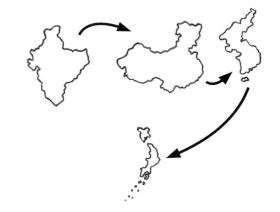

Letters of the Matching Cards	O	L
Country the Card Represents	India	Japan

2. Before it was influenced by countries on the mainland, Japan's original religion was Shinto, which expresses love and respect for nature. Its followers worship spirits called kami. Shinto stresses purifying whatever is unclean and celebrating life and the beauty of nature.

3. The Japanese adopted the Mahayana form of Buddhism, which came to Japan from China by way of Korea. This type of Buddhism says that all people can reach enlightenment. However, the religion of Shinto still survived and was sometimes blended with Buddhism.

Section 19.6

1.

Letters of the Matching Cards	M	K
Country the Card Represents	China	Japan

2. Before it was influenced by countries on the mainland, Japan had only a spoken language. Written documents were in Chinese.

3. The Japanese adopted the Chinese writing system and invented kanji and kana to adapt Chinese characters to their own language.

Section 19.7

1.

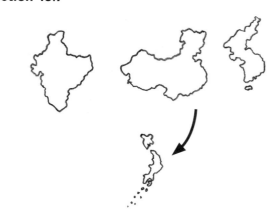

Letters of the Matching Cards	J	G
Country the Card Represents	China	Japan

2. The Japanese developed a new form of poetry called tanka that was based on Chinese poetry forms. A tanka poem has 31 syllables divided into lines of 5, 7, 5, 7, and 7 syllables.

Section 19.8

1.

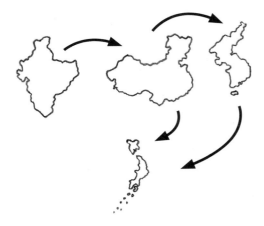

Letters of the Matching Cards	A	H
Country the Card Represents	China	Japan

2. Before they were influenced by countries on the mainland, Japanese sculptures consisted of clay figures that were probably meant to accompany or protect the dead.

3. Japanese sculptures of Buddha, like those of China and Korea, often show Buddha in the same pose. In contrast, Japanese sculptors preferred to work in wood and often added original touches to their carvings.

Section 19.9

1.

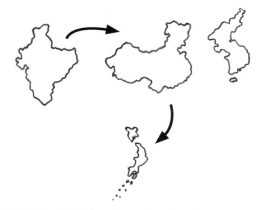

Letters of the Matching Cards	D	E
Country the Card Represents	India	Japan

2. In India, Buddhist monasteries had shrines called stupas, with bell-shaped roofs. The Chinese changed stupas to pagodas, having several stories and curved roofs. The Japanese adopted the Chinese pagoda design for their Buddhist temples.

Section 19.10

1.

Letters of the Matching Cards	N	B
Country the Card Represents	China	Japan

2. Before it was influenced by the countries on the mainland, Japan's music consisted of chanted poems, war songs, folk songs, and prayers. All were recited and used only a few notes.

3. The Japanese adopted a Chinese instrument called a sheng, a type of mouth organ, which they called a sho.

Heian-kyo: The Heart of Japan's Golden Age

What was life like for aristocrats during the Heian period?

Overview

In a Writing for Understanding activity, students learn about aristocratic life and the cultural accomplishments of Japan during the Heian period by "visiting" the home of a Japanese aristocrat. They learn how a Japanese aristocrat might act in certain situations, and then write a diary entry describing a day in the life of a Heian noble.

Objectives

In the course of reading this chapter and participating in the classroom activity, students will

Social Studies

- describe the golden age of literature, art, and drama in medieval Japan.
- explain the significance of the *Tale of Genji,* and its influence on modern Japanese culture.
- identify the causes that ended the Heian period and brought about the rise of the military class.

Language Arts

- write a coherent diary entry that structures sentences clearly and effectively.
- articulate the purpose and characteristics of a novel.

Social Studies Vocabulary

Key Content Terms Heian period, golden age, courtier, *Tale of Genji*

Academic Vocabulary aristocrat, conduct, significant, erode

Materials

History Alive! The Medieval World and Beyond

Interactive Student Notebooks

CD Track 11

Visual 20

Placards 20A–20G

Lesson Masters

- Information Masters 20A and 20B (1 transparency of each)
- Vocabulary Development handout (1 per student, on colored paper)

2 sheets of paper folded into fans with 12 folds

20 small stones

2 lightweight balls or paper squeezed into balls

string

Activity	Suggested Time	Materials
Preview	15 minutes	• Interactive Student Notebooks • Visual 20
Vocabulary Development	30–40 minutes	• *History Alive! The Medieval World and Beyond* • Interactive Student Notebooks • Vocabulary Development handout
Writing for Understanding	• Step 1, classroom set up 30 minutes • Steps 2–6, visiting the various "rooms" of the aristocrat's house 90 minutes • Step 7, writing the diary entry 30 minutes (4 regular periods) (2 block periods)	• *History Alive! The Medieval World and Beyond* • Interactive Student Notebooks • Placards 20A–20G • CD Track 11 • Information Master 20A (1 transparency) • Information Master 20B (1 transparency) • 2 sheets of paper folded into fans with 12 folds • 20 small stones • 2 lightweight balls or paper squeezed into balls • string
Processing (optional)		• Interactive Student Notebooks
Assessment	40 minutes	• Chapter 20 Assessment

Preview

1 **Use art to introduce the Heian period.** Project *Visual 20: The Golden Age of Japan* and analyze the painting as a class. Ask,

- What are some interesting details you notice in this painting?

- Who might have lived in a house like this?

- What do you think life was like for the people who lived here?

Visual 20

Tell students that during the Heian period, wealthy Japanese lived in mansions like this one. A house typically had two or three main buildings connected by covered walkways. Each building consisted of a single room. Decorated screens divided each large room into sections.

2 **Have students complete the Preview activity in their Interactive Student Notebooks.** Review the directions with students and ask if they have any questions.

3 **Have students share their responses in pairs or with the class.**

4 **Connect the Preview activity to the chapter.** Tell students that in the Preview activity they viewed the home of a wealthy aristocratic family during Japan's Heian period. As students read the chapter, they will discover how aristocrats lived during this period, a time in Japanese history in which manners were very important. The smallest social mistake could mean a person would never again be included in the social events of the upper class, and therefore, would be excluded from political power. Aristocrats enjoyed a life of luxury and leisure. Many devoted their days to such activities as creating the perfect perfume to wear to a party. It was also a time when the Japanese produced outstanding works of art and literature.

Vocabulary Development

1 **Introduce the Key Content Terms.** Have students locate the Key Content Terms for the chapter in their Interactive Student Notebooks. These are important terms that will help them understand the main ideas of the chapter. Ask volunteers to identify any familiar terms and suggest how they might be used in a sentence.

2 **Have students complete a Vocabulary Development handout.** Give each student a copy of the Vocabulary Development handout of your choice from the Reading Toolkit at the back of the Lesson Masters. These handouts provide extra Key Content Term practice and support, depending on your students' needs. Review the completed handout by asking volunteers to share one answer for each term.

> **Vocabulary Development: Metaphor**
>
> Explain that the term "golden age" is a metaphor that was used by Greek and Roman poets to refer to an ideal time of peace and prosperity. Talk about why we would refer to an ideal state as *golden,* and how this word carries connotations of goodness and value. To further explore the connotations of the metaphor, you might contrast the term "silver age"; you might also have students extend the metaphor to a period in their own lives or the lives of their parents, their ancestors, or others in their community.

Reading

1 **Introduce the Essential Question and have students read Section 20.1.**
Have students identify the Essential Question on the first page of the chapter: *What was life like for aristocrats during the Heian period?* Then have students read Section 20.1. Afterward, have students respond to these questions:

- What event marks the beginning of the Heian period in Japan?

- Why is this period often called Japan's golden age?

2 **Have students complete the Reading Notes for Chapter 20.** Assign Sections 20.2 to 20.10 during the activity, as indicated in the procedures for the Writing for Understanding. Remind students to use the Key Content Terms where appropriate as they complete their Reading Notes.

Writing for Understanding

1 **Before class, prepare materials and the classroom for the activity.** Follow these steps:

- Arrange your desks according to the diagram and connect them with string to create six small "rooms" that will represent the home of a Japanese aristocrat. Indicate "doors" through which students can walk to reach the various rooms.

- Create the following stations in the rooms. The directions for students are found on Placards 20A–20G. To make the activity run more smoothly, consider creating another set of placards from www.teachtci.com. Also, consider placing a few copies of *History Alive! Medieval World and Beyond* at each station for students to use as they complete their Reading Notes. (**Note:** Consider asking a parent or adult aide to help monitor stations during this activity.)

Station A: Tape Placard 20A on the wall as indicated in the diagram.

Station B: Place two paper fans and Placard 20B on the floor.

Station C: Place the CD player cued to CD Track 11, "Japanese Thoughts on Beauty," on a desk. Place Placard 20C on the floor.

Station D: Place Placard 20D on the floor.

Station E: Place Placard 20E on the floor.

Station F: Place Placard 20F on the floor.

Station G: Place a lightweight ball and 10 small stones on each of two desks as indicated. Place Placard 20G nearby.

Placards 20A–20G

2   Place students in pairs and have them read Section 20.2 and complete the Reading Notes. Have students sit with their partners in one of the rooms you have created to read Section 20.2 and complete the Reading Notes. This section provides background on how Heian-kyo came to be Japan's capital city.

3   Introduce the activity. Project *Information Master 20A: Procedures for Visiting a Japanese Noble's House* so that only the classroom map and the first paragraph show. Explain that in this lesson students will suppose they are aristocrats during the Heian period. They have just been invited to a noble's *shoen,* or house. The tape on the classroom floor (or string) represents the decorative screens used to divide a large room. As students move from room to room in the noble's home, they will find objects or situations they do not understand. They will use *History Alive! The Medieval World and Beyond* to discover how to behave in each situation. Afterward, they will write a diary entry about life during the Heian period.

Information Master 20A

4   Review the procedures for the activity. Uncover Steps 1 through 5 of Information Master 20A and review the directions with students.

5   Have pairs visit the stations. When pairs finish at each station, use the Guide to Reading Notes to check their work and, optionally, to award points.

6   Review how students chose to act in each situation. Once pairs have visited every room and completed their Reading Notes, read the "Situation" and "Problem" off each placard and have volunteers explain what they did in each circumstance, and why.

7   Have students read Section 20.10 and complete the Reading Notes for that section. When everyone has visited all stations, have students read Section 20.10 to learn about the influences of the Heian period on modern Japan.

8   Review directions for completing a diary entry about daily life during the Heian period. Project *Information Master 20B: Creating a Diary Entry* and go over the criteria. Remind students that a tanka has 31 syllables in five lines of 5, 7, 5, 7, and 7 syllables. Distribute paper for students to write their diary entries. (**Note:** You may wish to have students write rough drafts on scrap paper and final drafts on specially decorated paper, as was done during the Heian period. To create such paper, have students wet a piece of drawing paper and place large drops of watercolor paints on it, allowing the colored drops to run together. When the paper is dry, they can copy or print the diary entry onto it.)

Information Master 20B

Processing

1   Understand the intent of the Processing activity. The diary entry serves as this chapter's processing activity. Should you choose to not have students do the writing assignment, you might use the optional Processing activity in the Interactive Student Notebook.

2   Have students complete the Processing activity.

3   Have students share their answers with their partners or with the class.

Quicker Coverage

Omit the Room Set-Up Instead of setting up your room to resemble a noble's home, skip Steps 1, 3, 4, and 5. Instead, make transparencies of each placard. Read through the situations and problems on each placard as a class and discuss what students might do in each situation. Then have students read the sections indicated and complete their Reading Notes.

Omit the Diary Entry Instead of having students complete the diary entry in Step 8 of the activity directions, have them create a sensory figure for a Japanese aristocrat during the Heian period. Have them first draw their figure in the center of a piece of paper. Then, in five boxes around their figure, have them write the following sentence starters:

With my ears, I . . .

With my eyes, I . . .

With my hands, I . . .

With my mouth, I . . .

With my nose, I . . .

In each box, students should complete the sentences by describing a detail of aristocratic life during the Heian period. Challenge students to refer to a different aspect of court life in each sentence.

Deeper Coverage

Conduct a Wrap-up Activity To test students on their Heian period manners after they have finished their tour of the aristocrat's home and have completed their Reading Notes, read the following situations and ask students to state the correct response, based on their reading.

- **Situation 1**: You enter a room in the home of a wealthy Heian family. The nobleman welcomes you inside and requests that you take a seat. You see no chairs, only mats and cushions. Where is the proper place to sit? *(on the floor or on a cushion)*

- **Situation 2**: Once you are in the room, you notice that the noblewoman of the house sits behind a portable screen. Should you go behind the screen to greet her? *(No.)*

- **Situation 3**: You are a member of the sixth rank in the Heian court. Your neighbor is a member of the fourth rank. You wish to build a gatepost outside your home. Should you build it higher or lower than your neighbor's? *(lower)*

- **Situation 4**: Your cousin wrote you a poem and had it delivered to you. What are you now expected to do? *(Write a poem in response that has the same style, mood, and imagery as the original.)*

- **Situation 5**: You are a woman and you wish to write a personal letter to a friend. What style of writing should you use, katakana or hiragana? *(hiragana)*

Assessment

Mastering the Content

1. D	5. B	9. A	13. B
2. A	6. D	10. B	14. D
3. C	7. A	11. C	15. D
4. B	8. C	12. A	16. B

Applying Social Studies Skills

17. Sample answers: it is large; it has many buildings and gardens

18. Sample answers: stairs leading up to the door; posts raising the house above the ground

19. Sample answers: using trees and gardens; streams running through the grounds

Exploring the Essential Question

20. Answers should include all the elements requested in the prompt.

Scoring Rubric

Score	Description
3	Student completes a letter that addresses all four bulleted points. The letter is clearly stated, is supported by details, and demonstrates command of standard English conventions.
2	Student responds to most or all parts of the task, but the letter may lack details or not be clearly stated.
1	Student responds to at least one part of the task. The letter may contain factual and/or grammatical errors and may lack details.
0	Response does not match the task or is incorrect.

English Language Learners

Reduce the Diary Entry Alter the Writing for Understanding diary entry (see Information Master 20B) by making the tanka poem optional. Also, have students focus on writing about and illustrating only three key aspects of life as a Japanese noble during the Heian period. Finally, reduce the minimum length of the diary entry to one page.

Learners Reading and Writing Below Grade Level

Provide Additional Support for the Reading Notes Consider providing students with copies of Sections 20.3 through 20.9 with the paragraphs where they will find the answers to the Reading Notes questions highlighted or underlined.

Learners with Special Education Needs

Provide Support for the Writing Activity Help students write their tanka poems by having them review Section 19.7 from the previous chapter. Then project the annotated tanka poem below on a transparency, and have students practice pausing after each syllable and counting the syllables.

A/ ska/ter/ glides/ by (5 syllables)

and/ be/comes/ one/ with/ the/ ice (7 syllables)

mas/ter/ of/ her/ world (5 syllables)

I/ weep/ at/ such/ per/for/mance (7 syllables)

this/ po/e/try/ in/ mo/tion. (7 syllables)

Finally, have students write their own tanka poem, and have a classmate check its syllable count.

Advanced Learners

Modify the Activity Place an extra question at each station in the home of a Japanese noble to further challenge students.

- *Station A:* Would you rather have been an emperor or a member of the Fujiwara family during the Heian period? Why?
- *Station B:* How are the privileges of the top three ranks of the Heian court similar to the privileges of the upper class in the United States today? How are they different?
- *Station C:* Do you think people of the Heian court were more obsessed with beauty than people are today? Justify your opinion.
- *Station D:* Which piece of sculpture do you think should have more value, one carved from a single piece of wood or one that includes several pieces of carved wood joined together? Why?
- *Station E:* Reread Sei Shonagon's list of "Things That Should Be Short." What four items would you add to her list?
- *Station F:* Of the problems described in this section, which do you think contributed most to the downfall of the Heian court? Justify your opinion.
- *Station G:* What modern American game best compares to kemari? Justify your opinion.

Enrichment Resources

Find out more about the Heian period in Japan by exploring the following Enrichment Resources for *History Alive! The Medieval World and Beyond* at www.teachtci.com.

Enrichment Readings These in-depth readings encourage students to explore selected topics related to the chapter. You may also find readings that relate the chapter's content directly to your state's curriculum.

Internet Connections The recommended Web sites provide useful and engaging content that reinforces skills development and mastery of subjects within the chapter.

Literature Recommendations

The following books offer opportunities to extend the content in this chapter.

Jingu: The Hidden Princess by Ralph Pray (Walnut Creek, CA: Shen's Books, 2002)

Tale of Genji by Murasaki Shikibu (North Clarendon, VT: Charles E. Tuttle, 2000)

What Life Was Like for the Ancient Japanese by Fiona MacDonald (London: Anness Publishing, 2001)

Section 20.2

1. The emperor moved Japan's capital from Nara to Heian-kyo because he thought the priests' power was damaging to the government, and he wanted a larger, grander city for his capital.

2. Answers will vary. Sample answer: My life in Heian-kyo is filled with beauty and elegance. For instance, the mansion I live in has beautiful gardens and artificial lakes. Though the grounds of my home are large, they are surrounded by a well-kept stone wall. The large rooms of my home are divided by screens and connected by open-air hallways.

Section 20.3

1. If your class is doing the activity, students should bow to Fujiwara Michinaga because he led Japan and was shown respect by everyone around him.

2. The Fujiwara family gained and used power by marrying into the emperor's family, and they acted as advisers to the emperor.

3. Students' sketches will vary.

Section 20.4

1. If your class is doing the activity, students should not use the fan because it has too few folds for a person of their rank.

2. During the Heian period, rank was determined by the rank of a person's birth family.

3. Drawings will vary but should include nine ranks with the top three ranks labeled "nobles." The fourth and fifth ranks should be labeled "less important officials." The sixth through ninth ranks should be labeled "minor officials, clerks, and experts in certain fields."

Section 20.5

1. If your class is doing the activity, students' responses will vary. Possible response: I would tell her to use white powder on her face and touches of red on her cheeks. She should paint on a small red mouth, pluck her eyebrows, and paint new eyebrows high on her forehead. She should blacken her teeth.

2. During the Heian period, people were judged on whether or not they had good taste and on their family ties.

3. Students' sketches about Heian beauty, fashion, and manners will vary.

Section 20.6

1. If your class is doing the activity, students' responses about the kemari and the stone-balancing game will vary.

2. c. Festival of the Snake; e. bugaku; a. sumo wrestling; b. rango; d. kemari

3. Students' sketches illustrating an important idea about recreation during the Heian period will vary.

Section 20.7

1. If your class is doing the activity, students should praise Painting 2 because it shows the new Japanese style of painting adopted during the Heian period.

2. During the Heian period, sculptors began to carve statues from carefully selected pieces of wood that were then joined together.

3. Painters drew thin lines and filled them in with bright colors. Lines were made quickly to show movement. Scroll paintings showed scenes from right to left to show the passage of time. Interior scenes were painted as if viewed from above.

Section 20.8

1. If your class is doing the activity, students should borrow the *Tale of Genji* because it is a romance novel that follows the love life of Genji, a fictional prince.

2. People were expected to make up poetry in public, while men and women created poetry to charm one another. If someone received a poem from a family member or friend, he or she was expected to write a poem in response.

3. The *Tale of Genji* is significant even today because it serves as a model for the modern romance novel, is regarded as one of the world's great works of literature, and creates a vivid picture of Heian court life.

Section 20.9

1. If your class is doing the activity, students should have an unsympathetic attitude toward the poor in order to be accepted by the aristocrats.

2. The Heian period ended for these three reasons: (1) The wealthy owners of large estates paid no taxes, which weakened the imperial government. (2) Law enforcement broke down, and bandits roamed the land. (3) Struggles over land and power led to civil war and the rise of new military leaders.

3. Students' sketches will vary.

Section 20.10

Use the answers below to check students' spoke diagrams on the influences of the Heian period on present-day Japan.

Literature: Murasaki Shikibu and Sei Shonagon still influence Japanese writers, and their works are considered Japanese classics.

Poetry: Tanka poetry is still a vibrant part of Japanese literature.

Drama: Bugaku led to Japan's Noh theater in which a chorus sings a heroic story as performers dance and act it out.

The Rise of the Warrior Class in Japan

What was the role of the samurai in the military society of medieval Japan?

Overview

In this Experiential Exercise, students learn about the rise of a warrior class in Japan and the pivotal role these samurai played from the end of the 12th century to the 19th century.

Objectives

In the course of reading this chapter and participating in the classroom activity, students will

Social Studies

- analyze the rise of a military society in late 12th-century Japan and the role of the samurai.
- explain the roles of shogun, daimyo, and samurai in the lord-vassal system of medieval Japan and the values, customs, and traditions within this system.
- compare and contrast elements of Amida and Zen Buddhism.
- describe the lasting influence of the samurai through modern times.

Language Arts

- clarify word meanings through the use of definitions and examples.
- deliver dramatic presentations that summarize main ideas.

Social Studies Vocabulary

Key Content Terms shogun, samurai, daimyo, martial arts, Amida Buddhism, Zen Buddhism, Bushido, restoration

Academic Vocabulary successor, administer, sophisticated, supreme, inferior

Materials

History Alive! The Medieval World and Beyond

Interactive Student Notebooks

Visuals 21A–21E

Lesson Masters

- Information Master 21 (1 transparency)
- Student Handout 21 (1 copy)
- Vocabulary Development handout (1 per student, on colored paper)

construction paper, scissors, tape, string, and colored markers (for making props)

fine paintbrush, ink or dark paint, and paper (for Skit 4)

Activity	Suggested Time	Materials
Preview	10 minutes	• Interactive Student Notebooks
Vocabulary Development	30–40 minutes	• *History Alive! The Medieval World and Beyond* • Interactive Student Notebooks • Vocabulary Development handout
Experiential Exercise	90 minutes (2 regular periods) (1 block period)	• Visuals 21A–21E • construction paper, scissors, tape, string, and colored markers (for making props) • fine paintbrush, ink or dark paint, and paper (for Skit 4) • Information Master 21 • Student Handout 21 • Interactive Student Notebooks
Processing	20 minutes	• *History Alive! The Medieval World and Beyond* • Interactive Student Notebooks
Assessment	40 minutes	• Chapter 21 Assessment

Preview

1 **Have students complete the Preview activity in their Interactive Student Notebooks.** Review the directions with students, and ask if they have any questions.

2 **Have students share their responses in pairs or with the class.**

3 **Connect the Preview activity to the chapter.** Explain to students that, just as modern American soldiers need to be trained before heading off to war, Japanese samurai also needed very specific training. In this chapter, students will learn about the training of samurai, including the skills, knowledge, and values these warriors learned. However, they will discover that the samurai's training was very different from the training of modern American soldiers.

Vocabulary Development

1 **Introduce the Key Content Terms.** Have students locate the Key Content Terms for the chapter in their Interactive Student Notebooks. These are important terms that will help them understand the main ideas of the chapter. Ask volunteers to identify any familiar terms and suggest how they might be used in a sentence.

2 **Have students complete a Vocabulary Development handout.** Give each student a copy of the Vocabulary Development handout of your choice from the Reading Toolkit at the back of the Lesson Masters. These handouts provide extra Key Content Term practice and support, depending on your students' needs. Review the completed handout by asking volunteers to share one answer for each term.

Reading

1 **Introduce the Essential Question and have students read Section 21.1.** Have students identify the Essential Question on the first page of the chapter: *What was the role of the samurai in the military society of medieval Japan?* Then have students read Section 21.1. Afterward, have students use information from Section 21.1 and from the chapter opener image to propose some possible answers to the Essential Question.

2 **Have students complete the Reading Notes for Chapter 21.** Assign Sections 21.2 to 21.12 during the activity, as indicated in the procedures for the Experiential Exercise. Remind students to use the Key Content Terms where appropriate as they complete their Reading Notes.

Experiential Exercise

1 **Prepare materials and assign roles.** Make one copy of each page of *Student Handout 21: Preparing Skits for Samurai School*. Place students in groups of four and give each group a different Student Handout page. For classes with fewer than 32 students, consider omitting Skits 4 or 5 and just having students read those shorter sections and complete their Reading Notes. For classes with more than 32 students, consider creating larger groups for Skits 1, 7, or 8 and have the extra students help with the pantomime.

Student Handout 21

2 **Have students complete the Reading Notes for Section 21.2.** This reading supplies background information about the conditions that led to the rise of a warrior class in Japan. When students have completed the reading and the Reading Notes for the section, ask,

- How did Minamoto Yoritomo change Japanese government?

- What title was given to the head of the new government?

- How were loyal warriors rewarded?

- Who were the daimyos?

3 **Introduce the activity.** Project *Visual 21A: Samurai*. Ask,

- What do you see?

- What do you think this man's role was in the military society of Japan? Why?

Explain that this image shows a samurai. Samurai were important warriors in Japanese history. In this lesson, students will learn about the training of samurai, including skills they had to master. The class will enact a visit to a samurai school. Each group will create a skit or "lesson" about one aspect of the skills, knowledge, and values taught to samurai.

Visuals 21A–21E

4 **Review the directions for the activity.** Project *Information Master 21: Preparing Skits for Samurai School* and review the directions listed there. Ask if students have any questions.

5 **Have groups prepare their skits.** Direct them to where you have assembled materials they might use to make props. Remind groups to create short, simple skits. Allow students at least ten minutes to create their skits. (**Note:** Students should not pretend to perform religious ceremonies in their skits. Emphasize that the directions for Skit 6, Section 21.8, specify explanations, not act-it-outs. Skit 6 requires Visuals 21B–21E.)

Information Master 21

6 **Have groups present their skits or "samurai lessons" in front of the class.** Call on groups to present their skits in order by number: Skit 1, then Skit 2, and so on. Follow these steps for each group:

- Before each group begins its skit, have them announce which section of the book they read. As each group sets up, have observing students turn to that section of the book and locate the corresponding Reading Notes.

- After each samurai lesson has been presented, have the observing students read the section of the book that corresponds to the skit topic. During this time, have the skit members reflect on their performance by writing three things they did well in their skit and three things they could improve.

- Have observing students share three things from their reading that they saw in this skit and three things that were missing.

- Allow students to ask any questions of their samurai "Sensei" (SEN-say).

- Have the observing students complete the Reading Notes for this section. (**Note:** Consider assigning this step for homework the night after each skit has been presented.)

7   **Conduct a wrap-up discussion.** Ask,

- Which part of the samurai training did you think was most important? Least important?

- How do you think the training of a samurai differs from the training of an American soldier?

- What was the role of the samurai in the military society of medieval Japan?

8   **Have students complete the Reading Notes for Sections 21.11 and 21.12.**

Processing

In the Processing activity, students will create a class schedule for a young person who is new to samurai training.

Quicker Coverage

Skip Props for the Skits Instead of having students follow Step 2 on each of their role cards, which has them create a prop, have them simply complete Step 1 and pantomime as they read their lines during the skits.

Have Students Complete the Reading Notes During the Skits Instead of having students read each section of the book following each skit, instruct students to listen carefully during the skits and complete their Reading Notes as they observe. Remind students after each skit to ask any questions they need to complete their Reading Notes.

Deeper Coverage

Have Students Expand Their Skits Have students use the Internet or library books to find out more about samurai training to include in their presentations. Also, as lessons are being presented, encourage the presenters and the observing students to act as if they are truly attending samurai school. For example, the samurai instructors could call on students to demonstrate skills. They could also pose a quiz question for students to answer at the completion of each skit.

Assessment

Mastering the Content

1. D	5. A	9. B	13. A
2. B	6. B	10. B	14. A
3. C	7. A	11. C	15. D
4. D	8. C	12. D	16. C

Applying Social Studies Skills

17. Answers will vary. Sample answer: It is better just to go ahead and do things with determination than to go out of one's way to try to avoid trouble, as the trouble will happen anyway.

18. Answers will vary. Sample answer: Once a child has had the experience of being afraid, it will stay with him or her for life.

19. Answers will vary. Sample answer: Welcome challenges rather than trying to avoid them, because one gets more honor for facing a great challenge than for facing a small one.

Exploring the Essential Question

20. Answers should include all the elements requested in the prompt.

Scoring Rubric

Score	Description
3	Student completes a want ad that addresses at least five of the bulleted points. The want ad is clearly stated, supported by details, and demonstrates command of standard English conventions.
2	Student responds to most or all parts of the task, but the want ad may lack details or not be clearly stated.
1	Student responds to at least one part of the task. The want ad may contain factual and/or grammatical errors and may lack details.
0	Response does not match the task or is incorrect.

Tomoe Gozen: History or Legend?

1   **Use a Venn diagram to compare and contrast "history" and "legend."**
Draw a Venn diagram on the board. Label one side "History" and the other
"Legend." Label the middle section "Both." Ask students to suggest words
that describe "history" and add them to the diagram. Do the same for the
concept of "legend." Help students fill in any similarities in the overlapping
area. Point out that history is based on known facts, while legend includes
fictional elements, although it may be based on historical facts.

2   **Discuss how historians decide if something is history or legend.** Elicit from
students the idea that history is based on evidence from the past—written
documents, artifacts, or eyewitnesses. Events or people in a legend may have
been real, but historians need to have evidence—not just stories—to make
that determination.

3   **Have students read the Chapter 21 Reading Further in the Student
Edition.** When they finish, ask them how historians determined that Tomoe
Gozen was most likely a real person. Have students discuss whether they
are convinced or not, and why. Then have students tell about other historic
figures they know of who also became legends. For example, students may
know the story about George Washington and the cherry tree, which is
probably a legend, not a true historic event, although Washington was a real
person. Ask students why they think this story might have been told over and
over again. What does it say about Washington? What is its main message?

4   **Have students complete the Reading Further in their Interactive Student
Notebooks.** Discuss how comparing and contrasting helps students to analyze two ideas or items. Point out that comparing and contrasting helps to
distinguish items from each other and also helps to better clarify each one.
Ask, *How did the Venn diagram help you to write your summary?*

5   **Invite students to share their summaries.** Discuss with students some
reasons these two women might have become legends in Japanese culture.

English Language Learners

Modify the Activity During the Experiential Exercise, let students become a fifth member of a group and take a non-speaking role. For example, a student might demonstrate how to use a weapon while another student talks about it. Or, for Skits 2, 7 or 8, students might take a role in pantomiming during a demonstration.

Learners Reading and Writing Below Grade Level

Provide Support for Reading Provide students with a copy of the section that their group has been assigned to read. On the copy, have students highlight the sentences that will help them complete the sentences on their role cards. Encourage these students to make very clear "cue cards" with the statements they will read, as well as clear directions about what to do as they read them. For example, a cue card might read: "Samurai always go into battle dressed in heavy armor. This armor is unique (point to armor) because it is made of rows of small, coated metal plates and laced with silk cords."

Learners with Special Education Needs

Modify the Reading Notes Give students a copy of the Guide to Reading Notes with the answer to one question in each section omitted. As they listen to each skit, students can focus on the single question they are asked to answer. Remind them to review the answers for the other questions in each section.

Modify the Activity During the Experiential Exercise, let students become a fifth member of a group and observe its activities. Give student observers an extra copy of the role cards from Student Handout 21, and have them check off each role as it is developed by the group.

Shorten the Processing Activity Instead of having students design an entire class schedule for a young samurai student, ask them to instead choose what they think is the most important training for a samurai. Have students list that subject and then complete these sentences.

- Through this kind of training, a samurai learns to
- I think that _____ is the most important training for a samurai because

Advanced Learners

Enhance or Replace the Processing Activity In addition to or as a replacement for the Processing activity, have students create a Venn diagram that compares the training of Japanese samurai to that of modern American soldiers. Students can gather information for this Venn diagram by

- reviewing the list of skills, knowledge, and values from the Preview activity
- skimming Chapter 21 for information on Japanese samurai training
- using their knowledge of American military training or reading about basic training for the U.S. Army on the Internet

Once students have created this Venn diagram, challenge them to choose one element of Japanese samurai training that would be a useful addition to the preparation of American soldiers. Have them explain and justify their selection in a few sentences below their Venn diagram.

Enrichment Resources

Have students find out more about the development of samurai society in Japan by exploring the following Enrichment Resources for *History Alive! The Medieval World and Beyond* at www.teachtci.com.

Enrichment Readings These in-depth readings encourage students to explore selected topics related to the chapter. You may also find readings that relate the chapter's content directly to your state's curriculum.

Internet Connections The recommended Web sites provide useful and engaging content that reinforces skills development and mastery of subjects within the chapter.

Literature Recommendations

The following books offer opportunities to extend the content in this chapter.

Among Samurai and Shoguns: Japan 1000–1700 A.D. by the Editors of Time-Life Books (Alexandria, VA: Time-Life Books, 2000)

The Boy and the Samurai by Erik Christian Haugaard (Boston: Houghton Mifflin Company, 1991)

Sword of the Samurai: Adventure Stories from Japan by Eric Kimmel (New York: HarperCollins Children's, 2000)

Section 21.2

1. Shoguns rewarded samurai with land or appointments to offices and rewarded daimyos for their obedience and loyalty with land, money, and appointments to office. Daimyos helped the shoguns rule and rewarded samurai for their obedience and loyalty with land, money, and appointments to office. Samurai, in turn, provided protection and loyalty to daimyos. Samurai pledged to serve and protect the shogun.

2. After a century of warfare between daimyos for power, Tokugawa Ieyasu became shogun and established a strong military government.

Section 21.3

1. Answers will vary. Answers may include: helmet, iron mask, shoulder guards, shin guards, and metal sleeves.

2. Students should label the sword. A long curved sword was used to fight.

3. Answers will vary. Students might draw and label a bow and arrow or a spear.

Section 21.4

1. Answers will vary. Possible answer: Samurai learned to shoot accurately while riding horseback.

2. If a samurai's sword was lost or broken, he or she would continue to fight with other weapons such as fans or wooden staffs. They might also use martial arts.

3. Answers should include the name of the samurai, his or her ancestors, heroic deeds, and reason for fighting. Possible answer: My name is Tomoe Gozen. My father was a skilled samurai, as was my grandfather. I have won many battles. I will fight you today because you offended my personal honor.

Section 21.5

1. Students' responses will vary. Samurai were taught to think of themselves as already dead.

2. Answers will vary. Possible answer: Samurai might go for days without eating, march barefoot in the snow on long journeys, or hold stiff positions for hours without complaining.

3. Samurai were trained to always be alert because an attack could come when it was least expected. They were trained by being hit with no notice.

Section 21.6

1. Answers will vary. Possible answer: Calligraphy is the art of beautiful writing. I must practice it so I can be a student of culture as well as a warrior.

2. Haiku is a form of poetry that consists of three lines of five, seven, and five syllables.

Section 21.7

Drawings might include a tea caddy, a small bowl, a wooden dipper, a whisk, a scroll painting, a flower arrangement, or an urn.

Section 21.8

1. A samurai would prove his or her devotion to the Amida Buddha by repeating Amida's name over and over, up to 70,000 times a day.

2. According to Zen Buddhism, enlightenment can be achieved through meditation and through giving up logical thinking.

3. Students should write the koan, "What is the sound of one hand clapping?"

Section 21.9

1. Bushido was the samurai code, or "The Way of the Warrior." It called on samurai to be fair, honest, and fearless in the face of death. They were also expected to value loyalty and personal honor.

2. Answers will vary. Possible answer: I am always loyal to my lord.

Section 21.10

1. Students' drawings will vary. The drawing might show a woman in a fighting position and the same size as the male samurai.

2. Around the 12th century, women enjoyed respect and status. Some trained as samurai. However, by the 17th century they were under the control of men.

Section 21.11

Answers will vary. Possible answers:

In the left section: A shogun ruled in the name of an emperor. The samurai code was stricter than the code of chivalry, since it demanded that he kill himself to maintain his honor.

In the right section: A military leader might rule as king. The knights of Europe had a code of chivalry.

In the center section: Ties of loyalty and obligation bound rulers and those who served them. Rulers rose to power as military chiefs. Both societies had lords who built castles and held estates worked by peasants. Both societies had warriors bound by codes or loyalty, who wore armor, rode horses, and owned land.

Section 21.12

1. During World War II, Japanese suicide pilots, called kamikazes, sometimes crashed their planes into enemy ships.

2. Answers will vary. Possible answers: Martial arts are still studied. People continue to write haiku and use calligraphy. Zen gardens and tea ceremonies remain popular. Samurai ideals of loyalty and respect for rank are still alive in modern Japan.

Japan During Medieval Times

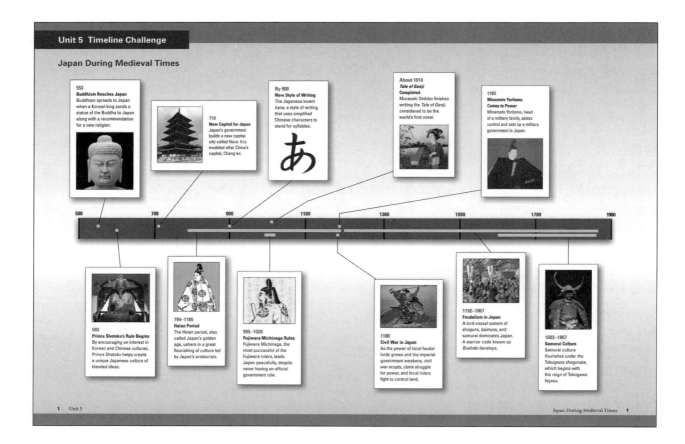

Unit 5 Timeline Challenge

Japan During Medieval Times

552
Buddhism Reaches Japan
Buddhism spreads to Japan when a Korean king sends a statue of the Buddha to Japan along with a recommendation for a new religion.

710
New Capital for Japan
Japan's government builds a new capital city called Nara. It is modeled after China's capital, Chang'an.

By 900
New Style of Writing
The Japanese invent kana, a style of writing that uses simplified Chinese characters to stand for syllables.

あ

About 1010
Tale of Genji **Completed**
Murasaki Shikibu finishes writing the *Tale of Genji*, considered to be the world's first novel.

1185
Minamoto Yoritomo Comes to Power
Minamoto Yoritomo, head of a military family, seizes control and sets up a military government in Japan.

583
Prince Shotoku's Rule Begins
By encouraging an interest in Korean and Chinese cultures, Prince Shotoku helps create a unique Japanese culture of blended ideas.

794–1185
Heian Period
The Heian period, also called Japan's golden age, ushers in a great flourishing of culture led by Japan's aristocrats.

995–1028
Fujiwara Michinaga Rules
Fujiwara Michinaga, the most successful of the Fujiwara rulers, leads Japan peacefully, despite never having an official government role.

1180
Civil War in Japan
As the power of local feudal lords grows and the imperial government weakens, civil war erupts, clans struggle for power, and local rulers fight to control land.

1192–1867
Feudalism in Japan
A lord-vassal system of shoguns, daimyos, and samurai dominates Japan. A warrior code known as *Bushido* develops.

1603–1867
Samurai Culture
Samurai culture flourishes under the Tokugawa shogunate, which begins with the reign of Tokugawa Ieyasu.

1 Unit 5

Japan During Medieval Times 1

Overview

This Timeline Challenge helps students review the main events and ideas of this unit while providing practice in reading and interpreting timelines. You can vary and expand the activity according to students' needs and the amount of time available.

Basic Procedure

1 **Introduce the timeline in the Student Edition.** Direct students to the Japan During Medieval Times Timeline at the end of Unit 5 in the Student Edition. You may wish to have students read aloud and discuss the timeline entries.

2 **Introduce the Timeline Challenge in the Interactive Student Notebook.** Direct students to the Unit 5 Timeline Challenge. Point out the two types of questions, "Timeline Skills" and "Critical Thinking," and model how to answer each type.

3 **Have students complete the Timeline Challenge.** Monitor students as they work. Use the Guide to Unit 5 Timeline Challenge to check their answers. You may wish to project a transparency of this page as you work through the questions with the class and conduct a discussion of the "Critical Thinking" questions.

4 **Complete the KWL chart.** Return to the KWL chart created at the beginning of the unit, and ask students to list the key information they have learned.

Classroom Timeline

1 **Prepare the Timeline Challenge Cards.** Copy and cut the cards from *Student Handout TC5: Unit 5 Timeline Challenge Cards.* You may wish to laminate the cards for future use.

2 **Create a timeline on a classroom wall.** On an empty wall or a large bulletin board, make a timeline with masking tape or colored paper. Mark off the time intervals in advance, or ask students to do so in class.

3 **Have students place the Timeline Challenge Cards.** Distribute cards to individual students or pairs and have them tape the cards to the timeline in the correct locations. Call on students to provide more information on the timeline topics to review main events and issues.

Student Handout TC5

Internet Research

1 **Review students' suggestions for additional timeline entries.** Have students share their answers to the last question of the Timeline Challenge.

2 **Have students conduct Internet research.** Ask students to choose and research one of their suggested events.

3 **Have students create additional Timeline Challenge Cards.** Direct students to research an appropriate image for their cards and then use the computer to create an illustrated card, complete with timeline entry.

Timeline Skills

Score 1 point for each correct answer.

1. Korea

2. Prince Shotoku encouraged an interest in Korean and Chinese cultures which blended into a unique Japanese culture.

3. It was modeled after the capital of China, Chang'an.

4. The development of a new style of writing, the reign of Fujiwara Michinaga, and the publication of the *Tale of Genji* all occurred during the Heian period.

5. Fujiwara Michinaga ruled despite having never held a government position.

6. The *Tale of Genji* is considered the world's first novel.

7. five years

8. Feudalism lasted for about seven centuries in Japan.

Critical Thinking

Score 1 to 3 points for each answer, depending on the thoroughness of the response.

9. Possible answers include:

a. *Korea:* Buddhism came to Japan through Korea in 552. Korean sculpture also influenced Japanese artists.

b. *China:* Chinese writing greatly influenced Japanese writing. Japan also adopted the pagoda design as an architectural style from China.

10. The Heian period was a time during which aristocrats led a great flourishing of Japanese culture. New forms of art and literature developed, including books such as the *Tale of Genji*, and a new style of painting called *yamato-e*, which expressed nonreligious scenes characterized by thin lines and vivid colors.

11. Japanese samurai were trained in swordsmanship. They learned how to how to avoid getting hit. They were given mental training, during which they learned self-control and preparedness. They were also trained in calligraphy.

12. Answers will vary. Students must explain why the events they chose merit inclusion.

Using Scores to Inform Instruction

Timeline Skills A score of 5 out of 8 indicates that students understand most of the key events in the unit.

Critical Thinking A score of 8 out of 12 indicates that students are able to think critically about most of the key issues in this unit.

If students score below these levels, consider reviewing timeline and critical thinking skills.

Civilizations of the Americas

Geography Challenge

Chapter 22: The Mayas
What led to the rise, flourishing, and fall of the Mayan civilization?
Response Group

Chapter 23: The Aztecs
How did the Aztecs rise to power?
Visual Discovery

Chapter 24: Daily Life in Tenochtitlán
What was daily life like for Aztecs in Tenochtitlán?
Writing for Understanding

Chapter 25: The Incas
How did the Incas manage their large and remote empire?
Experiential Exercise

Chapter 26: Achievements of the Mayas, Aztecs, and Incas
What were the significant achievements of the Mayas, Aztecs, and Incas?
Social Studies Skill Builder

Timeline Challenge

Civilizations of the Americas

Overview

This activity introduces geographic information essential to Unit 6. Students read and interpret maps to learn about the location, physical features, and climate of the areas inhabited by the Mayan, Incan, and Aztec civilizations. They annotate a map of Mexico, Central America, and South America and answer questions in their Interactive Student Notebooks, and then discuss critical thinking questions. Students' comprehension of content and proficiency in map-reading and higher-order thinking skills will help you gauge their readiness for the unit. The pages that follow include a completed map, answers to questions, a scoring guide to inform your teaching, and suggestions for modifications to meet specific student needs.

Essential Geographic Understandings

1. Location of Mexico, Central America, and South America

2. Key physical features: Andes Mountains, Mexico Plateau, Yucatán Peninsula, Atacama Desert, Amazon River

3. Location of the Incan, Mayan, and Aztec civilizations

4. Impact of physical geography on ways of life

Procedures

1 **Introduce the unit.** Tell students that in this unit they will learn about the civilizations of Mexico, Central America, and South America that flourished at about the same time as the other civilizations they have studied.

2 **Create a KWL chart.** Ask students to identify what they already know about these civilizations and what they want to learn. Use their responses to gauge how much additional background information they will need as you progress through the unit. Students will return to the KWL chart at the end of the unit and add the key information they have learned.

3 **Have students read Unit 6 "Setting the Stage" in the Student Edition.**

4 **Have students complete the Geography Challenge.** Monitor students as they work. Use the guide on the next two pages to check their answers. You may wish to project the map from the Interactive Student Notebook and have students annotate it as the class works through the map-reading questions. Make sure that students have grasped Essential Geographic Understandings 1 to 3.

5 **Discuss the "Critical Thinking" questions.** Help students understand the geographic relationships described in Essential Geographic Understanding 4.

Mexico, Central America, and South America

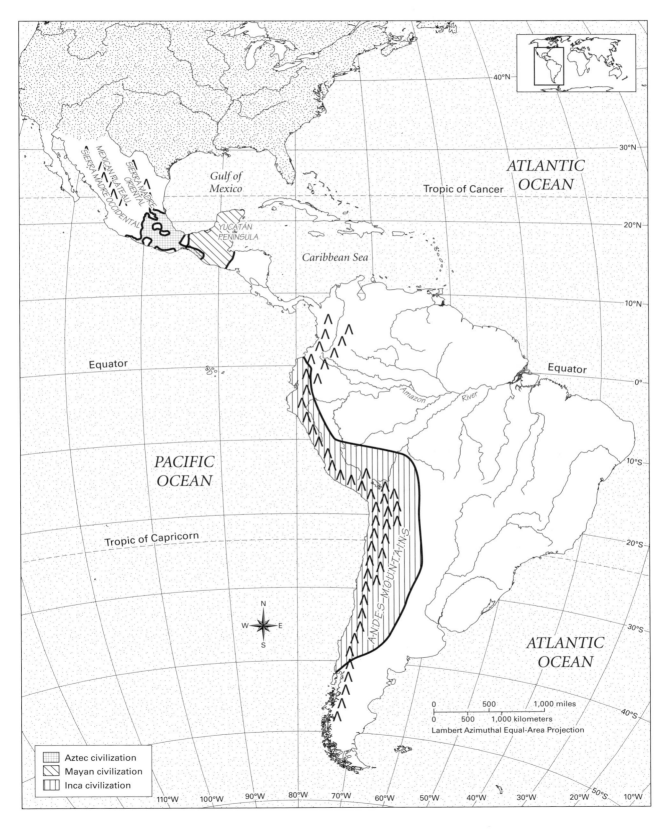

40°N

30°N

ATLANTIC OCEAN

Tropic of Cancer

Gulf of Mexico

20°N

SIERRA MADRE ORIENTAL

MEXICAN PLATEAU

SIERRA MADRE OCCIDENTAL

YUCATÁN PENINSULA

Caribbean Sea

10°N

Equator

Equator

0°

Amazon River

PACIFIC OCEAN

10°S

Tropic of Capricorn

ANDES MOUNTAINS

N
W   E
S

20°S

30°S

ATLANTIC OCEAN

0   500   1,000 miles
0   500   1,000 kilometers
Lambert Azimuthal Equal-Area Projection

40°S

Aztec civilization
Mayan civilization
Inca civilization

50°S

110°W   100°W   90°W   80°W   70°W   60°W   50°W   40°W   30°W   20°W   10°W

Geography Skills

Score 1 point for each correct answer. Use the map on the previous page to check shading and labeling.

1. Students should shade the Mayan civilization on the map, including the key.

2. Students should shade the Aztec civilization on the map, including the key.

3. Students should shade the Incan civilization on the map, including the key.

4. Students should label the Sierra Madre Occidental, Sierra Madre Oriental, Andes Mountains, Mexico Plateau, Yucatán Peninsula, and Amazon River.

5. The elevation of the land in central Mexico ranges from 6,500 feet to 13,000 feet above sea level. The principal climate zone is semiarid.

6. The high elevation and semiarid climate might have made transportation and farming difficult.

7. The land in the northern Yucatán Peninsula ranges in elevation from sea level to 700 feet, while in the southern Yucatán, the elevation ranges from 1,500 feet to 6,500 feet.

8. The climate in the north is tropical wet and dry, while the south is humid subtropical.

9. The steep hills and wet climate might have limited the size of farms and settlements.

10. The land in western South America rises to about 13,000 feet in the Andes Mountains. It has a highland climate.

11. High elevation would mean cold living conditions and difficult farming for the Incas.

Critical Thinking

Questions may have more than one correct answer. Score 1 to 3 points for each reasonable answer, depending on the strength of students' geographic reasoning. Possible answers are given here.

12. The Aztecs may have had the largest city because they had vast areas outside the city where food could be grown.

13. An economy based on agriculture might have been easiest in the Mayan civilization because they had a lot of low, flat land with enough rainfall to grow crops. Agriculture was probably most challenging for the Incas because of their steep land.

14. In order to trade, people need surplus goods, a desire for other goods, means of travel, and trading partners. Perhaps the Incas had an extensive trade system, as trade might have helped to unify such a large empire.

15. All three civilizations had enough water and fertile soil to grow crops.

Using Scores to Inform Instruction

Geography Skills A score of 8 out of 11 or better indicates that students have acquired sufficient geographic information to proceed with the unit.

Critical Thinking A score of 8 out of 16 or better indicates that students are beginning to understand the relationships between physical geography and the different ways in which people live.

Modifying Instruction

ELL or Learners with Special Education Needs Consider focusing on map-reading questions or limiting the number of "Critical Thinking" questions.

Students with Weak Map or Critical Thinking Skills Assign appropriate pages from the Social Studies Skills Toolkit in the back of the Lesson Masters.

The Mayas

What led to the rise, flourishing, and fall of the Mayan civilization?

Overview

In a Response Group activity, students use a Sacred Round to solve problems related to four aspects of Mayan culture.

Objectives

In the course of reading this chapter and participating in the classroom activity, students will

Social Studies

- explain the causes and effects of the rise and fall of the Mayan civilization.
- describe the structure of Mayan society, and the roles and functions of each class.
- analyze important aspects of Mayan culture, including class structure and slavery, warfare, family life, religious practices, and agricultural techniques.
- map the political and geographic features of the Mayan civilization.
- evaluate various theories to explain the sudden fall of the Mayan civilization.

Language Arts

- deliver a persuasive presentation with a clear position and effective evidence.

Social Studies Vocabulary

Key Content Terms Mayas, Mesoamerica, ceremonial center, hieroglyphic, social pyramid, ritual, sacrifice, slash-and-burn agriculture

Academic Vocabulary abandon, considerable, divine, sustain

Materials

History Alive! The Medieval World and Beyond

Interactive Student Notebooks

Lesson Masters

- Information Master 22 (1 transparency)
- Student Handout 22A (See Preview directions for quantities.)
- Student Handouts 22B–22D (1 for every 3 students)
- Vocabulary Development handout (1 per student, on colored paper)

Activity	Suggested Time	Materials
Preview	20 minutes	• Interactive Student Notebooks • Student Handout 22A (See Preview directions for quantities.)
Vocabulary Development	30–40 minutes	• *History Alive! The Medieval World and Beyond* • Interactive Student Notebooks • Vocabulary Development handout
Response Group	120 minutes (3 regular periods) (1.5 block periods)	• *History Alive! The Medieval World and Beyond* • Interactive Student Notebooks • Student Handouts 22B–22D (1 copy per 3 students) • Information Master 22 (1 transparency)
Processing	15 minutes	• Interactive Student Notebooks
Assessment	40 minutes	• Chapter 22 Assessment

Preview

1 **Prepare the classroom and materials for the Preview activity.** Clear a large space at the front of the room where students will create a physical model of the Mayan social pyramid, using their bodies. Have a sturdy chair available for one student to stand on. Make a copy of *Student Handout 22A: Role Cards,* and cut them out. You may need to make multiple copies of the page with Role Card D. You should have the following quantities:

- Role Card A: Mayan Ruler (1)
- Role Card B: Mayan Noble (1) and Mayan Priest (1)
- Role Card C: Mayan Merchants (2) and Mayan Artisans (2)
- Role Card D: Mayan Peasants (enough for the remaining students)
- Role Card E: Mayan Slaves (3)

Student Handout 22A

2 **Prepare to create a Mayan social pyramid.** Give each student a role card. Have them read their role cards. Then tell them that, as you call their role, they should follow the directions on their card. Tell students that some roles will be assigned to more than one student, so when they read the statement from their role card they may need to take turns. Remind students that they should listen carefully to what other students say about their roles.

3 **Have students create a Mayan social pyramid.** Have students come to the front of the classroom by role, beginning with Role Card A. As students come to the front of the classroom, place them as explained below. Allow each student in that role to read the statement on his or her role card before calling the next group.

- Role Card A: Have this student stand on a sturdy chair.
- Role Card B: Have these students stand side-by-side in front of the ruler.
- Role Card C: Have these students kneel side-by-side in front of the noble and priest.
- Role Card D: Have these students sit cross-legged, side-by-side, in front of the merchants and artisans.
- Role Card E: Have these students lay on the floor in front of the peasants.

Once students have completed the pyramid, have the lower three levels of the pyramid turn around and face the upper two. Then ask, What shape have you created with this arrangement of your bodies? After discussing this question, have students return to their desks.

4 **Have students complete the Preview activity in their Interactive Student Notebooks.** After students label the pyramid, discuss the following questions as a class. Have students record responses during the class discussion.

- What do you think this pyramid represents? *(the class structure of Mayan society)*

- What clues tell you who might be at the top level of the pyramid? The second level? The third? The fourth? The fifth? (*things people at each level said or did*)

- How do you think Mayan class structure affected people's lives? (*A few privileged people at the top had power and property; most people—those at the bottom—had little power and property and did the most manual labor.*)

5   **Connect the Preview activity to the chapter.** Remind students that in the Preview activity they created a model of the Mayan social pyramid and considered how the Mayan social structure might have affected people's lives. In the chapter, students will learn more about Mayan civilization, including class structure, family life, religious beliefs and practices, and agricultural techniques.

Vocabulary Development

1   **Introduce the Key Content Terms.** Have students locate the Key Content Terms for the chapter in their Interactive Student Notebooks. These are important terms that will help them understand the main ideas of the chapter. Ask volunteers to identify any familiar terms and suggest how they might be used in a sentence.

2   **Have students complete a Vocabulary Development handout.** Give each student a copy of the Vocabulary Development handout of your choice from the Reading Toolkit at the back of the Lesson Masters. These handouts provide extra Key Content Term practice and support, depending on your students' needs. Review the completed handout by asking volunteers to share one answer for each term.

Reading

1   **Introduce the Essential Question and have students read Section 22.1.** Have students identify the Essential Question on the first page of the chapter: *What led to the rise, flourishing, and fall of the Mayan civilization?* Then have students read Section 22.1. Afterward, have students carefully analyze the chapter opener image. Ask them to find words, phrases, or sentences in the text of Section 22.1 and connect them to visual details in the chapter opener image. Have several volunteers share the connections they found with the rest of the class.

2   **Have students complete the Reading Notes for Chapter 22.** Assign Sections 22.2 to 22.6 during the activity, as indicated in the procedures for the Response Group activity. Remind students to use the Key Content Terms where appropriate as they complete their Reading Notes.

> **Writing: Spelling Derivatives**
>
> As you review students' work, you can integrate coverage of spelling derivatives by noting the various noun and adjective forms of the following terms and calling attention to their spelling patterns: *Mayas/Mayan; Mesoamerica/Mesoamerican; ceremony/ceremonial; hieroglyph/hieroglyphic; rite/ritual; sacrifice/sacrificial.* Have students sort the pairs by patterns and note where the spelling does or does not change in the derivative.

Response Group

1 **Prepare the materials.** Prior to beginning this activity, do the following:

- Make a transparency of *Information Master 22: Solving Problems Using the Sacred Round.*

- Make one copy of *Student Handout 22B: Sacred Round* on card stock for every three students. You may want to cut the two rounds from each copy beforehand to save time during class.

- Make one copy of *Student Handout 22C: Sacred Round Calculations* for every three students.

- Make one copy of *Student Handout 22D: Guide to Glyphs on the Sacred Round* for every three students. (**Note:** Consider making Student Handouts 22B–22D different colors for easy identification.)

2 **Have students read Section 22.2 and complete the Reading Notes.** Tell students that this section provides background information on the Mayas. Then have students read and complete their Reading Notes.

3 **Place students in groups of three and introduce the activity.** Explain that in this activity students will complete an authentic task—using a Sacred Round—that will help them understand more about Mayan culture. Explain that the Sacred Round was a ritual calendar. Only Mayan priests could "read" the hidden meaning of the Sacred Round, which was used to determine the best days to plan, hunt, cure, do battle, and perform religious ceremonies. Students will use the Sacred Round and interpret its meaning to solve four problems dealing with different aspects of Mayan culture.

4 **Prepare students for the activity.** Distribute one copy of *Student Handout 22B: Sacred Round* and a pair of scissors to each group. Have students read the directions on the Student Handout that explain how to operate the two pieces of the Sacred Round. Then have students cut out their Sacred Round.

5 **Have students use the Sacred Round.** Explain that the Sacred Round has 260 days. Each day in the ritual calendar consists of a number, represented by dots and bars, and a day name, represented by a glyph (symbol).

- The smaller round contains the numbers. Ask students to look at this round and figure out what number a dot represents *(1)* and what number a bar represents *(5)*. Then ask them to calculate the highest number on the smaller round *(13: two bars and three dots)*.

- The larger round contains the day names. Ask students how many names, or hieroglyphs, are on the larger round *(20)*. Explain that the glyphs gave priests clues about whether certain days were prophetically good or bad for certain events.

- The first day on the ritual calendar is 1 Imix. Have students find these two points on their calendars (they are marked with arrows). Then have them fit the point of Imix into the notch for the single dot, or 1.

Information Master 22

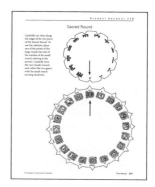

Student Handout 22B

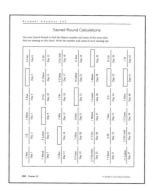

Student Handout 22C

Student Handout 22D

- Explain that to find the next day on the ritual calendar, they must carefully rotate the two rounds toward each other, fitting the next point into the next notch. The small round turns clockwise. Have students practice this and identify the next day on the calendar *(2 Ik)*. Repeat this a few times to make sure students understand how to use the Sacred Round.

Distribute one copy of Student Handout 22C to each group. Have groups use the Sacred Round to fill in the missing days on the handout.

6 **Review the directions for the activity.** Distribute one copy of Student Handout 22D to each group. Have students quickly review the glyphs and their translations. Then, check for understanding by asking students, Which of these calendar days might be a bad day to play a dangerous outdoor game? *Possible answers: Cimi (death) or Cauac (thunderstorm or rain).* Then project Information Master 22 and cover the four problems. Review the directions with students.

7 **Have students read and complete the activity.** Reveal the first problem and have students read Section 22.3 and complete their Reading Notes before using the Sacred Round to solve the problem. Then facilitate a discussion in which a presenter from each group explains their answer. Encourage presenters with different answers or rationales to respond to the previous speaker. (**Note:** You may want to have presenters stand on a chair, just as Mayan priests would stand on the top steps of the temple to address the people.) Then reveal the next problem, and rotate the role of the presenter each time groups discuss a new problem. Here are some possible responses:

- Problem 1: 13 Cimi might not be a good day to attack because Cimi means death and its symbol is a human skull. Others, however, might interpret this as a good sign.

- Problem 2: 7 Ben might be the best day for the wedding because the symbol for Ben, a maize seedling, combines parts of the names of the bride and groom. Others might wait until 1 Ahau.

- Problem 3: Preparations should begin on 9 Muluc. One interpretation is that this is a good day to start preparations because the symbol for Muluc is a drop of water.

- Problem 4: 9 Ik might be the best day to plant because the symbol for Ik is a germinating maize seed. Others might wait until 11 Kan.

8 **Debrief the activity.** Ask students,

- How did it feel to use the Sacred Round to solve problems?

- Why do you think Mayan priests—instead of some other group—were the only people who used the Sacred Round?

- What aspects of this experience support what you read about the Mayas?

Processing

Have students complete the Processing activity in their Interactive Student Notebooks. Students create glyphs to represent four important aspects of Mayan culture.

Quicker Coverage

Eliminate the Preview Activity The Preview activity helps students understand the structure of Mayan society and the role played by each social class. However, if you skip the Preview, students will still find this content in their reading and Reading Notes for Section 22.3.

Assign Reading for Homework Assign students to read Sections 22.3–22.6 the night before using the Sacred Rounds in class.

Deeper Coverage

Have Students Generate Questions After students have completed the Response Group activity using the Sacred Round, have them create one or two additional questions based on Mayan culture. Their questions should establish the following:

- the current day
- the dilemma—related to one of the four topics of Mayan culture: class structure, family life, religious beliefs and practices, or agricultural techniques
- the answer

Then choose a few student-generated questions for the class to answer using their Sacred Rounds.

Assessment

Mastering the Content

1. B	5. B	9. A	13. A
2. C	6. A	10. D	14. A
3. B	7. A	11. C	15. B
4. D	8. C	12. D	16. D

Applying Social Studies Skills

17. Answers will vary. Sample answer: Mayas played a ball game trying to hit a rubber ball through a stone ring. The losers of the game lost their lives.

18. Students should circle the pyramid.

19. the Observatory; Answers will vary. Sample answer: It was used for studying the night sky, gathering information to help make the calendar.

Exploring the Essential Question

20. Answers should include all the elements requested in the prompt.

Scoring Rubric

Score	Description
3	Student completes all six parts of the task. Arguments and questions are clearly stated, logically reasoned, and demonstrate command of standard English conventions. Parts 1a, 2a, and 3a should each have at least one accurate supporting detail (e.g., many non-farmers in cities, farming methods bad for soil, dependence on war for sacrifices and slaves).
2	Student responds to most or all parts of the task, but arguments and questions may lack relevance or not be clearly stated.
1	Student responds to at least one part of the task. Arguments and questions may contain factual and/or grammatical errors and may lack relevance.
0	Response does not match the task or is incorrect.

English Language Learners

Model the Activity During Step 5, walk through the use of the Sacred Round with these students, or with the class as a whole, until you feel they understand how to use it. During Step 7, walk through the first problem with students. Discuss each possible day with these students, or with the entire class, so they can understand how to identify days that will or will not work well in solving the problem.

Learners Reading and Writing Below Grade Level

Alter the Preview Activity Give students their role cards the day before so that they can practice what they are supposed to do and say during the experience. Or, consider giving these students the role of Peasant, which will be the role of the majority of the class. Instead of having every Peasant read his or her statement aloud, only call on four students who are confident readers.

Learners with Special Education Needs

Pare Down Reading Notes Limit the number of Reading Notes students must complete as follows:

- Each time Information Master 22 prompts students to read a section of the chapter and complete the corresponding Reading Notes, have these students focus on completing just one part of the Reading Notes for that section.

- Afterward, review the Reading Notes as a class, and have students fill in any missing parts of their notes. You might make a transparency of the Reading Notes to fill in along with the class.

Advanced Learners

Alter the Processing Activity In addition to the regular Processing activity, have students respond to a critical thinking question. Challenge them to use their critical thinking skills by responding to one of these questions:

- What can you do with the knowledge you gained about the ancient Mayas?

- What is a compelling reason why you should know this information?

- What do you think would have happened if the Mayan civilization had not suddenly disappeared?

Enrichment Resources

Find out more about the Mayas and their civilization by exploring the following Enrichment Resources for *History Alive! The Medieval World and Beyond* at www.teachtci.com.

Enrichment Readings These in-depth readings encourage students to explore selected topics related to the chapter. You may also find readings that relate the chapter's content directly to your state's curriculum.

Internet Connections The recommended Web sites provide useful and engaging content that reinforces skills development and mastery of subjects within the chapter.

Literature Recommendations

The following books offer opportunities to extend the content in this chapter.

The Gods and Goddesses of the Ancient Maya by Leonard Everett Fisher (New York: Holiday House, 1999)

Popul Vuh: A Sacred Book of the Maya by Victor Montejo (Vancouver: Groundwood-Douglas & McIntyre, 1999)

Rain Player by David Wisniewski (Boston: Houghton Mifflin Company, 1995)

Section 22.2

1. Check students' maps against the map below to make sure they have drawn in the boundary of the Mayan civilization; shaded the northern lowlands, southern lowlands, and highlands on the map and key; and labeled the Yucatán Peninsula and Petén Jungle.

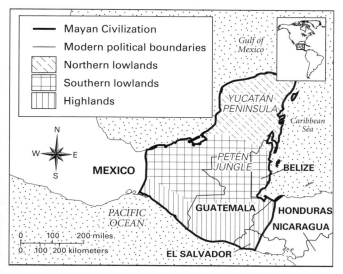

2. Symbols will vary. Possible achievements and explanations include:

   • Farming—The Olmecs turned from hunting and gathering to farming, and maize was an important crop.

   • Permanent Settlements—Farming allowed the Olmecs to create farming villages, which were linked by trade routes.

   • Capital City—The Olmecs' capital city boasted palaces, temples, and monuments.

   • Religious Centers—The Olmecs were the first Mesoamericans to develop large religious and ceremonial centers.

   • Calendar—The Olmecs were the first Mesoamericans to use a solar calendar.

3. Check students' timelines against the one below.

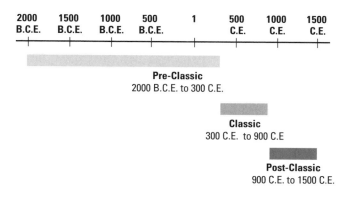

Section 22.3

Possible answers:

The Ruler Called the halach uinic, or "true man"; decided when and where to go to war; at religious ceremonies, wore a very tall headdress; might have been influenced by female family members.

Nobles and Priests Nobles knew how to read and write; nobles gathered taxes, supplies, and labor for important projects; nobles led peasant armies in times of war; priests led rituals and performed sacrifices.

Merchants and Artisans Merchants traveled by sea, rivers, and roads to trade with other city-states; merchants traded such goods as obsidian, jade, copal, and quetzal feathers; artists painted murals of Mayan life and important battles; artisans were skilled weavers and potters.

Peasants Peasant men worked mostly in the fields; peasant women generally worked at preparing food, weaving, and sewing; peasants also built temples and pyramids and served as soldiers; peasants sometimes attended royal weddings and religious ceremonies.

Slaves People could become slaves if their families sold them into slavery; soldiers of humble background who were captured in war were enslaved; people who committed serious crimes were enslaved; slaves were often sacrificed when their masters died.

Section 22.4

1. Possible answers:

That young woman is very pretty. I wonder if she also . . .
- knows how to keep a clean house.
- is a good cook.
- likes children.
- is a good weaver.

That young man is very handsome. I also hope that he is . . .
- a hardworking farmer.
- a good hunter.
- a skilled builder.
- a brave soldier.

Section 22.5

Students' webs will vary. Possible answers:

Sacred Round

- The Mayas' knowledge of astronomy and math let them develop a complex calendar system.
- The Sacred Round was made up of two cycles. One cycle was made up of the numbers 1 to 13; the other had 20 day names.
- The Sacred Round was used to determine the best days to plant, do battle, perform religious ceremonies, and many other activities.

Mayan Gods

- The Mayas believed in more than 160 gods.
- Primary gods were the god of rain, the god of corn, and the god of death.
- The jaguar was an important animal in the Mayan religion.

Pok-a-tok

- This is a ball game played by two teams of nobles.
- Players tried to hit a rubber ball through a stone hoop using their elbows, wrists, and hips.
- Members of the losing team may have been sacrificed.

Offerings and Sacrifices

- The Mayas made offerings of plants, food, flowers, feathers, jade, and shells.
- Animals, and sometimes humans, were sacrificed.

Section 22.6

Students' answers and drawings will vary. Possible answers:

Crops

- maize, or corn
- beans
- squash

Agricultural Techniques

- In the mountainous highlands, the Mayas used terraces to create more flat land on which to farm.
- In the swampy lowlands, the Mayas used raised earthen platforms surrounded by drainage canals.
- In the densely forested lowlands, the Mayas used slash-and-burn agriculture to clear land for farming.

Theories for Decline of the Mayan Civilization

- The population of Mayan cities grew faster than their farming systems (or food supplies) could sustain.
- There was uncontrolled warfare.
- Mayan city-states were invaded by groups from central Mexico.
- Drought may have caused massive crop failure.

The Aztecs

How did the Aztecs rise to power?

Overview

In a Visual Discovery activity, students learn about the origins of the Aztecs and the growth of their empire by analyzing images representing key stages in the development of the Aztec Empire and by using information students have learned through historical reenactments.

Objectives

In the course of reading this chapter and participating in the classroom activity, students will

Social Studies

- describe the beginnings of the Aztecs, how they arrived and survived in the Valley of Mexico, and the legend of their empire's beginnings.

- explain how the Aztecs built their capital of Tenochtitlán and describe the main features of the city.

- analyze Aztec warfare and other methods the Aztecs used to create and maintain their empire.

Language Arts

- ask probing questions to elicit information.

- answer interview questions persuasively with supporting details, reasons, and descriptions.

Social Studies Vocabulary

Key Content Terms Aztecs, mercenary, Tenochtitlán, alliance, plaza, causeway, conformity

Academic Vocabulary enormous, impressive, vital, capture

Materials

History Alive! The Medieval World and Beyond

Interactive Student Notebooks

Visuals 23A–23D

Lesson Masters

- Student Handouts 23A–23B (2 copies of each, cut apart)

- Vocabulary Development handout (1 per student, on colored paper)

Activity	Suggested Time	Materials
Preview	20 minutes	• Interactive Student Notebooks • Visual 23A
Vocabulary Development	30–40 minutes	• *History Alive! The Medieval World and Beyond* • Interactive Student Notebooks • Vocabulary Development handout
Visual Discovery	90 minutes (2 regular periods) (1 block period)	• *History Alive! The Medieval World and Beyond* • Interactive Student Notebooks • Visuals 23B–23D • Student Handouts 23A–23B (2 copies of each, cut apart)
Processing	20 minutes	• Interactive Student Notebooks
Assessment	40 minutes	• Chapter 23 Assessment

Preview

Visual 23A

1 Introduce the Preview image. Project *Visual 23A: The Story of the Aztecs.* Explain to students that this image tells much about the story of the Aztec people, including details about the founding of the Aztec Empire, the capital city of Tenochtitlán, and the Aztecs' relations with their neighbors. Tell students they will discover key parts of the Aztecs' story by carefully analyzing this image. Ask,

What are some of the interesting details you see? (**Note:** Consider having volunteers come to the screen to point out details.)

2 Have students analyze details of the beginnings of the Aztec Empire. Focus students' attention on the center of the image. Consider covering up other parts of the image so that students see only a square in the center showing the eagle on the cactus and the Aztec leader kneeling near it. Tell students that this part of the image provides clues about the beginnings of the Aztec Empire. Then ask,

- What kind of bird do you see in the center of this image?

- What is the eagle standing on?

- Who might the men be who are standing around the eagle?

- How does the man closest to the eagle differ from those who are farther away?

- What conclusions might you draw about the man closest to the eagle?

- Why might all these people be looking at the eagle on the cactus? *(According to legend, Aztec priests received a vision that they were to build their capital where they found an eagle perched on a cactus eating a serpent, or snake.)*

3 Have students analyze details of the Aztec capital city. Focus students' attention on the area inside the blue box in the top two-thirds of the image. Then ask,

- What might the blue border represent?

- What might the crossed blue strips represent?

- Based on these two clues, what might be interesting or unique about where this city was built? *(The Aztec capital, Tenochtitlán, was located on an island in Lake Texcoco in the Valley of Mexico. The city had canals running through it.)*

4 Have students analyze details of the Aztecs' relations with their neighbors. Focus student's attention on the area along the bottom third of the image. Then ask,

- What interesting details do you notice about the men in this part of the image?

- Who might these men be?

- What is happening to the temples?

- What conclusions can you draw about the Aztecs' relationships with their neighbors? (*The Aztecs tended to fight with, and often conquer, neighboring groups.*)

5 **Have students complete the Preview activity in their Interactive Student Notebooks.** Review the directions with them, and continue to project Visual 23A. After they have finished, have students share their work with a partner or have several volunteers briefly share their work with the class.

6 **Connect the Preview activity to the chapter.** Tell students that in the Preview activity they looked at an illustration depicting the origins of the Aztec Empire. Explain that in this lesson they will learn about the empire's rulers, the Aztecs, who had very humble beginnings, but rose to become one of the most powerful civilizations in the Americas.

Vocabulary Development

1 **Introduce the Key Content Terms.** Have students locate the Key Content Terms for the chapter in their Interactive Student Notebooks. These are important terms that will help students understand the main ideas of the chapter. Ask volunteers to identify any familiar terms and suggest how they might be used in a sentence.

2 **Have students complete a Vocabulary Development handout.** Give each student a copy of the Vocabulary Development handout of your choice from the Reading Toolkit at the back of the Lesson Masters. These handouts provide extra Key Content Term practice and support, depending on your students' needs. Review the completed handout by asking volunteers to share one answer for each term.

Reading

1 **Introduce the Essential Question and have students read Section 23.1.** Have students identify the Essential Question on the first page of the chapter: *How did the Aztecs rise to power?* Then have students read Section 23.1. Afterward, have students carefully analyze the chapter opener image. Then ask them to find words, phrases, or sentences in the text of Section 23.1 and connect them to visual details in the chapter opener image. Have several volunteers share the connections they found with the rest of the class.

2 **Have students complete the Reading Notes for Chapter 23.** Assign Sections 23.2 to 23.4 during the activity, as indicated in the procedures for the Visual Discovery. Remind students to use the Key Content Terms where appropriate as they complete their Reading Notes.

Visual Discovery

1 Put students in pairs and introduce the activity. Explain that students will analyze several images to learn about the development of the Aztec Empire.

2 Project *Visual 23B: The Founding of Tenochtitlán* and have students analyze the image. Help pairs carefully analyze the image by asking the questions below. Have students discuss their responses with their partners. Then choose a few pairs to share their responses with the class.

- What interesting or important details do you see?

- Who are the men on the left and right of the image? How do you think they feel about seeing this eagle?

- What important event in Aztec history might this image represent?

- Why do you think there are no other native peoples in this image?

- Do you think this was painted from the perspective of the Aztecs or from that of other groups living in the Valley of Mexico before the Aztecs arrived? How can you tell?

Visual 23B

3 Have students read Section 23.2 and complete the Reading Notes. Review the answers with the class, encouraging students to add key information to their Reading Notes as necessary.

4 Combine pairs into groups of four to prepare for the act-it-out. Give each group one card from *Student Handout 23A: Role Cards for the Founding of Tenochtitlán.* Assign at least four groups to be "actor groups" and the remaining groups to be "on-scene reporter" groups. Tell the actor groups to review their role cards and use information from their Reading Notes to generate ideas for how to accurately bring their characters to life and how to answer questions. Tell the reporter groups to review their cards and use their Reading Notes to prepare several questions to ask of the character on their role cards. Remind them that their job is not to ask trick questions, but rather to ask thoughtful questions that their assigned characters can answer.

Student Handout 23A

Give groups a few minutes to prepare and practice as you circulate around the room. (**Note:** You may want to check the reporters' questions to ensure that the characters will be able to answer them fairly easily and accurately.)

5 Conduct the act-it-out. Select one actor from each actor group to come up to the screen and step into the image in front of his or her character. (**Note:** It doesn't matter which character in the image each group chooses). Then, follow these steps:

- Have each actor bring his or her character to life by following Steps 1 and 2 on the role card.

- Act as a reporter and ask the actor one or both of the questions for which the actor has prepared answers in Step 3 of the role card. (**Note:** It will be easier to ask students questions from their role cards if you have students tape their role cards to their chests during the act-it-out).

- As you are questioning each actor, other actors should stay "frozen" until it is their turn.

- Select one or two students from each reporter group to ask questions of the characters.

6 **Project *Visual 23C: The City of Tenochtitlán* and have students analyze the image.** Ask,

- What interesting or important details do you see?

- What might some of the buildings or other details be used for?

- What do you think life is like in a city like this?

- How do you think the Aztecs were able to build a city like this?

7 **Have students read Section 23.3 and complete the Reading Notes.**

8 **Repeat Steps 2–5 for *Visual 23D: Aztec Warfare.*** Make the following modifications:

- Step 2: Use the following questions:

  What interesting or important details do you see?

  What do you think is happening?

  What does this image tell you about the Aztec style of warfare?

  What does this image tell you about the Aztecs' relationships with some of their neighbors? Why do you think their relationships were like this?

- Step 3: Read Section 23.4.

- Step 4: Use the role cards from *Student Handout 23B: Role Cards for Aztec Warfare.*

- Step 5: Select three actors to play the role of Aztec warriors and one to play the Tlaxcalan warrior (the figure on the left wearing feathers around his head). Have the actors step into the image in front of the character they will bring to life and freeze into position. Even though there is only one Aztec warrior in the image, have the Aztec Jaguar and Eagle warriors line up behind the actor who plays the new Aztec warrior.

9 **Debrief the activity.** Project Visual 23A again. Help students identify what they have learned about the Aztecs by asking the following questions. Have students first discuss each question with their partner, then call on a few pairs to share their response.

- What have you learned about the beginnings of the Aztecs in the Valley of Mexico? What details in this image support what you have learned?

- What have you learned about their capital city of Tenochtitlán? What details in this image support what you have learned?

- What have you learned about how the Aztecs managed their empire? What details in this image support what you have learned?

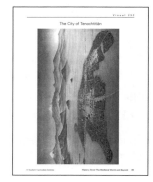

Visual 23C

Visual 23D

Student Handout 23B

Processing

Have students complete the Processing activity in their Interactive Student Notebooks. Students will design a flag depicting important details about the Aztec empire.

Quicker Coverage

Eliminate the Act-It-Outs While doing the Visual Discovery activity, eliminate Steps 4 and 5 as they apply to Visuals 23B and 23D.

Deeper Coverage

Connect the Reading to Visual 23C After students have read Section 23.3, give each pair four or five sticky notes. On each sticky note, have them write one detail from the image that is discussed in the text. For example, students might identify: causeways, plazas, canals, palaces, chinampas, or the Great Temple. Have pairs bring their sticky notes to the front of the classroom and stick them on the appropriate part of the image. Then debrief with students by reviewing the features they labeled. Consider encouraging students to really delve deeply into this activity by offering extra-credit points for pairs who identify features no one else labels.

Writing: Ask and Evaluate Research Questions

Another processing alternative is to have students identify both topics and specific research questions based on the content of the chapter. Ask what students would like to learn more about; then review and/or model ways, first, to generate research questions and, next, to evaluate those questions as good starting points for research.

Assessment

Mastering the Content

1. D	5. C	9. A	13. D
2. B	6. C	10. B	14. C
3. D	7. A	11. A	15. B
4. A	8. B	12. D	

Applying Social Studies Skills

16. 1250; 1325

17. Answers will vary. Sample answer: The Aztecs became independent and started building their own empire.

18. 1428; 1519

19. Sample answer: They wandered the deserts of northern Mexico as nomads.

Exploring the Essential Question

20. Answers should include all the elements requested in the prompt.

Scoring Rubric

Score	Description
3	Student completes both "sides" of the postcard, with a relevant drawing in the upper rectangle and text in the lower rectangle. Written comments are clearly stated, are supported by details, include at least three observations about Tenochtitlán and how it illustrates the power of the Aztecs, and demonstrate command of standard English conventions.
2	Student responds to most or all parts of the task, but written comments in the lower rectangle may lack details or not be clearly stated.
1	Student responds to at least one part of the task. Written comment(s) may contain factual and/or grammatical errors and may lack details.
0	Response does not match the task or is incorrect.

English Language Learners

Create Cue Cards for the Visuals Create simple cue cards that include the spiral questions you will ask students when they analyze each image during the Preview and Visual Discovery activity. For each spiral question you will ask, write an incomplete answer on a cue card. Create several identical cards for each spiral question. During the lesson, pass these out to students just prior to analyzing an image. Ask the spiral questions, and have students complete the statement on their cards. For example, cue cards for the image on Visual 23B might read as follows:

- An interesting detail I see in this image is
  _____.

- I think the men on the left and right of the image are _____. They are excited to see this eagle because _____.

- I think this image represents the following important event in Aztec history:
  _____.

- I think this painting was painted from the perspective, or viewpoint, of (choose one)
  — the Aztecs, because . . .
  — another group living in the Valley of Mexico, because . . .

Learners Reading and Writing Below Grade Level

Reduce Reading Note Requirements Reduce the number of questions that students must complete in the Reading Notes for each section by having them answer only the first two questions. At the completion of this lesson, give students a copy of Guide to Reading Notes 23 and allow them to use it to complete the third question. Similarly, you may want to provide some students with partial answers for the questions you have assigned them, omitting key words that they can fill in once they have read the appropriate section.

Learners with Special Education Needs

Assign a "Student Pointer" Assign a student to serve as the "student pointer" during the analysis of each visual. This student will point to the details that other students identify as important or interesting. Consider having this student use "magic paper" by doing the following:

- Give the student a sheet of paper to place over each detail on the screen.

- Have the student move three feet away from the screen, keeping the detail centered on the paper. This will magnify the detail for the rest of the class.

Add Non-Speaking Roles When conducting the act-it-out for Visual 23D, consider adding several non-speaking roles. Have the students play the roles of additional Aztec warriors. You can occasionally ask them easy yes-or-no questions that they can respond to by simply nodding or shaking their heads.

Assign "Interviewer" Roles Allow students to act as "interviewers" during the act-it-outs. Give these students copies of all the role cards for each act-it-out, with the two questions for each role highlighted. During the act-it-out, guide these students in asking each actor the questions for which they have prepared answers, rather than having them create their own.

Advanced Learners

Identify Bias Have students analyze "who's behind the paintbrush?" Right after students have analyzed the image on Visual 23D, and while other students may still be working to complete their Reading Notes, have these students respond to these questions:

- From which person's or group's perspective does this painting most likely come? What clues help you figure this out?

- In fact, this image is part of a mural painted from the perspective of the Tlaxcalans, sworn enemies of the Aztecs. How might it look different if it had been painted from the Aztec perspective?

- What additional information would you want or need to determine whether this image is an accurate portrayal of typical Aztec warfare?

Enrichment Resources

Find out more about the early Aztecs by exploring the following Enrichment Resources for *History Alive! The Medieval World and Beyond* at www.teachtci.com.

Enrichment Readings These in-depth readings encourage students to explore selected topics related to the chapter. You may also find readings that relate the chapter's content directly to your state's curriculum.

Internet Connections The recommended Web sites provide useful and engaging content that reinforces skills development and mastery of subjects within the chapter.

Literature Recommendations

The following books offer opportunities to extend the content in this chapter.

The Ancient Aztecs by Liz Sonneborn (Danbury, CT: Children's Press, 2005)

Aztec Times by Anthony Mason (New York: Simon & Schuster, 1997)

The Aztecs by John D. Clare (ed.) (New York: Barron's Educational Series, 2000)

Section 23.2

1. The Teotihuacáns and the Toltecs were two important groups who lived in the Valley of Mexico before the Aztecs. The Aztecs adopted the feathered serpent god, Quetzalcoatl, from the Teotihuacáns, and married into the Toltec royal line.

2. Answers will vary, but facial expressions might be unhappy or angry, since most groups initially thought that the Aztecs were barbarians, only worthy as mercenaries. The speech text should match the mood of the facial expression.

3. According to Aztec history, their priests were told to look for an eagle perched on a cactus and holding a snake in its beak. This would tell them where the Aztecs should build their new city. This location, on an island in the middle of Lake Texcoco, was a good site because there were plenty of fish and water birds to eat and the island was easy to defend.

Section 23.3

1. Students should draw chinampas and causeways.

2. Possible answers:

   • The Great Temple was one of the most important buildings in Tenochtitlán. It was 150 feet high. This is where important religious ceremonies took place, including human sacrifices.

   • The two-story Royal Palace was the home of the Aztec ruler, but also housed government offices, shrines, courts, storerooms, gardens, courtyards, an aviary, and a zoo.

3. Tenochtitlán had four wide avenues, which allowed people to move around easily. The city also had an aqueduct that carried fresh water into the city from miles away.

Section 23.4

1. Aztec tribute included food, cacao, gems, cotton, animals, animal skins, shells, building materials, or soldiers. This tribute was important because it was used to help feed the huge population of Tenochtitlán and to pay warriors, priests, officials, and servants.

2. Before a declaration of war, the Aztecs would request that the city join their empire as an ally. If they refused, after 60 days the Aztecs would declare war and attack the city. After the battle, captives were brought to Tenochtitlán. Some became slaves and others were sacrificed.

3. The Aztecs demanded that the city pay tribute, promise to obey the Aztec ruler, and honor the Aztec god. One advantage was that these conditions made it easy for the Aztecs to rule. One disadvantage was that most conquered people never felt any allegiance to the Aztecs, they resented paying tribute, and this led to a lack of unity in the empire.

Daily Life in Tenochtitlán

What was daily life like for Aztecs in Tenochtitlán?

Overview

In a Writing for Understanding activity, students research various aspects of daily life in Tenochtitlán. They "visit" the Great Market of Tenochtitlán and barter for information about additional aspects of daily life before creating illustrated journal entries from the perspective of a fictional Aztec character.

Objectives

In the course of reading this chapter and participating in the classroom activity, students will

Social Studies

- describe the class structure of Aztec society.
- research and teach other students about the daily lives of the Aztecs, including marriage, family life, food, markets, religious practices, and recreation.

Language Arts

- research and organize ideas for an illustrated journal.

Social Studies Vocabulary

Key Content Terms semidivine, hereditary, ward, polygamy

Academic Vocabulary elevate, emancipate, dispute

Materials

History Alive! The Medieval World and Beyond

Interactive Student Notebooks

Visual 24

Lesson Masters

- Information Masters 24A and 24B (1 transparency of each)
- Student Handout 24 (1 card per student)
- Vocabulary Development handout (1 per student, on colored paper)

sticky notes (2" x 1.5")

colored pencils

Activity	Suggested Time	Materials
Preview	10–15 minutes	• Interactive Student Notebooks • Visual 24
Vocabulary Development	30–40 minutes	• *History Alive! The Medieval World and Beyond* • Interactive Student Notebooks • Vocabulary Development Handout
Writing for Understanding	45 minutes (Phase 1) • Research three aspects of daily life in Tenochtitlán (1 class period) (.5 block period) 30–45 minutes (Phase 2) • "Trade" for information at the Great Market (1 class period) (.5 block period) 45 minutes (Phase 3) • Prepare rough drafts of journal entries (1 class period) (.5 block period)	• *History Alive! The Medieval World and Beyond* • Interactive Student Notebooks • Visual 24 • Information Masters 24A–24B (1 transparency of each) • Student Handout 24 (1 card per student) • sticky notes (2″ x 1.5″) • colored pencils
Processing (Optional)	20 minutes	• Interactive Student Notebooks
Assessment	40 minutes	• Chapter 24 Assessment

Preview

1 **Place students in pairs and have them complete the Preview activity.** Project *Visual 24: The Great Market of Tenochtitlán* and review the directions for the Preview activity in their Interactive Student Notebooks. Have pairs complete the Preview activity.

2 **Have volunteers share their answers.** Have volunteers share their answers to the three questions, particularly their hypotheses about the daily lives of the Aztecs.

3 **Connect the Preview activity to the chapter.** Tell students that in the Preview activity they looked at a famous mural, by Mexican artist Diego Rivera, depicting the Great Market of Tenochtitlán. By looking at the mural, they were able to see different aspects of Aztec daily life. In the chapter, students will learn more about six aspects of Aztec daily life—marriage, family life, food, markets, religious practices, and recreation.

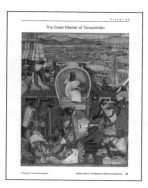

Visual 24

Vocabulary Development

1 **Introduce the Key Content Terms.** Have students locate the Key Content Terms for the chapter in their Interactive Student Notebooks. These are important terms that will help them understand the main ideas of the chapter. Ask volunteers to identify any familiar terms and how they might be used in a sentence.

2 **Have students complete a Vocabulary Development handout.** Give each student a copy of the Vocabulary Development handout of your choice from the Reading Toolkit at the back of the Lesson Masters. These handouts provide extra Key Content Term practice and support, depending on your students' needs. Review the completed handout by asking volunteers to share one answer for each term.

> **Vocabulary Development: Use Roots and Affixes**
>
> Introduce or review the following Greek and Latin roots and affixes: *semi,* meaning "half"; *here,* meaning "to stick"; *poly,* meaning "many"; and *gam,* meaning "marriage." Discuss how these meanings are related to the meanings of the vocabulary words *semidivine, hereditary,* and *polygamy.*

Reading

1 **Introduce the Essential Question and have students read Section 24.1.** Have students identify the Essential Question on the first page of the chapter: *What was daily life like for Aztecs in Tenochtitlán?* Then have students read Section 24.1. Afterward, have students carefully analyze the chapter opener image. Ask them to find words, phrases, or sentences in the text of Section 24.1 and connect to visual details in the chapter opener image. Have several volunteers share the connections they founds.

2 **Have students complete the Reading Notes for Sections 24.2–24.8.** Assign Sections 24.2 to 24.8 during the activity, as indicated in the procedures for the Writing for Understanding activity. Remind students to use the Key Content Terms where appropriate as they complete their Reading Notes.

Writing for Understanding

1   **Assign pairs to a side of the classroom.** Have half the pairs sit on either side of the classroom. It is very important for the activity that you have an equal number of pairs on each side of the room. If necessary, create some groups of three students to accomplish this.

2   **Have pairs complete the Reading Notes for Section 24.2.** Have pairs read Section 24.2 and complete the Reading Notes in their Interactive Student Notebooks. Afterward, have volunteers share with the class some of the important responsibilities or privileges of each class. Then ask,

    - What is similar about the social classes in Aztec and Mayan society? What is different?

    - To which class of Aztec society would you have wanted to belong? Why?

3   **Introduce the activity.** Explain that in this activity, students will create an illustrated journal from the perspective of someone living in the Aztec capital of Tenochtitlán. To gather the necessary information, they will first work with a partner to research three aspects of daily life. Then they will "visit" the Great Market of Tenochtitlán and trade for additional information.

Phase 1: Researching Three Aspects of Aztec Daily Life

1   **Assign pairs three sections to research.** Assign pairs on one side of the room ("odd pairs") to read and complete Reading Notes for Sections 24.3, 24.5, and 24.7, and pairs on the other side of the room ("even pairs") to read and complete Reading Notes for Sections 24.4, 24.6, and 24.8. Review the directions for the Reading Notes so that students understand how to complete them. Continue projecting Visual 24 and encourage students to use details from the image of the Great Market for ideas for their drawings. When pairs finish their notes for each section, have them bring their notes to you to be checked.

2   **Check students' work.** Use the Guide to Reading Notes to check students' work after they complete each section to make sure the notes are complete and accurate and the drawing of the market item is clear and appropriate.

3   **Have pairs prepare their items for market.** Once pairs have completed their three sections of assigned Reading Notes, distribute three small sticky notes to each student. Have each student draw one copy of each of the drawings of their three market items from their Reading Notes on the sticky notes. The drawings should be clear and colorful and include a short, simple label. Explain that they will use these extra drawings to barter, or trade, with other students later in the activity.

Phase 2: Bartering to Learn About Three More Aspects of Aztec Daily Life

1 Prepare the classroom. Move the desks to create a large open space in the middle of the room. Project Visual 24 again. Consider what you might do to enhance the "market" atmosphere, such as laying colorful rugs on the floor for students to sit on or creating an area with foods that might be sold in an Aztec market, such as woven baskets, tomatoes, chilis, avocados, corn, and chocolate.

2 Review the directions for trading at the Great Market. Have pairs sit together on the floor around the edges of the open space. They should have their Reading Notes "basket" and duplicate drawings in front of them. Project *Information Master 24A: Trading at the Great Market of Tenochtitlán* and review the directions.

3 Have students trade drawings and exchange information from their Reading Notes at the Great Market. Project Visual 24 again. Allow pairs ample time to trade drawings and information until everyone has completed all sections of the Reading Notes. Circulate to make sure pairs are explaining the information in their Reading Notes to one another and not just exchanging notebooks and copying. You may want to have cellophane tape or glue sticks available so students can better secure the drawings to their Reading Notes.

Information Master 24A

Phase 3: Creating an Illustrated Journal Entry

1 Review the directions for creating journal entries. Project *Information Master 24B: Creating an Illustrated Journal* and review the directions.

2 Assign roles for the journal entries. Explain that students will write their journal entries from the perspective of a fictional Aztec character. Distribute one card from *Student Handout 24: Biographical Sketches* to each student. Or, you may want to make a transparency of Student Handout 24 and let students choose their roles.

3 Have students write the rough draft of their journals. After students have prepared their rough drafts, consider using some technique, such as Peer Checking or Peer Read-Around, to allow students to get feedback on their writing. Have students prepare a final draft as homework.

Information Master 24B

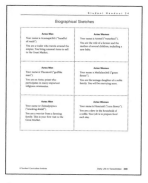

Student Handout 24

Processing (Optional)

1   **Understand the intent of the Processing activity.** The journal writing assignment serves as this chapter's Processing activity. Should you choose not to have students do the writing assignment, you might use the optional Processing activity in the Interactive Student Notebook.

2   **Have students complete the Processing activity.**

3   **Have students share their answers with their partners or with the class.**

Quicker Coverage

Alter Phase 1 of the Activity Divide the class into 12 equal-sized groups. Assign two groups of students to represent each section of the text (Sections 24.3–24.8). Have them follow the directions on their Reading Notes for their assigned section. Then have them prepare their items for market, according to Step 4 under Phase 1. During Phase 2, each group will need to meet and "trade" information with five other groups representing the other sections of the text.

Deeper Coverage

Have Students Present Journals

Have students present their journals by dramatically acting out one of their journal entries, either for classmates or for students in an elementary school classroom. Consider requiring them to assemble an appropriate costume or props for their presentation.

Assessment

Mastering the Content

1. B	5. A	9. A	13. B
2. D	6. B	10. C	14. D
3. C	7. C	11. D	15. A
4. A	8. D	12. B	16. C

Applying Social Studies Skills

17. over the causeways; by canoe

18. (a) 1893; (b) secondary

19. (a) expectant, eager, joyous; (b) opinion; (c) Sample answer: He was not there to see the people and has no way to know how they felt. He seems to be making up how the people felt just to help readers imagine the scene more vividly.

Exploring the Essential Question

20. Answers should include all of the elements requested in the prompt.

Scoring Rubric

Score	Description
3	Student completes all seven parts of the task. Selections and explanations are clearly stated, supported by details, and demonstrate command of standard English conventions.
2	Student responds to most or all parts of the task, but explanations may lack details or not be clearly stated.
1	Student responds to at least one part of the task. Explanations may contain factual and/or grammatical errors and may lack details.
0	Response does not match the task or is incorrect.

English Language Learners

Provide Writing Prompts Assist students with writing the illustrated journal in the Writing for Understanding activity by providing them with writing prompts or sentence starters. Here are three examples:

- My name is _____. Today, I visited the market in Tenochtitlán. Usually I spend my days doing activities such as . . .

- I had so much fun today. I visited the _____ and saw . . .

- I met an interesting person today while I was . . .

Learners Reading and Writing Below Grade Level

Modify the Writing Assignment Adapt Information Master 24B by asking students to create a postcard, instead of an entire journal entry, for each of their entries. Give them index cards, and have them draw a visual on the blank side of each postcard. Then instruct them to think of a sentence or two to describe each aspect of daily life in Tenochtitlán. Have them write a final draft of their postcard messages on the left side of the backs of the index cards. They should properly address their postcards with a name and address on the right side. All other requirements for this assignment can remain the same.

Learners with Special Education Needs

Create a Marketplace Stall For a student who might find the physical aspects of Phase 2 of the Writing for Understanding activity challenging, consider setting up an area (like a marketplace "stall") where other students can approach him or her to conduct trades.

Provide Support for the Writing Assignment For the illustrated journal, you might provide students with a copy of Information Master 24B with key directions highlighted. Allow students to keep this copy to share with parents or aides who may assist him or her with this assignment.

Modify the Note Taking While completing their Reading Notes, have all students write a sentence on their sticky note (Step 1 in Phase 1 of the Writing for Understanding), instead of a one-word label. They might need to use the space on the back of their sticky note if there is not room in front. This will help these students understand how this image connects to the Reading Notes during the trading round (Step 3 of Phase 2) of the activity.

Advanced Learners

Modify the Processing Activity Have students write their illustrated journal entries from the perspective of one of the two following people:

- A modern-day student who has been "dropped" into this ancient Aztec capital and who will be shadowing one of the six Aztec characters listed on Student Handout 24. In addition to the requirements on Information Master 24B, each entry should also include a paragraph in which the student compares modern society with that of the ancient Aztecs. For example, an entry might begin "Today, I went to the market with . . ." and go on to describe who that character is and the class to which he or she belongs. Then students would follow Steps 3–7 for this assignment, adding the step of making comparisons to modern-day life.

- A Mayan who is visiting one of the six Aztec characters listed on Student Handout 24. Again, the students should introduce themselves and the characters they are visiting, and then follow Steps 3–7 on Information Master 24B, in addition to comparing Mayan society with that of the ancient Aztecs.

Enrichment Resources

Find out more about Aztec daily life by exploring the following Enrichment Resources for *History Alive! The Medieval World and Beyond* at www.teachtci.com.

Enrichment Readings These in-depth readings encourage students to explore selected topics related to the chapter. You may also find readings that relate the chapter's content directly to your state's curriculum.

Internet Connections The recommended Web sites provide useful and engaging content that reinforces skills development and mastery of subjects within the chapter.

Literature Recommendations

The following books offer opportunities to extend the content in this chapter.

The Aztecs by Joanna Defrates (New York: McGraw-Hill Children's, 1993)

Aztecs and Maya: What Life Was Like for Ancient Civilizations in Central America by Fiona MacDonald (London: Anness Publishing, 2001)

Clothes and Crafts in Aztec Times by Imogen Dawson (Strongsville, OH: Gareth Stevens, 2000)

Section 24.2

Symbols/illustrations for each class will vary.

Ruler

Answers will vary, but may include:

- was considered semi-divine
- maintained the empire and decided when to wage war

Government Officials, Priests, and Military Leaders

Answers will vary, but may include:

- Officials in Tenochtitlán counseled the emperor, worked as judges, and governed the city's four districts; nobles throughout the empire ruled cities, collected tribute, or erected public buildings and roads.
- Priests conducted all religious rites and served individual gods; some priests ran schools to train boys for government jobs or the priesthood, others studied the sky.
- Girls could become priestesses.
- All Aztec men were trained as soldiers, and commoners could rise to power in the military by doing well in battle.

Commoners

Answers will vary, but may include:

- The pochteca were professional traders who enjoyed many privileges, like owning land and sending their children to the nobles' school.
- Craftspeople and artisans usually worked in their homes and traded their goods at markets, but some worked in the royal palace making items specially for the emperor.
- Most commoners were farmers, fishers, laborers, and servants who were loaned land by their local ward and had to pay tribute to the nobility in the form of crops, labor, or goods.

Peasants

Answers will vary, but may include:

- were free, but were considered inferior to commoners
- hired out their services to nobles

Slaves

Answers will vary, but may include:

- could own property, goods, and even other slaves
- their children were born free
- could be emancipated by working off a debt, upon completing their term of punishment for a crime, or when their masters died

Section 24.3

Students' drawings will vary. Possible answers:

- Most men married around age twenty, girls around age sixteen.
- A matchmaker, hired by the groom's family, helped set up the marriage and carried the bride to the ceremony.
- Aztec men could have more than one wife, but only one was the "primary" wife.
- Aztec women and men could divorce if they had good reason.

Section 24.4

Students' drawings will vary. Possible answers:

- Married women could own property or sell goods, and some older women practiced professions like matchmaking or midwifery.
- The woman's role of giving birth was as honored by the Aztecs as the man's role of fighting wars.
- Children of commoners were expected to help with chores around the house, like fetching wood and water, cleaning house, and grinding corn.
- All boys attended schools, where the sons of commoners trained to be soldiers and the sons of nobles trained for higher professions.

Section 24.5

Students' drawings will vary. Possible answers:

- Maize, the mainstay of the Aztec diet, was used to make common foods like tortillas and tamales.
- Aztec commoners raised turkeys and hunted wild game for food.
- From the waters around Tenochtitlán, Aztecs ate frogs, shrimp, insect eggs, and algae.
- The diet of wealthy Aztecs included cocoa, pineapples, oysters, and crabs.

Section 24.6

Students' drawings will vary. Possible answers:

- At the market, people bartered for all kinds of goods.
- The pochteca had a special place in the market where they sold such goods as gold, silver, and tortoise shells.
- Guards watched over the market to make sure sellers acted honestly.
- People came to the market to meet friends, gossip, and hear the day's news.

Section 24.7

Students' drawings will vary. Possible answers:

- Aztecs worshipped the sun and war god, Huitzilopochtli, as well as many other gods.
- Most Aztec rituals included blood sacrifices.
- Priests often pierced their skin with cactus spikes to offer their own blood.
- The Aztecs sacrificed humans on a much larger scale than other Mesoamerican groups.

Section 24.8

Students' drawings will vary. Possible answers:

- Patolli, a board game, was a favorite form of entertainment for the Aztecs.
- Tlachtli, played only by Aztec nobles, was a game in which players tried to hit a rubber ball through a small ring.
- The Aztecs believed that the tlachtli court represented the world and that the ball represented a heavenly body.

The Incas

How did the Incas manage their large and remote empire?

Overview

In an Experiential Exercise, students work in groups to role-play Incan chasquis (messengers) to communicate information about aspects of Incan culture to their classmates.

Objectives

In the course of reading this chapter and participating in the classroom activity, students will

Social Studies

- describe how the Incas built on the accomplishments of other cultures as they established their empire.

- explain the strategies the Incas used to maintain their large and remote empire.

- analyze various aspects of Incan civilization and culture, including class structure, family life, religion, and warfare.

- simulate the Incan message-relay system to identify how it helped the Sapa Inca control a far-flung empire.

Language Arts

- deliver oral summaries of content from the text.

- read expository text to connect the essential ideas to their own learning.

Social Studies Vocabulary

Key Content Terms Incas, ayllu, communal, oracle

Academic Vocabulary adapt, dedicate, alternative, rebellious

Materials

History Alive! The Medieval World and Beyond

Interactive Student Notebooks

Visual 25

Lesson Masters

- Information Master 25 (1 transparency)

- Student Handout 25 (4 copies, cut apart)

- Vocabulary Development handout (1 per student, on colored paper)

envelopes

traffic cones

Activity	Suggested Time	Materials
Preview	10 minutes	• Interactive Student Notebooks • Visual 25
Vocabulary Development	30–40 minutes	• *History Alive! The Medieval World and Beyond* • Interactive Student Notebooks • Vocabulary Development handout
Experiential Exercise	45 minutes (1 regular period) (.5 block period)	• *History Alive! The Medieval World and Beyond* • Interactive Student Notebooks • Student Handout 25 (4 copies, cut apart) • Information Master 25 (1 transparency)
Processing	20 minutes	• Interactive Student Notebooks
Assessment	40 minutes	• Chapter 25 Assessment

Preview

1 **Project *Visual 25: Machu Picchu.*** Then ask students,

   • What details do you see in this image?

   • What do you notice about the physical geography of this setting?

   • What might be some advantages to an empire having this geography? What might be some disadvantages?

   • Suppose you are the leader of the Inca Empire at its height. The empire extends more than a thousand miles north and south of your capital. What kind of communication system might you set up to get updates of important information from the far corners of your empire?

   As students discuss each question, have them record their responses in their Interactive Student Notebooks.

2 **Connect the Preview activity to the Chapter.** Tell students that in the Preview activity they analyzed an image of Machu Picchu, a religious and ceremonial center of the Incas. They also identified some of the geographic challenges of the Inca Empire, and predicted how leaders might have communicated with different parts of the empire. Explain that in this chapter, students will learn about the origins of the Inca Empire and discover how the Incas were able to control a huge territory that included such challenging geography as the Andes Mountains, a desert, and tropical rainforests.

Visual 25

Vocabulary Development

1 **Introduce the Key Content Terms.** Have students locate the Key Content Terms for the chapter in their Interactive Student Notebooks. These are important terms that will help them understand the main ideas of the chapter. Ask volunteers to identify any familiar terms and suggest how they might be used in a sentence.

2 **Have students complete a Vocabulary Development handout.** Give each student a copy of the Vocabulary Development handout of your choice from the Reading Toolkit at the back of the Lesson Masters. These handouts provide extra Key Content Term practice and support, depending on your students' needs. Review the completed handout by asking volunteers to share one answer for each term.

Reading

1 **Introduce the Essential Question and have students read Section 25.1.** Have students identify the Essential Question on the first page of the chapter: *How did the Incas manage their large and remote empire?* Then have students read Section 25.1. Afterward, have students use information from Section 25.1 and from the chapter opener image to propose some possible answers to the Essential Question.

2 **Have students complete the Reading Notes for Chapter 25.** Have students read Sections 25.2 through 25.6 and complete the corresponding Reading Notes before beginning the Experiential Exercise. Remind students to use the Key Content Terms where appropriate as they complete their Reading Notes.

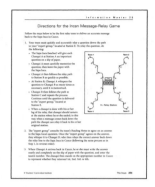

Information Master 25

Experiential Exercise

1 **Prepare materials for the Experiential Exercise.** Make a transparency of *Information Master 25: Directions for the Incan Message-Relay Game.* Make four copies of *Student Handout 25: Questions for the Incan Message-Relay Game.* Put all the questions for each round in a separate envelope and label them according to the round (i.e., Round 1, Round 2, etc.).

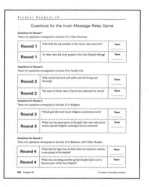

Student Handout 25

2 **Create four message-relay paths.** This activity is best conducted in a large open area, such as an outdoor field, the gymnasium, or the cafeteria. Set up the area as follows, and according to the diagram, below:

• Use masking tape or chalk to create a rectangle in the middle of the open area. Inside the rectangle, create four places for students to stand and label them *1st, 2nd, 3rd,* and *4th.* Consider any of the following options: use chalk to write the numbers, masking tape to tape the numbers on the ground; tape down pieces of paper with the numbers on them, or label traffic cones. Place a desk or table next to the rectangle (to serve as your supply station) and label it *Cuzco: Incan Capital.*

• From each of the four corners of the rectangle, step off about 15 to 20 paces (or as many as your space will allow). Mark each of the four endpoints with a large X, using masking tape or chalk, or with a traffic cone. These four locations are Station E for each of the four paths.

• Use masking tape, chalk, or cones to mark off and label four more relay stations on each path. Each Station A should be near the corners of the rectangle. The second, third, and fourth relay stations should be equidistant (about three or four paces) from each other and from the first and last relay stations.

• Finally, use masking tape, chalk, or string to create a curvy path that connects the relay stations.

(**Note:** If you do this activity in your classroom, clear the desks to the sides and create all four relay paths from the back of the room to an area at the front or from the center of the classroom to the corners.)

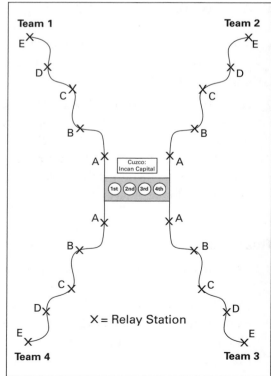

3 Introduce the Incan Message-Relay Game. Explain to students that they will now experience an important achievement of the Incas that helped them build and control their empire: their relay system. In this game, each team will relay a question about the Incan civilization along their path—just as Incan rulers used their roads to send messages to the far corners of their empire. Students at the last relay station on each path will use their Reading Notes to send an answer back along their path—just as Incan representatives would send information to the Incan ruler.

4 Create four teams of equal size and review the directions for the relay game. Project Information Master 25 and review the directions with students. Answer any questions about the rules, and then assign each group a number, 1–4.

5 Assign each team to a relay path. Take the class to the relay area you have created, making sure that all students bring their Reading Notes. Then assign each team to one of the four paths. Have four students on each team take their places at Stations A–D; these students are their team's chasquis. Have the remaining students gather at Station E, and make sure they have the group's Reading Notes open and ready to use; these students are their team's "expert group." Once teams are in position, consider doing a sample run of the activity by asking the first messengers a simple question such as, "What is your teacher's name?" Help any students or teams who still do not understand the directions.

6 Have students play Round 1 of the Incan Message-Relay Game. Follow these guidelines:

- For Step 1, give each Chasqui A the first question for Round 1. They must memorize the question before going to Relay Station B, as they cannot take it with them. Remind chasquis that they must stay on the path at all times.

- For Step 2, remind the "expert groups" that they should use their Reading Notes for Section 25.3 to answer the questions in Round 1.

- For Step 3, collect answers from the chasquis in the order they arrive back with their messages. (**Note:** This is important for the reviewing and scoring of the game later on.)

- Give each Chasqui A the second question for Round 1 and have them repeat the process.

7 Review the answers from Round 1. Use the following steps to review the questions and answers:

- Read the first question out loud.

- Read aloud the answer of the last team to arrive back in Cuzco. If it is correct, tell them they will receive five points if no other team has the correct answer. Then read aloud the answer of the next-to-last team, and repeat this process until you get to the team that arrived first. If their answer is correct, award them five points and the other teams receive nothing. If not, determine which team first arrived with the correct answer and award the five points to that team.

- Repeat this process for the second question.

8 Repeat Steps 6 and 7 for Rounds 2–4.

- For each new round, make sure the chasquis and "expert groups" on each team switch places. If you have fewer than 32 students, you may have some students who act as chasquis in consecutive rounds.

- Remind the "expert groups" that Round 2 corresponds to the Reading Notes from Section 25.4; Round 3 corresponds to Section 25.5; and Round 4 corresponds to Section 25.6.

- At the end of Round 4, tally the points for all the rounds and declare a winning team. You might consider an optional prize, such as extra credit, for the winning team.

9 Debrief the activity. Ask students,

- What was difficult or challenging about this system?

- What might have been the advantages of such a system for Incan leaders?

- What was the most interesting or important information you learned about Incan class structure, family life, religion, and relations with other peoples?

Processing

Have students complete the Processing activity. Students complete two Venn diagrams comparing and contrasting aspects of the Incan civilization to their own society.

Quicker Coverage

Jigsaw the Reading Introduce the activity and put students into four groups of equal size (Steps 3 and 4). Then have students number off, 1–4, in their large group. Have the 1s read and complete Reading Notes for Section 25.3, the 2s for Section 25.4, and so on. After students have completed their Reading Notes, have them take turns explaining their section to the rest of the group and have those students fill out their Reading Notes. When all Reading Notes are complete, proceed to Step 4 and review the directions for the activity with students.

Decrease Relay Questions Instead of having students do two questions for each relay round, choose just one question per round.

Deeper Coverage

Create Informational Posters Have students suppose that they have been hired to create informational posters to educate visitors to the Andes about the Incas. Students should work individually or in pairs to create their posters. Assign a quarter of the class to create a poster about the Incas with regard to each of the following topics: Class Structure (Section 25.3), Family Life (Section 25.4), Religion (Section 25.5), and Relations with Other Peoples (Section 25.6). Students should gather information for their posters from the text and from additional print or online resources. Each poster should include:

- a creative title that includes the topic (e.g., Religion).

- three to four visual elements, which might include maps, photos, illustrations, charts, graphs, etc.

- two to three paragraphs explaining the importance of their topic in Incan life, and how this helped the Incas manage their large and remote empire. These paragraphs should be broken up on different parts of their poster as they relate to the visual elements.

Increase Relay Game Difficulty To better reflect the challenging physical environment of the Andes, consider making it more difficult for the chasquis to relay messages down their relay paths by implementing one or more of the following suggestions.

- Place obstacles, such as classroom chairs, between relay stations; instruct students that they must climb over or go under the chairs to get to the next station.

- Have chasquis hop on one foot or place one foot in front of the other, heel-to-toe, to get from one station to another.

Assessment

Mastering the Content

1. C	5. A	9. C	13. B
2. B	6. D	10. D	14. A
3. A	7. D	11. B	15. C
4. C	8. B	12. A	16. D

Applying Social Studies Skills

17. Sample answer: in the Andes Mountains, northwest of Lake Titicaca

18. north-south; desert or Atacama Desert

19. Sample answer: The roads would probably be very steep to connect a road near sea level with one high in the Andes. Going from the coastal road to the mountain road would be especially hard because it is all uphill.

Exploring the Essential Question

20. Answers should include all the elements requested in the prompt.

Scoring Rubric

Score	Description
3	Student completes all four parts of the task. Explanations of potential benefits and drawbacks are clearly stated, supported by details, and demonstrate command of standard English conventions.
2	Student responds to most or all parts of the task, but explanations may lack details or not be clearly stated.
1	Student responds to at least one part of the task. Explanations may contain factual and/or grammatical errors and may lack details.
0	Response does not match the task or is incorrect.

English Language Learners

Pair Students for the Preview Activity Partner these students with a peer helper to complete the spiral questions in the Preview activity. Allow them to work together to complete the questions and discuss their responses. Students will feel more comfortable sharing their responses in a class discussion after having prepared with a partner.

Learners Reading and Writing Below Grade Level

Provide Support for Reading Notes Copy the Guide to Reading Notes for students, but omit key words from each answer, which students can then fill in as they read or participate in the class discussion.

Learners with Special Education Needs

Modify the Activity For a student who might be challenged by the physical aspects of the class activity, consider having that student rotate between the role of Chasqui D and joining the "expert group" during alternating rounds. The student will never have to move very far during the activity. Alternatively, you could post the student at one station, and have the other chasquis run to that student's relay station to deliver and receive messages.

Provide Support During the Activity Provide students with a completed copy of the Guide to Reading Notes that they can use during the Incan Message-Relay Game. You might also allow these students to have a peer helper who stays with them during the game and assists them during the relay.

Alter the Processing Activity Have these students choose only one topic to compare and contrast. Also consider including sentence starters for each of the three sections within the Venn diagrams to guide students as they write; for example:

- In the Incan civilization, these two things differ from the way I live today:
- My society and the Incan civilization have these two things in common:
- The way I live today differs from the way the Incas lived in these two ways:

Advanced Learners

Extend the Processing Activity As an extension to the Processing activity, have students do one or more of the following:

- Complete Venn diagrams for all four topics.
- List as many similarities and differences as they can think of, rather than only two of each.
- Create additional Venn diagrams that compare and contrast the Incan and Mayan or the Incan and Aztec civilizations.

Enrichment Resources

Find out more about the Incas by exploring the following Enrichment Resources for *History Alive! The Medieval World and Beyond* at www.teachtci.com.

Enrichment Readings These in-depth readings encourage students to explore selected topics related to the chapter. You may also find readings that relate the chapter's content directly to your state's curriculum.

Internet Connections The recommended Web sites provide useful and engaging content that reinforces skills development and mastery of subjects within the chapter.

Literature Recommendations

The following books offer opportunities to extend the content in this chapter.

The Ancient Incas: Chronicles from National Geographic by Fred L. Israel (New York: Chelsea House, 1999)

Inca Town by Fiona MacDonald (Danbury, CT: Franklin Watts, 1999)

Machu Picchu: The Story of the Amazing Incas and Their City in the Clouds by Elizabeth Mann (New York: Firefly Books, 2000)

Section 25.2

1. Peru, Ecuador, Bolivia, Chile, and Argentina

2. Symbols and one-sentence explanations will vary, but students will likely choose two of the following options for each culture.

   - Moches: built cities, dug irrigation canals, developed special classes of workers

   - Chimus: built well-planned cities, used elaborate irrigation methods, built good roads, created a message system using runners

3. Physical obstacles included tropical rainforest, high mountains, and raging rivers. To overcome these obstacles, the Incas built an elaborate system of roads (about 15,000 miles' worth) that linked all corners of the empire. They sent messages along these roads by means of an elaborate relay system. They built messenger stations every couple of miles, and shelters were placed every 15 to 30 miles to give travelers places to rest.

Section 25.3

1. The emperor, or Sapa Inca, was at the top of the Incan class structure. His authority to rule came from Inti, the sun god, whom the Incas believed was the ancestor of the Sapa Inca.

2. The Capac Incas were the highest level of nobles and were relatives of the emperor. The governors, or apus, of the four quarters of the empire were Capac Incas. So were most of the leaders of government, the army, and the priesthood.

3. Curacas were leaders of local groups brought into the Inca Empire. Many collected taxes. Others served as inspectors who made sure everyone followed Incan law. They also managed the allyus.

4. Most people were commoners who worked as farmers and herders.

Section 25.4

1. The emperor owned the land, and the Incan government loaned it to each ayllu. The ayllu grew crops and produced goods on the land.

2. The mit'a was a public duty tax, paid in labor by men of the ayllu. To pay the tax, men might repair roads, build storehouses, or work in mines.

3. The sons of nobles were tutored by amautas, and learned such subjects as religion, geometry, history, and military strategy. The children of most commoners received no formal education.

4. Incan men married in their early 20s, women at 16. Sometimes their families arranged the marriage. When a couple agreed to marry, they held hands and exchanged sandals.

Section 25.5

1. The most important Incan god was Inti, the sun god. Inti was important because the Incas believed that the emperors descended from Inti and because Inti was also the god of agriculture.

2. Some sacrifices, like throwing corn on a fire, happened regularly. In many rituals, the Incas sacrificed live animals. They also practiced human sacrifice, but only on sacred occasions or in times of a natural disaster.

3. Girls were between eight and ten when selected as Chosen Women. In the convents, they studied the Incan religion, learned to prepare special food and drink for religious ceremonies, and wove garments for the Sapa Inca and the Coya.

4. Some Chosen Women became mamaconas, or teachers, in the convents. Some left to work in temples or shrines. Others became wives of nobles or of the Sapa Inca. A few were sacrificed at important religious ceremonies.

Section 25.6

1. The Sapa Inca sent a delegate to tell the tribe that the Incas wanted to include these people in their empire. In this way, the Incas were able to convince many groups to join the empire without having to go to war.

2. Groups that resisted had to fight the Incan army and usually lost. Often the tribe lost many of its men. Sometimes, rebellious groups were forced to move to a different part of the Inca Empire.

3. When a tribe became part of the Inca Empire, its leaders had to build a sun temple. Local leaders and their sons traveled to Cuzco to learn Incan laws and Quechua, the official language.

4. The Incas believed that the Sapa Inca continued to rule the lands he conquered even after death. Each new Sapa Inca had to establish his own source of wealth and power by conquering new lands.

Achievements of the Mayas, Aztecs, and Incas

What were the significant achievements of the Mayas, Aztecs, and Incas?

Overview

In a Social Studies Skill Builder activity, students learn about important achievements of the Mayas, Aztecs, and Incas by identifying and categorizing a series of artifacts representing achievements of the three civilizations, which they "discover" in a fictitious museum.

Objectives

In the course of reading this chapter and participating in the classroom activity, students will

Social Studies

- explain the significance of the achievements of the Mayas, Aztecs, and Incas in the areas of science and technology, arts and architecture, and language and writing.

- identify and categorize a series of artifacts from the Mayan, Aztec, and Incan civilizations.

Language Arts

- respond to persuasive messages with questions, challenges, or affirmations.

Social Studies Vocabulary

Key Content Terms solar year, stele, glyph, dialect, pictograph, suspension bridge, trephination

Academic Vocabulary vocabulary, abstract, drastic, ingenious

Materials

History Alive! The Medieval World and Beyond

Interactive Student Notebooks

Placards 26A–26D (2 sets)

Visual 26

CD Tracks 12 and 13

Lesson Masters

- Information Masters 26A and 26B (1 transparency of each)

- Student Handout 26 (1 copy, cut apart)

- Vocabulary Development handout (1 per student, on colored paper)

Activity	Suggested Time	Materials
Preview	10 minutes	• Interactive Student Notebooks
Vocabulary Development	30–40 minutes	• *History Alive! The Medieval World and Beyond* • Interactive Student Notebooks • Vocabulary Development handout
Social Studies Skill Builder	90–120 minutes (2–3 class periods) (1–1.5 block periods)	• *History Alive! The Medieval World and Beyond* • Interactive Student Notebooks • Placards 26A–26D (2 sets) • CD tracks 12 and 13 • Information Masters 26A and 26B (1 transparency of each) • Student Handout 26 (1 copy, cut apart)
Processing	30–45 minutes	• Visual 26 • Interactive Student Notebooks
Assessment	40 minutes	• Chapter 26 Assessment

Preview

1 Have students complete the Preview activity in their Interactive Student Notebooks. Students consider important achievements of the past 50 years and predict whether they will still be in use 500 to 1,000 years from now.

2 Have students share their responses. When students are finished, have them share their responses with another student, or choose a few volunteers to share their responses with the class.

3 Connect the Preview activity to the chapter. In the Preview activity, students considered some of the important achievements of the past 50 years, and thought about whether or not these things would be used by people in the future. Tell students that in this chapter they will learn about lasting achievements of the Mayas, Aztecs, and Incas. During the activity, students will then take on the role of museum curators to categorize historic artifacts pertaining to these three civilizations.

Vocabulary Development

1 Introduce the Key Content Terms. Have students locate the Key Content Terms for the chapter in their Interactive Student Notebooks. These are important terms that will help them understand the main ideas of the chapter. Ask volunteers to identify any familiar terms and suggest how they might be used in a sentence.

2 Have students complete a Vocabulary Development handout. Give each student a copy of the Vocabulary Development handout of your choice from the Reading Toolkit at the back of the Lesson Masters. These handouts provide extra Key Content Term practice and support, depending on your students' needs. Review the completed handout by asking volunteers to share one answer for each term.

Reading

1 Introduce the Essential Question and have students read Section 26.1. Have students identify the Essential Question on the first page of the chapter: *What were the significant achievements of the Mayas, Aztecs, and Incas?* Then have students read Section 26.1. Afterward, have students carefully analyze the chapter opener image. Then ask them to find words, phrases, or sentences in the text of Section 26.1 and connect them to visual details in the chapter opener image. Have several volunteers share the connections they found, with the rest of the class.

2 Have students complete the Reading Notes for Chapter 26. Assign Sections 26.2 to 26.4 during the activity, as indicated in the procedures for the Social Studies Skill Builder. Remind students to use the Key Content Terms where appropriate as they complete their Reading Notes.

> **Reading: Trace Main Idea/Perspective**
>
> Review the main idea of this chapter: *The Mayas, Aztecs, and Incas left a lasting legacy.* Ask students to identify ways (including examples and explanations) that the author develops this perspective in the chapter. Note how history texts not only tell sequences of events but often, among other purposes, make cases for why things occurred as they did, and how events influenced future generations.

Social Studies Skill Builder

1 Arrange the classroom and prepare the materials. Follow these steps:

- Create a "museum basement" by setting up two identical sets of artifact stations, four on one side of the room and four on the other. Place two or three desks together to create each station (see the classroom map). Set the last two stations (Stations 4) fairly close together.

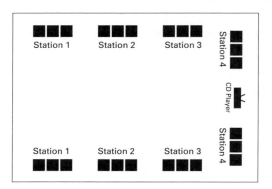

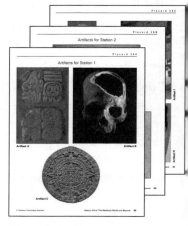

Placards A–D

- Create an additional set of placards. Place one copy of Placard 26A at each Station 1, one copy of Placard 26B at each Station 2, one copy of Placard 26C at each Station 3, and one copy of Placard 26D at each Station 4. Put the CD player between the two Station 4 areas, cued to CD Track 12, "Audio Artifact K." This and CD Track 13, "Audio Artifact L," are the two audio artifacts at Station 4.

- Cut out the cards from a copy of *Student Handout 26: Achievement Cards.*

- To create a more authentic "museum basement" atmosphere, consider using these creative touches: place placards on the floor beneath each station; use a spray can of artificial spider web to drape each station in cobwebs; turn off the lights and illuminate the classroom with a desk lamp.

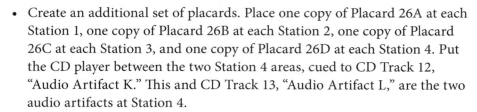
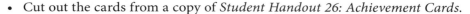

Student Handout 26

2 Place students in pairs and introduce the activity. Explain that students are about to take on the role of museum curators. First, they will read and take notes about the achievements of the Mayas, Aztecs, or Incas. Then, acting as curators at work in the basement of a museum, they will find, identify, and categorize visual and audio artifacts and place them in the appropriate wing of an American civilizations' museum. Assign half the pairs to use the stations on one side of the room and half to use the others.

3 Review the directions with students. Project *Information Master 26A: Designing Museum Exhibits* and review the steps of the activity with students.

4 Have students complete the activity. Give each pair their first "achievement card" from Student Handout 26, and have them begin. Allow ample time for completing the activity. (**Note:** You may want to check student's work on Part 2 of the Reading Notes by having them record the artifact letters first, then bring their Reading Notes to you for verification before they sketch and label each artifact.) Point out to students that two artifacts are on the CD. For these two, students should draw a symbol to stand for each one.

Information Master 26A

5 Review the Reading Notes. After the activity, review the Reading Notes as a class. Students should have categorized the artifacts as follows:

Mayan Achievements
- Artifact A: Mayan glyphs
- Artifact F: Mayan numbers
- Artifact I: Mayan mural
- Artifact J: Mayan corbel vault

Aztec Achievements
- Artifact C: Aztec calendar
- Artifact D: Aztec pictographs
- Artifact H: Aztec sculpture (sacrificial knife handle)
- Artifact K: Aztec poem

Incan Achievements
- Artifact B: Incan surgery
- Artifact E: Incan quipu
- Artifact G: Incan feather cloth
- Artifact L: Incan music

6 Debrief the activity. Have students complete a series of critical thinking challenges, as follows:

- Clear space in front of a white board or the chalkboard. Draw three large X's on the board, a few feet apart. Change the labels on each X for each challenge, as shown on *Information Master 26B: Critical Thinking Challenges.*

- Project Information Master 26B. Reveal one challenge at a time and have students follow the directions. For each challenge, call on several students who are not standing at the board to justify their partner's position.

Information Master 26B

Processing

1 Project *Visual 26: Artifact from Acapulco, Mexico.* Ask the class,

- What interesting details do you see?

- What materials do you think were used to create this artwork? *(tiles)*

- What do you call artwork that is made from small fragments of shells, glass, or colored tiles? *(a mosaic)*

- Do you see any clues about when this work of art was created and by whom? *(In the lower right corner of the image are the initials D. R. and the roman numeral LVI. It was created by Mexican muralist Diego Rivera in 1956.)*

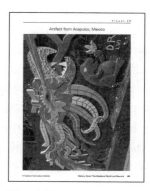

Visual 26

2 Have students complete the Processing activity. Review the directions with students, and have them complete the activity. Students create a mosaic of the key achievements of the Mayas, Aztecs, and Incas. First they create a planning drawing and then either draw or, using cut pieces of colored paper, paste a final mosaic on the page that follows.

Quicker Coverage

Jigsaw the Activity Assign an equal number of pairs to each civilization (for example, four pairs to read about and find artifacts for the Mayas, four pairs for the Aztecs, and four pairs for the Incas). After pairs have read about and found the artifacts for their civilization, do the following:

- Have all the pairs that studied each civilization meet together in a larger group.

- Give each civilization group a transparency of the blank Reading Notes for the section related to their civilization.

- Have each group use a transparency marker to complete the Reading Notes for their civilization on the transparency.

- Using an overhead projector, have each group quickly present their Reading Notes to the rest of the class. Make sure that groups adequately explain the achievements and their significance in Part 1 and the artifacts they examined in Part 2.

Eliminate the Debrief After students complete the Social Studies Skill Builder activity and the class has reviewed the Reading Notes, skip the debrief with the critical thinking challenges and move to the Processing activity.

Deeper Coverage

Create an Interactive Museum Assign each pair one artifact from the activity (in a large class, you may need to form groups of three or four per artifact). Alternatively, you may want to have groups research new artifacts that were not part of the activity for this museum exhibit. Have students create a replica of their artifact, and write a one-paragraph explanation of its significance. Then, do the following:

- Have students meet in larger groups, by civilization. Each large group should decide how to set up their museum exhibit in a way that will create interest for museum visitors.

- Once each civilization group has set up its museum exhibit, regroup students into six or nine smaller groups. Each group should have an equal number of students from each civilization.

- Have small groups rotate through the three museum exhibits. At each exhibit, the students from that civilization group should act as "docents," pointing out the artifacts and helping to explain their significance.

Assessment

Mastering the Content

1. D	5. A	9. A	13. D
2. C	6. B	10. B	14. B
3. B	7. C	11. C	15. A
4. A	8. D	12. D	16. C

Applying Social Studies Skills

17. stone

18. Answers will vary. Sample answer: had developed strong and complex building techniques and knowledge of engineering

19. Answers will vary. Sample answer: worshipped a sun god; had a very complicated calendar system; studied astronomy

Exploring the Essential Question

20. Answers should include all the elements requested in the prompt.

Scoring Rubric

Score	Description
3	Student describes a relevant achievement in each of the nine boxes. Descriptions are clearly stated, supported by details, and demonstrate command of standard English conventions.
2	Student responds to most or all parts of the task, but descriptions may lack details or not be clearly stated.
1	Student responds to at least one part of the task. Descriptions may contain factual and/or grammatical errors and may lack details.
0	Response does not match the task or is incorrect.

Walking Across Space: Incan Rope Bridges

1 **Use a KWL chart to explore the topic of Incan rope bridges.** Draw a KWL chart on the board. Ask students to copy the chart. As a class, fill in the first two columns by identifying what students already know and what they want to learn about Incan rope bridges. Have students complete their own charts with items from the board or others that they may think of. Do not erase the chart.

2 **Have students read the Chapter 26 Reading Further.** When students have finished reading, ask them to complete the last column of the KWL chart by filling in what they have learned about Incan rope bridges. Use students' suggestions to complete the class chart on the board.

3 **Discuss the reasons why people might travel to watch the Apurimac rope bridge being rebuilt.** Based on the reading and their own ideas, ask, *Why do you think people attend the bridge-rebuilding in Peru?* Ask students why they might or might not attend the event themselves. List their responses in the form of a T-chart.

4 **Have students complete the Reading Further activity in their Interactive Student Notebooks.** Students will write persuasive paragraphs designed to attract tourists to see the rebuilding of the Apurimac rope bridge. Have students exchange their drafts with a partner. Partners should review the drafts to improve organization and the use of persuasive words, and to strengthen arguments. Finally, have students evaluate their own paragraphs using the rubric.

5 **Invite students to read their paragraphs aloud to the class.** Ask the class to evaluate the persuasive effects of the paragraphs. Ask, *Would you be persuaded to make the trip? Why or why not?*

English Language Learners

Create Illustrated Achievement Cards After the Social Studies Skill Builder, have students create illustrated achievement cards by doing the following:

- Distribute index cards to pairs.

- On each card, have pairs quickly sketch one of the artifacts from the activity.

- On the other side, have them write, in their native language or in English, a brief description of the achievement the artifact represents. (For example: These bars and dots, or Mayan numbers, represent Mayan achievements in mathematics.)

- Have pairs review and sort their cards to help prepare for assessment or to assist in preparing artifacts to include in their Processing assignment.

Learners Reading and Writing Below Grade Level

Assist Students in Finding Artifacts Consider providing these students with copies of Sections 26.2 through 26.4 of *History Alive! The Medieval World and Beyond.* As they are instructed to read each section, encourage them to highlight the names of any artifacts and achievements they come across. Then, when these students visit the stations during the Social Studies Skill Builder activity, guide them to use their highlighted copies to help them determine which artifacts match the civilization they have just read about, by having them look only at the highlighted portions of their notes.

Learners with Special Education Needs

Create Artifact Packets Create a packet of artifacts that students can analyze and manipulate at their desks, rather than walking to the various stations. If appropriate, reduce the number of artifacts they need to review.

Create Larger Groups Consider creating some groups of three for students who may need additional help and support to complete the Social Studies Skill Builder activity.

Adapt the Processing Activity Modify the Processing activity for these students by doing any or all of the following:

- Reduce the number of tiles students must create for each civilization.

- Tell students which color to use for each civilization.

- Create a short list compiled from the Reading Notes that provides students with easy-to-draw achievements that they may choose from each of the three civilizations. For example, for the Incas, the list might include a system of roads, suspension bridges, stone buildings, music, and feather tunics.

Advanced Learners

Create New Museum Exhibits Have students work in small groups to research visuals of additional Mayan, Aztec, or Incan artifacts to create a new museum exhibit. They can then act as docents to lead the class through their museum. Establish specific criteria for this assignment, such as the following:

- Identify two additional pieces of art or artifacts from each of the Mayan, Aztec, and Incan civilizations.

- Discuss the reasons why each piece of art or artifact might have been created and what it can tell us about life in that civilization.

- Use proper pronunciation when presenting titles or names identifying the art and artifacts.

Enrichment Resources

Find out more about the major Mesoamerican civilizations by exploring the following Enrichment Resources for *History Alive! The Medieval World and Beyond* at www.teachtci.com.

Enrichment Readings These in-depth readings encourage students to explore selected topics related to the chapter. You may also find readings that relate the chapter's content directly to your state's curriculum.

Internet Connections The recommended Web sites provide useful and engaging content that reinforces skills development and mastery of subjects within the chapter.

Literature Recommendations

The following books offer opportunities to extend the content in this chapter.

Aztecs and Incas: A Guide to the Pre-Colonized Americas in 1504 by Sue Nicholson (New York: Larousse Kingfisher Chambers, 2000)

Eyewitness: Aztec, Inca and Maya by Elizabeth Baquedano (New York: Dorling Kindersley, 2000)

The Mystery of the Ancient Maya by Carolyn Meyer and Charles Gallenkamp (New York: Simon & Schuster, 1995)

Section 26.2

Part 1: Mayan Achievements

Students' explanations of each achievement's significance will vary. Achievements may include:

Science and technology: astronomical observatories, accurate calendar, understanding of mathematics, use of zero

Arts and architecture: murals, steles, weaving, corbel vault

Language and writing: hieroglyphics, around 30 dialects of Mayan language

Part 2: Mayan Artifacts

Students' drawings will vary.

Artifact A, Placard 26A: glyphs

Artifact F, Placard 26 B: numbers

Artifact I, Placard 26C: mural

Artifact J, Placard 26D: corbel vault

Section 26.3

Part 1: Aztec Achievements

Students' explanations of each achievement's significance will vary. Achievements may include:

Science and technology: chinampas, causeways, solar calendar

Arts and architecture: poetry, dance, sculpture, stone temples

Language and writing: Nahuatl language, pictographs

Part 2: Aztec Artifacts

Students' drawings will vary.

Artifact C, Placard 26 A: calendar

Artifact D, Placard 26B: pictographs

Artifact H, Placard 26C: sculpture

Artifact K, Placard 26 D/CD Track 12: poetry (Students may produce a symbol to stand for this artifact.)

Section 26.4

Part 1: Incan Achievements

Students' explanations of each achievement's significance will vary. Achievements may include:

Science and technology: system of roads, suspension bridges, terraces, irrigation canals, trephination

Arts and architecture: textiles, goldsmithing, music, stone buildings

Language and writing: Quechua language, quipus

Part 2: Inca Artifacts

Students' drawings will vary.

Artifact B, Placard 26A: surgery

Artifact E, Placard 26 B: quipu

Artifact G, Placard 26C: feather cloth

Artifact L, Placard 26D/CD Track 13: music (Students may produce a symbol to stand for this artifact.)

Civilizations of the Americas

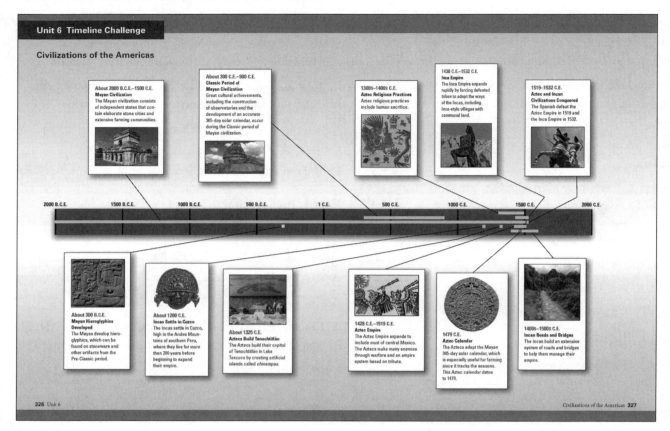

Unit 6 Timeline Challenge

Civilizations of the Americas

About 2000 B.C.E.–1500 C.E.
Mayan Civilization
The Mayan civilization consists of independent states that contain elaborate stone cities and extensive farming communities.

About 300 C.E.–900 C.E.
Classic Period of Mayan Civilization
Great cultural achievements, including the construction of observatories and the development of an accurate 365-day solar calendar, occur during the Classic period of Mayan civilization.

1300s–1400s C.E.
Aztec Religious Practices
Aztec religious practices include human sacrifice.

1438 C.E.–1532 C.E.
Inca Empire
The Inca Empire expands rapidly by forcing defeated tribes to adopt the ways of the Incas, including Inca-style villages with communal land.

1519–1532 C.E.
Aztec and Incan Civilizations Conquered
The Spanish defeat the Aztec Empire in 1519 and the Inca Empire in 1532.

2000 B.C.E.   1500 B.C.E.   1000 B.C.E.   500 B.C.E.   1 C.E.   500 C.E.   1000 C.E.   1500 C.E.   2000 C.E.

About 300 B.C.E.
Mayan Hieroglyphics Developed
The Mayas develop hieroglyphics, which can be found on stoneware and other artifacts from the Pre-Classic period.

About 1200 C.E.
Incas Settle in Cuzco
The Incas settle in Cuzco, high in the Andes Mountains of southern Peru, where they live for more than 200 years before beginning to expand their empire.

About 1325 C.E.
Aztecs Build Tenochtitlán
The Aztecs build their capital of Tenochtitlán in Lake Texcoco by creating artificial islands called *chinampas*.

1428 C.E.–1519 C.E.
Aztec Empire
The Aztec Empire expands to include most of central Mexico. The Aztecs make many enemies through warfare and an empire system based on tribute.

1479 C.E.
Aztec Calendar
The Aztecs adapt the Mayan 365-day solar calendar, which is especially useful for farming since it tracks the seasons. This Aztec calendar dates to 1479.

1400s–1500s C.E.
Incan Roads and Bridges
The Incas build an extensive system of roads and bridges to help them manage their empire.

326 Unit 6   Civilizations of the Americas 327

Overview

This Timeline Challenge helps students review the main events and ideas of this unit while providing practice in reading and interpreting timelines. You can vary and expand the activity according to students' needs and the amount of time available.

Basic Procedure

1 **Introduce the timeline in the Student Edition.** Direct students to the Civilizations of the Americas Timeline at the end of Unit 6 in the Student Edition. You may wish to have student volunteers read aloud the timeline entries, and then discuss them as a class.

2 **Introduce the Timeline Challenge in the Interactive Student Notebook.** Direct students to the Unit 6 Timeline Challenge. Point out the two types of questions, "Timeline Skills" and "Critical Thinking," and model how to answer each type.

3 **Have students complete the Timeline Challenge.** Monitor students as they work. Use the Guide to Unit 6 Timeline Challenge to check their answers. You may wish to project a transparency of this page as you work through the questions with the class and conduct a discussion of the "Critical Thinking" questions.

4 **Complete the KWL chart.** Return to the KWL chart created at the beginning of the unit, and ask students to list the key information they have learned.

Classroom Timeline

1 **Prepare the Timeline Challenge Cards.** Copy and cut the cards from *Student Handout TC6: Unit 6 Timeline Challenge Cards.* You may wish to laminate the cards for future use.

2 **Create a timeline on a classroom wall.** On an empty wall or a large bulletin board, make a timeline with masking tape or colored paper. Mark off the time intervals in advance, or ask students to do so in class.

3 **Have students place the Timeline Challenge Cards.** Distribute cards to individual students or pairs and have them tape the cards to the timeline in the correct locations. Call on students to provide more information on the timeline topics to review main events and issues.

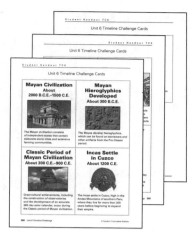

Student Handout TC6

Internet Research

1 **Review students' suggestions for additional timeline entries.** Have students share their answers to the last question of the Timeline Challenge.

2 **Have students conduct Internet research.** Ask students to choose and research one of their suggested events.

3 **Have students create additional Timeline Challenge Cards.** Direct students to research an appropriate image for their cards and then use the computer to create an illustrated card, complete with timeline entry.

Timeline Skills

Score 1 point for each correct answer.

1. about 3,500 years

2. Mayan hieroglyphics were developed during the Pre-Classic period.

3. During the Classic period, the Mayas constructed observatories and developed a 365-day solar calendar.

4. more than 200 years

5. The Aztecs built Tenochtitlán in Lake Texcoco by creating artificial islands called chinampas.

6. The Aztecs made many enemies through warfare and an empire system based on tribute.

7. The Incas forced defeated tribes to adopt the ways of the Incas, including Inca-style villages with communal land.

8. In order to manage their empire, the Incas built an extensive system of roads and bridges.

9. The Spanish defeated the Aztec and Inca empires in the 16th century.

Critical Thinking

Score 1 to 3 points for each answer, depending on the thoroughness of the response.

10. The four theories are: (1) The population of Mayan cities grew faster than their farming systems could sustain, (2) There was uncontrolled warfare, (3) Mayan city-states were invaded by groups from central Mexico, and (4) Drought may have caused massive crop failure. Students' choices and explanations will vary but they should defend their choices.

11. The Aztec Empire expanded by inviting neighboring cities to join them as allies, and by conquering them if they did not join the empire willingly. Conquered groups had to pay tribute to the Aztec tax collectors. The constant warfare and the heavy demands for tribute led the Aztecs to make many enemies among their conquered peoples.

12. The main challenges the Incas faced in controlling their large empire were related to geography. Large mountain ranges, tropical rainforests, and swift rivers dominated the land. The Incas built an extensive system of roads and bridges that allowed for communication, tax collection, and travel. The Incas were arranged in communal farming villages. To feed their population, they often built terraces and canals, and they farmed a variety of crops that grew well in their region.

13. Answers will vary. Students must explain why the events they chose merit inclusion.

Using Scores to Inform Instruction

Timeline Skills A score of 6 out of 9 indicates that students understand most of the key events in the unit.

Critical Thinking A score of 8 out of 12 indicates that students are able to think critically about most of the key issues in this unit.

If students score below these levels, consider reviewing timeline and critical thinking skills.

UNIT **7**

Europe's Renaissance and Reformation

Europe's Renaissance and Reformation

Overview

This activity introduces geographic information essential to Unit 7. Students read and interpret maps to learn about the political geography of Western and Central Europe as a launching point for their study of the Renaissance and Reformation. They annotate a map of western and central Europe and answer questions in their Interactive Student Notebooks, and then discuss critical thinking questions. Students' comprehension of content and proficiency in map-reading and higher-order thinking skills will help you gauge their readiness for the unit. The pages that follow include a completed map, answers to questions, a scoring guide to inform your teaching, and suggestions for modifications to meet specific student needs.

Essential Geographic Understandings

1. Location of the Italian city-states, the Papal States, and the Holy Roman Empire

2. Key physical features: Cities of Rome, Florence, Milan, Venice

3. Understanding the impact of location on the economies of the Italian city-states

4. Realizing the influence of the Roman Catholic Church, particularly on those areas in close proximity to its seat of power

Procedures

1 **Introduce the unit.** Tell students they will learn about two movements that took place in Europe, the Renaissance and the Reformation.

2 **Create a KWL chart.** Ask students to identify what they already know about the Renaissance and the Reformation and what they want to learn. Use their responses to gauge how much additional background information they will need as you progress through the unit. Students will return to the KWL chart at the end of the unit and add the key information they have learned.

3 **Have students read Unit 7 "Setting the Stage" in the Student Edition.**

4 **Have students complete the Geography Challenge.** Monitor students as they work. Use the guide on the next two pages to check their answers. You may wish to project the map from the Interactive Student Notebook and have students annotate it as the class works through the map-reading questions. Make sure that students have grasped Essential Geographic Understandings 1 to 3.

5 **Discuss the "Critical Thinking" questions.** Help students understand the geographic relationships described in Essential Geographic Understanding 4.

Europe, About 1500

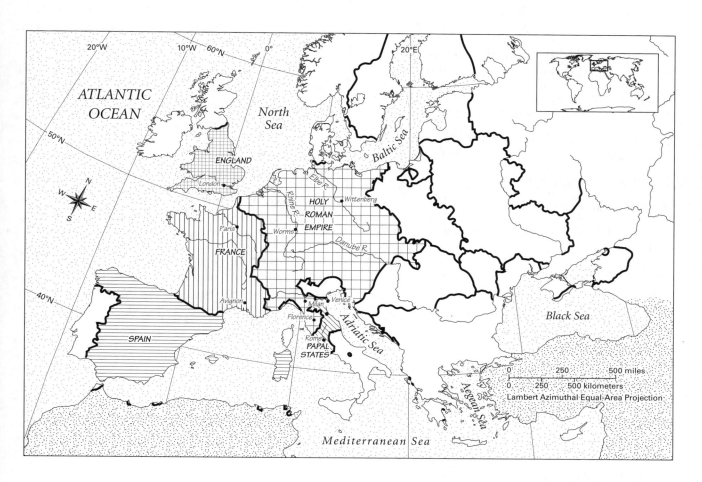

Geography Skills

Score 1 point for each correct answer. Use the map on the previous page to check shading and labeling.

1. Students should label Venice, Florence, Milan, Madrid, Paris, London, Worms, and Wittenberg.

2. Check students' maps for shading and labeling of the Holy Roman Empire.

3. Students should label Rome and shade the Papal States.

4. England is an island nation.

5. Avignon is located in France.

6. Students should label the Elbe River, Rhine River, and Danube River.

7. The city-state of Venice is located on the Adriatic Sea.

8. Venice, because it was conveniently located along the coast, between the rest of Europe and Asia and Africa.

Critical Thinking

Questions may have more than one correct answer. Score 1 to 3 points for each reasonable answer, depending on the strength of students' geographic reasoning. Possible answers are given here.

9. A religious movement may have spread from Wittenberg to Europe by means of the Rhine River.

10. The removal of the papal residence to Avignon might have weakened the power of the Papal States and strained the relationship between that area and the Church. It might also have weakened the control of the Church over the Italian city-states. The move might have strengthened the power of France.

Using Scores to Inform Instruction

Geography Skills A score of 5 out of 8 or better indicates that students have acquired sufficient geographic information to proceed with the unit.

Critical Thinking A score of 6 out of 9 or better indicates that students are beginning to understand the relationships between physical geography and the different ways in which people live.

Modifying Instruction

ELL or Learners with Special Education Needs Consider focusing on map-reading questions or limiting the number of "Critical Thinking" questions.

Students with Weak Map or Critical Thinking Skills Assign appropriate pages from the Social Studies Skills Toolkit in the back of the Lesson Masters.

The Renaissance Begins

What changes in Europe led to the Renaissance?

Overview

In a Visual Discovery activity, students trace the changes in Europe that led to the birth of the Renaissance, and then create a live Renaissance tableau.

Objectives

In the course of reading this chapter and participating in the classroom activity, students will

Social Studies

- identify elements of classical, medieval, and Renaissance art.
- connect the importance of the growth of towns, the rise of a money economy, and the development of independent city-states to the birth and spread of Renaissance ideas.
- explore how humanism encouraged a new way of thinking that affected many aspects of European life during the Renaissance.

Language Arts

- use definitions and examples to explain the meanings of new words.
- communicate effectively the perspective of a historical character.

Social Studies Vocabulary

Key Content Terms Renaissance, classical art, city-state, republic, humanism, humanities, individualism

Academic Vocabulary currency, territory, emphasis, contrast

Materials

History Alive! The Medieval World and Beyond

Interactive Student Notebooks

Visuals 27A–27E

Lesson Masters

- Student Handout 27 (1 role card per every 4 students)
- Information Master 27 (1 transparency)
- Vocabulary Development handout (1 per student, on colored paper)

Activity	Suggested Time	Materials
Preview	15 minutes	• Interactive Student Notebooks • Visual 27A
Vocabulary Development	30–40 minutes	• *History Alive! The Medieval World and Beyond* • Interactive Student Notebooks • Vocabulary Development handout
Visual Discovery	90 minutes (2 regular periods) (1 block period)	• *History Alive! The Medieval World and Beyond* • Visuals 27B–27E • Student Handout 27 (1 role card per every 4 students) • Information Master 27 (1 visual)
Processing	20 minutes	• Interactive Student Notebooks
Assessment	40 minutes	• Chapter 27 Assessment

Preview

1 **Introduce a visual metaphor for the Renaissance.** Project *Visual 27A: A Visual Metaphor for the Renaissance* and have students analyze the illustration. For the first two questions below, cover up the title of the visual. Then, ask,

- What interesting details do you see?

- What is being shown in this image?

- The title of this image is "A Visual Metaphor for the Renaissance." What do you think a *visual metaphor* is?

2 **Have students complete the Preview activity in their Interactive Student Notebooks.** Review the directions and see if students have any questions.

3 **Have students share their responses as a class or with a partner.**

4 **Connect the Preview activity to the chapter.** Explain to students that they will now explore the key changes in Europe that made way for a rebirth in classical arts and learning. Just as the illustration in the Preview activity suggests, Renaissance Europe experienced growth and a flowering of new ideas in architecture, arts, and learning. Students will learn that fueling this growth and change were travel and commerce, the growth of city-states, and the development of the philosophy known as humanism.

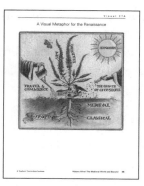

Visual 27A

Vocabulary Development

1 **Introduce the Key Content Terms.** Have students locate the Key Content Terms for the chapter in their Interactive Student Notebooks. These are important terms that will help them understand the main ideas of the chapter. Ask volunteers to identify any familiar terms and suggest how they might be used in a sentence.

2 **Have students complete a Vocabulary Development handout.** Give each student a copy of the Vocabulary Development handout of your choice from the Reading Toolkit at the back of the Lesson Masters. These handouts provide extra Key Content Term practice and support, depending on your students' needs. Review the completed handout by asking volunteers to share one answer for each term.

Reading

1 **Introduce the Essential Question and have students read Section 27.1.** Have students identify the Essential Question on the first page of the chapter: *What changes in Europe led to the Renaissance?* Then have students read Section 27.1. Afterward, have students use information from Section 27.1 and from the chapter opener image to propose some possible answers to the Essential Question.

> **Vocabulary Development: Use Roots and Affixes**
>
> Point out or guide students to recognize the Greek and Latin roots and affixes that will help them with the meanings of the vocabulary terms. These include the Latin prefix *re-*, meaning "again," plus a form of the Latin root *nasci*, "to be born"; the Latin root *humanus*, "human," plus the Greek suffix *–ism*, which can refer to a theory, a system, an action, or a process, or the plural of the Latin suffix *–ity*, which often refers to a state or quality; the Latin prefix *in-*, meaning "not," plus the Latin root *dividere*, "to divide," plus the Greek suffix *–ism*.

2 Have students complete the Reading Notes for Chapter 27. Assign Sections 27.2 to 27.5 during the activity, as indicated in the procedures for the Visual Discovery. Remind students to use the Key Content Terms where appropriate as they complete their Reading Notes.

Visual Discovery

1 Prepare materials and put students into pairs. You will need one role card from *Student Handout 27: Renaissance Role Cards* for every four students. After making the appropriate number of copies, cut apart the role cards.

2 Introduce the activity. Tell students they will work in pairs to explore various aspects of society that contributed to the flowering of the arts and learning during the Renaissance.

3 Project *Visual 27B: Classical, Medieval, or Renaissance?* and have students analyze the three images. Ask,

- What interesting details do you see?

- What similarities do you see among these three pieces of art?

- What differences do you see?

- Which one do you think is the oldest? Why?

- Which one do you think was created most recently? Why?

4 Have students read Section 27.2 and complete Part 1 of the Reading Notes. This section provides background on the causes that led to the Renaissance.

5 Have students complete Part 2 of the Reading Notes. Review the characteristics of art from the three periods—classical, medieval, and Renaissance—by analyzing the three pieces of art provided as examples in Section 27.2 of the book. Use the following background information as a reference for these pieces of art shown in this section:

- Example of Classical Art: Roman Copy of *Myron's Discobolus,* Statue, circa 450 B.C.E. This statue is a Roman copy of a Greek statue that was probably created to celebrate the achievement of a famous athlete, perhap his Olympic victory. Notice how his strong, defined body is carefully arranged into simple and harmonious shapes. He is neither an ordinary man nor a god, but he represents an ideal man in Greek society.

- Example of Medieval Art: *Narthex Tympanum,* Sculpture, 1120 C.E. This sculpture was made to fit into an arched niche, called a tympanum, over the entrance doors to a church in France. The figure in the center is Jesus, who is sending his apostles all over the world to preach. The figures in the scenes surrounding them, and in the long line across the bottom, are people around the world waiting for the apostles. Making the figures' bodies look realistic was not important to this artist. The artist's intention was to tell a story and convey religious meaning.

Student Handout 27

Visual 27B

- Example of Renaissance Art: *The School of Athens,* Raphael, Mural, about 1510 C.E. This mural was created to decorate an entire wall of a room in the pope's palace in Rome. It shows an imaginary gathering of the great thinkers of ancient Greece in a large, open building. It is arranged to frame the two most important philosophers, Plato and Aristotle, who stand in the center. The building recalls the architecture of classical antiquity and uses perspective to create depth.

6 **Project Visual 27B again and have students determine the time period for each work of art shown.** Tell students that they will now complete Part 3 of their Reading Notes for Section 27.2 by using what they learned from their reading and in Part 2. They will determine in what period each work of art on the visual was created. Give pairs of students a set amount of time, such as five minutes, to discuss and record their answers.

7 **Have pairs share their ideas.** For each artwork, ask students to identify the period in which they think it was created by raising one finger for classical, two for medieval, and three for Renaissance. Then have pairs explain their choices by pointing out specific details in each image to support their answers.

8 **Project *Information Master 27: Details About Renaissance Artwork* and reveal the answers.** Reveal each painting one at a time and discuss when each was created, as well as the details from each piece that act as clues.

9 **Project *Visual 27C: The Growth of Trade and Commerce* and have students analyze the image.** Ask,

- What interesting details do you see?

- What kinds of objects do you see?

- What are the people doing?

- Who do you think are the merchants?

- Who do you think are the customers?

10 **Have students read Section 27.3 and complete the corresponding Reading Notes.** Have them carefully examine the image in the book as they read. Then have partners discuss and record their answers to the questions in the corresponding Reading Notes.

11 **Place pairs into groups of four and distribute role cards.** Give each group one role card from Student Handout 27. Help each group choose a character in the projected image who they think would correspond to the one listed on their role card.

12 **Have groups prepare for the act-it-out.** Have groups review their role cards and use information from their Reading Notes to generate ideas for how to accurately bring their characters to life. Give them a few minutes (or more time if you would like them to gather or create props or costumes) to prepare and practice.

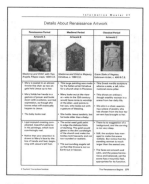

Information Master 27

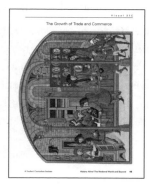

Visual 27C

13 Conduct the act-it-out. Select one student from each group to come up to the screen and step into the image in front of his or her character. Then have the other three students in each group bring their characters to life by following the steps on their role cards. Acting as a reporter, ask the questions the students have prepared to answer.

14 Project *Visual 27D: The Influence of Italian City-States* and have students analyze this image. Ask,

- What interesting details do you see?

- Describe the geographic features that surround this city. How is the city protected?

- What visual clues tell you that this is a prosperous city?

- Why might this city be an exciting and interesting place to live?

Visual 27D

15 Have students read Section 27.4 and complete the corresponding Reading Notes. Explain that the image they analyzed is a 15th-century map of the city of Florence, Italy. Then have students read and complete Section 27.4 of their Reading Notes.

16 Project *Visual 27E: The Growth of Humanism* and have students analyze the image. Ask,

- What interesting details do you see?

- Describe the objects in the image.

- What do you think this man is doing?

- In what ways does this image show influences of the Renaissance?

Visual 27E

17 Have students read Section 27.5 and complete the corresponding Reading Notes. Explain that the image they analyzed shows astronomer and clockmaker Nicholas Kratzer, who was born in Germany about 1487. In his late twenties, he went to England and became astronomer to Henry VIII, as well as a friend of English humanist Sir Thomas More. Then have students read and complete Section 27.5 of their Reading Notes.

Processing

Have students complete the Processing activity. Students re-examine the visual metaphor from the Preview activity and write an explanation of its meaning.

Quicker Coverage

Do Step 6 of the Visual Discovery as a Class Instead of having pairs match the paintings with their time periods, discuss each painting as a class and as you reveal the answers on Information Master 27.

Skip the Act-it-Out After students analyze Visual 27C and complete their Reading Notes, have them skip Steps 10 through 12 in which they prepare for and conduct the act-it-out.

Deeper Coverage

Create an Additional Act-it-Out After students have completed Steps 15 and 16 in the Visual Discovery, create an act-it-out for Visual 27E by writing role cards similar to those found on Student Handout 27. On each role card, list one of the following characters: Nicholas Kratzer, Monarch or City-State Leader, Catholic Church Leader, Petrarch. Then, on each role card, instruct students to be prepared to:

- explain who they are.
- describe their views on humanism.
- answer one or two questions to explain how their beliefs do or do not express Renaissance humanism.

Once students have prepared for this act-it-out, have one student from each group stand up. Conduct the act-it-out by asking these students the questions.

Assessment

Mastering the Content

1. A	5. B	9. C	13. B
2. D	6. C	10. A	14. A
3. B	7. D	11. C	15. C
4. A	8. B	12. D	16. C

Applying Social Studies Skills

17. cloth making; banking

18. silk, spices, perfume (any one or more)

19. Genoa

Exploring the Essential Question

20. Answers should include all the elements requested in the prompt.

Scoring Rubric

Score	Description
3	Student completes the Web site home page, accurately describing causes of the Renaissance. Information on the Web page is clearly stated, supported by details, and demonstrates command of standard English conventions.
2	Student responds to most or all parts of the task, but the Web page may lack details or not be clearly stated.
1	Student responds to at least one part of the task. The web page may contain factual and/or grammatical errors and may lack details.
0	Response does not match the task or is incorrect.

English Language Learners

Assist with Reading Notes For the Reading Notes for Part 3 of Section 27.2, consider giving students a partially completed chart to help them determine which period is represented by each piece of art. For the final row, provide students with the following information:

- Classical period: The woman is in a scene from her daily life; the poses are harmonious and balanced; the faces of the figures are very calm.
- Medieval period: Figures look flat and not real.
- Renaissance period: Figures look realistic; facial expressions are revealing; there is a full landscape in the background; there is perspective.

Learners Reading and Writing Below Grade Level

Provide Reading Support Before students read Section 27.2, consider providing them with three index cards labeled *Classical Art, Medieval Art,* and *Renaissance Art* for taking notes. As they read, have them answer this question for each period: *What are some characteristics of this style of art?* Encourage them to list words and brief phrases that will help them distinguish each style. For example, on the "classical art" card, they might write the following:

- balance, harmony
- lifelike figures (sometimes too perfect)
- nude or draped in togas
- active figures, calm faces
- heroes or people doing everyday tasks
- little depth or background detail

Encourage students to use these cards when they complete their Reading Notes and Step 6 of the Visual Discovery.

Learners with Special Education Needs

Provide Cue Cards Create simple cue cards for the spiral questions you will ask students when they analyze each image in the Visual Discovery. For each question you plan to ask, write an incomplete answer on a cue card. Create several identical cards for each spiral question. During the lesson, pass these out to students just prior to analyzing an image. Have students complete the statements on their cards. For example, cue cards for the image on Visual 27C might read as follows:

- An interesting detail I see in this image is
- These people are
- The merchants are the people who
- The customers are the people who

Add Additional Act-it-Out Roles Consider allowing students who may be hesitant to participate in the act-it-outs to take on the role of reporters. Provide them with a copy of all the role cards with the questions in Step 3 highlighted. After the actors have performed Steps 1 and 2, guide students to ask the actors these questions.

Advanced Learners

Provide an Alternate Processing Activity Have students write an essay in which they compare and contrast the artwork created in two of these three periods: classical, medieval, and Renaissance. In their essays, students should be sure to include

- the main purpose of art created during each period
- at least three characteristics of art created during each period

Enrichment Resources

Find out more about the Renaissance by exploring the following Enrichment Resources for *History Alive! The Medieval World and Beyond* at www.teachtci.com.

Enrichment Readings These in-depth readings encourage students to explore selected topics related to the chapter. You may also find readings that relate the chapter's content directly to your state's curriculum.

Internet Connections The recommended Web sites provide useful and engaging content that reinforces skills development and mastery of subjects within the chapter.

Literature Recommendations

The following books offer opportunities to extend the content in this chapter.

Eyewitness: Renaissance by Alison Cole (New York: Dorling Kindersley, 2000)

The Renaissance and the New World by Giovanni Caselli (New York: McGraw-Hill, 1998)

The Smile by Donna Jo Napoli (New York: Dutton Juvenile, 2008)

Section 27.2

Part 1 See the chart below for answers.

CAUSE	CAUSE	CAUSE
In the Late Middle Ages, merchants and Crusaders brought back goods and ideas from the East, including classical learning.	The Roman Catholic Church kept knowledge of ancient times alive by copying documents that survived from the classical period.	Europeans also read classical works that came by way of Muslim scholars.

EFFECT
This flow of ideas led to a rediscovery of ancient Greek and Roman culture.

Part 2 See the chart below for answers.

	Classical	Medieval	Renaissance
Purpose of this type of art	To show the importance of ordinary people, civic leaders, and gods and goddesses	To teach religion to people who could not read or write	To show the importance of people and nature
Two style characteristics of each example in your book	Possible answers: figure is nude; body is active and in motion; face is calm and without emotion	Possible answers: highlights Jesus who is larger than other figures; figures are all fully dressed in stiff clothing	Possible answers: lifelike three-dimensional figures; figures are shown in motion; colors reflect lighting

Part 3 See the chart below for answers.

	Classical	Medieval	Renaissance
Letter identifying the artwork	C	B	A
Two or three style characteristics in this piece of art	The woman is in a scene from her daily life; the poses are harmonious and balanced; the faces of the figures are very calm; no background or sense of perspective	Mary is larger than the other figures; figures look flat, not real	Figures look realistic; facial expressions are revealing; full landscape in background; has depth

Section 27.3

1. In the 13th century, Mongol conquests made it safe to travel along the Silk Road. Marco Polo's travels sparked a greater interest in the East, and helped encourage the transport of food, art, and luxury goods along the trade route.

2. An increase in trade led to a new, money economy. It also helped craftspeople, merchants, and bankers become more important in society.

3. Factor: The Growth of Trade and Commerce

   Merchants and bankers grew wealthy and could afford to pay for new buildings and art to beautify their cities. Growing trade meant that more classical texts, art, and artifacts were passed along trade routes, sparking interest in classical culture.

Section 27.4

1. Italian city-states were powerful cities in Renaissance Italy that ruled the surrounding towns and countryside. They were independent and were often republics governed by elected councils. Sometimes, in reality, they were ruled by rich merchants, guilds, or powerful families.

2. Because of their central Mediterranean location, Italian city-states became major centers of trade and business.

3. Factor: The Influence of Italian City-States

   Their wealth encouraged a growth in art and learning. Rich families supported the creation of art, new buildings, and centers of learning, such as universities and hospitals.

Section 27.5

1. Renaissance humanists believed that people could shape their own lives and achieve great things.

2. Renaissance humanists studied classical art, architecture, government, history, poetry, and language.

3. The Church taught that laws were made by God and required people to follow its teachings without question. It also emphasized life after death as opposed to life on Earth. Renaissance humanists believed that people should question everything, and tried to balance religious faith with an active interest in human existence.

4. Factor: The Growth of Humanism

   People began to change their ideas about many things, such as government, social class, and religion. They tried to improve upon the art, architecture, and ideas of the classical period, which led to new discoveries, new ways of studying things, and new inventions in many areas of life.

Florence: The Cradle of the Renaissance

What advances were made during the Renaissance?

Overview

In an Experiential Exercise, students take a "walking tour" of Florence, visiting seven sites to learn about various aspects of the Renaissance. Students apply their knowledge by creating a scrapbook page about their visit to Florence.

Objectives

In the course of reading this chapter and participating in the classroom activity, students will

Social Studies

- identify and explain Renaissance advances in architecture and engineering, painting, sculpture, literature, science, and mathematics.

- describe Florentine politics, as reflected in the work of Machiavelli, as well as Florentine commerce and trade.

- discuss the factors that made Florence an important cultural center during the Renaissance.

- explain how various advances made during the Renaissance reflect humanist thinking and ideals.

Language Arts

- write captions and a summary.

- demonstrate an understanding of grammar and sentence structure.

Social Studies Vocabulary

Key Content Terms Florence, Donatello, Michelangelo, secular, Dante Alighieri, Leonardo da Vinci, Niccolò Machiavelli

Academic Vocabulary intense, texture, analyze

Materials

History Alive! The Medieval World and Beyond

Interactive Student Notebooks

Visual 28

Placards 28A–28G

Lesson Masters
- Station Directions 28A–28G (2 copies)
- Station Materials 28A (2 copies)
- Station Materials 28B (1 per every four students, cut apart)
- Information Master 28 (1 transparency)
- Vocabulary Development handout (1 per student, on colored paper)

1 beach ball

2 small mirrors

clay or sculpting material

masking tape

basket or cardboard box

Activity	Suggested Time	Materials
Preview	10 minutes	• Interactive Student Notebooks • Visual 28
Vocabulary Development	30–40 minutes	• *History Alive! The Medieval World and Beyond* • Interactive Student Notebooks • Vocabulary Development handout
Experiential Exercise	120–150 minutes (3 class periods) (1.5 block periods)	• *History Alive! The Medieval World and Beyond* • Placards 28A–28G • Station Directions 28A–28G (2 copies) • Station Materials 28A (2 copies) • Station Materials 28B (1 per every four students, cut apart) • Information Master 28 (1 transparency) • 1 beach ball • 2 small mirrors • clay or sculpting material • basket or cardboard box • masking tape
Processing	20 minutes	• Interactive Student Notebooks
Assessment	40 minutes	• Chapter 28 Assessment

Preview

1 Have students examine an image of Florence. Project *Visual 28: Florence, Italy,* and have students analyze the image. Ask,

- What interesting details do you see here?

- How would you describe this city? The geographic features surrounding the city?

- What are the city's most noticeable features?

2 Have students complete the Preview activity in their Interactive Student Notebooks. Review the directions with students. After all students have completed the Preview activity, allow them to share their responses, encouraging them to come up to the visual and point out items they circled.

3 Connect the Preview activity to the chapter. Explain to students that they will be taking a "walking tour" of Florence to learn about many of the advances made there during the Renaissance. Florence became Italy's leading cultural center during the Renaissance and was the birthplace of many important writers, artists, and thinkers. In this chapter, students will be introduced to many of these people and will discover how their achievements affected Renaissance life and ideas.

Visual 28

Vocabulary Development

1 Introduce the Key Content Terms. Have students locate the Key Content Terms for the chapter in their Interactive Student Notebooks. These are important terms that will help them understand the main ideas of the chapter. Ask volunteers to identify any familiar terms and suggest how they might be used in a sentence.

2 Have students complete a Vocabulary Development handout. Give each student a copy of the Vocabulary Development handout of your choice from the Reading Toolkit at the back of the Lesson Masters. These handouts provide extra Key Content Term practice and support, depending on your students' needs. Review the completed handout by asking volunteers to share one answer for each term.

Reading

1 Introduce the Essential Question and have students read Section 28.1. Have students identify the Essential Question on the first page of the chapter: *What advances were made during the Renaissance?* Then have students read Section 28.1. Afterward, have students respond to these questions:

- Describe the city of Florence.

- How did Florence become such a wealthy city?

- Why do you think Florence has been called the "cradle of the Renaissance"?

2 **Have students complete the Reading Notes for Chapter 28.** Assign Sections 28.2 to 28.9 during the activity, as indicated in the procedures for the Experiential Exercise. Remind students to use the Key Content Terms where appropriate as they complete their Reading Notes.

Experiential Exercise

1 **Before class, prepare materials and the classroom for the activity.** Follow these steps:

* Arrange the desks to create seven stations as shown in the diagram. (**Note:** This activity works best in a large space. Consider setting up the stations in a gymnasium, library, or other large space.)

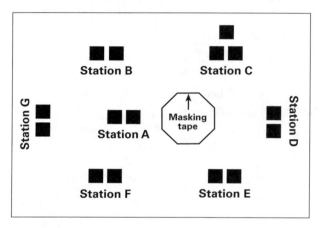

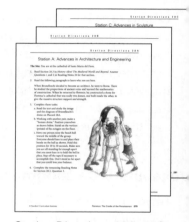

Station Directions 28A–28G

* Set up the stations. Choose one of these two options:

  Option 1: Set up the stations yourself, following the directions on the back of each placard.

  Option 2: Have students set up the stations.

* Have masking tape available for attaching items to desks and walls.

* At each station, place both copies of one of *Station Directions 28A–28G* and the corresponding placard, along with the other required materials in a one-gallon plastic bag. (**Note:** To make the activity run more smoothly, consider creating another set of placards.) You may want to place copies of *History Alive! The Medieval World and Beyond* at each station. Otherwise, students will have to carry their books and their Interactive Student Notebooks with them.

* If you have students set up each station, tell them that directions on the back of each placard describe how to set up each station and show what the station should look like. For bigger classes, have students create two set-ups at each station.

Placards 28A–28G

- Only one octagon and one beach ball are needed for Station A, though students may need assistance in creating the masking-tape octagon.

- If stations must be dismantled at the end of a class, have students return all the materials to the bag, throwing away any tape, so that the stations can be quickly reconstructed.

2 Pair students and introduce the activity. Have students sit on the floor near the center of the room. Explain that they will now assume the roles of modern tourists taking a walking tour of Florence. At each of seven sites, they will read a section of *History Alive! The Medieval World and Beyond*, perform a task, and record notes in their Interactive Student Notebooks.

3 Have students read Section 28.2 and complete the corresponding Reading Notes. Explain that this section provides background information about Florence and why the Renaissance was centered there.

4 Introduce students to the walking tour. Project *Information Master 28: Directions for the Walking Tour* and review the directions with students. Quickly review the procedures at each station to give them a general idea of what to do. (**Note:** You might find it helpful to invite a few adult aides to assist in monitoring this activity.)

5 Have pairs begin their tour. Assign each pair of students a different station to start from. When a pair finishes at a station, have them raise their hands to indicate they are ready for you to check their work. Use the Guide to Reading Notes to check their answers. Continue until most pairs have visited all the stations.

6 Hold a class discussion. Have students sit with their partners. Ask,

- What aspects of Renaissance Florence did you most enjoy learning about?

- What things did you learn about the Italian Renaissance that you didn't know before?

- What were some of the advances made during the Renaissance?

- Why do historians call Florence the "cradle of the Renaissance"?

At this time, you may want to announce the results of the vote on Machiavelli's ideas from Station F.

Station Materials 28A

Station Materials 28B

Information Master 28

Processing

1 **Have students complete the Processing activity.** Students create a scrapbook page that describes Renaissance Florence. Review the steps with students. Allow them time to create their pages. You might want to have their peers edit their picture captions and paragraph.

2 **Have students share their scrapbook pages with their partners or with the class.**

Quicker Coverage

Shorten the Activity Reduce from seven to three the number of stations students visit. Set up only Stations A–F. Have half the pairs visit Stations A–C and the other half visit D–F. Then have a pair who visited Stations A–C join a pair who visited Stations D–F. In these new foursomes, have students share what they learned at each station, as well as their answers to the Reading Notes. Have students complete those sections of Reading Notes for the stations they did not visit. All students will need to complete the Reading Notes for Section 28.9, but will omit Question 3, which pertained to Station G in the activity.

Abbreviate the Processing Activity Instead of assigning the scrapbook page, have students annotate the image in the Processing activity with at least two facts they learned from their reading and from their walking tour of Florence.

Deeper Coverage

Conduct a Wrap-Up Activity Follow these steps:

• Create a spectrum by placing a 10- to 15-foot strip of masking tape along the floor at the front of the room. On the board, above opposite ends of the spectrum, write "Most Significant Advancement" and "Least Significant Advancement." Remind students of the purpose of a spectrum.

• Remove the placards from the wall and assign one to each pair (**Note:** Do not assign Placard 28G). You may have more than one pair assigned to a placard.

• Tell students that based on their reading and completed Reading Notes, they should determine where on the spectrum they would place their placard.

• Have one student represent each advancement and come forward to stand on the spectrum where the pair thinks their contribution belongs. Tell students to hold their placards in front of their chests.

• Challenge the other students to identify advancements they believe are misplaced. Encourage discussion about where the advancements should be placed. The purpose of this activity is not to find "correct" locations, but to have students support their opinions.

Assessment

Mastering the Content

1. D	5. C	9. C	13. D
2. A	6. C	10. A	14. A
3. B	7. D	11. D	15. B
4. B	8. A	12. B	16. C

Applying Social Studies Skills

17. because a person is only born to a throne through luck, while a person who gains it himself or herself has worked to deserve it

18. Answers will vary. Sample answer: He is questioning where people come from and what happens after death. Not only is he questioning religious teachings, he is also depending on his own thoughts, not Church teachings.

19. primary source; Answers will vary. Sample answer: Petrarch lived at the time and was part of the Renaissance, not somebody writing about it later or from the outside.

Exploring the Essential Question

20. Answers should include all the elements requested in the prompt.

Scoring Rubric

Score	Description
3	Student writes a short paragraph in each of the three boxes, complying with all three bulleted requirements. Paragraphs are clearly stated, supported by details, and demonstrate command of standard English conventions.
2	Student responds to most or all parts of the task, but paragraphs may lack details or not be clearly stated.
1	Student responds to at least one part of the task. Paragraph(s) may contain factual and/or grammatical errors and may lack details.
0	Response does not match the task or is incorrect.

English Language Learners

Modify the Preview Activity Allow students to work in pairs as they complete the Preview activity. Let them discuss the five details they would circle in the image and what each might reveal about the city. Also, for some students, consider reducing the number of details they must identify from five to three.

Learners Reading and Writing Below Grade Level

Provide Reading Support Provide students with a copy of Guide to Reading Notes 28 with some sections completed for them. For the sections that are already completed, have students highlight key words and phrases in each answer as they visit these stations and are instructed to read and complete the Reading Notes. For the other sections, consider providing partial answers with key words omitted for students to fill in as they read.

Learners with Special Education Needs

Modify the Processing Activity Consider reducing from six to three the number of images for which students must write captions. Also, consider giving students the following prompts to help them write the paragraph.

- I learned many interesting things about Florence. For example, I learned that
- I also learned _____ about _____.
- Finally, I found out that
- My visit to Florence really helped me understand advances during the Renaissance in the following ways:

Advanced Learners

Extend the Activity Have students research additional examples of advances that originated in Florence during this time period. Instruct students to create a slide show or poster-board presentation highlighting these advances with images from Internet resources. Use these guidelines to assign this task:

- Using the Internet or additional resources from the library, find at least three more examples of advances that originated in Florence during the Renaissance.
- Include an illustration or photograph of each advance.
- Write a brief caption that describes each advance, tells who was responsible for it, and explains how it differs from what had come before.

Enrichment Resources

Find out more about Florence and the advances of the Renaissance by exploring the following Enrichment Resources for *History Alive! The Medieval World and Beyond* at www.teachtci.com.

Enrichment Readings These in-depth readings encourage students to explore selected topics related to the chapter. You may also find readings that relate the chapter's content directly to your state's curriculum.

Internet Connections The recommended Web sites provide useful and engaging content that reinforces skills development and mastery of subjects within the chapter.

Literature Recommendations

The following books offer opportunities to extend the content in this chapter.

The Apprentice by Pilar Molina Llorente (New York: Farrar, Straus & Giroux, 1994)

Leonardo and His Times by Andy Crawford (New York: Dorling Kindersley, 2000)

The Medicis: A Ruling Dynasty by Heather Lehr Wagner (New York: Chelsea House, 2005)

Section 28.2

1. Because of its ideal location on the Arno River, Florence became a center for trade and commerce. It also was dominated by the Medici family, who helped Florence become a banking center for Europe.

2. The city's residents could afford to be patrons of artists and thinkers.

3. Some travelers came to do business, while others came to study art. Still others came to learn at the city's schools and libraries.

Section 28.3

1. Renaissance buildings were modeled on ancient ruins. They had Greek- and Roman-inspired features such as arches, columns, and domed roofs. Renaissance architects also designed public buildings and spaces where citizens could interact based on the humanist ideal of good citizenship.

2. Brunelleschi used eight stone arches that leaned against each other. The arches were supported by hoops of iron, wood, and brick.

3. Sentences should be completed as follows:

   • On our dome, the parts of our bodies that supported the most weight were our legs and feet.

   • On Brunelleschi's dome, the parts that supported the most weight were the arches.

   • The feet on our dome were like the bottom of the arches, or the base, on Brunelleschi's dome.

   • The beach ball on our dome was like the lantern on Brunelleschi's dome.

   • The bodies on our dome were like the arches on Brunelleschi's dome.

Section 28.4

1. Renaissance figures were realistic like classical figures, but with emotions. Renaissance art showed the influence of humanism by depicting real people of all classes and self-portraits.

2. Possible answers: Renaissance painters used geometry to divide space, perspective to make scenes look more realistic, careful shading to make figures more realistic, and oil paint to redo work and to reveal new details and textures.

3. Possible answers:

Detail from Image	Perspective Technique
People	The figures closer to the viewer seem bigger; those farther away seem smaller.
Columns	The columns look flat when viewed straight on, but seen from another angle they appear to have three-dimensions.
Mountains	The mountains are pale and blurry to show they are in the distance.
Placement of Mary and Jesus	The viewer's eyes are drawn toward the vanishing point, where Mary and Jesus are.

Section 28.5

1. Renaissance sculptors created figures that were three-dimensional, freestanding, looked like real people, and showed emotion.

2. Donatello's *David* is a life-size statue that shows personality and mood and is natural and lifelike. Michelangelo's *David* is enormous, ideally beautiful, and shows complex emotions.

3. Students' responses will vary.

Section 28.6

1. Renaissance writers wrote about secular topics and about personal experiences. They used more individual styles and expressed thoughts and feelings about life. Unlike medieval writers, who wrote primarily in Latin, Renaissance writers wrote in their own vernacular, or local language.

2. Dante's *The Divine Comedy* highlights strong emotions and the experiences of individuals. It is also a social commentary and includes real people.

3. Image A: *Paradiso;* Image B: *Purgatorio;* Image C: *Inferno*

Section 28.7

1. During the Renaissance, people used a new approach: they questioned old ideas, made careful observations, performed experiments, and analyzed the results.

2. Students' sketches will vary. Their sketches could include circulation, the workings of the eye, the effect of the moon on Earth's tides, maps, bridges, weapons, or an underwater diving suit.

3. Drawing A: flying machine; Drawing B: four-wheeled armored tank; Drawing C: proportions of a man's head; Drawing D: physics and geometry calculations

Section 28.8

1. The Medici family was involved in or controlled most aspects of city life. They were able to pay a strong army, built palaces, sponsored art that made the city beautiful and famous, and were watchful for plots against them.

2. Machiavelli wrote about how politics and government functioned and how rulers could make their states strong. *The Prince* shocked people with its cold realism. Yet, it was a modern work because it separated religion from government and was concerned with the real-world operations of government and politics.

3. Students' interpretation of quotations will vary. Possible answers:

   Quotation 1: A political leader should master the art of war above all else.

   Quotation 2: Appear as if you have virtuous and admirable qualities, but be willing to display the opposite qualities when necessary.

   Quotation 3: The actions we take are considered acceptable or unacceptable based on the results we achieve.

Section 28.9

1. The woolen-cloth and banking industries helped Florence become the center of the Renaissance.

2. The Old Market was crowded and smelly; it supplied everyday goods, such as food and housewares. The New Market was orderly and clean; it supplied cloth and banking services.

3. Students' charts will vary. The third column of their completed chart should show a zero balance at the bottom.

Leading Figures of the Renaissance

In what ways have various leading figures of the Renaissance affected modern society?

Overview

In a Response Group activity, students create illustrated pedestals for ten prominent Renaissance figures that highlight the figures' lives and achievements. Groups then examine the pedestals in the class "gallery," identify which Renaissance figure each represents, and discuss two critical thinking questions related to these figures.

Objectives

In the course of reading this chapter and participating in the classroom activity, students will

Social Studies

- understand how the Renaissance spread from Italy to other parts of Europe.
- summarize key aspects of the lives and achievements of Renaissance figures, such as Leonardo da Vinci, Michelangelo, and William Shakespeare.
- describe and evaluate key advances made by ten prominent Renaissance figures.

Language Arts

- use definitions and examples to explain the meanings of new words.
- read expository text to connect the essential ideas to their own learning.

Social Studies Vocabulary

Key Content Terms Johannes Gutenberg, New World, William Shakespeare, Miguel Cervantes

Academic Vocabulary available, emotional, proportion, orbit, authorize

Materials

History Alive! The Medieval World and Beyond

Interactive Student Notebooks

Lesson Masters

- Student Handout 29A (1 page per group)
- Student Handout 29B (1 per every 3 students plus 1 transparency)
- Information Masters 29A–29C (1 transparency each)
- Vocabulary Development handout (1 per student, on colored paper)

butcher paper

Activity	Suggested Time	Materials
Preview	10 minutes	• Interactive Student Notebooks
Vocabulary Development	30–40 minutes	• *History Alive! The Medieval World and Beyond* • Interactive Student Notebooks • Vocabulary Development handout
Response Group	150 minutes (3 class periods) (1.5 block periods)	• *History Alive! The Medieval World and Beyond* • Interactive Student Notebooks • Student Handout 29A (1 page per group) • Student Handout 29B (1 per every 3 students plus 1 transparency) • Information Masters 29A–29C (1 transparency each) • butcher paper
Processing	20 minutes	• Interactive Student Notebooks
Assessment	40 minutes	• Chapter 29 Assessment

Preview

1 **Have students complete the Preview activity in their Interactive Student Notebooks.** Students choose someone they think has been influential in the past century and discuss that person's talents and achievements.

2 **Have students share their responses in pairs or with the class.**

3 **Connect the Preview activity to the chapter.** Explain that just as there were influential people in recent history, whom students identified in the Preview activity, the Renaissance period was filled with influential and talented people who greatly affected the world around them. In this chapter, students will learn about the lives and achievements of ten leading Renaissance figures.

Vocabulary Development

1 **Introduce the Key Content Terms.** Have students locate the Key Content Terms for the chapter in their Interactive Student Notebooks. These are important terms that will help them understand the main ideas of the chapter. Ask volunteers to identify any familiar terms and how they might be used in a sentence.

2 **Have students complete a Vocabulary Development handout.** Give each student a copy of the Vocabulary Development handout of your choice from the Reading Toolkit at the back of the Lesson Masters. These handouts provide extra Key Content Term practice and support, depending on your students' needs. Review the completed handout by asking volunteers to share one answer for each term.

Reading

1 **Introduce the Essential Question and have students read Section 29.1.** Have students identify the Essential Question on the first page of the chapter: *In what ways have various leading figures of the Renaissance affected modern society?* Then have students read Section 29.1. Afterward, have students respond to the following:

- Describe Europe from the 14th through the 16th centuries.

- Explain one reason why there was so much creative energy during the Renaissance.

- Explain why Leonardo da Vinci is considered to be the ideal "Renaissance person."

2 **Have students complete the Reading Notes for Chapter 29.** Assign Sections 29.2 to 29.12 during the activity, as indicated in the procedures for the Response Group activity. Remind students to use the Key Content Terms where appropriate as they complete their Reading Notes.

Response Group

1 **Place students in groups of three and introduce the activity.** Explain that students will first read about a prominent Renaissance figure, such as Leonardo da Vinci. They will create a pedestal for that figure and illustrate it with six images that represent that person's life and achievements. The pedestals will be placed together to create a "gallery" of Renaissance greats. After reading about all the figures, students will determine which figure belongs to each pedestal. Finally, the heads (or "busts") of the figures will be attached to their respective pedestals, or revealed, to complete the gallery.

2 **Have students read Section 29.2 and complete the Reading Notes for this section.** Tell students that this section explains how developments such as the printing press helped to spread Renaissance ideas throughout Europe.

3 **Distribute materials and review the steps for completing a bust and a pedestal of a Renaissance figure.** Assign each group a figure by giving them one page from *Student Handout 29A: Renaissance Figures.* Students can peek at the handout to find out which figure they have been assigned, but should then place the handouts face down to keep the figures' identities secret. Also, give each group a copy of *Student Handout 29B: Creating an Illustrated Pedestal,* markers, pencils, and scratch paper. Project a transparency of Student Handout 29B and review the steps with the class.

4 **Have students create their busts and pedestals.** Encourage groups to work quietly, as if they are in a museum gallery and, also, so as not to let others overhear the identity of their figure. Monitor their progress, initialing Student Handout 29B as they complete each step. Project *Information Master 29A: Pedestal Template* and, when groups begin Step 2 on Student Handout 29B, have them trace the template onto a sheet of butcher paper 3 to 4 feet long. Make sure the tracing is the right size for the addition of the head, which students will add later. (**Note:** You may want to anchor your projector so that all the pedestals are the same size. You may also decide to have students cut out their pedestals so they appear to be freestanding.)

5 **Have students arrange and display their pedestals to create the feeling of a gallery.** Have groups keep the heads face down at their desks or covered in some other way.

6 **Project *Information Master 29B: Identifying the Pedestals* and review the steps listed there.** Ask students if they have any questions. Then assign groups different sections of the chapter to read to start the identification process. Continue until most groups have completed their Reading Notes and matched all the pedestals with a Renaissance figure.

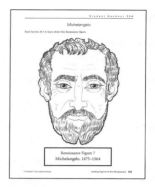

Student Handout 29A

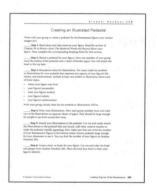

Student Handout 29B

Information Master 29A

Information Master 29B

7 Have students share their answers and reveal "who's who." Stand by one of the pedestals and ask, Which great Renaissance figure does this pedestal commemorate? Ask volunteers to share their group's answer and point out details that helped them determine the answer. Then ask the group that worked on the pedestal to tape their figure's head to the pedestal or to reveal it. Have one member of the group present the figure by summarizing the information on the pedestal and then sharing one thing for which their figure is most remembered. Continue the process until all ten figures have been identified and presented.

8 Have students participate in a Response Group discussion. First, set up a human bar graph in your classroom by taking the ten pedestals that groups created and lining them up along the board. Clear some space in front of the board. Project *Information Master 29C: Critical Thinking Questions* and reveal only Critical Thinking Question A. Then, do the following:

Information Master 29C

- Give groups time to discuss which of the ten leading figures they believe best answers Critical Thinking Question A. Make sure that they have details from their Reading Notes to support their choice.

- Have each group send one person to stand in front of the Renaissance figure they chose as most likely to win the award for "Most Original Idea or Talent." As students come to the board, have them form in a single line—like bars on a graph—in front of the figure they chose.

- As students remain standing in the bar graph, ask these questions:

  According to our human bar graph, who is most likely to win the award for "Most Original Idea or Talent"?

  According to our human bar graph, who is least likely to win the award for "Most Original Idea or Talent"?

  What evidence can you identify to support your choice for the figure who is most likely to win the award for "Most Original Idea or Talent"? Have seated students answer this question.

9 Have students participate in a second Response Group discussion. Repeat Step 8 with Critical Thinking Question B on Information Master 29C. Ask groups to choose a different person to send to the board. Ask these questions:

  According to our human bar graph, who most affected modern society?

  According to our human bar graph, who least affected modern society?

  What evidence can you identify to support your choice for who most affected modern society?

Processing

Have students complete the Processing activity in their Interactive Student Notebooks. Students will make a seating plan for a dinner party, which all ten leading Renaissance figures will attend.

> **Listening and Speaking: Oral Conventions**
>
> This activity is an ideal place to insert a mini-lesson on pronouns and antecedents. As students discuss and present their "most original" and most influential person, remind them that all the pronouns they use (such as *he, him, they,* and *them*) need to refer back to a clear antecedent, which, in this case, should be the person or people they are discussing. Remind students to avoid unclear references such as "They say" or "They believe" when those statements refer to no one in particular.

Quicker Coverage

Eliminate the Matching In Step 6 of the Response Group directions, have students post their heads on their pedestals to reveal the figures' identities. Then have students circulate and complete their Reading Notes by reading the information on the pedestals. For any Reading Notes questions that the pedestals do not address, have students turn to that section in Chapter 29 and fill in any missing information.

Omit the Group Discussions Eliminate Steps 8 and 9 in the Response Group directions, and simply have students create the pedestals, post them, and then match the pedestals to their Renaissance figures.

Reuse the Pedestals Once a class of students has created pedestals and done this activity, save the pedestals to use for future classes. Then, skip Steps 3 through 5 in the Response Group activity, and just have students match the pedestals to their reading and discuss the Critical Thinking Questions in Steps 8 and 9.

Deeper Coverage

Research Additional Renaissance Figures Have students use the Internet or books from the library to identify one additional person from the Renaissance whose talents or achievements were significant. Students should research information about the person's background, as well as list his or her talents or achievements. Some people you may wish students to consider are:

- Desiderius Erasmus: humanist philosopher
- Guillaume Dufay: composer and musician
- Baldassare Castiglione: writer
- Aldus Pius Manutius: writer and publisher
- Leon Alberti: architect
- Gerardus Mercator: mapmaker
- René Descartes: philosopher, mathematician

Assessment

Mastering the Content

1. B	5. C	9. B	13. D
2. D	6. D	10. A	14. D
3. A	7. B	11. B	15. A
4. C	8. A	12. C	16. C

Applying Social Studies Skills

17. scientists, people who made advances in science

18. the other people were not mainly writers

19. Leonardo made contributions in many different fields

Exploring the Essential Question

20. Answers should include all the elements requested in the prompt.

Scoring Rubric

Score	Description
3	Student completes a fictitious journal entry that complies with all three bulleted points. Journal entries are clearly stated, supported by details, and demonstrate command of standard English conventions.
2	Student writes a journal entry that complies with two of the bulleted points; or journal entry may address all three points but may lack details or not be clearly stated.
1	Student addresses at least one of the bulleted points. Journal entry may contain factual and/or grammatical errors and may lack details.
0	Response does not match the task or is incorrect.

From Gutenberg to the Internet

1   **Prepare students to read the Chapter 29 Reading Further.** Ask, *What different forms of communication do we use today? How are books and magazines different from movies, CDs, videos, and the Internet? Does anyone know how long printing has existed?*

2   **Have a volunteer read aloud the introduction to the Chapter 29 Reading Further.** Ask, *What are some kinds of ideas that might spread more quickly because of printing? For example, how might printing help to spread scientific or scholarly information?*

3   **Have students read the Chapter 29 Reading Further.** Discuss the following terms to be sure that students understand them: *sue* (as in lawsuit), *business partnership*, and *pension*. Ask students to suggest how to use each word in a sentence.

4   **Discuss the key facts that students learned from the Reading Further.** Ask, *What motivated Gutenberg to develop a printing press? What technical problems did he have to solve? What business problems interfered with his progress on the press? What made the Gutenberg Bible so extraordinary?*

5   **Have students complete the Reading Further in their Interactive Student Notebooks.** Students will write a persuasive essay in which they argue whether print media (books, newspapers) or the Internet is a superior form of communication. Review the nature of supporting details. Write the following argument on the board as the center of a word web: *The Internet communicates information faster than books do.* Then have the class brainstorm for details that support the argument, and add them to the word web.

7   **Ask volunteers to read aloud their essays.** Invite students to share questions and comments. Encourage the class to politely ask questions that challenge classmates' arguments and ask for further supporting details or evidence.

English Language Learners

Adapt the Preview Activity Allow students to work in pairs, if needed, to choose a figure and discuss or research the person's talents and why he or she was chosen. Also, consider reducing, from three to one or two, the number of talents some students must list.

Learners Reading and Writing Below Grade Level

Shorten the Activity Lower from ten to five or six the number of figures that students must read about in the Response Group activity. For the remaining figures, provide students with a copy of Guide to Reading Notes 29 with answers for those sections. Have students highlight key words or phrases in the answers that may help them decide which pedestal corresponds to each figure.

Learners with Special Education Needs

Prepare Students for the Activity Give students photocopies of Sections 29.3 through 29.12 from *History Alive! The Medieval World and Beyond* ahead of time and ask them to highlight information in each section that may later help them complete the Reading Notes. This will allow them to complete the Reading Notes during the class time as other students are both reading the text and completing their notes.

Modify the Processing Activity Reduce the number of dinner guests from ten to six. Have students choose which six guests they would invite. They can write one sentence explaining why they chose each guest (for example, because that guest might have more interesting or entertaining stories to tell) or complete a seating chart for those six guests and explain why they sat them where they did.

Advanced Learners

Extend the Processing Activity Have students imagine some of the conversations that might take place around the dinner table. Instruct students to "eavesdrop" on some of the conversations and add speech bubbles to their seating plan to show what various guests might say to one another. Encourage students to include comments on other guests' talents and achievements, as well as anything in their personal histories or backgrounds, training, or work that the guests might have in common.

Enrichment Resources

Find out more about leading figures of the Renaissance by exploring the following Enrichment Resources for *History Alive! The Medieval World and Beyond* at www.teachtci.com.

Enrichment Readings These in-depth readings encourage students to explore selected topics related to the chapter. You may also find readings that relate the chapter's content directly to your state's curriculum.

Internet Connections The recommended Web sites provide useful and engaging content that reinforces skills development and mastery of subjects within the chapter.

Literature Recommendations

The following books offer opportunities to extend the content in this chapter.

Elizabethan England by Ruth Ashby (Tarrytown, NY: Marshall Cavendish Corp., 1999)

Leonardo's Horse by Jean Fritz (New York: Putnam, 2001)

Nicolaus Copernicus: Father of Modern Astronomy by Barbara A. Somervill (Mankato, MN: Compass Point Books, 2005)

Section 29.2

1. Renaissance ideas were spread by merchants who moved from Italy throughout Europe, visitors who traveled to Italy, and scholars who went to Italy to learn and then returned home eager to share what they had learned.

2. His printing press used movable type, meaning the characters could be rearranged and used again on other printing jobs. He also cast his type in metal instead of using wooden blocks.

3. Books and pamphlets could now be produced much more cheaply and quickly, and all of this new printed matter allowed ideas to spread more quickly, as well.

Section 29.3

1. Name: Michelangelo

   Title (from section title): Sculptor and Painter

   Lived (years of birth and death): 1475–1564

   From (the place): near Florence, Italy

   Personality and Training: He was ambitious, religious, and said to have a bad temper. He studied art, especially painting and sculpture.

   Talents and Achievements: He was a very talented painter and sculptor. His art shows emotions and human beauty. His sculpting seems to bring figures to life. His work influenced others. Three of his greatest sculptures are the *Pietà, David,* and *Moses.* One of his painted masterpieces is the ceiling of the Sistine Chapel in Rome.

2. Pedestal 7; Answers will vary.

Section 29.4

1. Name: Titian

   Title (from section title): Painter

   Lived (years of birth and death): about 1488–1576

   From (the place): the Italian Alps

   Personality and Training: Persuasive and generous, he studied painting, including fresco painting and examples of art from Rome and Florence.

   Talents and Achievements: He was known for his use of color and lively brushwork that made his paintings come alive and show personality. He created many paintings of myths and Bible stories, as well as portraits of royalty. His color and brushwork techniques are still copied today.

2. Pedestal 3; Answers will vary.

Section 29.5

1. Name: Albrecht Dürer

   Title (from section title): Artist

   Lived (years of birth and death): 1471–1528

   From (the place): Nuremberg, Germany

   Personality and Training: Fashionable, confident, and intellectual, he studied goldsmithing, painting, printmaking, math, Latin, and classical literature and sculpture. He traveled and met humanists.

   Talents and Achievements: He blended detailed German painting with Italian techniques of perspective and idealized beauty. He had a talent for engravings and woodcuts. He painted religious figures, myths, self-portraits, and court portraits. He wrote essays about art to advise other artists.

2. Pedestal 9; Answers will vary.

Section 29.6

1. Name: Nicolaus Copernicus

   Title (from section title): Scientist

   Lived (years of birth and death): 1473–1543

   From (the place): Torun, Poland

   Personality and Training: A creative, free thinker, he went to the University of Krakow and studied medicine, law, and astronomy in Italy.

   Talents and Achievements: Skilled in observation and math, he studied what he really saw in the skies, not what he was supposed to. He proposed the theory that Earth and other planets orbit the sun. This theory was attacked by the Church, but influenced key scientists, and is part of the basis of modern astronomy.

2. Pedestal 10; Answers will vary.

Section 29.7

1. Name: Andreas Vesalius

    Title (from section title): Scientist

    Lived (years of birth and death): 1514–1564

    From (the place): Brussels, Belgium

    Personality and Training: He was hard-working, curious, confident, and gloomy and distant at times. He earned a medical degree.

    Talents and Achievements: A good observer and an independent thinker, he studied dead human bodies and made important discoveries, such as that the human heart has four chambers. He wrote the first modern medical textbook, which included illustrations based on his drawings.

2. Pedestal 1; Answers will vary.

Section 29.8

1. Name: Isabella I

    Title (from section title): Queen of Spain

    Lived (years of birth and death): 1451–1504

    From (the place): Castile, Spain

    Personality and Training: She was intelligent, strong-willed, brave, and a devoted Catholic. Her schooling was limited. She studied Latin as an adult and sponsored fine art.

    Talents and Achievements: She was a forceful woman and held her own in court politics. Her marriage to Ferdinand allowed the couple to unite Spain. She sponsored Columbus's voyages, which led to the European discovery of the "New World."

2. Pedestal 4; Answers will vary.

Section 29.9

1. Name: Elizabeth I

    Title (from section title): Queen of England

    Lived (years of birth and death): 1533–1603

    From (the place): London, England

    Personality and Training: Strong-minded and independent, but also flexible and willing to listen to good advice, she was a gifted scholar, highly educated, and spoke five languages.

    Talents and Achievements: A flexible and thoughtful ruler, she changed unpopular policies and strengthened England's economy. She had political skill and inspired love and loyalty. She supported theater, education, culture, trade, and exploration. Under her rule, England became richer and more powerful.

2. Pedestal 8; Answers will vary.

Section 29.10

1. Name: William Shakespeare

    Title (from section title): Poet and Playwright

    Lived (years of birth and death): 1564–1616

    From (the place): Stratford-on-Avon, England

    Personality and Training: Quiet, a bit mysterious, and a keen observer, he thought deeply about life and had a sense of humor. He studied Latin, classical literature, and acting. His work shows knowledge of many subjects.

    Talents and Achievements: An actor, poet, and playwright, he had a way with words and an understanding of human behavior. People admire his beautiful sonnets. He wrote 38 plays. Many of his plays are still popular today and his works have added to the English languge.

2. Pedestal 2; Answers will vary.

Section 29.11

1. Name: Miguel Cervantes

   Title (from section title): Writer

   Lived (years of birth and death): 1547–1616

   From (the place): near Madrid, Spain

   Personality and Training: He was adventurous, courageous, and had a biting sense of humor. He may have studied with humanist priests, but much of his education came from his experiences.

   Talents and Achievements: He was a gifted writer with a talent for satire. He wrote many plays, poems, and novels. His masterpiece, *Don Quixote,* is a satire that pokes fun at tales of heroic knights and at Spanish society. It is a masterpiece of world literature.

2. Pedestal 5; Answers will vary.

Section 29.12

1. Name: Leonardo da Vinci

   Title (from section title): Renaissance Person

   Lived (years of birth and death): 1452–1519

   From (the place): near Florence, Italy

   Personality and Training: He was brilliant, extremely curious, a vegetarian, a keen observer, and an independent thinker. He trained under a master painter and sculptor in Florence. He studied art, music, math, anatomy, architecture, and engineering.

   Talents and Achievements: He was a painter, sculptor, architect, and engineer. He sketched inventions that were far ahead of their time. His *Mona Lisa* shows perspective, balance, detail, and a rich use of light, color, and shade.

2. Pedestal 6; Answers will vary.

The Reformation Begins

What factors led to the weakening of the Catholic Church and the beginning of the Reformation?

Overview

In a Visual Discovery activity, students explore the factors that contributed to the weakening of the Catholic Church and then examine the leaders whose ideas led to Reformation.

Objectives

In the course of reading this chapter and participating in the classroom activity, students will

Social Studies

- summarize corrupt practices and key events that weakened the Catholic Church.

- describe the theological, political, and religious ideas of major figures during the Reformation.

- understand Martin Luther's theological and political ideas and how they led to the Reformation.

- examine factors that contributed to the spread of Protestant ideas throughout Europe.

Language Arts

- use definitions and examples to explain the meanings of new words.

- read expository text to connect the essential ideas to their own learning.

Social Studies Vocabulary

Key Content Terms indulgence, simony, Reformation, Protestant, Martin Luther, denomination

Academic Vocabulary saint, doctrine, thesis, treaty

Materials

History Alive! The Medieval World and Beyond

Interactive Student Notebooks

Visuals 30A–30C

Lesson Masters

- Information Master 30

- Student Handout 30A (enough for 1 certificate per student)

- Student Handout 30B (1 copy per every 4 students)

- Vocabulary Development handout (1 per student, on colored paper)

Activity	Suggested Time	Materials
Preview	45 minutes	• *History Alive! The Medieval World and Beyond* • Interactive Student Notebooks • Information Master 30 • Student Handout 30A (enough for 1 certificate per student)
Vocabulary Development	30–40 minutes	• *History Alive! The Medieval World and Beyond* • Interactive Student Notebooks • Vocabulary Development handout
Visual Discovery	45 minutes (1 class period) (.5 block period)	• *History Alive! The Medieval World and Beyond* • Interactive Student Notebooks • Visuals 30A–30C • Student Handout 30B (1 copy per every 4 students)
Processing	20 minutes	• Interactive Student Notebooks
Assessment	40 minutes	• Chapter 30 Assessment

Preview

1   **Understand the intent of the Preview activity.** The Preview activity that appears in the Interactive Student Notebook is not the real activity for this chapter. It is intended to distract students from the actual Preview activity. In the actual activity, students are led to believe that they can purchase academic points. This allows them to make comparisons to the Catholic Church's practice of selling indulgences in the Late Middle Ages. To make certain that you have enough time to complete this activity and debrief it, set aside one regular class period (half a block schedule period) in which to complete each of the Preview and Reading sections of this lesson. Also, be sure to inform your school administrators about the activity in advance.

2   **Prepare materials for the Preview activity.** Cut one certificate per student from *Student Handout 30A: Certificates of Purchase Points.* Make a copy of *Information Master 30: Memo from the Principal.* During the activity, you may want to have this fictional memo delivered to class.

Student Handout 30A

3   **Discuss the new school "policy."** Tell students you have received a memo from the principal about a new school policy. Then read Information Master 30 aloud. Ask students if they have any questions or concerns. Acknowledge questions and concerns, but adopt a neutral stance and make it clear that you must carry out the policy whether or not you agree with it. Some students may realize that this policy is similar to the sale of indulgences by the Church. Discreetly ask them to hold their comments for a discussion later.

4   **Allow students to buy "Purchase Points."** Distribute one "Certificate of Purchase Points" from Student Handout 30A to each student. Have students who wish to buy points raise their hands. Collect their money and completed certificates. This will allow you to easily return the money to students at the end of the period. For those students who do not wish to purchase points immediately, explain that they can take their certificate home, discuss the matter with their parents, and submit the certificate and money tomorrow.

Information Master 30

5   **Have students complete the Preview activity in their Interactive Student Notebooks.** Students will decide how to respond to a new school policy that they believe is unfair. (**Note:** This Preview question is not intended to relate to the purchasing of points, but serves to distract students from realizing that the school policy allowing the purchasing of points is fabricated.)

6   **Have students share their answers in pairs or with the class.**

7   **Connect the Preview activity to the chapter.** Explain that the decisions students just made in the Preview activity—whether or not to speak out against an unfair practice—parallels historic fact: many Europeans during the 1500s had to decide whether or not to protest against unfair practices of the Catholic Church. In this chapter, students will learn about these unfair practices as well as about the people who tried to reform the Church. Finally, they will be introduced to one man who ignited a new movement called the Reformation.

Vocabulary Development

Note: It is important in this lesson to debrief the Preview activity. The Preview debrief occurs in the Reading section of the Procedures, so you may wish to do Vocabulary Development at a later point in the lesson.

1 **Introduce the Key Content Terms.** Have students locate the Key Content Terms for the chapter in their Interactive Student Notebooks. These are important terms that will help them understand the main ideas of the chapter. Ask volunteers to identify any familiar terms and how they might be used in a sentence.

2 **Have students complete a Vocabulary Development handout.** Give each student a copy of the Vocabulary Development handout of your choice from the Reading Toolkit at the back of the Lesson Masters. These handouts provide extra Key Content Term practice and support, depending on your students' needs. Review the completed handout by asking volunteers to share an answer for each term.

Reading

1 **Introduce the Essential Question and have students read Section 30.1.** Have students identify the Essential Question on the first page of the chapter: *What factors led to the weakening of the Catholic Church and the beginning of the Reformation?* Then have students read Section 30.1. Afterward, have students use information from Section 30.1 and from the chapter opener image to propose some possible answers to the Essential Question.

2 **Have students read about corruption in the Catholic Church.** Have students read Section 30.2 through the end of the subsection "Worldliness and Corruption Within the Church."

3 **Debrief the Preview activity.** Ask students if they see a connection between their reading of Section 30.2 and the new school policy announced in the memo. Some students may recognize that the school, like the Roman Catholic Church, is attempting to raise funds by asking students to purchase something they ordinarily would have to earn. Once students understand the parallel, reveal to them that the policy was fabricated. Return the money and certificates you collected. Then hold a discussion to help students make comparisons between the activity and the practice of selling indulgences. Ask,

- How did you feel when the memo was read?
- What did you like about the policy?
- What did you dislike?
- Do you think this policy is justifiable? Why or why not?
- How did you feel when I did not speak against the policy?
- How did you decide whether to purchase points?

Writing: Spell Derivatives

The Key Concept Terms are useful for reviewing how to spell some derivatives correctly. Guide students to break the following terms into bases and affixes: *Re-form-ation; Pro-test-ant;* and *de-nominat(e) + ion.* Review the simple addition of most prefixes, as well as the spelling changes that occur with the addition of some suffixes, such as when the final *e* is dropped before adding the noun-making suffix *–ion.*

4 Have students complete Question 1 of the Reading Notes for Section 30.2 in their Interactive Student Notebooks. They should refer to the reading and to their experience with "grade indulgences." Use the Guide to Reading Notes to discuss their connections.

5 Have students read the rest of Section 30.2 and complete their Reading Notes for this section.

6 Have students complete the Reading Notes for Chapter 30. Assign Sections 30.3 to 30.5 during the activity, as indicated in the procedures for the Visual Discovery. Remind students to use the Key Content Terms where appropriate as they complete their Reading Notes.

Visual Discovery

1 Place students in pairs and have them analyze *Visual 30A: Early Calls for Reform.* Project the visual, which shows reformer Jan Hus about to be executed. Ask,

Visual 30A

- What interesting details do you see?

- Why might this man be tied up?

- What might be about to happen to him?

- This man, Jan Hus, is about to be burned at the stake. What might he have done to receive such harsh punishment? *(Hus spoke out against the corruption within the Catholic Church. He was arrested, charged with heresy, and sentenced to execution.)*

- Why do you think the Catholic Church would order the execution of certain individuals? *(Leaders of the Catholic Church were upset by Hus's criticism of the Church's wealth and the pope's authority. They were alarmed by his assertion that Jesus, not the pope, was the head of the Church.)*

2 Have students read Section 30.3 and complete the corresponding Reading Notes. Have students share their responses. Then use the Guide to Reading Notes to review the main points with the class.

3 Have students analyze *Visual 30B: Martin Luther Breaks Away from the Church.* Project the visual, which shows Martin Luther after he has nailed his Ninety-Five Theses to the church door in Wittenberg, Germany. Ask,

Visual 30B

- What interesting details do you see?

- Describe the man holding the scroll. What do you think he has just done?

- What are some of the reactions to the document hanging on the church door?

- Based on the reactions of the people gathered, what might be written on the document?

- What kind of personality traits would a person have to have to question or challenge the Catholic Church at this time?

4   Have students read Section 30.4 and complete the corresponding Reading Notes. Have students share their responses. Then use the Guide to Reading Notes to review the main points with the class.

5   Have students prepare for and conduct an act-it-out. Place pairs of students in groups of four. Give each group a copy of *Student Handout 30B: Creating an Act-It-Out About Martin Luther.* Briefly review the handout with the class. Then assign one of the four characters to each group. Monitor the groups' progress as they prepare for the act-it-out. When they are ready, project Visual 30B and choose four students to assume the roles of the four characters. Ask the questions from Student Handout 30B that they have prepared to answer. Conduct the act-it-out again with another group of four students.

Student Handout 30B

6   Have students analyze *Visual 30C: Other Leaders of the Reformation.* Project Visual 30C, which shows a German bookseller at a public marketplace. Explain that book publishing was a powerful force in the distribution of religious pamphlets during the Reformation. Ask,

- What interesting details do you see here?

- Why do you think a crowd has gathered around the man on the right?

- The man on the left is distributing a pamphlet about Protestant ideas. How do people seem to be responding to the pamphlet?

- How does the monk on the left seem to be reacting to this scene?

7   Have students read Section 30.5 and complete the corresponding Reading Notes. Have students share their responses. Then use the Guide to Reading Notes to review the main points with the class.

Visual 30C

Processing

Have students complete the Processing activity in their Interactive Student Notebooks. Students draw facial features for six people involved with or affected by the Reformation, and write about how each might feel about the need for reform.

Quicker Coverage

Eliminate the Act-It-Out Skip Step 5 in the directions for the Visual Discovery where students conduct the act-it-out about Martin Luther.

Skip the Preview Activity Instead of presenting the memo on Information Master 30 to students, complete only Steps 5–7 of the Preview activity. Then, during the Reading portion of the main activity, skip Step 3, and just have students read Section 30.2 and complete the Reading Notes there. Note that students will not be able to complete Question 1 of the Reading Notes for Section 30.2.

Deeper Coverage

Conduct a Wrap-up Activity Once students have completed their Reading Notes for the entire chapter, assign groups of four students to one of the following figures from this chapter: John Wycliffe, Jan Hus, Catherine of Siena, Desiderius Erasmus, Martin Luther, Huldrych Zwingli, John Calvin, King Henry VIII, or William Tyndale. Explain that each group must prepare a 30- to 45-second "commercial" arguing why their figure should be inducted into the Reformation Hall of Fame. Commercials should include the following:

- a catchy slogan that highlights the candidate's contribution to the reform of the Catholic Church or the spread of the Reformation
- a visual, such as a poster, sign, or banner, that highlights the candidate's background and accomplishments
- a short speech that argues why the candidate deserves to be inducted

Once all commercials have been presented, have students vote on who they think deserves the honor, and ceremoniously announce the top three candidates who will be inducted.

Assessment

Mastering the Content

1. D	5. C	9. A	13. B
2. D	6. A	10. D	14. C
3. B	7. B	11. D	15. B
4. C	8. A	12. A	16. A

Applying Social Studies Skills

17. Coverdale Bible

18. the printing press had not yet been invented

19. Answers will vary. Possible answer: With so many translations already in print, the Catholic Church gave up on trying to keep the Bible in Latin only and published its own translation to compete with the Protestant ones.

Exploring the Essential Question

20. Answers should include all the elements requested in the prompt.

Scoring Rubric

Score	Description
3	Student completes all six parts of the task. Sentences placed in the outline are clearly stated, supported by details, and demonstrate command of standard English conventions.
2	Student responds to most or all parts of the task, but sentences in outline may lack details or not be clearly stated.
1	Student responds to at least one part of the task. Sentences in outline may contain factual and/or grammatical errors and may lack details.
0	Response does not match the task or is incorrect.

English Language Learners

Add Support to the Activity Refer to the bulleted questions in Steps 1, 3, and 6 of the Visual Discovery Activity to create a list of questions you plan to ask about each of the three visuals. Allow students a few moments to analyze the images in pairs, using the questions as their guide, before you begin the class analysis. This may help some students feel more comfortable taking part in the class discussion.

Learners Reading and Writing Below Grade Level

Support the Reading Notes Provide students with a copy of Guide to Reading Notes 30 with key words and phrases omitted for them to fill in as they read. For Section 30.3, for example, the answer to Question 1 might be reformatted as follows:

Wycliffe questioned the _____ authority and attacked _____ and immoral behavior by clergy. He said the _____, not the Church, was the ultimate religious authority. Against Church tradition, he had the _____ translated into _____.

Learners with Special Education Needs

Modify the Processing Activity Reduce the number of individuals for which students need to draw facial expressions and write explanations. Allow students to choose only four individuals.

Advanced Learners

Extend the Processing Activity Follow these directions.

1. Have students suppose that the writings of the following reformists—Wycliffe, Hus, Erasmus, Luther, Zwingli, Calvin, Henry VIII, and Tyndale—will be collected into pamphlets to highlight the reforms they believe are needed in the Catholic Church.

2. The editors of the pamphlets want to organize these writings into two or three pamphlets, with similar views represented in each pamphlet.

3. Have students choose which reformists had similar ideas on reforms needed in the Catholic Church.

4. Students should list the reformists they have chosen to present in each pamphlet and what three to five major points or arguments will be made in each pamphlet. They can divide the reformists into two or three groups depending on what they see as the commonalities and differences among their arguments.

Enrichment Resources

Find out more about the events that led to the Reformation by exploring the following Enrichment Resources for *History Alive! The Medieval World and Beyond* at www.teachtci.com.

Enrichment Readings These in-depth readings encourage students to explore selected topics related to the chapter. You may also find readings that relate the chapter's content directly to your state's curriculum.

Internet Connections The recommended Web sites provide useful and engaging content that reinforces skills development and mastery of subjects within the chapter.

Literature Recommendations

The following books offer opportunities to extend the content in this chapter.

Bible Smuggler by Louise A. Vernon (Scottdale, PA: Herald Press, 1967)

The Printing Press: A Breakthrough in Communication by Richard Tames (Chicago: Heinemann, 2000)

The Reformation: History Through Sources by Michael Mullett (Chicago: Heinemann, 1998)

Section 30.2

See the chart below for answers

Classroom Activity	Historical Connection
The school attempted to raise money by selling points to students.	• The Church attempted to increase its financial holdings by selling indulgences to Catholics.
Students who performed poorly on assignments were told they could still earn high grades by buying points.	• Catholics who sinned believed they could avoid doing good deeds to make up for their sins by buying indulgences.
Students who honored the academic process or couldn't afford to buy points were troubled by the policy, believing it was wrong or unfair.	• Catholics who honored Church teachings or couldn't afford to buy indulgences were troubled by the selling of indulgences, believing the practice was invalid, corrupt, or unfair.

Answers will vary. Possible answers: a. Popes became entangled in political disputes that prompted many to question the popes' authority. b. The Great Schism lessened people's respect for the papacy. c. The Catholic Church sold offices in a practice called simony.

Section 30.3

Wycliffe questioned the pope's authority and attacked indulgences and immoral behavior by clergy. He said the Bible, not the Church, was the ultimate religious authority. Against Church tradition, he had the Bible translated into English.

Hus wanted to end corruption among the clergy. He also wanted the Bible and the mass to be available in the people's everyday language, rather than in Latin.

3. Catherine showed that people could lead spiritual lives that went beyond the usual norms of the Church. She emphasized personal experience of God over Church doctrine.

4. Erasmus was a humanist priest who wanted to reform the Church. He wrote *The Praise of Folly*, a satire of society, including abuses within the Church. His criticism of the Church added to people's desire to question its teachings.

Section 30.4

1. Luther was outraged by the sale of indulgences. He posted the Ninety-Five Theses to express his ideas about this practice and other issues.

2. Luther believed that salvation came from faith; the Church preached good works. Luther said the Bible was the ultimate religious authority; the Church taught that it was the pope and Church teachings. Luther said all Christians were priests and should read the Bible for themselves; the Church had official priests and did not feel that people needed to read the Bible. Luther claimed that most Church sacraments had no basis in the Bible; the Church upheld non-biblical sacraments, such as marriage.

3. He refused to take back his teachings and was declared a heretic by the Holy Roman emperor. The emperor forbade the printing of his writings.

Section 30.5

1. Answers may appear in any order: a. People were tired of abuses and ready for change.
b. The printing press helped spread Luther's ideas.
c. Government leaders learned they could win independence from the Catholic Church.

2. Huldrych Zwingli and John Calvin began new churches in Switzerland.

3. Henry VIII split from the Church so that he could divorce and remarry, and so that he no longer had to share power and wealth with the Church.

4. Tyndale was a priest and scholar who translated books of the Bible into English. He adopted Protestant views and was burned at the stake. His translations were used as a basis for the King James Bible.

The Spread and Impact of the Reformation

What were the effects of the Reformation?

Overview

In a Social Studies Skill Builder activity, students explore the beliefs and practices of three denominations of Protestantism, and then create an illustrated cause-and-effect poster to show how the Reformation affected Europe and the world.

Objectives

In the course of reading this chapter and participating in the classroom activity, students will

Social Studies

- list and compare key beliefs and practices of Lutheranism, Calvinism, and Anglicanism.

- analyze how the Counter-Reformation revitalized the Catholic Church.

- locate and label Catholic and Protestant regions on a map of Europe.

- identify the locations of Christian missions in the early modern period.

- describe the long- and short-term causes and effects of the Reformation.

Language Arts

- use definitions and examples to explain the meanings of new words.

- read expository text to connect the essential ideas to their own learning.

Social Studies Vocabulary

Key Content Terms Lutheranism, Calvinism, theocracy, Anglicanism, Counter-Reformation, nationalism, absolute monarchy, Puritans

Academic Vocabulary reform, error, consequently, clarify

Materials

History Alive! The Medieval World and Beyond

Interactive Student Notebooks

Lesson Masters

- Information Masters 31A and 31B (1 transparency of each)

- Vocabulary Development handout (1 per student, on colored paper)

butcher paper, 12" x 18" construction paper or poster board

Activity	Suggested Time	Materials
Preview	20 minutes	• *History Alive! The Medieval World and Beyond* • Interactive Student Notebooks • Information Master 31A (1 transparency)
Vocabulary Development	30–40 minutes	• *History Alive! The Medieval World and Beyond* • Interactive Student Notebooks • Vocabulary Development handout
Social Studies Skill Builder	50 minutes (1 regular class period) (.5 block period)	• *History Alive! The Medieval World and Beyond* • Information Master 31B (1 transparency) • butcher paper, 12″ x 18″ construction paper or poster board
Processing	20 minutes	• Interactive Student Notebooks
Assessment	40 minutes	• Chapter 31 Assessment

Preview

1 **Examine Christian religions.** Project a transparency of *Information Master 31A: Main Branches of Christianity.* Have students examine the diagram carefully. Ask students the questions below, one at a time. Have students record their response to each question in their Interactive Student Notebooks before sharing their thoughts with the class.

- What do you see?

- What are the three main branches of Christianity? *(Protestant, Roman Catholic, Eastern Orthodox)*

- Why do you think all the branches are considered part of Christianity? *(All the branches center on belief in Jesus Christ. All are based on the teachings of the Bible.)*

- Find Lutheranism, Calvinism, and Anglicanism on the diagram. To which larger branch do they belong? *(Protestant)*

- Have you seen examples of these different forms of Christianity in your community? In what ways? *(Answers might include church buildings, schools, flyers, local newspapers, etc.)*

- How do you think Catholic leaders may have reacted to the growing number of Protestant churches in the 15th and 16th centuries? *(Catholic leaders may have been alarmed at the rapid spread of Protestantism, and they may have wanted to bring unity back to the Catholic Church.)*

2 **Connect the Preview activity to the chapter.** Explain that in this Preview activity, students identified some different denominations of Christianity today. In this chapter, they will look more closely at the beliefs and practices of three groups that broke away from the Roman Catholic Church during the Reformation, and then examine how the Catholic Church tried to stop the spread of Protestantism. Finally, they will explore how the Reformation affected Europe and, ultimately, the rest of the world.

Vocabulary Development

1 **Introduce the Key Content Terms.** Have students locate the Key Content Terms for the chapter in their Interactive Student Notebooks. These are important terms that will help them understand the main ideas of the chapter. Ask volunteers to identify any familiar terms and suggest how they might be used in a sentence.

2 **Have students complete a Vocabulary Development handout.** Give each student a copy of the Vocabulary Development handout of your choice from the Reading Toolkit at the back of the Lesson Masters. These handouts provide extra Key Content Term practice and support, depending on your students' needs. Review the completed handout by asking volunteers to share one answer for each term.

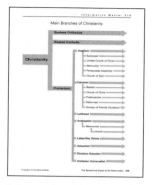

Information Master 31A

Reading: Informational Materials

Guide students to name ways in which the diagram differs in structure and purpose from a paragraph in a textbook. Also, ask students to name ways in which the diagram is more effective or less effective in conveying information than a traditional paragraph would be. Return to a discussion of the structure of informational materials when students work with their cause-and-effect diagrams at the end of the chapter. Note how diagrams condense and telegraph key information.

Reading

1 **Introduce the Essential Question and have students read Section 31.1.** Have students identify the Essential Question on the first page of the chapter: *What were the effects of the Reformation?* Then have students read Section 31.1. Afterward, have students use information from Section 31.1 and from the chapter opener image to propose some possible answers to the Essential Question.

2 **Have students complete the Reading Notes for Chapter 31.** Assign Sections 31.2 to 31.6 during the activity as indicated in the procedures for the Social Studies Skill Builder. Remind students to use the Key Content Terms where appropriate as they complete their Reading Notes.

Social Studies Skill Builder

1 **Prepare materials.** Cut large squares of butcher paper for half the class. Alternatively, gather large pieces of construction paper (roughly 12" x 18") or pieces of poster board.

2 **Project Information Master 31B and have students analyze the cause-and-effect diagram.** Project the diagram on *Information Master 31B: Creating an Illustrated Cause-and-Effect Poster.* Ask,

- What details do you see on this diagram?

- What kind of diagram is this and how can you tell?

- According to the diagram, how many major causes of the Reformation were there? *(2)* What was the first one? *(corruption within the Church)*

3 **Divide the class into pairs and introduce the activity.** Continue to project the diagram on Information Master 31B. Explain to students that they will be adding both visual and written information to this diagram to plan and then create an illustrated cause-and-effect poster. Tell students that they will add their own illustrations and annotations to create a graphic representation of the content covered in this chapter.

4 **Prepare for the activity.** Give each pair of students a large piece of paper. Project Information Master 31B and have pairs copy the diagram, leaving room on the right side to add additional effects and examples .

5 **Review the causes of the Reformation.** Have students turn to Section 30.2 in the previous chapter and, with their partners, review the major events that led to the Reformation. On the left side of the diagram, have students add the one missing cause and illustrate both causes.

6 **Have students read Sections 31.2–31.4 and complete the corresponding Reading Notes in their Interactive Student Notebooks.** These sections discuss the key beliefs and practices of Lutheranism, Calvinism, and Anglicanism.

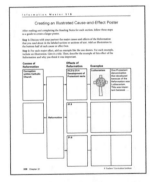

Information Master 31B

7 Continue to project Information Master 31B and have students illustrate their diagrams for Sections 31.2–31.4. Remind students to illustrate the effects they have added to their diagrams with drawings, graphics, images from the Internet, or photocopied photos. Encourage pairs to be creative and to use color when designing and completing their posters.

8 Have students read Section 31.5 and complete the corresponding Reading Notes in their Interactive Student Notebooks.

9 Have students illustrate their diagrams for Section 31.5. Project Information Master 31B and monitor students as they illustrate their diagrams.

10 Have students read Section 31.6 and complete the corresponding Reading Notes in their Interactive Student Notebooks.

11 Have students illustrate their diagrams for Section 31.6. Project Information Master 31B and monitor students as they illustrate their diagrams.

12 Conduct a wrap-up discussion. Ask,

- How did the Reformation affect the Catholic Church?
- How did the Reformation affect Europe?
- How did the Reformation affect the rest of the world?

Processing

Have students complete the Processing activity in their Interactive Student Notebooks. Students will complete a Venn diagram to compare and contrast aspects of Catholicism and Protestantism during the Reformation.

Writing: Organization and Focus

Before students complete the Processing activity, remind them to use transitions to link their sentences and help unify their writing. Review transitions that students might use, such as *one effect, the most important effect, in addition, also, furthermore,* and *nevertheless.*

Quicker Coverage

Provide Copies of the Diagram Instead of having students copy the cause-and-effect diagram from the projected Information Master in Step 4 of the activity, consider enlarging the copy of the diagram and providing it to each pair of students. Students can then paste it onto a larger sheet of butcher paper and complete Steps 5 through 12 of the activity.

Provide Causes in the Diagram Instead of having students review the causes of the Reformation in Step 5 of the activity, fill in that part of the diagram in advance and simply review those causes quickly as a class. For the first cause, consider drawing a stack of money to represent the sale of indulgences. For the second cause, "Political Conflicts with European Rulers," consider drawing a crown and a cross to represent the conflicts between the pope and different monarchs.

Deeper Coverage

Expand the Cause-and-Effect Poster Once students have completed the activity as written, encourage them to think about the continued effects of the Reformation. Ask,

- What are some additional effects of the different Protestant religions that developed?
- What are some additional effects of the Catholic Counter-Reformation?
- What are some additional effects of persecuted groups seeking freedom to worship? The spread of Christianity throughout the world? The religious wars and persecution?

Have students add these additional effects to the right side of their posters.

Assessment

Mastering the Content

1. A	5. C	9. A	13. A
2. D	6. D	10. D	14. D
3. C	7. B	11. C	15. B
4. B	8. B	12. A	16. C

Applying Social Studies Skills

17. England was Protestant and Ireland was Catholic.

18. English North America was Protestant and Spanish Mexico was Catholic.

19. they were most likely Catholic, while most of the people already in the United States were Protestant.

Exploring the Essential Question

20. Answers should include all the elements requested in the prompt.

Scoring Rubric

Score	Description
3	Student writes appropriate descriptions in each of four parts of the Venn diagram according to instructions: one distinct effect of the religion in the outer part of each circle and one shared effect in the center part of the diagram. Descriptions are clearly stated and demonstrate command of standard English conventions.
2	Student responds to most or all parts of the task, but descriptions may not be clearly stated.
1	Student responds to at least one part of the task. Descriptions may contain factual and/or grammatical errors.
0	Response does not match the task or is incorrect.

English Language Learners

Add Support to the Activity Provide a version of the cause-and-effect diagram that has additional boxes filled in to help guide students during the activity.

Learners Reading and Writing Below Grade Level

Break Down the Reading Have students read Section 31.2 as a class or in pairs. Then, as a class, complete the first row of the chart in the Reading Notes for that section. Finally, have students read Section 31.3 and complete the next row of the chart, and so on.

Learners with Special Education Needs

Provide Annotations for the Diagram Provide students with the effects that follow to serve as annotations for their planning diagrams. Students should place these annotations in the appropriate place on the diagram and add an illustration.

- After the Thirty Years' War, Europe was divided into Catholic and Protestant territories.
- Ignatius of Loyola founded a new order of Catholicism, the Society of Jesus, which was dedicated to spreading their faith around the world.
- King Henry VIII founded Anglicanism in 1534, creating a new Protestant denomination that blended elements of Catholicism and Protestantism.
- Lutheranism began in Germany in 1521. It taught that salvation was received through faith, and it placed importance on discipline and strong families.

- Fearing the spread of Protestant ideas, the pope established the Roman Inquisition.
- The Reformation planted seeds of democratic ideas, and helped people be more willing to resist authority.
- The Council of Trent met more than 20 times to clarify Catholic teachings and to correct abuses.
- John Calvin founded a new Protestant denomination, Calvinism, which taught predestination and the Bible as the true source of authority and urged communities to set up theocracies.
- Catholics and Protestants worked to spread their faiths, bringing Christianity to many other areas of the world.

Advanced Learners

Eliminate the Model Diagram Instead of projecting the model of the cause-and-effect diagram shown on Information Master 31B, have students create the diagrams themselves. Instead of having students copy the diagram in Step 4 of the activity, draw a basic cause-and-effect diagram on the board that has one box labeled, "Effects of the Reformation" and three arrows protruding from the right of the box. As they read, have students determine the three major effects of the Reformation, label these on their diagram in large boxes, and then complete the diagram by following the directions on Information Master 31B.

Enrichment Resources

Find out more about the effects of the Reformation by exploring the following Enrichment Resources for *History Alive! The Medieval World and Beyond* at www.teachtci.com.

Enrichment Readings These in-depth readings encourage students to explore selected topics related to the chapter. You may also find readings that relate the chapter's content directly to your state's curriculum.

Internet Connections The recommended Web sites provide useful and engaging content that reinforces skills development and mastery of subjects within the chapter.

Literature Recommendations

The following books offer opportunities to extend the content in this chapter.

Behind the Mask: The Life of Queen Elizabeth I by Jane Resh Thomas (New York: Clarion Books, 1998)

King Henry VIII and the Reformation in World History by Richard Worth (Berkeley Heights, NJ: Enslow, 2001)

Martin Luther by Sally Stepanek (New York: Chelsea House, 1986)

Sections 31.2 to 31.4

Possible answers are listed below. Similarities are underlined in each column.

	Lutheranism	Calvinism	Anglicanism
Origins of the Denomination	founded by Martin Luther in Germany in 1521	founded by John Calvin in Switzerland in 1541	founded by King Henry VIII in 1534
Beliefs About Sin and Salvation	believed that <u>salvation was a gift from God received by people if they sincerely believed in Jesus, were sorry for their sins</u>, and accepted the Bible as truth; Luther called this "justification by faith."	believed in predestination, the idea that God already knows who will be saved in the afterlife and who will be condemned; thought that people's destinies were revealed by their behavior: those who behaved well were saved; those who sinned were not	believed baptism washed away original sin; <u>believed in justification by faith: to go to heaven, people needed to believe in God, regret their sins</u>, and receive God's mercy
Beliefs About the Ultimate Source of Authority	<u>believed that the Bible was the only true source of religious guidance</u>; rejected the authority of church councils and the pope	<u>believed the Bible was the only source of religious guidance</u>; believed that communities should be governed according to God's laws and therefore, when people sinned, they were also committing a crime	<u>based beliefs on the Bible</u>; the monarch, assisted by the Archbishop of Canterbury, was the main interpreter of the Bible; other clergy helped uphold the monarch's ideas; believers could interpret beliefs in their own ways as long as they were loyal to the monarch

	Lutheranism	Calvinism	Anglicanism
Rituals and Worship	kept some Catholic practices and added new Lutheran ones; church looked much like a Catholic Church (with altar, crucifix, and candles); services had some similarities to Catholic mass, such as Communion, Bible readings, sermons, and hymns; also had differences, such as prayers in German instead of Latin and two sacraments instead of seven	believers attended services up to five times a week; sermons were long and explained how to live according to the Bible; churches were very simple, with wood panels and benches; no paintings, statues, or stained glass windows; used only the two sacraments mentioned in the Bible: baptism and Communion; could sing only words from the Bible	High church service was formal and like the Catholic mass; Low Church service was more like the Lutheran service; services were held in former Catholic Church buildings; most of the decorations were removed, the inside was painted white, and the Ten Commandments were painted on the wall; hymns, and eventually services, were in English instead of Latin, so everyone could take part; used only the two sacraments mentioned in the Bible: baptism and Communion
Community Life	emphasized strict discipline and large, strong families; children taught to pray before meals and bed	believed that communities should be theocracies, governed by God through religious leaders; laws were based on the Bible and were very strict; swearing, dancing and playing cards were not allowed; homes could be inspected to see if families were obeying the laws; people who broke laws were severely punished or banished	communities were not all alike: High Church communities were mostly wealthy; Low Church communities had mostly middle- and working-class people; heresy mostly ceased to be a crime; people could worship as they liked, as long as they did not attack the monarch or the Anglican Church

Section 31.5

1. This meeting of Catholic Church leaders began in 1545 to combat corruption in the Catholic Church and to resist Protestantism. The council rejected predestination and justification by faith alone, and reaffirmed the Catholic belief in seven sacraments and in the Church's authority to interpret the Bible. It required better training of clergy, calling for priests and bishops to spend more time preaching, and it corrected many abuses committed by clergy.

2. The Society of Jesus was a new order, also known as the Jesuits, formed by Ignatius of Loyola during the Counter-Reformation to preach, educate people, and perform public services. The Jesuits were dedicated teachers and missionaries.

3. The Society of Jesus (or Jesuits) founded schools and colleges, brought Europeans back to the Catholic Church, and spread Catholicism in Africa, Asia, and the Americas.

4. The Church looked to Catholic rulers to support it and to win back lands lost to Protestantism. The pope started the Roman Inquisition, which condemned people whose views were considered dangerous. The Church published a list of books that Catholics were forbidden to read, and dealt harshly with those it labeled heretics.

3. See the chart for correct answers.

Areas of the World Where Catholic Missionaries Traveled	Areas of the World Where Protestant Missionaries Traveled
India, China, Japan, Southeast Asia	Ceylon, India, Indonesia
Canada, the Mississippi Valley	English colonies in North America
American Southwest, Mexico, South America	

Section 31.6

1. Students should shade the following areas:

   Protestant: much of the Holy Roman Empire, Norway, Sweden, and Denmark, part of Prussia; Switzerland, Scotland, the Netherlands, parts of France, England

   Catholic: Portugal, Spain, Italy, France, southern Holy Roman Empire, Hungary, Poland, Ireland

2. Protestants emphasized being true to their own consciences. This belief made people more willing to question authority. Some persecuted groups, such as the Puritans, even fled, seeking freedom to worship in their own ways. In addition, leaders of Protestant churches were elected by congregation members, instead of the powerful.

Europe's Renaissance and Reformation

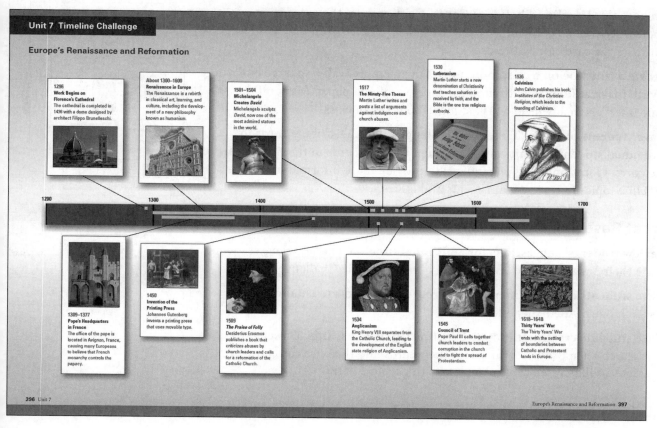

Unit 7 Timeline Challenge

Europe's Renaissance and Reformation

1296
Work Begins on Florence's Cathedral
The cathedral is completed in 1436 with a dome designed by architect Filippo Brunelleschi.

About 1300–1600
Renaissance in Europe
The Renaissance is a rebirth in classical art, learning, and culture, including the development of a new philosophy known as humanism.

1501–1504
Michelangelo Creates *David*
Michelangelo sculpts *David*, now one of the most admired statues in the world.

1517
The Ninety-Five Theses
Martin Luther writes and posts a list of arguments against indulgences and church abuses.

1530
Lutheranism
Martin Luther starts a new denomination of Christianity that teaches salvation is received by faith, and the Bible is the one true religious authority.

1536
Calvinism
John Calvin publishes his book, *Institutes of the Christian Religion*, which leads to the founding of Calvinism.

1200   1300   1400   1500   1600   1700

1309–1377
Pope's Headquarters in France
The office of the pope is located in Avignon, France, causing many Europeans to believe that French monarchy controls the papacy.

1450
Invention of the Printing Press
Johannes Gutenberg invents a printing press that uses movable type.

1509
The Praise of Folly
Desiderius Erasmus publishes a book that criticizes abuses by church leaders and calls for a reformation of the Catholic Church.

1534
Anglicanism
King Henry VIII separates from the Catholic Church, leading to the development of the English state religion of Anglicanism.

1545
Council of Trent
Pope Paul III calls together church leaders to combat corruption in the church and to fight the spread of Protestantism.

1618–1648
Thirty Years' War
The Thirty Years' War ends with the setting of boundaries between Catholic and Protestant lands in Europe.

Overview

This Timeline Challenge helps students review the main events and ideas of this unit while providing practice in reading and interpreting timelines. You can vary and expand the activity according to students' needs and the amount of time available.

Basic Procedure

1 **Introduce the timeline in the Student Edition.** Direct students to the Europe's Renaissance and Reformation Timeline at the end of Unit 7 in the Student Edition. You may wish to have students read aloud and discuss the timeline entries.

2 **Introduce the Timeline Challenge in the Interactive Student Notebook.** Direct students to the Unit 7 Timeline Challenge. Point out the two types of questions, "Timeline Skills" and "Critical Thinking," and model how to answer each type.

3 **Have students complete the Timeline Challenge.** Monitor students as they work. Use the Guide to Unit 7 Timeline Challenge to check their answers. You may wish to project a transparency of this page as you work through the questions with the class and conduct a discussion of the "Critical Thinking" questions.

4 **Complete the KWL chart.** Return to the KWL chart created at the beginning of the unit, and ask students to list the key information they have learned.

Classroom Timeline

1 **Prepare the Timeline Challenge Cards.** Copy and cut the cards from *Student Handout TC7: Unit 7 Timeline Challenge Cards*. You may wish to laminate the cards for future use.

2 **Create a timeline on a classroom wall.** On an empty wall or a large bulletin board, make a timeline with masking tape or colored paper. Mark off the time intervals in advance, or ask students to do so in class.

3 **Have students place the Timeline Challenge Cards.** Distribute cards to individual students or pairs and have them tape the cards to the timeline in the correct locations. Call on students to provide more information on the timeline topics to review main events and issues.

Student Handout TC7

Internet Research

1 **Review students' suggestions for additional timeline entries.** Have students share their answers to the last question of the Timeline Challenge.

2 **Have students conduct Internet research.** Ask students to choose and research one of their suggested events.

3 **Have students create additional Timeline Challenge Cards.** Direct students to research an appropriate image for their cards and then use the computer to create an illustrated card, complete with timeline entry.

Timeline Skills

Score 1 point for each correct answer.

1. Brunelleschi designed a dome that would not collapse.

2. The pope's relocation of his headquarters led may Europeans to believe the papacy was controlled by the French monarchy.

3. the Renaissance

4. The printing press allowed books and pamphlets to be published more easily, which helped ideas spread more quickly throughout Europe.

5. Michelangelo created *David* in about three years.

6. The publication of Erasmus's book and Martin Luther's posting of the Ninety-Five Theses both helped to cause the Reformation.

7. Calvinism was founded after the publication of *Institutes of the Christian Religion*.

8. The Council of Trent was a meeting of Catholic leaders intended to combat corruption in the church and fight the spread of Protestantism.

9. Possible answer: Boundaries were set between Protestant and Catholic lands in Europe.

Critical Thinking

Score 1 to 3 points for each answer, depending on the thoroughness of the response.

10. Humanist ideals included a belief that all people had the ability to control their own lives and to achieve greatness. These ideals also sought to balance religious faith with an emphasis on individual dignity and an interest in nature and human society. These ideals affected people's thinking about social standing and caused people to value an individual's achievements more than his or her class or family. Humanists also taught people to use their minds to question everything, a belief that encouraged Renaissance thinking.

11. Answers will vary but could include:

   Leonardo da Vinci: He was an accomplished painter, sculptor, architect, engineer, and inventor. He studied a wide variety of scientific and mathematical principles. He studied circulation and the workings of the eye. He also learned about the effects of the moon on the Earth's tides.

   William Shakespeare: He wrote numerous poems and plays that showed his deep understanding of human behavior and emotions. Not only are his plays still extremely popular, they have influenced many writers.

12. Answers will vary but could include:

   Martin Luther: He challenged the Catholic Church by arguing against church abuses and indulgences. He later founded a new denomination known as Lutheranism, which was the first Protestant church.

   John Calvin: He published a book that became one of the most influential works of the Reformation. He also tried to establish a Christian state in Geneva that would be ruled by God through the Calvinist church leaders.

13. Answers will vary. Students must explain why the events they chose merit inclusion.

Using Scores to Inform Instruction

Timeline Skills A score of 6 out of 9 indicates that students understand most of the key events in the unit.

Critical Thinking A score of 8 out of 12 indicates that students are able to think critically about most of the key issues in this unit.

If students score below these levels, consider reviewing timeline and critical thinking skills.

Europe Enters the Modern Age

Geography Challenge

Chapter 32: The Age of Exploration
How did the Age of Exploration change the way Europeans viewed the world?

Experiential Exercise

Chapter 33: The Scientific Revolution
How did the Scientific Revolution change the way people understood the world?

Visual Discovery

Chapter 34: The Enlightenment
How have the ideas of the Enlightenment influenced modern government?

Response Group

Timeline Challenge

Europe Enters the Modern Age

Overview

This activity introduces geographic information essential to Unit 8. Students read and interpret maps to learn about European voyages of discovery from the 1400s to the 1600s. They annotate a map of the world and answer questions in their Interactive Student Notebooks, and then discuss critical thinking questions. Students' comprehension of content and proficiency in map-reading and higher-order thinking skills will help you gauge their readiness for the unit. The pages that follow include a completed map, answers to questions, a scoring guide to inform your teaching, and suggestions for modifications to meet specific student needs.

Essential Geographic Understandings

1. Approximate routes of the major European voyages of discovery

2. Key physical features: continents of the world, major oceans and seas

3. Understanding of the relative location of the other continents to Europe

4. Understanding of the movement of people and goods from the 15th through the 17th centuries

Procedures

1 **Introduce the unit.** Tell students that in this unit they will learn about the European Age of Exploration, the Scientific Revolution, and the Enlightenment.

2 **Create a KWL chart.** Ask students to identify what they already know about the Age of Exploration and what they want to learn. Use their responses to gauge how much additional background information they will need as you progress through the unit. Students will return to the KWL chart at the end of the unit and add the key information they have learned.

3 **Have students read Unit 8 "Setting the Stage" in the Student Edition.**

4 **Have students complete the Geography Challenge.** Monitor students as they work. Use the guide on the next two pages to check their answers. You may wish to project the map from the Interactive Student Notebook and have students annotate it as the class works through the map-reading questions. Make sure that students have grasped Essential Geographic Understandings 1 to 3.

5 **Discuss the "Critical Thinking" questions.** Help students understand the geographic relationships described in Essential Geographic Understanding 4.

The Age of Exploration

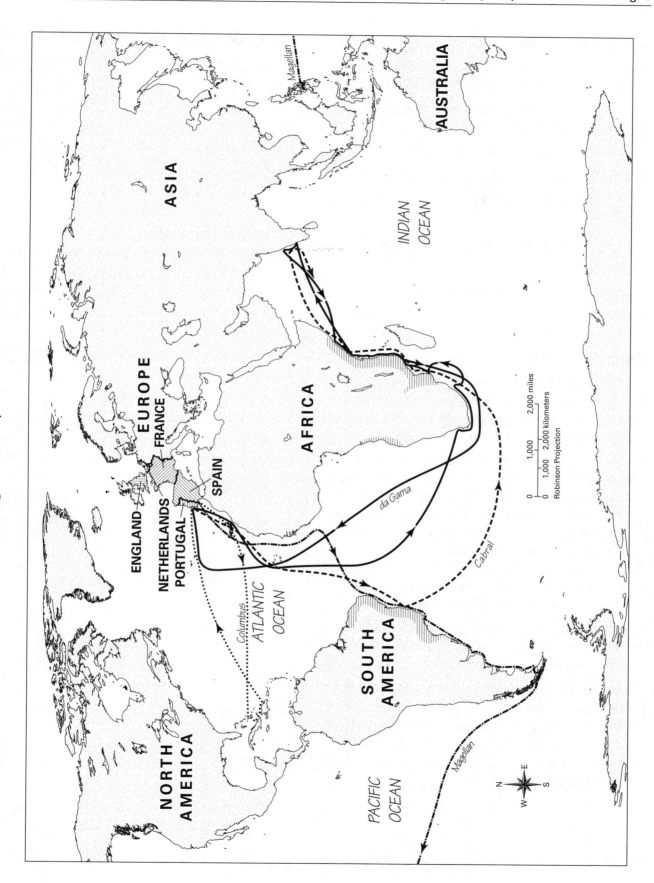

Geography Skills

Score 1 point for each correct answer. Use the map on the previous page to check shading and labeling.

1. Students should label the Atlantic Ocean, Pacific Ocean, and Indian Ocean.

2. Check students' maps for da Gama's route.

3. Check students' maps for Cabral's route.

4. By 1600, Portugal had claimed territory or cities in South America, Africa, and Asia.

5. Check students' maps for Columbus's route.

6. Check students' maps for Magellan's route.

7. England, France, and the Netherlands sent explorers to North America's east coast.

Critical Thinking

Questions may have more than one correct answer. Score 1 to 3 points for each reasonable answer, depending on the strength of students' geographic reasoning. Possible answers are given here.

8. Da Gama sailed south along the west coast of Africa, rounded Africa at the Cape of Good Hope, sailed up the east coast of Africa, and then sailed east across the Indian Ocean to Asia. He then traveled the same route in reverse back to Portugal, except that he now stayed much closer to the African coast for the entire journey. The route was extremely long, which was why European monarchs were looking for a faster, shorter route.

9. Columbus's expedition reveals that Europeans at the time did not know that North and South America existed.

10. Accept reasonable answers. Students may say that Portugal had the best sailors, ships, and maps. They may also point out that Portugal was a small country and wanted to add to its territory or that Portugal was led by rulers who wanted to explore lands beyond Europe.

Using Scores to Inform Instruction

Geography Skills A score of 4 out of 7 or better indicates that students have acquired sufficient geographic information to proceed with the unit.

Critical Thinking A score of 6 out of 9 or better indicates that students are beginning to understand the relationships between physical geography and the different ways in which people live.

Modifying Instruction

ELL or Learners with Special Education Needs Consider focusing on map-reading questions or limiting the number of "Critical Thinking" questions.

Students with Weak Map or Critical Thinking Skills Assign appropriate pages from the Social Studies Skills Toolkit in the back of the Lesson Masters.

The Age of Exploration

How did the Age of Exploration change the way Europeans viewed the world?

Overview

In an Experiential Exercise, students explore "uncharted territory" to discover some of the rewards, challenges, and dangers during the Age of Exploration. Students then compare their experience to those of actual European explorers.

Objectives

In the course of reading this chapter and participating in the classroom activity, students will

Social Studies

- identify the motivations and key advances in knowledge and technology that led to the Age of Exploration.
- map the important European expeditions during the Age of Exploration.
- identify and explain the effects of the Age of Exploration—including the exchange of goods and ideas—on people in various parts of the world.
- describe the economic effects of exploration, including the origins of modern capitalism, the growth of the cottage industry, mercantilism, and new patterns of trade.

Language Arts

- summarize reading materials, including the main idea and details.
- use definitions, examples, and restatement to clarify meanings of new words.

Social Studies Vocabulary

Key Content Terms Age of Exploration, cartography, colony, epidemic, capitalism, market economy, cottage industry, mercantilism

Academic Vocabulary starve, detrimental, inflation, policy

Materials

History Alive! The Medieval World and Beyond

Interactive Student Notebooks

Lesson Masters
   Student Handouts 32A–32B (See Planning Guide for copies.)

- Information Masters 32A–32C (1 transparency of each)

- Vocabulary Development handout (1 per student, on colored paper)

pink, green, and blue copy paper

shoeboxes (3)

masking tape or string

transparency marker

Activity	Suggested Time	Materials
Preview	10 minutes	• Interactive Student Notebooks
Experiential Exercise	45–50 minutes (1 regular period) (.5 block period)	• *History Alive! The Medieval World and Beyond* • Student Handout 32A (4 copies on pink paper, 3 copies on blue paper, 1 copy on green paper; all cut in half) • Student Handout 32B (1 copy on pink, blue, and green paper; all cut in half) • 5 pieces of pink paper, 7 of green paper, and 7 of blue paper (cut in half) • Information Masters 32A–32C (1 transparency of each)
Vocabulary Development	30–40 minutes	• *History Alive! The Medieval World and Beyond* • Interactive Student Notebooks • Vocabulary Development handout
Processing	30–40 minutes	• Interactive Student Notebooks
Assessment	40 minutes	• Chapter 32 Assessment

Preview (optional)

1   **Understand the intent of the Preview activity.** The activity serves as the Preview for this lesson. In the event that you cannot do the activity, suggested directions for an optional Preview activity appear below.

2   **Have students complete the Preview activity in their Interactive Student Notebooks.** Students examine the motives for, and evaluate the value of, U.S. exploration of space today.

3   **Have students share their responses with a partner or with the class.**

4   **Connect the Preview activity to the chapter.** Tell students that in the Preview activity they examined some of the motives for U.S. exploration of space. In this chapter, they will study explorers who sailed for Portugal, Spain, England, and other European countries in the 15th and 16th centuries. They will learn about the motives for exploration, routes explored, items exchanged between Europeans and other peoples, and positive and negative effects of this exploration throughout the world.

Experiential Exercise

1   **Prepare the materials and classroom for the activity.** Set up the activity by doing the following:

- Make one transparency each of Information Masters 32A, 32B, and 32C.

- Get 11 sheets of pink copy paper. Make 4 copies of *Student Handout 32A: Riches Cards,* 1 copy of *Student Handout 32B: Danger Cards,* and leave the rest blank. Cut the pink paper in half to get 4 Danger Cards, 8 Riches Cards, and 10 blank cards.

- Get 12 sheets of blue copy paper. Make 3 copies of Student Handout 32A, 1 copy of Student Handout 32B, and leave the rest blank. Cut the blue paper in half to get 4 Danger Cards, 6 Riches Cards, and 14 blanks.

- Get 10 sheets of green copy paper. Make 1 copy of Student Handout 32A, 1 copy of Student Handout 32B, and leave the rest blank. Cut the green paper in half to get 4 Danger Cards, 2 Riches Cards, and 14 blanks.

- Push the desks to the sides of the room. Lay the papers face down, according to the diagram on the next page. (**Note:** You may want to organize the desks as in the diagram, and place one piece of paper on top of each desk. Students can then reach or crawl across the desks as necessary to "explore" and get their piece of paper.) Use masking tape or string to section off a corner of your room. Use two pieces of masking tape or string to divide that area into three equal-sized rows. Place a box at the end of each row marked with the team color.

    Have students take care not to bend, rip, or fold the paper during the activity. Then, the only preparation you will need to repeat with other classes is to reposition the pieces of paper on the floor according to the classroom map. You might also consider laminating them for easy re-use.

Student Handout 32A

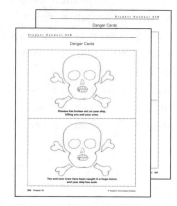

Student Handout 32B

2 **Introduce the activity.** Explain to students that they will play a game in which they will explore the three "territories" they see laid out in the classroom. These are areas they know little or nothing about. Tell students they will work in teams to find and collect "riches" in their assigned territory. Along the way, they will experience some of the typical challenges, dangers, and rewards of exploration.

3 **Divide the class into three groups of equal size.** Assign one group to be the blue team, one as the pink team, and one as the green team. Show teams where to stand. Have them line up single-file in their assigned rows. Then tell students they will explore the "territory" of the classroom with the colored paper that corresponds to their team color.

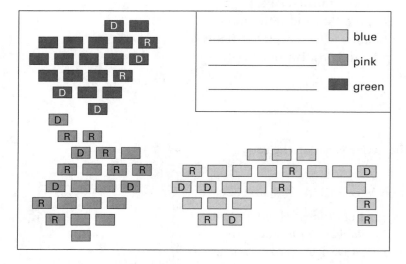

4 **Explain the rules of the game.** Project *Information Master 32A: Exploration Game Rules.* Use a piece of paper to cover the transparency. Review the rules one at a time. (**Note:** As you reveal each additional step, you can use the map to illustrate the rules, such as: showing students which papers are on the edges of the territories they will explore, versus which papers are in the interiors, or showing them which box to put their papers in after they return from their exploration.)

5 **Conduct the game.** Project *Information Master 32B: Exploration Game* to facilitate the game. You will need to reveal one row at a time. In the first few rounds, teams that have an X in their box do not get to send out an explorer. Each time a team turns over a Riches Card, record +1 for that round. Each time a team turns over a Danger Card, record –1 for that round. Teams receive a 0 for a blank piece of paper. (**Note:** There are more pieces of paper for each team than there are rounds in the game. This is to represent the idea that explorers did not reach every part of the territory they discovered.)

Information Master 32A

Information Master 32B

6 Debrief the activity. Have students sit with their teams and respond to these questions:

- How did it feel to play the game?

- What were some of the difficulties or dangers of being an explorer? *(Students should mention storms, food shortages, disease and violent encounters with native peoples.)*

- What were some of the rewards? *(Students might mention adventure, riches, and excitement.)*

- What factors contributed to the blue and pink teams ending up with more riches than the green team? *(They began earlier than the green team, and the territories they explored happened to have more riches.)*

- When real explorers explored new lands, who was greatly affected by this exploration, but was not represented in this game? *(The native inhabitants of each area.)*

- How do you think native inhabitants would feel about or respond to what happened during the game? *(They might feel angry and threatened as explorers began exploring and then claiming their lands, and taking things of value from their lands.)*

7 Connect the activity to the chapter. In the activity, students took on the role of explorers who were exploring "uncharted territory." They were rewarded for their efforts, but they also experienced "danger" and setbacks. In the chapter, students will study explorers who sailed for Portugal, Spain, England, and other European countries. Students will learn about routes the explorers followed, items exchanged between Europeans and other peoples, and positive and negative effects of exploration throughout the world.

Vocabulary Development

1 Introduce the Key Content Terms. Have students locate the Key Content Terms for the chapter in their Interactive Student Notebooks. These are important terms that will help them understand the main ideas of the chapter. Ask volunteers to identify any familiar terms and suggest how they might be used in a sentence.

2 Have students complete a Vocabulary Development handout. Give each student a copy of the Vocabulary Development handout of your choice from the Reading Toolkit at the back of the Lesson Masters. These handouts provide extra Key Content Term practice and support, depending on your students' needs. Review the completed handout by asking volunteers to share one answer for each term.

Reading

1 Introduce the Essential Question and have students read Section 32.1.
Have students identify the Essential Question on the first page of the chapter:
How did the Age of Exploration change the way Europeans viewed the world?
Then have students read Section 32.1. Afterward, ask students,

- Why did European explorers make these daring voyages?

- What does the term "New World" tell us about how Europeans viewed the world until the 1400s?

2 Have students read and complete the Reading Notes for Sections 32.2 and 32.3. Put students from the same activity groups in pairs or groups of three. Assign these new groups to read Sections 32.2 and 32.3 and complete the corresponding Reading Notes. Remind students to use the Key Content Terms where appropriate as they complete their Reading Notes.

3 Have students connect the activity to their reading. Project a transparency of *Information Master 32C: Making Connections to the Age of Exploration.* Cover everything except the column headings and have students create a T-chart in their notebooks with these headings. Then reveal the first row and have students copy the text from the Information Master, and complete the missing information to draw connections between the activity and history. After pairs have discussed and completed the first row, hold a class discussion about the connections, and record them on the transparency. Then reveal the second and third rows, repeating this process for each row. Use the guide below to ensure that students make all relevant connections.

Information Master 32C

Classroom Activity	Age of Exploration
• The object of the game was for teams to **explore new territory and find riches.**	• European motives to explore were: to find new trade routes to Asia, gain new knowledge, earn fame and wealth, and spread Christianity.
• The blue team started the game and had several turns before the pink and green teams joined in.	• Portugal's explorers began the Age of Exploration. They explored **routes around the tip of Africa, on to India and the Moluccas (Spice Islands).**
• **The blue team explored the territory closest to "home," and brought back riches from that territory.**	• Portugal's explorers brought back valuable items from known places—such as gold and slaves from Africa, and silks, jewels, and spices from India and the Moluccas.

4 **Have students read and complete the Reading Notes for Sections 32.4 and 32.5.**

5 **Have students connect the activity to their reading.** Reveal the fourth and fifth rows, repeating the process used in Step 3 for each row. Use the guide below to ensure that students make all relevant connections.

Classroom Activity	Age of Exploration
• The pink team started after the blue team, and explored a territory farther away from "home."	• *Spain followed Portugal into the Age of Exploration. However, starting with Columbus, Spanish routes of exploration were westward.*
• *The pink team found lots of riches in new territories they explored.*	• Spain brought huge amounts of gold and silver and exotic foods from new lands they explored in the Americas.

6 **Have students read and complete the Reading Notes for Section 32.6.**

7 **Have students connect the activity to their reading.** Reveal the sixth through eighth rows, repeating the process used in Step 3 for each row. Use the guide below to ensure that students make all relevant connections.

Classroom Activity	Age of Exploration
• The green team was the last to enter the game. They explored a different territory than the blue and pink teams.	• *England, France, and the Netherlands began their explorations after Portugal and Spain. They concentrated their early explorations in North America.*
• *The green team explored new territories, but found fewer riches.*	• England, France, and the Netherlands found fewer riches, mostly fish and furs, in the areas of North America they explored.
• Students on all teams uncovered Danger Cards, which detracted from what they had gained by finding riches.	• *Explorers faced many dangers, including running out of food, being lost at sea, attacked by native people, and falling ill.*

8 **Have students read and complete the Reading Notes for Section 32.7.**

Processing

Have students complete the Processing activity in their Interactive Student Notebooks. Students identify the positive and negative effects of European exploration, and then answer the Essential Question.

Quicker Coverage

Eliminate Rounds in the Activity Allow teams to send out multiple explorers in later rounds. Modify the rounds as follows:

- Rounds 1 and 2: one explorer at a time from only the blue team
- Rounds 3 and 4: one explorer at a time from the only the blue and pink teams
- Rounds 4 to the end: two or three explorers at a time for each team

Each individual explorer should still pick up only one piece of paper, but sending out multiple explorers at a time will cut down on the number of rounds. You may choose to stop at Round 8 or Round 9, depending on how many explorers go out in each round.

Deeper Coverage

Research Explorers Assign each student an explorer from this chapter to research. Several students will research the same explorer. Have students gather research showing whether the explorer's impact was positive or negative. A positive impact might be increased wealth for the home country; a negative impact might be the diseases Europeans introduced to native populations. Then have students create both a "wanted poster" and a "commemorative plaque" for their explorer. The requirements for each assignment are below. Alternatively, you might allow them to choose one or the other, depending on whether they thought their explorer's impact was more positive or more negative. Display all together the posters and plaques for each explorer. Have students conduct a quick gallery walk to learn more about each explorer.

Wanted poster should include:

- name and picture or drawing of explorer
- a sentence explaining why people should watch out for this explorer
- two to three examples of the negative impact of this explorer's journeys

Commemorative plaque should include:

- name and picture or drawing of explorer
- a sentence explaining why people should honor this explorer
- two to three examples of the positive impact of this explorer's journeys

Assessment

Mastering the Content

1. D	5. B	9. D	13. A
2. A	6. C	10. D	14. D
3. C	7. A	11. B	15. C
4. B	8. A	12. C	16. B

Applying Social Studies Skills

17. Portugal, Spain

18. 112

19. Answers will vary. Sample answers: Explorers sailed for anyone who would pay them; Italy produced many good sailors. Explorers had to look outside their home countries for sponsors because Italian city-states were happy with the old trade routes and did not want to develop new ones.

Exploring the Essential Question

20. Answers should include all the elements requested in the prompt.

Scoring Rubric

Score	Description
3	Student completes all five empty boxes. Views in boxes are clearly stated, supported by details, and demonstrate command of standard English conventions.
2	Student responds to most or all parts of the task, but views may lack details or not be clearly stated.
1	Student responds to at least one part of the task. Views may contain factual and/or grammatical errors and may lack details.
0	Response does not match the task or is incorrect.

Bartolomé de Las Casas: From Conquistador to Protector of the Indians

1 **Preview the following vocabulary terms.**

   • Review the term *conquistador*. Explain that the concept covers both the soldiers and those who took part in defeating the Indians in the Americas.

   • Introduce the term *encomienda*. Explain that it is the Spanish term for the system of giving land grants to the conquistadors as a reward for their services. The conquistadors also were awarded a number of native people to work in mines or on Spanish lands. Emphasize that the native labor was forced labor.

2 **Have students read the Chapter 32 Reading Further.** After students complete the reading, review the meaning of *primary source* and have students find examples of primary sources in the Reading Further. Discuss how some primary sources inform readers, while others seek to persuade them about a topic.

3 **Have students complete the Chapter 32 Reading Further in their Interactive Student Notebooks.** Students will write a Weblog (blog) entry about a contemporary human-rights issue. Before they begin writing, help them brainstorm a list of human-rights issues.

English Language Learners

Modify the Reading Notes Provide students with a copy of the Reading Notes with the routes already drawn on the maps for Sections 32.3–32.6. Have students label the routes as they read each section.

Provide Activity Directions The day before you plan to do the Experiential Exercise, assign students to their teams. Make a copy of the activity directions on Information Master 32A and review them with students. Allow students to take a copy home with them to review. This will help them to better understand the game as they play it.

Learners Reading and Writing Below Grade Level

Modify Note Taking Pair these learners with other students who are reading and writing at or above grade level. As partners work together to complete the Reading Notes, have the student reading at or above grade level record the answers in his or her set of Reading Notes. Be sure to give below-grade-level learners something concrete to do—such as looking for the answer to the next question—while their partner writes the answer for each Reading Notes question. Later, make a photocopy of the Reading Notes for the other partner.

Learners with Special Education Needs

Allow for Nonparticipation Explain the classroom activity to students ahead of time. Allow them to decide whether they wish to participate. If they choose to observe instead, give them a copy of the completed chart from Steps 3, 5, and 7 of the Reading directions in the Lesson Guide. Format this so that only the entries in the "Classroom Activity" column are exposed. As the activity unfolds, have these students circle each item from this column that they observe, and record a note about what they saw happen. After the activity, ask them to share which items they observed and to describe specifically what they saw.

Advanced Learners

Extend the Reading Notes After students complete the reading and Reading Notes for each section of 32.3–32.6, have them grade each country according to the "report card" below. Students should assign a letter grade for each category and should write a short explanation of why they gave that grade. Have them use the letter grades below. You may want to copy this "report card" onto your board or make a large copy of it for students.

	Impact on European Country	Impact on the World	Impact on Native Inhabitants of Areas Explored
Section 32.3 Portuguese exploration			
Section 32.4 Early Spanish exploration			
Section 32.5 Later Spanish exploration			
Section 32.6 English/ French/ Dutch exploration			

A Excellent
B Very Good
C Average
D Poor
F Fail

Enrichment Resources

Find out more about the European Age of Exploration by exploring the following Enrichment Resources for *History Alive! The Medieval World and Beyond* at www.teachtci.com.

Enrichment Readings These in-depth readings encourage students to explore selected topics related to the chapter. You may also find readings that relate the chapter's content directly to your state's curriculum.

Internet Connections These recommended Web sites provide useful and engaging content that reinforces skills development and mastery of subjects within the chapter.

Literature Recommendations

The following books offer opportunities to extend the content in this chapter.

Beyond the Sea of Ice: The Voyages of Henry Hudson by Joan E. Goodman and Bette Duke (Richmond Hill, ON: Firefly, 1999)

Francisco Pizarro and the Conquest of the Inca by Gina De Angelis (New York: Chelsea House, 2000)

The Travels of Hernán Cortés by Deborah Crisfield (Austin: Raintree-Steck Vaughn, 2000)

Section 32.2

1. Rankings and justifications will vary, but motives may include: desire to find new trade routes to Asia, excitement over the opportunity for new knowledge, chance to earn fame and glory, chance for adventure, the desire to claim new lands' riches and wealth, and to spread Christianity.

2. Cartography: Improved mapmaking led to more accurate maps, which helped explorers by making navigation easier. Ship design: Improved ship design, such as new caravels, improved navigation and the ability to explore along coastlines. Compass and astrolabe: Improved compass and astrolabe gave more accurate direction and distance measurements, and helped sailors travel more safely on the open seas. Weapons: Weapons using gunpowder and steel swords gave Europeans a huge military advantage over native peoples.

Section 32.3

1. See the map in the student book for correct routes.

2. Vasco da Gama was important to Portuguese exploration because he brought the first load of valuable spices from India directly back to Portugal, which made Portugal even more eager to trade directly with Indian merchants.

Pedro Cabral was important to Portuguese exploration because he reached the east coast of Brazil and claimed it for Portugal. He then established a trading post in India and signed trade treaties there. This paved the way for the Portuguese to take control of the eastern sea routes to Asia, and to build forts and trading posts in India.

3. Answer will vary, but may include:

brought gold and slaves from Africa to Europe

found a sea route to India

brought back spices and other goods, such as porcelain, incense, jewels, and silk

attacked towns in India, the east coast of Africa, and the Moluccas in an attempt to take the spice trade away from Muslim traders

- broke hold of Muslim and Italian control over Asian trade, which reduced the prices of Asian goods, such as spices and fabrics, and made them more affordable to people in Europe

- established colonies in Brazil, bringing great suffering to the native people.

- brought millions of enslaved West Africans to Brazil

Section 32.4

1. See the map in the student book for correct routes.

2. Christopher Columbus was important to Spanish exploration because he discovered the West Indies and paved the way for further exploration of a new (to Europeans) land mass—the Americas—between Europe and Asia.

Ferdinand Magellan was important to Spanish exploration because he discovered a strait connecting the Atlantic and Pacific, allowing ships to continue on to Asia. After he was killed, Magellan's crew completed their voyage, becoming the first people to circumnavigate the globe.

3. Answers will vary but may include:

- revealed the existence of the Americas— a "New World" to Europeans

- opened up a westward route to the Indies

- showed that it was possible to sail completely around the world

- proved that Columbus had indeed found a "New World"

- Spain began settlements in the West Indies, and earned great wealth.

- sent Europe new crops, such as sweet potatoes and pineapples

- Spanish settlement was extremely detrimental to the native peoples of the West Indies.

- brought millions of enslaved Africans to work in their American colonies

Section 32.5

1. See the map in the student book for correct routes.

2. Hernán Cortés was important to Spanish exploration because he defeated the Aztecs.

   Francisco Pizarro was important to Spanish exploration because he conquered the Incas.

3. Answer will vary, but may include:

   • rapidly expanded Spain's foreign trade and overseas colonization

   • Wealth from the Americas made Spain one of the world's richest and most powerful countries.

   • Ships brought corn and potatoes to Spain, and these crops grew well in Europe.

   • An increased food supply helped spur a population boom in Europe.

   • Europeans were introduced to new luxury items, such as chocolate.

   • Inflation resulted from the increased amount of gold and silver in Spain's economy.

   • The Spanish introduced new animals, such as horses, cattle, sheep, and pigs, to the Americas.

   • The Aztecs and Incas lost much of their cultures along with their wealth.

   • Many native peoples became laborers for the Spanish or died from European diseases.

Section 32.6

1. See the map in the student book for correct routes.

2. John Cabot was important to English exploration because he made England's first voyage of discovery and first land claims in the New World.

   Giovanni da Verrazano was important to French exploration because he explored the Atlantic coast and gave France its first claims in the Americas.

   Henry Hudson was important to Dutch and English exploration because he tried to find a northwest passage through North America to the Pacific Ocean. He explored the Hudson River, which led to Dutch settlement in the area, and claimed Hudson Bay in Canada for the English.

3. Answers will vary, but may include:

   • found rich resources of cod and other fish, which led European fishing boats to regularly visit the region

   • Europeans began trading with Native Americans for whale oil and otter, beaver, and fox furs.

   • Europeans set up a number of trading posts in North America.

   • English exploration contributed to a war between England and Spain.

   • After the defeat of the Spanish Armada, other European countries took an active role in trade and colonization around the world.

Section 32.7

1. As merchants gained wealth by trading and selling goods from around the world, they used their profits to finance more voyages and to start trading companies. Other people then began to invest money in these companies and share in their profits. Soon this type of shared ownership was applied to other kinds of businesses.

2. In a market economy, goods are sold for prices set by the open market, meaning that the price of an item depends on what people will pay for it. In turn, this usually depends on how much of the item is available, and how many people want to buy it.

3. A cottage industry is a small-scale manufacturing business in which people worked out of their homes (cottages). Typically, this involved turning raw materials into finished products, such as spinning wool into thread, or weaving thread into cloth. This was a step toward the later system of factories operated by capitalists.

4. Mercantilism is an economic policy that relied on the belief that building wealth was the best way to build a country's power. Nations looked to their colonies to supply raw materials for their industries, and then profited by turning these raw materials into finished goods they could sell to other countries and back to their own colonies.

The Scientific Revolution

How did the Scientific Revolution change the way people understood the world?

Overview

In a Visual Discovery activity, students analyze a series of images to examine key scientists, inventions, and discoveries of the Scientific Revolution. Students "step into" these images to bring them to life.

Objectives

In the course of reading this chapter and participating in the classroom activity, students will

Social Studies

- explain how the Renaissance, Greek rationalism, and global exploration provided a foundation for the Scientific Revolution.

- analyze images to determine the impact of scientific theories proposed during this period by scientists such as Copernicus, Kepler, Galileo, and Newton.

- identify the key elements of the scientific method, as advanced by Bacon and Descartes.

- evaluate the contributions of key individuals and inventions of the Scientific Revolution.

Language Arts

- ask probing questions to elicit information.

- clarify the meanings of new words through the use of definition and example.

Social Studies Vocabulary

Key Content Terms Scientific Revolution, rationalism, geocentric theory, heliocentric theory, gravity, mass, scientific method, hypothesis

Academic Vocabulary telescope, lens, formula, microscope

Materials

History Alive! The Medieval World and Beyond

Interactive Student Notebooks

Visuals 33A–33D

Lesson Masters

- Student Handout 33 (2 copies)
- Vocabulary Development handout (1 per student, on colored paper)

Activity	Suggested Time	Materials
Preview	20–25 minutes	• Interactive Student Notebooks • Visual 33A
Vocabulary Development	30–40 minutes	• *History Alive! The Medieval World and Beyond* • Interactive Student Notebooks • Vocabulary Development handout
Visual Discovery	75–90 minutes (2 regular periods) (1 block period)	• *History Alive! The Medieval World and Beyond* • Interactive Student Notebooks • Visuals 33B–33D • Student Handout 33 (2 copies, role cards cut apart)
Processing	20 minutes	• Interactive Student Notebooks
Assessment	40 minutes	• Chapter 33 Assessment

Preview

1 **Prepare for the Preview activity.** In this Preview activity, students will briefly experience what it may have been like to live during the Scientific Revolution, when many people were questioning traditional teachings and beliefs. You will need to "teach" students Ptolemy's geocentric theory, using the questions and guiding them in the following steps. It is important that you act as though this remains the currently accepted scientific theory.

2 **Have students complete the Preview activity in their Interactive Student Notebooks.** After students have drawn their diagrams, have them share their drawings with a partner. Encourage students to update their diagrams and labels, based on feedback from their peers.

3 **Ask students the following questions about their diagrams.** Remember that you are acting as though Ptolemy's geocentric theory is still upheld today.

- What is at the center of our system of planets? *(Expect students to say, "The sun." Then correct them and say something like, "No, I think you mean that Earth is at the center and other planets orbit around it.")*

- What is the closest body that orbits Earth? *(Expect students to say, "The moon." Congratulate them on getting this one right.)*

- What is the next closest body that orbits Earth? *(Expect students to say something like, "Nothing else orbits Earth, all the planets orbit the sun." Act disbelieving and say, "What? No, everyone knows that Mercury is the next planet that revolves around Earth.")*

- What is the next closest body that orbits Earth? *(Expect students to become frustrated or indignant. Tell them, "This is unbelievable. Since you seem to have the wrong information, let's have a quick review of how this all works.")*

4 **Project** *Visual 33A: Ptolemy's Geocentric Theory* **and explain Ptolemy's theory.** In a serious tone, describe Ptolemy's geocentric theory as if it were the common scientific teaching of today, as it was at the early part of the Scientific Revolution. Use the image as a visual aid to make the following points:

- Through the use of reason and critical thinking, the Greek thinker Ptolemy proved more than two thousand years ago that Earth is at the center of the universe.

- As all serious scientists today agree, Earth does not move. However, the moon, sun, and planets revolve around Earth. The moon is the closest to Earth, then Mercury, Venus, the sun, Mars, Jupiter, and finally, Saturn. A sphere, beyond the planets, contains the stars.

- As students should have already learned in their science classes, this is known as the geocentric theory. It accurately explains how our universe is structured.

Visual 33A

5   **Debrief the experience.** Ask students,

- How did you feel while learning about Ptolemy's geocentric theory of the universe?

- Do you believe Ptolemy's theory is correct? Why or why not?

    Assure students that Earth does orbit the sun, and only the moon orbits Earth—just as they have learned in their science classes. Explain that what they just experienced was a situation that, to some extent, replicated the frustrations scientists during the Scientific Revolution might have encountered. Then ask students, If today's scientists believed Ptolemy's theory, what steps might you take to disprove the theory?

6   **Have students answer this final Preview activity question.** Ask students the question below. You may want to have a quick discussion in which some students share their situations, and the steps they took, with the rest of the class.

- Describe a time when many people strongly believed something to be true, but you didn't. (Or imagine what this might feel like.) How did you try to change their minds? Were you successful?

7   **Connect the Preview activity to the chapter.** Remind students that in the Preview activity they experienced what is was like during the Scientific Revolution, a period in which thinkers began to question the conclusions of Aristotle and other traditional sources. These thinkers developed a new approach to science called the scientific method, which led to many new discoveries and important inventions. Many of these discoveries disproved traditional teachings and beliefs that had been accepted for hundreds of years. In the chapter and activity, students will learn about the scientists who led the Scientific Revolution, and about their new theories, discoveries, and inventions.

Vocabulary Development

1   **Introduce the Key Content Terms.** Have students locate the Key Content Terms for the chapter in their Interactive Student Notebooks. These are important terms that will help them understand the main ideas of the chapter. Ask volunteers to identify any familiar terms and suggest how they might be used in a sentence.

2   **Have students complete a Vocabulary Development handout.** Give each student a copy of the Vocabulary Development handout of your choice from the Reading Toolkit at the back of the Lesson Masters. These handouts provide Key Content Term extra practice and support, depending on your students' needs. Review the completed handout by asking volunteers to share one answer for each term.

Reading

1 Introduce the Essential Question and have students read Section 33.1.
Have students identify the Essential Question on the first page of the chapter:
How did the Scientific Revolution change the way people understood the world?
Then have students read Section 33.1. Afterward, have students carefully
analyze the chapter's opening images. Then ask students to find words,
phrases, or sentences in the text of Section 33.1 that connect to visual details
in the chapter opening images. Have several volunteers share the connections
they found with the rest of the class.

2 Have students complete the Reading Notes for Chapter 33. Assign Sections
33.2 to 33.7 during the activity, as indicated in the procedures for the Visual
Discovery activity. Remind students to use the Key Content Terms where
appropriate as they complete their Reading Notes.

Visual Discovery

1 Prepare the materials and the classroom. Set up your classroom so that all
pairs in the activity will be able to see the screen clearly. Make two copies of
Student Handout 33: Role Cards for Act-It-Out. You will need to cut apart the
role cards prior to the activity.

2 Place students in pairs and introduce the activity. Explain to students
that in this activity they will analyze images to learn how the key scientists,
inventions, and discoveries of the Scientific Revolution changed the way
people understood the world.

3 Have pairs complete the Reading Notes for Section 33.2. Tell students
that this section will provide background information on the roots of the
Scientific Revolution. Have students read Section 33.2 and complete the
corresponding Reading Notes in their Interactive Student Notebooks.

4 Have students analyze the image of Copernicus. Project *Visual 33B:
Copernicus's Heliocentric Theory.* Help students carefully analyze the image
by asking,

- What interesting or important details do you see? *(Make sure students
  notice the following: The man is on a rooftop; he appears to be looking at the
  sky; he appears to be recording information about what he sees.)*

- What do you see on the diagram to the man's right? *(The sun is in
  the center, with planets revolving around it. The moon is revolving
  around Earth.)*

- What do you see on the diagram on the left? *(The sun is in the center with
  planets circling around it. One planet* (Earth) *has another body* (the moon)
  orbiting it.)

- How does the diagram to the right differ from Ptolemy's diagram, which
  you saw in the Preview activity? *(Ptolemy's diagram had Earth at the
  center, with the sun and other planets orbiting Earth. This diagram has the
  sun at the center, with Earth and the other planets orbiting the sun.)*

Student Handout 33

Visual 33B

- Why might people have opposed the ideas in this diagram? (*The ideas in this diagram were against the accepted teachings of Ptolemy and the teachings of the Bible and Aristotle, which had long been major sources guiding most Europeans' thinking about the natural world.*)

Tell students that this is a painting of the Polish astronomer Nicolaus Copernicus, who is credited with developing the heliocentric theory. At the time, many people did not believe his theory.

5 **Have pairs complete the Reading Notes for Section 33.3.** Have pairs read Section 33.3 and complete the corresponding Reading Notes in their Interactive Student Notebooks. You may want to use the Guide to Reading Notes to review answers to these questions with students before moving on.

6 **Repeat Steps 4 and 5 for the image of Galileo.** Use *Visual 33C: Galileo Galilei* and the following spiral questions to help students analyze the image:

Visual 33C

- What interesting details do you see? (*Make sure that students notice the following: The man in the center is pointing out a telescope; the men around him are wearing robes; one man is looking through the telescope.*)

- What might the man in the center be discussing? (*the telescope*)

- Who might the other men be? How do they seem to be reacting to what the man in the center is saying? (*They might be religious or political leaders. Some are listening, others are discussing. Some seem curious while others seem doubtful.*)

- If the man is describing some discoveries he has made using the telescope, what might those discoveries be? (*They might have to do with the orbit of the planets, the sun, or the stars. They likely support what Copernicus and Kepler observed about the planets moving around the sun.*)

- Why might it be risky for this man to share such information with others? (*Because Copernicus's heliocentric theory contradicted the teachings of Aristotle and the Bible, this man might encounter resistance, especially from leaders of the Catholic Church.*)

Tell students that this is a painting of the Italian scientist Galileo Galilei showing his telescope to the Venetian senate. Then have students read and complete Reading Notes for Section 33.4.

7 **Have students prepare for an act-it-out.** Create eight groups of equal size. Give each group one role card cut from Student Handout 33. Pass out the four role cards to four groups and assign them to be "actor groups" who will bring their characters to life. Tell actor groups to review their role cards and use information from their Reading Notes to generate ideas. Then pass out the second set of four role cards to the remaining groups and assign them to be "reporter groups" who will write two or three additional questions for their character. Remind reporter groups that they should write good questions that the character should be able to answer, not trick questions. Give students a few minutes to prepare and practice.

8 **Conduct the act-it-out.** Select one student from each actor group to come up to the screen and freeze in the appropriate position in front of their character. Remind students to stay frozen until you, as an on-the-scene reporter, ask them one or two of the questions the actor is prepared to answer. After asking each actor his or her questions, call on the appropriate reporter group to ask an additional question of that actor.

9 **Repeat Steps 4 and 5 for the image of Newton.** Use *Visual 33D: Isaac Newton* and the following spiral questions to help students analyze the image:

Visual 33D

- What interesting or important details do you see? *(Make sure students notice the following: The man is sitting under an apple tree and looking at an apple that has fallen to the ground; the man has a science book that includes a diagram of the heliocentric theory; there is a telescope in the background, to the right.)*

- What does the man seem to be noticing? *(the apple on the ground)*

- What is the law that explains why an apple falls to the ground? *(the law of gravity)*

- How does the law of gravity also explain why planets travel around the sun? *(It explains that, because the sun's mass is larger than that of the planets, the planets are trapped in the sun's gravity and orbit the sun rather than drifting off into space.)*

- Why do you think the discovery of the law of gravity was so important? *(It explained why the planets orbit the sun, as well as explaining why objects on Earth fall to the ground—e.g., why the moon orbits Earth, why an apple falls to the ground instead of drifting up to the sky, why you always land after you jump.)*

  Tell students that this is a painting of the English scientist Isaac Newton, who discovered the law of gravity. Then have students read and complete the Reading Notes for Section 33.5.

10 **Have pairs complete the Reading Notes for Sections 33.6 and 33.7.** Have pairs read Sections 33.6–33.7 and complete the corresponding Reading Notes in their Interactive Student Notebooks. Review the answers, encouraging students to add key information to their notes. (**Note:** You may want to assign this step as homework.)

Processing

Have students complete the Processing activity. Students will evaluate the contributions of key individuals during the Scientific Revolution.

Quicker Coverage

Skip the Act-It-Out After analyzing Visual 33C in Step 6, skip Steps 7 and 8 in which students prepare for and conduct an act-it-out.

Deeper Coverage

Create Additional Act-It-Outs Create act-it-outs for Visual 33B and Visual 33D. Write role cards for Copernicus and Newton, following the set-up of the role cards on Student Handout 33. Use the directions in Steps 7 and 8 of the Visual Discovery to conduct each additional act-it-out. During Step 8, have one student from each actor group represent the scientist in that image, and ask each actor a different question from the role card.

Assessment

Mastering the Content

1. C	5. A	9. B	13. C
2. B	6. C	10. A	14. A
3. B	7. D	11. B	15. C
4. D	8. A	12. D	

Applying Social Studies Skills

Answers will vary. Sample answers:

16. seek the truth

17. sometimes our senses mislead us

18. himself

19. because he is the one doing the thinking, he must exist

Exploring the Essential Question

20. Answers should include all the elements requested in the prompt.

Scoring Rubric

Score	Description
3	Student completes all three parts of the task. Statements are clearly stated, supported by details, and demonstrate command of standard English conventions.
2	Student responds to most parts of the task, but statements may lack details or not be clearly stated.
1	Student responds to at least one part of the task. Statements may contain factual and/or grammar errors and may lack details.
0	Response does not match the task or is incorrect.

English Language Learners

Create Cue Cards for Images Create simple cue cards for the spiral questions you will ask students when they analyze each image. For each spiral question you plan to ask, write an incomplete answer on a cue card. During the lesson, pass these out to students just prior to analyzing an image. Ask the questions, and have students complete the statement on their cards. For example, cue cards for the image on Visual 33B might read as follows:

- An interesting or important detail I see in this image is
- On the diagram on the man's right I see
- This diagram is different from Ptolemy's diagram because
- I think people might have been against the ideas in this diagram because

Support the Act-It-Out If you choose one of these students to be the actor during the act-it-out, provide additional support by telling him or her ahead of time which of the questions from the role card you will ask. Have the student(s) work with a peer to practice giving a verbal response to that question.

Learners Reading and Writing Below Grade Level

Modify the Reading Notes Provide some additional structure for students as they complete the Reading Notes by giving them a copy of the Guide to Reading Notes with key words omitted from each answer. Students can complete the answers and fill in the missing words as they read.

Learners with Special Education Needs

Create Additional Roles Consider allowing some students to participate in the act-it-out in nonspeaking roles. For example, one student could be an adviser to the Italian leader, seated to his left. Another could be one of the spectators watching Galileo present and explain his telescope.

Modify the Processing Activity Copy Sections 33.3 to 33.7 of *History Alive! The Medieval World and Beyond* and highlight the individuals mentioned in the Processing activity. Also, highlight one or two discoveries or inventions for which each was responsible. Give students these pages to use as they complete the Processing activity.

Advanced Learners

Extend the Processing Activity Extend the assignment for some students by having them each write an acceptance speech for the individual they elected to receive the gold medal. In their acceptance speeches, students should:

- include the names of the other two medal winners and why it is an honor to be named among them
- thank anyone who has helped them. This could include people who supported their ideas or other scientists or inventors who improved their ideas.
- discuss how they believe their invention, discovery, or contribution will affect the world in the future

Enrichment Resources

Find out more about the Scientific Revolution by exploring the following Enrichment Resources for *History Alive! The Medieval World and Beyond* at www.teachtci.com.

Enrichment Readings These in-depth readings encourage students to explore selected topics related to the chapter. You may also find readings that relate the chapter's content directly to your state's curriculum.

Internet Connections These recommended Web sites provide useful and engaging content that reinforces skills development and mastery of subjects within the chapter.

Literature Recommendations

The following books offer opportunities to extend the content in this chapter.

Galileo and the Universe by Steve Parker (New York: Chelsea House, 1995)

Isaac Newton by Tony Allan (Chicago: Heinemann Library, 2001)

Johannes Kepler and the New Astronomy by James R. Voelkel (New York: Oxford, 2001)

Section 33.2

1. The Bible and the teachings of Aristotle guided most Europeans' thinking about the natural world during the Middle Ages.

2. Possible answers:

   • Renaissance: As Renaissance scholars rediscovered the culture of ancient Greece and Rome, they learned about a greater variety of works than just those of Aristotle. They were influenced by Greek rationalism. They began to believe that reason could be used to discover basic truths about the world. Reason and observation became a key part of modern science.

   • Age of Exploration: Before the Age of Exploration, scholars believed there were only three continents. The discovery of the Americas proved them wrong, and such discoveries encouraged Europeans to question traditional teachings.

Section 33.3

1. Students should draw a diagram of the solar system, with the sun at the center and the planets orbiting it. The three labels on their diagram should be:

   • The sun is at the center of the universe.

   • Earth and the other planets orbit the sun.

   • Earth also turns on its own axis every 24 hours.

2. Kepler figured out that the orbits of the planets were ovals, or ellipses, not circles. Then he wrote precise mathematical laws describing the movements of the planets around the sun.

Section 33.4

1. Galileo discovered that the surface of the moon is not perfectly smooth, that moons travel around Jupiter, and that Venus passes through phases.

2. Galileo's discoveries showed that moons travel around other planets, so Earth could not be the only center of motion in the universe. Galileo also showed that Venus travels around the sun.

3. The idea that Earth was the center of the universe was part of an entire system of belief approved by the Catholic Church. Church leaders feared that attacks on the geocentric theory could lead people to question the teachings of the Church.

Section 33.5

1. Newton's law of gravity says that all objects have a force of attraction, or gravity, between them. The strength of the force depends on the masses of the objects and the distance between them.

2. Copernicus, Kepler, and Galileo said that the planets revolve around the sun. Newton's work explained why they do so.

Section 33.6

1. Francis Bacon believed that people could gain knowledge through scientific investigation that depended on close observation. Rene Descartes prized logic and mathematics, and thought that to gain reliable knowledge, people should doubt every statement until logic proved it. These ideas helped to create a new approach to science that was based on logic, mathematics, and observation.

2. Students' diagrams and symbols will vary but should include the following consecutive steps:

   • State a question or a problem.

   • Form a hypothesis.

   • Conduct an experiment to test the hypothesis.

   • Measure data and record results.

   • Analyze the data to determine if the hypothesis is correct.

Section 33.7

Students' sketches will vary.

- The telescope makes distant objects seem closer, allowing us to study distant planets and stars.

- The microscope makes small objects seem larger, allowing us to examine tiny organisms, such as bacteria.

- The barometer measures the change in atmospheric pressure, which helps us to study and predict the weather.

- The thermometer measures temperature, allowing us to study and track data about the weather.

The Enlightenment

How have the ideas of the Enlightenment influenced modern government?

Overview

In this Response Group activity, students "visit" an Enlightenment-era salon to learn about the ideas of five important Enlightenment thinkers. Students then analyze excerpts from significant historical documents and try to match them to the correct source.

Objectives

In the course of reading this chapter and participating in the classroom activity, students will

Social Studies

- describe the roots of the Enlightenment.

- explain the key ideas of five Enlightenment thinkers—Hobbes, Locke, Montesquieu, Voltaire, and Beccaria.

- explain the influence of Enlightenment thought on later democratic thinking and institutions.

- analyze excerpts from important historical documents to identify the Enlightenment thinkers whose ideas are expressed in each.

Language Arts

- clearly state a position and provide a detailed explanation of a rationale.

- analyze text to identify a cause-and-effect pattern.

Materials

History Alive! The Medieval World and Beyond

Interactive Student Notebooks

Visual 34

Lesson Masters

- Information Masters 34A, 34C, and 34D (1 transparency of each)

- Information Master 34B (2 copies of each head, A–E)

- Student Handout 34 (1 copy, cut apart)

- Vocabulary Development handout (1 per student, on colored paper)

Social Studies Vocabulary

Key Content Terms Enlightenment, constitutional monarchy, bill of rights, social contract, natural rights, separation of powers, despotism, religious tolerance

Academic Vocabulary insight, behalf, arbitrary

Activity	Suggested Time	Materials
Preview	10 minutes	• Interactive Student Notebooks • Visual 34
Vocabulary Development	30–40 minutes	• *History Alive! The Medieval World and Beyond* • Interactive Student Notebooks • Vocabulary Development handout
Response Group	Phase 1 75–90 minutes (2 regular periods) (1 block period) Phase 2 45–50 minutes (1 regular period) (.5 block period)	• *History Alive! The Medieval World and Beyond* • Interactive Student Notebooks • Information Master 34A (1 transparency) • Information Master 34B (2 copies of each head, A–D) • Information Masters 34C and 34D (1 transparency of each) • Student Handout 34 (1 copy, cut apart)
Processing	20–25 minutes	• Interactive Student Notebooks
Assessment	40 minutes	• Chapter 34 Assessment

Preview

Visual 34

1 **Analyze an image from the Enlightenment.** Project *Visual 34: Madame Geoffrin's Salon* or refer students to the large image in the chapter opener. Ask students the following questions, one at a time. Have students record their responses in their Interactive Student Notebooks before sharing their thoughts with the class.

- What are four interesting details you see in this image?

- What conclusions can you draw about the people at this gathering? Give one piece of evidence to support each conclusion.

- What kinds of ideas might people discuss at a gathering like this, and why?

- In what ways might these people spread the ideas discussed at this gathering?

Consider having students come to the image and point out the details that they note in the first question or use as supporting evidence in the second and third questions.

2 **Connect the Preview activity to the chapter.** Explain to students that in the Preview activity they analyzed an image of a French Enlightenment salon, an informal gathering of thinkers, at the home of Madame Geoffrin. (**Note:** In the complete image on Visual 34, Madame Geoffrin is toward the right side of the image. She appears in a blue dress and a black bonnet). People attending salons shared their thoughts on such topics as government, art, society, and religion. Intellectuals who attended these gatherings often wrote about the ideas that they discussed there, thus spreading those ideas to others. These thinkers were products of the Enlightenment, a time when educated Europeans began to believe that reason was the key to human progress. In the chapter, students will learn about key Enlightenment thinkers, and how their ideas affected modern democratic thinking and institutions.

Vocabulary Development

1 **Introduce the Key Content Terms.** Have students locate the Key Content Terms for the chapter in their Interactive Student Notebooks. These are important terms that will help them understand the main ideas of the chapter. Ask volunteers to identify any familiar terms and suggest how they might be used in a sentence.

2 **Have students complete a Vocabulary Development handout.** Give each student a copy of the Vocabulary Development handout of your choice from the Reading Toolkit at the back of the Lesson Masters. These handouts provide extra Key Content Term practice and support, depending on your students' needs. Review the completed handout by asking volunteers to share one answer for each term.

Reading

1 Introduce the Essential Question and have students read Section 34.1.
Have students identify the Essential Question on the first page of the
chapter: *How have the ideas of the Enlightenment influenced modern
government?* Then have students read Section 34.1. Afterward, have
students use information from Section 34.1 and from the chapter opener
image to propose some possible answers to the Essential Question.

2 Have students complete the Reading Notes for Section 34.2. Tell students
that this section will introduce them to the roots of the Enlightenment. Have
students read Section 34.2 and complete the corresponding Reading Notes in
their Interactive Student Notebooks. Remind students to use the Key Content
Terms where appropriate as they complete their Reading Notes.

3 Have students complete the Reading Notes for Sections 34.3 to 34.9.
Assign Sections 34.3 to 34.9 during the activity, as indicated in the procedures for the Response Group activity. If your class is not doing the activity,
remind students not to complete item 4 in each section through Section 34.7.

Information Master 34A

Response Group

Put students in groups of three and introduce the activity. Tell students that
they are about to "visit" an Enlightenment salon, or social gathering, where
they will meet five of the most influential thinkers of the Enlightenment. Then
they will play a game called "Whose Idea Was This, Anyway?" in which they
analyze excerpts from important historical documents to determine which
Enlightenment thinker's idea is represented in each.

Student Handout 34

Phase 1

1 Prepare for Phase 1 of the activity. Prepare the materials and the classroom
as follows:

- Make a transparency of *Information Master 34A: Reading Activity Directions.*
- Make a copy of *Student Handout 34: Enlightenment Thinker Cards* and cut
the cards apart.
- Make two copies of *Information Master 34B: Head of Enlightenment Thinker.*

Tape one set of the heads, at even intervals, along one wall of the classroom.
Post the other set on the opposite wall.

2 Project Information Master 34A and review the directions. Once you are
certain students understand the process, assign half the groups to use one
wall of Enlightenment Thinkers during the activity, and the other half
of the groups to use the opposite wall. Then give each group of three an
Enlightenment Thinker Card from Student Handout 34.

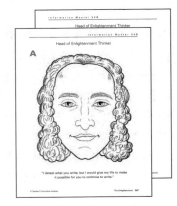

Information Master 34B

Pairs will read Sections 34.3 to 34.7, one at a time (in a different order, depending on their Enlightenment Thinker Card), and complete the corresponding Reading Notes. (**Note:** To save time in class, you might want to have students skim the section and identify the quotation in class, then complete the Reading Notes for Sections 34.3 to 34.7 for homework.)

3 **Debrief Phase 1 with students.** Go to one of the walls on which the Enlightenment Thinkers' heads are posted, and one by one, identify each thinker. Then ask students,

- With which Enlightenment thinker's ideas do you most agree? Least agree?

- How might these ideas have helped shape government at the time? Today?

- Which thinker do you think might have the greatest influence on your life today, and why?

Phase 2

1 **Prepare for Phase 2 of the activity.** Make a transparency of *Information Master 34C: "Whose Idea Was This, Anyway?" Game Directions* and *Information Master 34D: Excerpts from Enlightenment Documents.*

2 **Project Information Master 34C and review the directions.**

3 **Play the game.** Continue projecting Information Master 34C and walk students through each step. Use the following tips to help the game run smoothly.

- **Step 1:** After groups have chosen their Presenter in the first round, have them rotate the role (to the right) for each additional round.

Information Master 34C

- **Step 2:** For each round of the game, project Information Master 34D and reveal one excerpt as you read it aloud. Conceal the remaining excerpts and the answers at the bottom. Consider giving groups one minute to carefully reread the excerpt and to ask about any words they don't understand. (**Note:** If you have limited class time, you might want to do only Rounds 1 to 4.)

- **Step 3:** Give groups two to three minutes to analyze the excerpt and their Reading Notes to try to match the excerpt to an Enlightenment thinker.

- **Step 4:** Call on several Presenters whose groups selected other Enlightenment thinkers, and ask them to explain their selections.

The answers for each round can be found on the bottom of Information Master 34D.

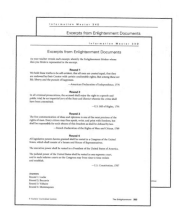

Information Master 34D

4 **Have students read Sections 34.8 and 34.9 and complete the their Reading Notes.** These sections discuss the impact of the Enlightenment on government, and the contributions of women to the Enlightenment.

Processing

Have students complete the Processing activity in their Interactive Student Notebooks. Students find a newspaper article or photograph that represents an idea of one of the Enlightenment thinkers they studied in this chapter.

Quicker Coverage

Eliminate Phase 1 of the Activity Skip Phase 1 of the activity, in which students match quotations to the Enlightenment thinkers. Instead, have students complete the Reading Notes for Sections 34.3 to 34.7 the night before beginning the activity. Start the activity by arranging students in groups of three, and then proceed to the directions for Phase 2. In Step 4 on Information Master 34C game directions students go to the wall and stand in front of the appropriate Enlightenment thinker posted there (from Phase 1). You will need to post one set of Information Master 34B, labeled, along the wall, so that students can complete that step of the Response Group activity.

Eliminate Phase 2 of the Activity Conduct Phase 1 of the activity as directed, then skip Phase 2 in which students play the game "Whose Idea Was This, Anyway?"

Deeper Coverage

Use Volunteers in Phase 1 of the Activity Instead of posting Information Master 34B on the wall during Phase 1, invite adult volunteers to play the roles of the "Enlightenment thinkers." Cut out the heads from Information Master 34B for the volunteers to wear as masks. (You may need to enlarge them as you photocopy the pages of the Information Master.) Have the "Enlightenment thinkers" read their quotations to each group. If students are stumped, allow them to ask yes/no questions, such as, "Did you live in England?" or "Were you ever arrested?" (**Note:** To ensure that the volunteers are well prepared, you will need to give each one an advance copy of the text pertaining to his or her character. You might also encourage volunteers to do additional research or to wear a costume to more dramatically portray their characters.)

Assessment

Mastering the Content

1. A	5. B	9. D	13. B
2. C	6. D	10. B	14. A
3. B	7. D	11. A	15. D
4. A	8. C	12. C	16. C

Applying Social Studies Skills

17. John Locke

18. 1st Amendment

19. Answers will vary. Sample answer: protecting the rights of the accused; promising a speedy, public, and local trial

Exploring the Essential Question

20. Answers should include all the elements requested in the prompt.

Scoring Rubric

Score	Description
3	Student completes a cartoon that complies with all three bulleted points. Cartoon is clearly presented, connects Enlightenment ideas to a current event or topic, and demonstrates command of standard English conventions.
2	Student responds to most or all parts of the task, but cartoon may lack details or not be clearly presented.
1	Student responds to at least one part of the task. Cartoon may contain grammatical errors and/or show a misunderstanding of Enlightenment ideas and their implications.
0	Response does not match the task or is incorrect.

English Language Learners

Provide Support in Phase 1 On Information Master 34B, highlight the key words within each quotation that might help students link the quotation to their Reading Notes.

Provide Support in Phase 2 These students will find it difficult to understand the 18th-century language of the documents on Information Master 34D. Consider rewriting the excerpts to simplify them. For example, you might rewrite the excerpt in Round 1 as follows: *All people are born equal and have God-given rights— such as life, liberty, and the pursuit of happiness—that cannot be taken away.*

Learners Reading and Writing Below Grade Level

Create Mixed-Ability Groups Pair these students with peers who are working above grade level and can help them understand the quotations in Phase 1 and the excerpts in Phase 2. You might consider adding a step to each phase in which students discuss the quotation's or excerpt's meaning before they identify the thinker. Also, consider having groups complete together only one set of Reading Notes and one copy of Student Handout 34B. Then allow them to copy it for the other group members after that activity is over.

Learners with Special Education Needs

Create Roles in Phase 1 of the Activity Instead of having students take Reading Notes and identify the related Enlightenment thinker by his quotation, have them portray the thinkers. Provide each student with the quotation for his or her thinker the day before you plan to teach this lesson. Encourage them to practice reading the quotation aloud. Also, have them read the section on their assigned thinker, and give them a copy of the Guide to Reading Notes. During class, as groups visit each thinker, these actors can read the quotation aloud to the other students. You might consider having them cut out their thinker's head from Information Master 34B, and wear it as a mask.

Modify the Processing Activity Consider using one of these two options:

- Provide students with a list of appropriate topics for the articles they will be asked to find. Appropriate topics include the following:
  - human rights (John Locke)
  - democratic principles, such as elections, trials, and so on (John Locke)
  - separation of powers within the government, such as Congress as lawmakers, the president as executor of laws, and so on (Montesquieu)
  - religious freedom (Voltaire)
  - capital punishment; fair punishment for criminals (Beccaria)
  - women's rights (Adams, de Gouges, Wollstonecraft)

- Gather a few articles you believe are appropriate for this Processing activity, and provide students with a small portfolio of articles from which to choose. Consider labeling each with the name of a thinker from this chapter or one of the topics listed above to help students focus on the information they should highlight in the article.

Advanced Learners

Evaluate Thinkers Using a Spectrum Have students place the five thinkers along a spectrum, based on how influential they have been to American ideas about society and government. Ask students to draw this spectrum and to place each thinker where they think he belongs in relation to the others.

←—————————————————————→

Least Influential to
American Ideas

Most Influential to
American Ideas

Enrichment Resources

Find out more about the Enlightenment by exploring the following Enrichment Resources for *History Alive! The Medieval World and Beyond* at www.teachtci.com.

Enrichment Readings These in-depth readings encourage students to explore selected topics related to the chapter. You may also find readings that relate the chapter's content directly to your state's curriculum.

Internet Connections The recommended Web sites provide useful and engaging content that reinforces skills development and mastery of subjects within the chapter.

Literature Recommendations

The following books offer opportunities to extend the content in this chapter.

John Locke: Champion of Modern Democracy by Graham Faiella (New York: Rosen Publishing, 2005)

People at the Center of the Enlightenment by Gail B. Stewart (Farmington Hills, MN: Blackbirch Press, 2005)

A Young Person's Guide to Philosophy by Jeremy Weate (New York: Dorling Kindersley, 1998)

Section 34.2

1. Scientists during the Scientific Revolution and Enlightenment thinkers both applied observation and reason to their study of the world.

2. Like Renaissance humanists and Protestants during the Reformation, Enlightenment thinkers rejected authority and upheld the freedom of individuals to think for themselves.

3. They saw the laws of nature as evidence of an intelligent Creator and human progress as a sign of God's goodness. Their approach to moral problems also reflected Christian values, such as respect for others and for a moral law.

4.

Old Belief	New Idea
• Christian faith was based largely on trust in the Bible as God's word. • Ideas about right and wrong were based on religious teachings. • Kings had a divine right to rule.	• Humans are perfectly able to discover truth for themselves. • Ideas about right and wrong should be based on rational insight. • People have individual rights that government must respect.

Section 34.3

1. Hobbes was influenced by the English Civil War, and the chaos, disorder, and discontent that characterized that period and after, when England was ruled by the House of Commons.

2. Hobbes argued that humans are naturally cruel, selfish, and greedy, and want power. Without laws, people would always be in conflict. Governments are created to protect people from themselves, as they are incapable of making decisions that are good for society as a whole. Only a ruler with absolute authority can maintain an orderly society.

3. Hobbes is important because he was one of the first thinkers to apply the tools of the Scientific Revolution to problems of politics; later, most thinkers came to different conclusions, and most countries moved away from absolute monarchies.

4. Hobbes was Enlightenment thinker C. He said: "The condition of man . . . is a condition of war of everyone against everyone."

Section 34.4

1. Locke was influenced by a long English tradition of laws limiting the monarch's power. He approved of Parliament's checks on the king's power and of the English Bill of Rights, which strengthened Parliament as the representative of the people.

2. Locke argued that monarchs did not have a divine right to rule. Instead, the true basis of government was a social contract among free people. The purpose of government was to protect people's natural rights, including the rights to life, liberty, and property. In exchange for this protection, people gave government the power to rule on their behalf.

3. His theory that a government's authority was based on the consent of the governed and the idea that government could be overthrown if it failed to respect people's rights had wide influence and was ultimately echoed in the American Declaration of Independence.

4. Locke was Enlightenment thinker E. He said: "Man . . . hath by nature a power . . . to preserve his property—that is, his life, liberty, and estate—against the injuries and attempts of other men."

Section 34.5

1. Montesquieu was influenced by his Catholic upbringing, his practice of law, and his experience as president of the local parliament. He was also critical of French institutions such as the king's court and the Catholic Church.

2. Montesquieu described his theory of how governments should be organized. He believed the best way to protect political liberty was to divide power among three branches of government. The legislative branch would make the laws, the executive branch would enforce the laws, and the judicial branch would interpret the laws. Under this separation of powers, no one branch would be too powerful.

3. Montesquieu's ideas were very influential among the men who wrote the U.S. Constitution. They made the separation of powers a key part of the American system of government.

4. Montesquieu was Enlightenment thinker <u>D.</u> He said: "When the legislative and executive powers are united in the same person, or in the same body of magistrates, there can be no liberty."

Section 34.6

1. Voltaire believed passionately in reforming society in the name of justice and human happiness.

2. Voltaire warned against oppression and used humor to attack the French court and the power of the Catholic clergy. He strongly favored a constitutional monarchy with a separation of powers. He was especially concerned with freedom of thought and speech, and championed religious tolerance.

3. Voltaire's ideas about religious tolerance and free speech greatly influenced early American political thinkers, who included these protections in the U.S. Bill of Rights.

4. Voltaire was Enlightenment thinker <u>A.</u> He said: "I detest what you write, but I would give my life to make it possible for you to continue to write."

Section 34.7

1. Beccaria objected to the harsh practices, such as torture, that were common in his day. He was also opposed to trials being held in secret, as well as to corrupt judges and capital punishment.

2. Beccaria argued that laws exist to preserve security and order. Punishments should be severe enough only to stop people from committing crimes, but need not be brutal. He also argued that a person accused of a crime should receive a fair and speedy trial, and that torture and capital punishment should never be used. He further argued that persons who commit the same crime should receive the same punishment.

3. Beccaria's ideas about rights and punishment

influenced reform movements throughout Europe. Many laws concerning crime and punishment in the United States also reflect his ideas.

4. Beccaria was Enlightenment thinker <u>B.</u> He said: "For a punishment to be just it should consist of only such gradations of intensity as suffice to deter men from committing crimes."

Section 34.8

1. Frederick the Great of Prussia, Catherine the Great of Russia, and Joseph II of Austria were all considered "enlightened despots." Some enlightened despots founded universities and scientific societies, introduced religious reforms, and ended torture and capital punishments.

2. Declaration of Independence: Locke—natural rights, social contract; Constitution: Montesquieu—separation of powers; Bill of Rights: Voltaire—freedom of religion and speech; Beccaria—right to a speedy trial

Section 34.9

- Madame Geoffrin: hosted salons in her home where the brightest talents in Europe could meet for lively talk about the latest ideas; also provided financial support to the Encyclopedists

- Abigail Adams: strongly supported American independence; argued for equal rights, political representation, and education for women

- Olympe de Gouges: wrote the Declaration of the Rights of Woman and of the Female Citizen; argued for women's equality with men in every aspect of public and private life

- Mary Wollstonecraft: argued for women to have the same rights and opportunities as men; believed that education was the key to women gaining equality with and freedom from men

Europe Enters the Modern Age

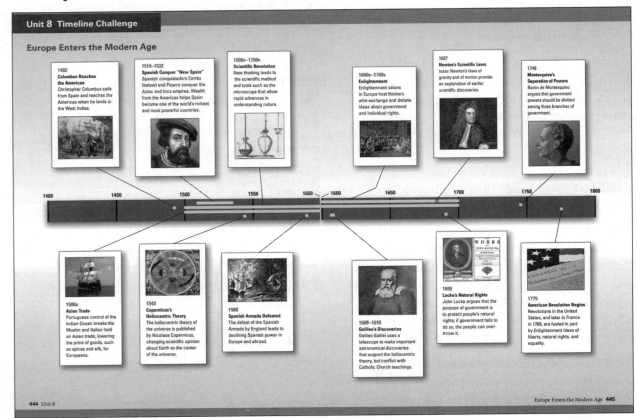

Unit 8 Timeline Challenge

Europe Enters the Modern Age

1492
Columbus Reaches the Americas
Christopher Columbus sails from Spain and reaches the Americas when he lands in the West Indies.

1519–1532
Spanish Conquer "New Spain"
Spanish conquistadors Cortés (below) and Pizarro conquer the Aztec and Inca empires. Wealth from the Americas helps Spain become one of the world's richest and most powerful countries.

1500s–1700s
Scientific Revolution
New thinking leads to the scientific method and tools such as the microscope that allow rapid advances in understanding nature.

1600s–1700s
Enlightenment
Enlightenment salons in Europe host thinkers who exchange and debate ideas about government and individual rights.

1687
Newton's Scientific Laws
Isaac Newton's laws of gravity and of motion provide an explanation of earlier scientific discoveries.

1748
Montesquieu's Separation of Powers
Baron de Montesquieu argues that government powers should be divided among three branches of government.

1500s
Asian Trade
Portuguese control of the Indian Ocean breaks the Muslim and Italian hold on Asian trade, lowering the price of goods, such as spices and silk, for Europeans.

1543
Copernicus's Heliocentric Theory
The heliocentric theory of the universe is published by Nicolaus Copernicus, changing scientific opinion about Earth as the center of the universe.

1588
Spanish Armada Defeated
The defeat of the Spanish Armada by England leads to declining Spanish power in Europe and abroad.

1609–1610
Galileo's Discoveries
Galileo Galilei uses a telescope to make important astronomical discoveries that support the heliocentric theory, but conflict with Catholic Church teachings.

1690
Locke's Natural Rights
John Locke argues that the purpose of government is to protect people's natural rights; if government fails to do so, the people can overthrow it.

1775
American Revolution Begins
Revolutions in the United States, and later in France in 1789, are fueled in part by Enlightenment ideas of liberty, natural rights, and equality.

444 Unit 8

Europe Enters the Modern Age **445**

Overview

This Timeline Challenge helps students review the main events and ideas of this unit while providing practice in reading and interpreting timelines. You can vary and expand the activity according to students' needs and the amount of time available.

Basic Procedure

1 **Introduce the timeline in the Student Edition.** Direct students to the Europe Enters the Modern Age Timeline at the end of Unit 8 in the Student Edition. You may wish to have students read aloud and discuss the timeline entries.

2 **Introduce the Timeline Challenge in the Interactive Student Notebook.** Direct students to the Unit 8 Timeline Challenge. Point out the two types of questions, "Timeline Skills" and "Critical Thinking," and model how to answer each type.

3 **Have students complete the Timeline Challenge.** Monitor students as they work. Use the Guide to Unit 8 Timeline Challenge to check their answers. You may wish to project a transparency of this page as you work through the questions with the class and conduct a discussion of the "Critical Thinking" questions.

4 **Complete the KWL chart.** Return to the KWL chart created at the beginning of the unit, and ask students to list the key information they have learned.

Classroom Timeline

1 **Prepare the Timeline Challenge Cards.** Copy and cut the cards from *Student Handout TC8: Unit 8 Timeline Challenge Cards.* You may wish to laminate the cards for future use.

2 **Create a timeline on a classroom wall.** On an empty wall or a large bulletin board, make a timeline with masking tape or colored paper. Mark off the time intervals in advance, or ask students to do so in class.

3 **Have students place the Timeline Challenge Cards.** Distribute cards to individual students or pairs and have them tape the cards to the timeline in the correct locations. Call on students to provide more information on the timeline topics to review main events and issues.

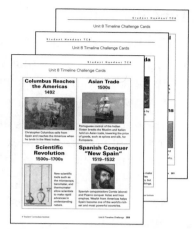

Student Handout TC8

Internet Research

1 **Review students' suggestions for additional timeline entries.** Have students share their answers to the last question of the Timeline Challenge.

2 **Have students conduct Internet research.** Ask students to choose and research one of their suggested events.

3 **Have students create additional Timeline Challenge Cards.** Direct students to research an appropriate image for their cards and then use the computer to create an illustrated card, complete with timeline entry.

Timeline Skills

Score 1 point for each correct answer.

1. Spain finished conquering the Aztec and Inca empires 40 years after Columbus reached the Americas.

2. The prices of Asian goods in Europe dropped in the 16th century because Portugal broke the Muslim and Italian hold on Asian trade.

3. New scientific tools developed during the Scientific Revolution include the microscope, barometer, and thermometer.

4. Copernicus's heliocentric theory was significant because it changed scientific opinion about Earth as the center of the universe.

5. The English defeat of the Spanish Armada was important because it marks the decline of Spanish power in Europe and abroad.

6. Enlightenment ideas were spread through European salons where thinkers exchanged and debated ideas about government and individual rights.

7. Galileo's important astronomical discoveries put him in conflict with the Catholic Church.

8. Newton's laws provided an explanation of earlier scientific discoveries.

9. Locke argued that the purpose of government is to protect people's natural rights, and if it fails to do so, the people can overthrow it.

10. The American Revolution in 1775 and French Revolution in 1789 were based on, or resulted from, Enlightenment ideas.

Critical Thinking

Score 1 to 3 points for each answer, depending on the thoroughness of the response.

11. Answers will vary. Students may choose any theory, law, discovery, or invention from the Scientific Revolution, provided that they supply a concrete explanation of the significance of their choice.

12. The establishment of executive, legislative, and judicial branches represents Montesquieu's ideas about the separation of powers.

13. Portugal explored parts of Africa and Asia, and set up trading ports in cities along the coasts. The Portuguese gained control of the Indian Ocean, and were able to bring more Asian goods to Europe at a lower cost. They also explored Brazil, made it a colony, and brought African slaves there. Spain mostly explored the New World, and conquered two of the most powerful empires in the Americas, the Aztecs and the Incas. Their exploration and colonization made them one of the richest countries in the world. The English mostly explored North America, and were able to establish trading posts and colonies, but did not initially gain as much wealth as the Portuguese and Spanish did.

14. Answers will vary. Students must explain why the events they chose merit inclusion.

Using Scores to Inform Instruction

Timeline Skills A score of 7 out of 10 indicates that students understand most of the key events in the unit.

Critical Thinking A score of 8 out of 12 indicates that students are able to think critically about most of the key issues in this unit.

If students score below these levels, consider reviewing timeline and critical thinking skills.

This pacing guide suggests how many instructional days to allot to each chapter, including activities and assessment, for teaching the course in 50-minute classes, five times per week.

Unit 1: Europe During Medieval Times	
Geography Challenge	1 day
Ch. 1: The Legacy of the Roman Empire	3 days
Ch. 2: The Development of Feudalism in Western Europe	4 days
Ch. 3: The Roman Catholic Church in Medieval Europe	5 days
Ch. 4: Life in Medieval Towns	5 days
Ch. 5: The Decline of Feudalism	4 days
Ch. 6: The Byzantine Empire	5 days
Timeline Challenge	1 day

Unit 2: Islam in Medieval Times	
Geography Challenge	1 day
Ch. 7: The Origins and Spread of Islam	4 days
Ch. 8: Learning About World Religions: Islam	4 days
Ch. 9: Muslim Innovations and Adaptations	4–5 days
Ch. 10: From the Crusades to New Muslim Empires	3 days
Timeline Challenge	1 day

Unit 3: The Culture and Kingdoms of West Africa	
Geography Challenge	1 day
Ch. 11: Early Societies in West Africa	4 days
Ch. 12: Ghana: A West African Trading Empire	4 days
Ch. 13: The Influence of Islam on West Africa	4 days
Ch. 14: The Cultural Legacy of West Africa	4–5 days
Timeline Challenge	1 day

Unit 4: Imperial China	
Geography Challenge	1 day
Ch. 15: The Political Development of Imperial China	4 days
Ch. 16: China Develops a New Economy	5 days
Ch. 17: Chinese Discoveries and Inventions	4–5 days
Ch. 18: China's Contacts with the Outside World	4–5 days
Timeline Challenge	1 day

Unit 5: Japan During Medieval Times	
Geography Challenge	1 day
Ch. 19: The Influence of Neighboring Cultures on Japan	4 days
Ch. 20: Heian-kyo: The Heart of Japan's Golden Age	4 days
Ch. 21: The Rise of the Warrior Class in Japan	4 days
Timeline Challenge	1 day

Unit 6: Civilizations of the Americas	
Geography Challenge	1 day
Ch. 22: The Mayas	4 days
Ch. 23: The Aztecs	4 days
Ch. 24: Daily Life in Tenochtitlán	5 days
Ch. 25: The Incas	3 days
Ch. 26: Achievements of the Mayas, Aztecs, and Incas	5 days
Timeline Challenge	1 day

Unit 7: Europe's Renaissance and Reformation	
Geography Challenge	1 day
Ch. 27: The Renaissance Begins	4 days
Ch. 28: Florence: The Cradle of the Renaissance	5 days
Ch. 29: Leading Figures of the Renaissance	5 days
Ch. 30: The Reformation Begins	4 days
Ch. 31: The Spread and Impact of the Reformation	3 days
Timeline Challenge	1 day

Unit 8: Europe Enters the Modern Age	
Geography Challenge	1 day
Ch. 32: The Age of Exploration	4 days
Ch. 33: The Scientific Revolution	4 days
Ch. 34: The Enlightenment	5 days
Timeline Challenge	1 day

History Alive! The Medieval World and Beyond — Skills Correlation

	Map Skills	Comparing and Contrasting	Sequencing Events	Creating a Timeline	Analyzing Cause and Effect	Making Predictions	Recognizing the Role of Chance, Error, and Oversight in History	Framing Questions to Research	Distinguishing Fact from Opinion	Selecting Useful Information	Selecting Credible Sources: Primary Sources	Selecting Credible Sources: Secondary Sources	Drawing Sound Conclusions	Identifying Frame of Reference and Point of View	Identifying Bias, Stereotyping, and Propaganda	Conducting a Cost-Benefit Analysis	Interpreting Political Cartoons
Unit 1: Europe During Medieval Times																	
Geography Challenge	•	•				•							•				
Ch. 1: The Legacy of the Roman Empire	•				•	•	•			•			•				
Ch. 2: The Development of Feudalism in Western Europe		•	•		•	•			•							•	
Ch. 3: The Roman Catholic Church in Medieval Europe		•	•		•	•				•	•		•				
Ch. 4: Life in Medieval Towns	•	•			•	•			•	•				•			
Ch. 5: The Decline of Feudalism			•		•	•	•		•				•	•			
Ch. 6: The Byzantine Empire		•	•		•				•	•	•		•	•	•		
Timeline Challenge			•	•	•								•				
Unit 2: Islam in Medieval Times																	
Geography Challenge	•				•	•							•				
Ch. 7: The Origins and Spread of Islam	•	•	•			•			•	•	•		•			•	
Ch. 8: Learning About World Religions: Islam		•				•			•	•	•		•				
Ch. 9: Muslim Innovations and Adaptations	•	•							•	•	•	•	•		•		
Ch. 10: From the Crusades to New Muslim Empires	•	•	•	•	•	•			•	•		•	•		•	•	
Timeline Challenge			•	•	•								•			•	

History Alive! The Medieval World and Beyond — Skills Correlation	Map Skills	Comparing and Contrasting	Sequencing Events	Creating a Timeline	Analyzing Cause and Effect	Making Predictions	Recognizing the Role of Chance, Error, and Oversight in History	Framing Questions to Research	Distinguishing Fact from Opinion	Selecting Useful Information	Selecting Credible Sources: Primary Sources	Selecting Credible Sources: Secondary Sources	Drawing Sound Conclusions	Identifying Frame of Reference and Point of View	Identifying Bias, Stereotyping, and Propaganda	Conducting a Cost-Benefit Analysis	Interpreting Political Cartoons
Unit 3: The Culture and Kingdoms of West Africa																	
Geography Challenge	●					●							●				
Ch. 11: Early Societies in West Africa	●	●	●		●	●		●			●	●	●	●		●	
Ch. 12: Ghana: A West African Trading Empire	●				●	●		●			●	●	●	●		●	
Ch. 13: The Influence of Islam on West Africa		●	●		●	●		●			●	●	●				
Ch. 14: The Cultural Legacy of West Africa		●			●	●					●	●	●				
Timeline Challenge			●	●									●				
Unit 4: Imperial China																	
Geography Challenge	●	●				●							●				
Ch. 15: The Political Development of Imperial China		●	●		●	●	●	●		●			●	●		●	●
Ch. 16: China Develops a New Economy		●	●		●			●			●	●			●	●	
Ch. 17: Chinese Discoveries and Inventions		●			●		●	●			●		●				
Ch. 18: China's Contacts with the Outside World	●	●	●	●	●		●	●			●	●	●			●	
Timeline Challenge		●	●	●									●				

History Alive! The Medieval World and Beyond — Skills Correlation

	Map Skills	Comparing and Contrasting	Sequencing Events	Creating a Timeline	Analyzing Cause and Effect	Making Predictions	Recognizing the Role of Chance, Error, and Oversight in History	Framing Questions to Research	Distinguishing Fact from Opinion	Selecting Useful Information	Selecting Credible Sources: Primary Sources	Selecting Credible Sources: Secondary Sources	Drawing Sound Conclusions	Identifying Frame of Reference and Point of View	Identifying Bias, Stereotyping, and Propaganda	Conducting a Cost-Benefit Analysis	Interpreting Political Cartoons
Unit 5: Japan During Medieval Times																	
Geography Challenge	•												•				
Ch. 19: The Influence of Neighboring Cultures on Japan	•		•		•	•				•	•			•			
Ch. 20: Heian-kyo: The Heart of Japan's Golden Age					•	•				•	•		•	•			
Ch. 21: The Rise of the Warrior Class in Japan		•	•	•	•	•			•	•	•			•			
Timeline Challenge			•	•									•				
Unit 6: Civilizations of the Americas																	
Geography Challenge	•	•				•											
Ch. 22: The Mayas	•	•			•	•			•		•		•	•		•	
Ch. 23: The Aztecs			•	•	•	•			•	•	•		•	•	•	•	
Ch. 24: Daily Life in Tenochtitlán		•				•			•	•	•			•	•		
Ch. 25: The Incas	•	•	•		•	•			•	•				•		•	
Ch. 26: Achievements of the Mayas, Aztecs, and Incas		•			•	•			•	•	•			•			
Timeline Challenge			•	•									•				

History Alive! The Medieval World and Beyond — Skills Correlation

	Map Skills	Comparing and Contrasting	Sequencing Events	Creating a Timeline	Analyzing Cause and Effect	Making Predictions	Recognizing the Role of Chance, Error, and Oversight in History	Framing Questions to Research	Distinguishing Fact from Opinion	Selecting Useful Information	Selecting Credible Sources: Primary Sources	Selecting Credible Sources: Secondary Sources	Drawing Sound Conclusions	Identifying Frame of Reference and Point of View	Identifying Bias, Stereotyping, and Propaganda	Conducting a Cost-Benefit Analysis	Interpreting Political Cartoons
Unit 7: Europe's Renaissance and Reformation																	
Geography Challenge	•				•								•				
Ch. 27: The Renaissance Begins	•	•			•	•		•		•	•	•	•	•	•		
Ch. 28: Florence: The Cradle of the Renaissance		•			•	•		•			•	•					
Ch. 29: Leading Figures of the Renaissance		•			•	•		•			•	•	•				
Ch. 30: The Reformation Begins		•	•		•	•		•		•			•				
Ch. 31: The Spread and Impact of the Reformation	•	•			•	•		•			•	•		•	•		
Timeline Challenge		•	•	•									•				
Unit 8: Europe Enters the Modern Age																	
Geography Challenge	•												•				
Ch. 32: The Age of Exploration	•	•			•	•	•	•		•	•		•	•		•	
Ch. 33: The Scientific Revolution		•			•	•			•	•	•				•	•	
Ch. 34: The Enlightenment		•			•	•				•	•						•
Timeline Challenge		•	•	•													

Placards

Chapter 20
427: Sei Shonagon in Ivan Morris, trans. and ed., *The Pillowbook of Sei Shonagon* (New York: Columbia University Press, 1991). From FROM THE COUNTRY OF EIGHT ISLANDS by Hiroaki Sato and Burton Watson, copyright © 1981 by Hiroaki Sato and Burton Watson. Used by permission of Doubleday, a division of Random House, Inc.

Chapter 28
428: Niccolò Machiavelli, *The Prince,* trans. Luigi Ricci (London: Grant Richards, 1903). Niccolò Machiavelli, in Peter Loptson, ed., *Readings on Human Nature* (Orchard Park, NY: Broadview Press, 1998). Ibid.

Lesson Guide

Photographs

Cover: Gina Martin/Getty Images

Title page: Gina Martin/Getty Images

Art

Chapter 19
240–242: Len Ebert.

Placards

Photographs

1: Granger Collection, NY 2: The Art Archive/Harper Collins Publishers 3: Atlantide Phototravel/Corbis 4: Asier Villafranca/Shutterstock 5: TCI 6: The Art Archive/Real Collegiata San Isidoro Leon/Gianni Dagli Orti 7: Northwind Picture Archives 8: DEA/C SAPPA/De Agostini Editore/Photolibrary 9: Erich Lessing/Art Resource, NY 10: Angelo Hornak/Corbis 11: Anger O/Jupiter Images 12: Dennis Marsico/Corbis 13: Stephen Finn/Shutterstock 14: Victoria & Albert Museum, London/Art Resource, NY 15: R&S Michaud/Woodfin Camp 16: TCI. 17: Stock Montage 18: Stock Montage 19: Aramco World 20: Photo.com 21: Leinad-Z, Wikipedia Commons 22: Aramco World 23: Mark Karrass/Corbis 24: Abbas/Magnum Photos 25: Paul Almasy/Corbis 26: Liba Taylor/Corbis 27: John Elk Photography 28: Hulton-Deutsch Collection/Corbis 29: Lawrence Manning/Corbis 30: Frederic Noy/AFP Photo/Getty Images 31: Marc and Evelyn Bernheim/Woodfin Camp & Associates 32: Science & Society Picture Library, London 33: TCI. 34: Ontario Science Centre, Toronto 35: Science Museum, London/HIP/Scala/Art Resource, NY 36: Ontario Science Centre, Toronto 37: Ontario Science Centre, Toronto 38: The Trustees of the Imperial War Museum, London. IWM #IB 2759/c 39: Vassil/Wikipedia Commons 40: Ontario Science Centre, Toronto 41: The Art Archive/Victoria and Albert Museum London/Eileen Tweedy 42: Fujita Museum of Art, Osaka, Japan 43: Katariina Jarvinen/Shutterstock 44: Plush Studios/Blend Images/Corbis 45L: Office of Shoso-in Treasure House, Nara, Japan 45R: The Art Archive/Private Collection Paris/Gianni Dagli Orti 46: TCI 47: Carl & Ann Purcell/Corbis 48: Courtiers playing football (Kemari) at Hokoju (detail), 1500–1573.

The Avery Brundage Collection, B60D20; Asian Art Museum of San Francisco. Reproduced by permission 49B: RapidEye/iStockphoto.com 49TL: Kwamikagami/Wikimedia Commons 49TR: The Art Archive/Archaeological Museum, Lima, Peru/Dagli Orti 50T: Gianni Dagli Orti/Corbis 50BL: Werner Forman/Art Resource, NY 50BR: Werner Forman Archive/Corbis 51T: Courtesy of William Siegal Galleries, Santa Fe, New Mexico, Orange Feather Tunic, Inca Culture, Peruvian Highlands, 1400–1532 C.E., photo by Lorran Meares 51BR: Charles & Josette Lenars/Corbis 51BL: Werner Forman Archive/Art Resource 52: Adalberto Rios Szalay/Photolibrary 53: Bill Ross/Corbis 54: Francis G. Mayer/Corbis 55: iStockphoto.com 56T: The Art Archive/Biblioteca Nazionale Marciana, Venice, Italy/Dagli Orti 56BL: The Granger Collection, New York 56BR: British Museum, London/The Bridgeman Art Library 57TL: Shutterstock 57TR: Janaka Dharmasena/123RF.com 57BL: Accademia, Venice, Italy/Scala/Art Resource, NY 57BR: Alinari Archives/Corbis 58: Erich Lessing/Art Resource, NY

Art

Chapter 28
53: Susan Jaekel 54–59 (back): Doug Roy